The Social Contract from Hobbes to Rawls

The concept of the social contract has been central to political thought since the seventeenth century. Contract theory has been used to justify political authority, to account for the origin of the state and to provide foundations for moral values and the construction of a just society. In *The Social Contract from Hobbes to Rawls*, leading scholars from Britain and America survey the history of contractarian thought and the major debates in political theory which surround the notion of the social contract.

The book examines the critical reception to the ideas of classical contractarians such as Hobbes, Locke and Rousseau, moving on to consider the impact of contemporary thinkers such as Rawls and Gauthier. It incorporates discussion of the importance of the contract in international relations theory and looks at feminist responses to contractarianism. Challenging the notion that there is a single tradition that can be traced back beyond Hobbes to classical Greece, three distinct traditions are identified alongside a series of anti-contractarian arguments which have played a role in shaping the debate to the present day. Together, the essays provide a comprehensive introduction to theories and critiques of the social contract within a broad political theoretical framework.

Editors: **David Boucher** is Senior Lecturer in Politics at the University of Wales, Swansea. His most recent book is *A Radical Hegelian* with Andrew Vincent. **Paul Kelly** is Lecturer in Politics at the University of Wales, Swansea. He is the author of *Utilitarianism and Distributive Justice: Jeremy Bentham and the Civil Law*.

Contributors: Dario Castiglione, John Charvet, Diana Coole, Murray Forsyth, Bruce Haddock, Jeremy Jennings, Rex Martin, Margaret Moore, Martyn P. Thompson, Jeremy Waldron, Lawrence Wilde and Howard Williams.

The Social Contract from Hobbes to Rawls

Edited by David Boucher
and Paul Kelly

Routledge
Taylor & Francis Group

LONDON AND NEW YORK

First published 1994
by Routledge
11 New Fetter Lane, London EC4P 4EE

Transferred to Digital Printing 2004

Simultaneously published in the USA and Canada
by Routledge
29 West 35th Street, New York, NY 10001

Typeset in Monotype Times New Roman by
the EPPP Group at Routledge

British Library Cataloguing in Publication Data
A catalogue record for this book is available from the British Library.

Library of Congress Cataloging in Publication Data
a catalog record for this book has been requested.

ISBN   0–415–10845–4
ISBN   0–415–10846–2 (pbk)

Printed and bound by Antony Rowe Ltd, Eastbourne

Contents

Contributors

David Boucher is Senior Lecturer in Politics at the University of Wales, Swansea. He has published widely in the philosophy of history, political theory and the history of thought in international relations. He is author of Texts in Context (1985), *The Social and Political Thought of R. G. Collingwood* (1989) and co-author with A. Vincent of *A Radical Hegelian* (1993); he is the editor of R. G. Collingwood's *Essays in Political Philosophy* (1989) and *New Leviathan* (1992). He is currently completing a book on theories of international relations from Thucydides to Marx (to be published by Clarendon Press).

Dario Castiglione is Lecturer in Politics at the University of Exeter, having previously been at the Australian National University. He is the author of articles on Hume and the social contract.

John Charvet is Reader in Politics at the London School of Economics. He has published widely in political philosophy and the history of political thought. He is the author of *The Social Problem in the Philosophy of Rousseau* (1974), *A Critique of Freedom and Equality* (1981) and *Feminism* (1982).

Diana Coole is Senior Lecturer in Politics at Queen Mary and Westfield College, University of London. She has published widely in contemporary political philosophy, feminism and postmodernism. Her publications include *Women in Political Theory* (2nd edn, 1993). Dr Coole is currently completing a book on politics and negativity.

Murray Forsyth is Professor of International Politics at the University of Leicester. His numerous publications include *Unions of States: The Theory and Practice of Confederation* (1981), *Reason and Revolution: The Political Thought of the Abbé Sieyes* (1987) and *Federalism and Nationalism* (1989); he edited, with Maurice Keens-Soper and John Hoffman, *A Guide to the Political Classics Vols I* and *Vol II* (1988 and 1993).

Bruce Haddock is Senior Lecturer in Politics and Head of Department at the University of Wales, Swansea. He has published widely in the philosophy of history, political theory and the history of ideas. He is the author of *An Introduction to Historical Thought* (1980) and *Vico's Political Thought* (1986);

he is currently completing a study of Italian federalism, 1830–65. Dr Haddock is also joint editor of the journal *Collingwood Studies*.

Jeremy Jennings is Senior Lecturer in Politics at the University of Wales, Swansea. His publications include *Georges Sorel: The Character and Development of his Thought* (1985) and *Syndicalism in France: A Study of Ideas* (1990); he is the editor and translator of *Intellectuals in Twentieth Century France: Mandarins and Samurai* (1993). He is currently completing an edition of Sorel's *Reflections on Violence* and writing a book on political ideas in France from 1789 (to be published by Clarendon Press).

Paul Kelly is Lecturer in Politics at the University of Wales, Swansea. He is author of *Utilitarianism and Distributive Justice: Jeremy Bentham and the Civil Law* (1990) and is completing a new edition of Jeremy Bentham's writings on political economy as part of the new *Collected Works of Jeremy Bentham*. He is also completing a study of the legal and political theory of Ronald Dworkin. Dr Kelly is review editor of *Utilitas: A Journal of Utilitarian Studies*.

Rex Martin is Professor of Philosophy at the University of Kansas, in Lawrence, and Professor of Politics at the University of Wales, Swansea. Among his numerous publications are *Historical Explanation: Re-enactment and Practical Inference* (1977), *Rawls and Rights* (1985) and *A System of Rights* (1993); he has also edited, with M. Singer, *G. C. MacCallum: Legislative Intent, and Other Essays on Law, Politics and Morality* (1993).

Margaret Moore is Assistant Professor of Political Science at the University of Waterloo, Canada. She has published a number of articles on contemporary political philosophy and is author of *The Foundations of Liberalism* (1993). She is currently working on *Justice, Gender and the Politics of Identity*.

Martyn P. Thompson is Professor of Political Theory at Tulane University, New Orleans. He was previously Professor of Intellectual History and Literary Studies in the University of Tübingen. He has published several articles and books on the history of social contract theory and is co-editor of the annual *Politisches Denken Jahrbuch*. He is currently completing a historical study of Defoe and early Whiggism.

Jeremy Waldron is Professor of Law at the University of California at Berkeley. He has published widely in political philosophy and legal theory and his many publications include *Nonsense Upon Stilts: Bentham, Burke and Marx* (1987), *The Right to Private Property* (1988), *The Law* (1990) and most recently *Liberal Rights: Collected Papers, 1981–1991* (1993). He is also editor of *Theories of Rights* (1984).

Lawrence Wilde is Reader in Politics at The Nottingham Trent University. He is author of *Marx and Contradiction* (1989) and *Modern European Socialism* (1994). He is co-editor with M. Cowling of *Approaches to Marx* (1989).

Howard Williams is Professor of Political Theory in the Department of International Politics at the University of Wales, Aberystwyth. He has published numerous books including *Marx* (1980), *Kant's Political Philosophy* (1983), *Heraclitus, Hegel and Marx's Dialectic* (1988), *Concepts of Ideology* (1988) and *Political Theory in International Relations* (1991); he has edited *Essays on Kant's Political Philosophy* (1992).

Preface

In this collection of essays on the social contract and its critics from Hobbes to the present day we do not pretend to provide a history of a unified tradition. Instead the essays are engagements with social contract theory which testify to the importance of the idea in modern political thought and contemporary political philosophy. The contributors approach the issues historically and philosophically and as such the essays make a worthwhile contribution to illuminating the history of the idea of a social contract and to the ongoing debates which serve to illustrate the diversity and continued interest in contractarian thinking.

Taken together the essays in the the volume provide a companion to courses in the history of political thought and modern political philosophy. That said, we do not presume that the authors or the texts considered cover all the interesting and diverse uses to which social contractarian arguments have been put. The emphasis of the volume is upon what is usually regarded as classical contractarianism and its modern progeny, but the first essay does attempt to give an indication of the much wider variety of contractarian arguments invoked for all kinds of purposes throughout the ages.

In a philosophical text of this sort the use of gender-specific terms such as 'man' and 'mankind' is unavoidable, especially given that some of the classical thinkers consciously exclude women from the category of citizens, subjects or full moral individuals. To avoid confusion within each chapter, we have chosen not to impose a false gender neutrality, but we would like to point out that such terms are intended to be inclusive unless the context indicates otherwise.

This collection began its life as contributions to a conference on the social contract and its critics held at Gregynog, the University of Wales Conference Centre, near Newtown in Powys, January 1993. Additional contributions were invited in order to give a more comprehensive characterization of the various aspects of contractarianism. The only essay to have appeared in print previously is that by Jeremy Waldron and we are indebted to *The Review of Politics* (1989, vol. 51, no. 1) for granting permission to republish it. The original contributor of the Locke chapter pulled out of the project at the last minute and we are grateful to both Jeremy Waldron and Martyn P.

Thompson for stepping in at such short notice. All of the contributors have been exemplary in meeting the editors' deadlines and we wish to express our appreciation for making our job much less arduous than it otherwise would have been. Finally we would like to acknowledge our debt to Caroline Wintersgill of Routledge who gave us every encouragement to pursue this project.

David Boucher
Paul Kelly
University of Wales, Swansea

1 The social contract and its critics

An overview

David Boucher and Paul Kelly

Whilst social contract theory never really fell into abeyance it is certainly true that it has enjoyed a renaissance of interest following the publication of Rawls's *A Theory of Justice* in 1971. Since then, not only has it become a recurrent feature of contemporary political philosophy, but also there has been a renewed interest in the historical origins of social contract theory and the classic contractarians, Hobbes, Locke, Rousseau and Kant. With this interest has come attempts to trace the social contract 'tradition' further back beyond Hobbes to the ancient Greeks, and to construct 'models' or definitions of the social contract which can incorporate all putative contractarian thinkers.[1]

Rather than provide a *précis* of the contributions to this volume, we want in this introductory essay to challenge one of the assumptions of similar commentaries on the social contract, namely that there is a single unified tradition or a single model or definition of the contract. Instead we identify a number of traditions in which the *contract* takes on a distinct character and serves a specific end. Social contract theories for the purpose of our discussion fall into three broad categories, moral, civil and constitutional. Whilst these are not mutually exclusive categories, there is nevertheless a tendency for one of these types to predominate in any one thinker. The *moral* and *civil* theories tend to raise the more philosophically interesting questions, and the contractarians discussed in these essays tend to fall into one of these two categories. Nevertheless, we will also briefly explore the third category to illustrate the diversity of contractarian thinking and to emphasize the disjunctures that exist between these categories in order to undermine the thesis advanced by so many recent commentators that there is a single unbroken tradition stretching back from Rawls and Gauthier through Hobbes to the ancient Greeks. The second theme of this essay will be to illustrate the diversity of responses by anti-contractarians even to the *moral* and *civil* versions of contract theory. It is our contention that these anti-contractarian arguments form an integral part of any account of contractarian thinking.

VARIETIES OF CONTRACTARIANISM: MORAL, CIVIL AND CONSTITUTIONAL

The idea of the social contract when examined carefully is seen to have very few implications, and is used for all sorts of reasons, and generates quite contrary conclusions. The reason why it is such a flexible tool in the hands of the theorist is that the choice posited, when one is posited, is variable. The choice may be to create society; civil society; a sovereign; procedural rules of justice; or morality itself. It may be a choice of contract that binds in perpetuity, or one renewed with each succeeding generation. The choice may be historical, ideal or hypothethical, its expression explicit or tacit, and the contractees may be each individual contracting with every other, individuals contracting with their rulers and God (and the various permutations to which such a combination gives rise), the heads of families agreeing among themselves, corporations or cities contractually bound to a superior, or the people as a body contracting with a ruler or king. Furthermore, the motivation for the choice may be a religious duty, personal security, economic welfare, or moral self-righteousness. We are not, then, confronted with one social contract, but with a variety of traditions, each adopting contractarianism for its own purposes.

Given the diversity of the character of social contract theory it would be unwise to try to give an operational definition of something so heterogeneous. In developing our thesis that there is not one contract tradition but at least three, there is no better place to start than ancient Greece. Many commentators trace the source of social contract theory to the ancient Greeks' distinction between nature and convention. The idea of an agreement as the source of the origin and organization of political society can, it is claimed, be found in the sophists Antiphon and Hippias, as well as in Thrasymachus and Glaucon. The writings of Epicurus are similarly taken to ground justice in self-interest. Socrates' *Crito*, on the other hand, is taken to illustrate the implied contract and its concomitant obligations between citizen and state.[2]

The case for putative Greek founders is at best tenuous. Glaucon in criticism of conventional moral constraints attributes the origin of justice not to a natural aversion to inflict injuries, but to a desire to avoid them being inflicted upon oneself by others.[3] This merest of hints can, of course, be related to Hobbes's theory where it is argued that there is no justice or injustice in the state of nature, it being only the will of the sovereign subsequent to the social contract that establishes right and wrong. Hobbes's theory, however, is more a theory of the origin and legitimacy of political obligation and sovereignty than an attempt to ground morality in mutual consent. (The *civil* as opposed to the *moral* character of Hobbes's argument is emphasized in Forsyth's Chapter 2.) Indeed, it is Hobbes's denial of the possibility of morality by agreement that makes the sovereign necessary to impose it.

Moral contractarianism

Perhaps a better comparison can be made between Glaucon and modern moral contractarians such as John Harsanyi, John Mackie and especially David Gauthier, all of whom in their different ways ground moral principles in the creative self-interest of individuals who adopt constraints on their behaviour in order to maximize benefits.[4] In this category we can also include James Buchanan, although his position is perhaps more ambiguous than that of Gauthier or Mackie because his moral scepticism makes him less inclined to offer his arguments as an alternative foundational morality, nevertheless that is in effect what he offers. Gauthier, on the other hand, clearly attempts to ground morality in the rational agreements of utility maximizers who from their different bargaining positions negotiate constraints.[5] His is not, however, a utilitarian theory in that its concern is not with the aggregate benefit of all or the majority, but rather with the relative benefit of each individual. That said, Gauthier's argument is intended only to ground a very narrow conception of 'morality' as he claims the bargain applies only to the distribution of the 'cooperative surplus', that is the difference in the economic product of a society that results from social cooperation. The bargaining position from which each individual starts is shaped by a Lockian conception of property rights. Consequently, what each individual bargains for is the 'maximum relative benefit', or the maximum benefit that an individual could hope to achieve compared with what each would have achieved by the deployment of his or her property in the absence of social cooperation. It is precisely this restriction in the scope of the bargain and Gauthier's own account of what might be called the original position from which the bargain has been struck that has lead to the criticism that he cannot be said to provide a contractarian basis for morality. (See Moore's Chapter 12.)

It is true that at a superficial level Glaucon and Gauthier appear similar in offering a contractarian ethics in that they both deny a distinction between moral and prudential rationality; deny the claim that justice is anything more than an instrumental good, and refuse to attribute content to individual rationality. Gauthier is, nevertheless, significantly different in that his conclusions, unlike Glaucon's, depend on a reasoned justification of in-strumental rationality related to a theory of bargaining out of which contractually binding moral constraints emerge. To the question 'why should I act morally?' Gauthier answers, because it is rational to do so – instrumental rationality and morality are equated. (Moore's essay is an examination and critique of this claim.)

Glaucon's position is quite different: he argues that the weak benefit at the expense of the strong, and that the powerful are *irrational* for agreeing to constraints on their behaviour. Possession of Gyges ring is but an extreme illustration of this point. It is the force of law and the fear of sanctions that constrain Glaucon's maximizers, whereas it is the gentler force of reason and the fear of long-term reduced benefits that constrain Gauthier's utility maximizers.

Whereas *moral* contractarians such as Gauthier want to limit the moral and governmental constraints on individuals, that is not the purpose of the Greek 'contractarians' Antiphon, Hippias, Glaucon, Thrasymachus and Epicurus. Instead of legitimizing society and authority by grounding them in consent, they ridicule the conventional basis of law and morality. The only Greek theorist that appears to have some claim to use a contract as a constraint on the scope of law is Lycophron, the evidence for which is a brief mention by Aristotle. In arguing that the purpose of government is to promote virtue, Aristotle contends:

> Otherwise, the political association becomes a mere alliance differing only in respect of place from those alliances whose members live at some distance from one another; and the law becomes mere convention, 'a guarantor of mutual justice', as the sophist Lycophron said, powerless to make the citizens into good and just men.[6]

Civil contractarianism

When compared with the non-Hobbesian classic contract theorists of the seventeenth and eighteenth centuries the Greek connection is even more dubious. These theorists (including to some extent Hobbes himself) are best described as *civil* contractarians. *Civil* contractarianism is that form of social compact, whether historical or hypothetical, whose role is either to legitimize coercive political authority, or to evaluate coercive constraints independently of the legitimation of the authority from which they derive. The contract may include provision for a governmental compact as in Grotius or Pufendorf, or merely determine where sovereignty lies, as in Locke or Rousseau. Most importantly the *civil* contractarians posit moral and rational constraints upon conduct that are not merely the result of preferences, but which are consolidated, extended or transformed by the social contract.

For *civil* contractarians there is no question of agreement *creating* morality, although agreements may generate moral or political obligations. The institution of civil or political society in a social compact is designed to secure pre-existing moral rights and duties. For Grotius, Pufendorf and Locke the state of nature, whether historical or hypothetical, is a social condition regulated by God's moral law.[7] (On the context of Locke's argument see Thompson's Chapter 4.) Grotius is emphatic that the contract that establishes civil society constitutes a legal community consonant with man's natural sociability, and consistent with the mutual recognition and protection of his moral rights. The obligation to keep our agreements is not a consequence of living in civil society, but the necessary corollary under the natural law of our rationality and sociability.[8] For Pufendorf, unlike Hobbes, justice and injustice do not depend upon a sovereign.[9] Individuals have natural obligations in a state of nature, some congenital and others adventitious or incurred by agreement. These obligations are, however, imperfect given that their discharge is uncertain. The civil sovereign created by the elaborate three-stage compact, comprising two contracts and one decree, converts imperfect into perfect obligations by adding to them the weight of civil law and authority. Both imperfect and perfect rights and obligations, as Haakonssen rightly suggests, 'have an equal moral foundation in natural law'.[10]

Both Pufendorf and Locke identify two natural obligations which predispose us to institute political society and sovereignty. We have a duty to God under the natural law of self-preservation and in so far as it is consistent with this, the preservation of others.[11] For Locke self-preservation and the preservation of mankind are rights derived from prior duties imposed upon men by God. The inconveniences of the state of nature, particularly the uncertainty of application, interpretation and execution of the law of nature makes the discharge of our obligations to God precarious. The establishment of a political power to which each individual is subject, and the continuing legitimacy of that power depends upon the consent of the people. Because each person is naturally free, equal and independent, no one can become politically subjected to another without his consent.[12] (See Waldron's Chapter 3.) Does consent, then, constitute the ground for political obligation? It is unlikely that Locke would have viewed the matter in these terms. (See Thompson's Chapter 4.)

The obligation to preserve mankind in general and ourselves in particular seems difficult to discharge in the state of nature, and the enjoyment of our property which is a condition of self-preservation seems particularly precarious in the state of nature. Political society is meant to remedy these defects, and comes into existence when the executive power of each in the state of nature is given up to society as a whole, and when a legislative authority is empowered to give the law of nature certainty and an executive power is authorized to enforce it.

It is, then, our obligation of self-preservation, which appears to be a right against other people, but which is in fact an obligation to God who having made us, owns us, which is the rational basis for being obliged to a government which enhances one's prospects of self-preservation.[13] Consent identifies the occasion on which our moral obligations become political, and is an acknowledgement of the legitimacy of the political power to which we are subjected, and not as such our ground for obeying it.

A variation of this 'Lockian' argument has recently been advanced by Robert Nozick in *Anarchy, State and Utopia*.[14] For Nozick, individuals in the pre-political state are bearers of rights to life, liberty and property; these rights are absolute, negative side constraints, but unlike Locke's natural rights they are not derived from God's natural law, rather they are taken to be the conditions for a conception of the person as a free and equal subject. Unfortunately for Nozick and subsequent commentators these rights are never adequately explained or defended. However, whereas Locke argues our duty to preserve ourselves provides the rational basis for political obligations, Nozick argues that our rights create no duties other than those we freely assume. How then is the state possible? It is in answer to this that Nozick develops a peculiar 'invisible hand' version of the social contract.

Nozick's argument takes the following form, in the state of nature each individual has the same fundamental rights including rights of enforcement. Given the inconveniences of the 'Lockian' state of nature individuals will group together into protective agencies or else consent to a protective agency to provide security and regularity in enforcement. These protective agencies acquire no special rights not already held by the individuals who consent to them as they are set up with the sole limited purpose of maintaining security. Over time the need to protect the members of a protective association will lead to the establishment of a dominant protective agency in a given territory. In the case of 'independents' who do not freely transfer their executive rights to the dominant protective agency, the dominant protective agency can enforce its will as a means of prohibiting the effects of dangerous private enforcements of justice upon its members, as long as it provides compensation in terms of security and protection. Thus while no one has expressly consented to the establishment of the state, and without relying on the problematic notion of tacit consent, we have the emergence via an invisible hand process of an ultraminimal state. There are a number of crucial difficulties with Nozick's account, namely how we get from an ultraminimal state in which protection is provided only to those who purchase protection services to the minimal state in which all are protected. This is a redistributive question and the success of Nozick's argument depends upon whether he can show how the good of protection differs from other desirable goods.

However, the important point is that while Nozick's argument avoids direct recourse to the social contract, his invisible hand explanation provides a contractarian reason for us to acknowledge the legitimacy of political obligations even if they are only to a much reduced state. Nozick's argument is significant in modern contractarian debates because it is confined exclusively to the origin of our political obligations and consciously denies the redistributive implications that are central to Rawls's contractarian theory of justice.

Although Nozick self-consciously allies himself with a 'Lockian' tradition, it is clear that his theory is significantly different from Locke's. What Nozick does, however, is stimulate a re-evaluation and development of 'Lockian' arguments as a source for contemporary political theory in the same way that Gauthier, Kavka and Buchanan use Hobbes's argument. However, the most significant of the classic *civil* contractarians from the perspective of the modern resurgence of interest in contract theory is Immanuel Kant.

Kant and Rousseau are also conventionally associated with the idea of a classic tradition having its roots in ancient Greece, but neither bears any relation to the position of Glaucon. Both conceive of the contract as a hypothesis which sheds light on the human condition. For Rousseau it describes the mechanism by which moral transformation takes place – that is, from activity guided by the particular will or self-interest, to that inspired by one's real or rational will and the common good. In Kant's case it is a requirement of reason, a standard by which the practice of sovereigns can be evaluated.

Rousseau is at once contemptuous and praising of the idea of a social contract. He is dismissive of those thinkers like Grotius, Hobbes, Locke and Pufendorf who read back into the natural condition attributes and desires peculiar to civil society. In his 'Discourse on the Origin and Foundations of Inequality Among Men' the idea of contract or consent is used to show how artificial inequalities, such as those of honour, prestige, power and privilege, as opposed to natural inequalities like age, strength, ability and health, are institutionalized and compounded at a certain stage of social development by the establishment of political authority designed to protect the interests of those with unequal advantages. Rousseau argues that:

> Such was, or should have been, the origin of society and laws, which gave new fetters to the weak and new forces to the rich, irretrievably destroyed natural liberty, established forever the law of property and of inequality, changed adroit usurpation into an irrevocable right, and for the profit of a few ambitious men henceforth subjected the entire human race to labour, servitude and misery.[15]

Having spoken of the idea of contract as a device to compound the iniquitous inequalities correlative with social development, he uses it in *The Social Contract* to transform this political society, thoroughly corrupted by self-interest, into a just body politic. (See Jennings's Chapter 6.)

Rousseau at once wants to emulate the strong community spirit and denial of individualism found in Sparta, while at the same time wanting to present a voluntarist theory of political obligation which legitimizes sovereign authority by grounding it in consent. It is clear, however, that the consent required is that which chooses right, rather than creates it, and what is chosen can hardly be described as an act of free will. A charismatic Lawgiver with remarkable powers of persuasion and deceit claims authority for a fundamental constitution from a superhuman source, the implication of which is some form of Divine retribution if it is not imposed upon the people by themselves, and the adoption of which with proper guidance from the Lawgiver, Civil Religion and the Censorial Tribunal, will make them into the kind of moral people they would have had to have been to have chosen the fundamental laws freely.[16] The 'common masses' are simply incapable of understanding the complexities of what such a great Legislator has to propose: 'For an emerging people to be capable of appreciating the sound maxims of politics and to follow the fundamental rules of statecraft, the effect would have to become the cause'.[17]

Kant's use of the social contract is consistent with his moral theory and optimism about the capacity for human potentialities to flourish. His political philosophy, like his metaphysics or moral theory, is formulated independently of empirical evidence. The concept of the will that legitimizes political authority, he claims, is a necessary hypothesis and the social contract itself is a requirement of reason, not as an account of the origin of political society, but as a rational criterion of the just polity.[18] (See Williams's Chapter 7.) Consent is not the ground of political obligation in Kant and therefore breaches of the contract are not justifications for rebellion.[19] Obligation is demanded as a dictate of reason on the ground that the ruler is the upholder and administrator of the system of public legal justice within which morality operates, and which if undermined by civil disobedience would retard progress. The value of the person as an end in himself or herself constrains rulers in how they should treat their subjects. In invoking the idea of a social contract Kant is providing a way of thinking about laws and social arrangements which are appropriate to the value of autonomous persons. Politics, Kant claims, must be subordinate to morality, that is, 'politics must bend the knee before right' and no ruler can avoid having his or her public and private conduct judged according to the principle of right however much he or she 'may also devise a hundred excuses and subterfuges to get out of deserving them in practice'.[20] Incessant national and international scrutiny and the exemplars to be found in the conduct of other rulers provide the impetus to progress towards the correspondence of morality and politics.

Perhaps the most famous restatement of a Kantian contract theory is provided by John Rawls's *A Theory of Justice*.[21] Rawls uses the concept of a social contract not simply to choose his two principles of justice, but as a device which underpins his conception of a just society as a fair system of social cooperation between individuals who are free and equal. Rawls's resurrection of the Kantian contract tradition not only has stimulated a series of what have come to be known as 'contractualist' thinkers including Brian Barry and T. M. Scanlon, but also has provoked a new tradition of anti-contractarians known as communitarians, whom we will discuss in the second section of this chapter.

As with Kant, Rawls does not use social contract arguments to explain the origin of political authority but rather to characterize a form of political association; this is what Rawls means by describing the ideal or just society as a fair system of social cooperation. However, not only is Rawls distinctive because of his use of the metaphor of society as a fair agreement, but also he uses the contract device to justify the choice of the two principles which make up his conception for 'justice as fairness'. It is this use of the contract as a theory of justification in normative political theory that has underpinned the claim that Rawls's *A Theory of Justice* has marked a rebirth of normative political theory.

The use of the contract to justify his two principles of justice has led to the greatest controversy surrounding his theory and has in part prompted his recent restatement of his theory in *Political Liberalism*.[22] The contract is not designed as a bargaining situation in which the participants decide upon principles that should govern their behaviour and in that way his theory differs from *moral* contractarians such as Gauthier. Instead the contract is designed as a device of 'representation', to show individuals why they have reasons for acknowledging the impartial or neutral political perspective embodied in 'justice as fairness'. The two principles of justice are identified independently of the contract, thus highlighting the difference with *moral* contractarianism, in which the principles of morality are the result of a bargain in the original contract. However, given that individuals have a tendency to partiality, why should they adopt these principles of justice? Rawls answers this question with his idea of a fair initial agreement guaranteed by a 'veil of ignorance'. His point is that these principles would be chosen as fair terms of cooperation in circumstances where no individual was able to tailor alternative principles to his advantage. The 'veil of ignorance' not only denies individuals knowledge of the particular features of their personality, such as beliefs, desires, aspirations and moral commitments, but also denies them specific knowledge about their society. Given these constraints no individuals could choose principles that advantage them at the expense of others. Consequently, by adopting this model of a fair initial choice situation the participants have reasons for adopting fair principles of social cooperation.

While much of the criticism that Rawls's theory has attracted has focused on the implications of his account of 'justice as fairness', a major source of criticism has focused on his contractarianism. Communitarians have claimed that the social contract serves no real purpose as it does not provide individuals with a reason for going behind the hypothetical 'veil of ignorance' in the first place. Unless they are already inclined to adopt an impartial perspective then the contract will not work. This has led Rawls in his recent work to re-emphasize that the contract is only a model or 'representative device' and that the real motivation for adopting 'justice as fairness' is provided from individuals' comprehensive moral perspectives, and to recast his theory as a *political* rather than a full ethical theory. (See Kelly's Chapter 13.)

Other critics of Rawls who are sympathetic to his enterprise, such as Barry and Scanlon,[23] have abandoned Rawls's conception of the original position and 'veil of ignorance', but retain the idea of society or justified moral principles as the outcome of a fair agreement. This form of contractarianism is commonly referred to as 'contractualism' to distinguish it from *moral* contractarianism. For 'contractualists' the agreement does not result in the choice of principles whether political or moral but it does offer criteria of justification. In Scanlon's case a criterion of whether a principle counts as moral is whether it could not reasonably be rejected. Scanlon's argument goes significantly beyond either the early or late Rawls in that he applies this criterion to the whole of morality, not just *political* morality or justice. However, it has been argued that Scanlon, despite abandoning the 'original position', does not advance significantly beyond Rawls, because of his reliance on a conception of 'reasonableness'. This concept is no less problematic than a direct appeal to substantive moral principles, because whether someone regards the actions of another as unreasonable will at least in part depend on his or her moral or ethical commitments. An appeal to a public conception of 'reasonableness' simply begs the question about an impartial or neutral grounding for liberal political or moral principles. This inability of modern-day Kantians to ground an Archimedean point from which an impartial perspective can be justified has given rise to a debate within modern liberal political philosophy about the value of the contractarian enterprise as a strategy of justification. Whilst there is likely to remain a significant Kantian component in liberal political philosophy, the use of the social contract device as a foundation is of less importance, as can be seen in Rawls's later work where the idea of a *political* society as a fair association of free and equal individuals has a higher profile than the device of the 'original position' and 'veil of ignorance'. Whilst it would be premature to write the obituary of social contract theory, from the perspective of liberal political theory we are perhaps entering a *post*-contractarian age. (See Chapters 13 and 14 by Kelly and Martin.)

Constitutional contractarianism

There is a third broad category of contractarianism that was extensively invoked during the middle ages, and which continued in various guises to be invoked concurrently with *civil* contractarianism. Its modern-day corollary may be found in modern constitutionalism in which the rights and duties of the sovereign and subject are legally defined. It is essentially a juristic conception with its sources in the Roman Law jurists, the covenants of the Old Testament, commercial law, and the feudal contractual arrangements into which lords and vassals entered, and into which kings formally entered with their vassals.[24] In this respect civil society itself is not necessarily posited to rest upon consent, it is instead the relationship between the ruler and the ruled that is said to be contractual, explicitly or implicitly, and which specifies or implies the respective rights and duties of the contractees. The agreement, then, is not among individuals, but between the people, normally narrowly conceived, and the ruler. The idea of arbitrary and absolute rule was anathema to the people of the middle ages.[25] Thomas Aquinas, for example, thought that men naturally cohere into society, and that it was equally as natural that someone should take charge of those matters that pertain to the common good. A community that elects its own leader even if it contracts obedience in perpetuity can justifiably depose a tyrant who subverts the common good; 'since he had not acted faithfully in discharging the royal office, so the covenant made by his subjects might likewise not be kept'.[26] Where the right to place a ruler over a community lies elsewhere, for example, in the hands of the Emperor, it is that authority to which a community must appeal to act, and ultimately to God if satisfaction is not attained.

During a period when law was the fundamental category in terms of which all physical, moral and social relations were conceived, in which the cosmos was hierarchically ordered by law, and one's station had both rights and duties juridically attached, the individual subject, or collectives of subjects, stood at the centre of an array of contractual engagements which might include the idea of a contract among subjects; between subjects and a ruler; between a ruler and collective rights bearers, like cities, or guilds; between a ruler and God, and between God and the subjects of a ruler. Law was, in its secular form, understood as a repository of customs and practices and no clear conception of the ruler making law, rather than declaring it, emerged during the middle ages. The idea that legislation is an integral aspect of political practice, rather than the declaration of what to a large extent already exists in convention, custom and natural law, found clear theoretical expression in Marsilius of Padua's conviction that the will of the legislator was the source of law.[27] The legislator for him was the people (or the weightier part thereof) from whom the authority of law derived, and which was more likely to be obeyed if understood as self-imposed. Although Marsilius does not use contractual language, the idea of conditional government was pervasive throughout the middle ages. The conditions were often specified as inherent in the terms of appointment, as Manegold of Lautenbach famously illustrates towards the end of the eleventh century: 'is it not plain', he argues, that a tyrant 'falls from the dignity granted to him? Since it is evident that he has broken the contract by virtue of which he was appointed'.[28] Such language persisted throughout the early modern period and even James I who believed that kingly authority was rightly compared with that of a father, felt compelled to admit that certain obligations towards his people were bestowed upon him on taking the coronation oath, but they were not, he insisted, contractual.[29] In *A Speech to the Lords and Commons* (1610), James conceded that as king he had tacitly accepted to obey the laws and protect the people of his kingdom, and in the coronation oath expressly promised to do so. Kingship degenerates into tyranny, he contends, when this pact is broken. He does not, however, allow what was commonly attached to the idea of contract, a qualified right of resistance, or duty to God to depose a tyrant who subverts God's laws.[30] The ground for such a view he had given in the earlier tract. When a party to a contract breaks its terms only a superior judge can adjudicate the merits of the claim. No party can release himself from the contract because he thinks another party has broken its terms. If there were such a pact between king and subjects only God can judge if it has been broken, and administer punishment accordingly.[31]

The idea of a contemporaneous contract as a constraint on ruler and ruled reflected the social relations and practices of the time and had little bearing on the broader question of the legitimacy of the political authority itself. The answer to this question was sought in the idea of an original contract between the people and the sovereign in the distant past and binding upon successive generations. This view was developed during the fourteenth and fifteenth centuries by such writers as Engelbert of Volersdorf (1250–1311), John of Paris (d. 1306), and Nicholas of Cusa (1401–64). Only rarely is the original contract explicitly purported to be an agreement among individuals constitutive of the community,[32] and instead refers to the pact between the community and its ruler, with a great deal of equivocation and contradiction in explanation of the origin of the contracting community itself.[33] Even in later thinkers like Richard Hooker (1554–1600), who tried to show that political society was both natural and a human artefact, we should not confuse its emergence by common consent with the idea that it is founded in contract.[34] He believed that the implied compact between the community and its ruler was perpetually renewed in the coronation oath. In his view corporations like the state are immortal. Those persons living now are alive in their ancestors, and their ancestors live on in them. The consent of our ancestors bind us in perpetuity. Political obligation does not, however, rest upon consent, but is commanded by God. The choice of government may have been at the discretion of the people, but those upon whom office is conferred 'hold it by divine right'. He goes on to say that 'God doth ratify the works of that Sovereign authority which *Kings* have received by men'.[35]

The religious controversies of the sixteenth century gave rise to numerous tracts by Huguenots, such as Hotman, Beza and Mornay, and the radical Calvinist Buchanan, in which consent and contract in relation to the community and its ruler is invoked in various degrees to claim the freedom of religious worship for their own denominations, and to establish theories of resistance largely grounded in an implied contractual duty to God. Similarly in the Thomist revival of the sixteenth century, in such writers as Vitoria, Molina and Suarez, the language of consent and contract figures,[36] but certainly not as prominently as the searchers for the pedigree of social contract theory would like.[37]

If Socrates is to be commandeered as a proto-contractarian it is to this heterogeneous tradition of constitutional contract theory that he is perhaps best related in so far as passing reference to political agreements is deemed sufficient for membership.

After convincing Crito that an honourable man keeps his promises, Socrates does suggest that the enjoyment of the protection of the laws constitutes an implied agreement to obey,[38] but it does not, however, generate mutual obligations. Dissatisfaction with the laws does not constitute grounds for resistance. The appeal by the laws to Socrates to honour his obligations relies much more heavily upon the notion of natural rather than voluntarily incurred obligations. The Laws describe Socrates as their 'child and servant', and themselves as 'his parents' and 'guardians'. In comparison to Socrates' congenital parents his country is described as 'far more precious, more venerable, more sacred, and held in greater honour both among gods and among all reasonable men', and against which violence 'is a far greater sin'.[39] Socrates is being compelled to obey the laws as a son is naturally obliged to obey his parents. Furthermore it may plausibly be suggested that Socrates be compared more fruitfully with modern communitarianism than with contractarianism. There is not the slightest implication that individuals have an identity apart from the community, nor that the community is the product of individual consenting wills. Indeed, the laws claim responsibility for shaping Socrates into the person he is, and even imply that in so far as they have made him, they own him, he is their servant and must obey.

The strong sense of will and voluntarism that are characterisitic of the contract theories of the seventeenth and eighteenth centuries, and which have their roots in the medieval period, barely finds expression in the Greek world.[40] The purpose of the so-called Greek contractarians was to suggest that the origin of law and justice was conventional, not that they were legitimized by consent. In such writers as Antiphon and Glaucon the suggestion is that moral constraints are a confidence trick perpetrated upon the strong by the weak.

It now remains in this section to examine what among those classic contract theorists the social contract creates, and why for most of these thinkers it necessitates sub-dividing the world into smaller political units to which citizens owe their primary obligations (for variations upon these themes see Charvet's Chapter 10.)

SOCIAL CONTRACT AND THE STATE

The social contract tradition that informs modern contractarianism, and the search for philosophical foundations to moral and political obligation, is undoubtedly the classic form of the seventeenth and eighteenth centuries associated with Grotius, Hobbes, Pufendorf, Locke, Rousseau and Kant. The most notable of the twentieth century's earlier revivals is explicitly an attempt to overcome the deficiencies of the contract theories of Hobbes, Locke and Rousseau, by developing an account of what they lacked, namely a theory of the non-social community.[41] It is undeniable that Rawls, Nozick, Buchanan and Gauthier derive inspiration from this same tradition which is the central focus of this volume.

The classic contractarians had a preoccupation, in differing degrees, however, that distinguishes them from not only Ancient Greek and medieval, but also modern contract theorists. That preoccupation is with the personality of the state. Like earlier and later contractarians the classic *civil* contractarians assume the sub-division of the world into smaller political units. The desire for security, in one guise or another, and improved material and cultural benefits, acts as the catalyst to transform a potentially hostile state of nature into multiple political units, the legitimacy of which is based upon authority and not force. Whether the state of nature is posited as a universal moral community, or a mere aggregate of atomistic individuals, the inconveniences consequent upon a lack of legitimate authority provide the mechanism for the transformation. The possession of non-moral natural rights as perpetual sources of conflict *inter homines*, or moral defects resulting from the Fall, or even the existence of some degenerates unable to uphold the law of nature (in all, or most of its characterizations) makes it imperative that individuals subordinate themselves to political authority.[42] In Hobbes, for example, civil society unites otherwise morally unrelated individuals, whereas in Grotius, Locke, Pufendorf and Vattel civil society, with its consequent obligations, is superimposed upon a universal moral community, thus giving rise to potential conflicts between one's duties as a citizen and a human being. The existence of self-complete and self-sustaining political communities, at least for security purposes, is justified on prudential grounds.[43] Although the product of human artefact and will, states are nevertheless natural in so far as they better facilitate God's purpose of the preservation of mankind.

In such writers as Vitoria and Grotius the universal moral community of humankind is posited as a real constraint upon the activities of states, whereas Locke, Pufendorf, Wolff and Vattel gradually place the state at the centre of international relations. These writers essentially validate a process that achieved formal recognition and was greatly facilitated by the Peace of Westphalia in 1648. The state becomes the principal moral entity through which the interests of individuals are expressed in the international society of states. The primary obligation of the citizen *de facto* belongs to the state, and that of the state to its citizens, and only to humanity as a whole as a secondary consideration.

In Vitoria, for instance, we find the suggestion that God has implanted in men a natural sociableness which impels them towards *societas*. He is adamant, however, that political power is not derived from the people. Whereas a community by consent, express or implied, confers authority upon a ruler, just as the College of Cardinals elects the Pontiff, the power exercised by the ruler or pope, is a gift bestowed by God.[44] The partnerships or communities existing by consent or succession do not override the fact that the whole world 'is in a sense a commonwealth', and that within it Christendom constitutes 'a single commonwealth and a single body'.[45] The inhabitants of the whole world are subject to natural law and the law of nations (*jus gentium*). Although not without inconsistency, Vitoria equates the law of nations with human positive law and maintains that the whole world is bound by it. No political community or state has a right to act in ways detrimental to the interests of the larger community.[46] It was in this context that Vitoria robustly defended the American Indian against the claims to dominion by the Spanish Empire and the Papacy.[47] Grotius, of course, was an even greater champion of the law of nations, 'deriving its authority from the consent of all, or at least of many nations'.[48] Despite the existence of states as self-sustaining 'lesser social units' individuals continue to be 'fellow-citizens of that common society which embraces all mankind'.[49] The law of nations was for Grotius, like Vitoria, only one of a range of moral constraints upon the activities of nations in their relations with each other. The natural law is ultimately the foundation of the law of nations, and its subjects are not the abstract entities of states, but instead individuals whether they are rulers, merchants or travellers.

The gradual centralization of military power, diplomatic representation, the right of declaring war and making treaties during the sixteenth and seventeenth centuries became reflected in the articulation of a more abstract conception of the state. At first the concepts of *societas* (partnership) and *universitas* (corporation) inherited from Roman Law and medieval juristic scholasticism proved inadequate. A *universitas*, but not a *societas*, could be authoritatively endowed with a fictitious personality (*person ficta*) to make it a subject under law with a capacity for proprietary rights. This status, however, had to be conferred by a higher authority. In this respect, to conceptualize a state as a corporation, a fictitious personality, implied a higher temporal conferring authority. Furthermore, the corporation was not deemed a moral agent capable of doing wrong. It had no will and no soul.[50] If the state was not a corporation it had to be a *societas*, or partnership which was itself conducive to the language of agreement and consent.

In order to place the state at the centre of international law, a much stronger conception of the state as a moral personality, and of the obligation of individuals to it, had to be developed. Classic contractarian theorists gave substance to the idea of the state as a deliberative moral agent with rights and duties commensurate with its higher will and personality. This is a preoccupation that is absent from Greek, Romano-medieval and modern versions of contractarianism.

It was commonplace to compare the state in its relations with other states with the individual in a state of nature whether or not it was regulated by a moral natural law. Both Hobbes and Pufendorf posit this analogy, and at the same time deny international law the status of law proper because of the lack of a sovereign enforcer. States in their relations for Hobbes are subject to an amoral, and for Pufendorf a moral natural law, and in each case the social contract creates the person of the state demanding almost complete obedience. That they should advocate a form of absolutism is not at all surprising, given the economic and social devastation resulting from the Thirty Years War and the English Civil War.

The person that Hobbes's contractees create is an artificial man with much greater strength and power than any natural man. The soul that animates this artificial man is sovereignty.[51] The unity of the multitude is achieved in the representation of one person: 'For it is the *Unity* of the Representer, not the *Unity* of the Represented, that maketh the Person *One*'.[52] The sovereign essentially represents the people and is the embodiment of their unity. The conception is, however, little more than a metaphor and the office of the state remained tied to the person of the ruler. Pufendorf thought Hobbes's depiction of the state as an artificial man ingenious,[53] but his own characterization goes much further. He attributes to the state an individuality and personality distinct from the people who institute it, and the person of the ruler entrusted with its authority. The state is for Pufendorf a *composite* moral person with a will and capacity to bear rights and duties that none of the individuals, or *simple* moral persons comprising it, could claim in their own right. The subordination and intermingling of wills integral to the social contract creates the state which is 'the most powerful of moral societies and persons'.[54] To view the state as a moral person and to place it at the centre of international relations and to make it the principal subject of the law of nations became a commonplace among contractarians. Following Christian Wolff both Vattel and Thomas Reid are typical examples. For Vattel the state 'becomes a moral person having an understanding and a will peculiar to itself, and susceptible at once of obligations and of rights'.[55] Reid argues that: 'A Nation incorporated and united into one Political Body becomes by this Union and Incorporation a Moral Person. It has a Public Interest and good which it ought to pursue as every private man pursues his own private good. It has an understanding and Will'.[56] It is in Rousseau, of course, among the contractarians, that we find the elevation of the subject to the status of citizen and sovereign, and the most dramatic transformation of the multitude into a moral body, or 'public person' with a will more real than that of its constituent parts.[57]

Contractarianism does not, however, sit well with the conception of the state as a moral person because the superior moral entity is made to rest upon the particular or capricious wills of its constituent parts, and more often than not becomes indistinguishable from the person of the ruler or monarch. In fact, the idea of the person of the state becomes much more powerful, and in the hands of some much more dangerous, when set free from contractarian arguments. Hegelians and post-Hegelian German philosophers asserted the organic unity, individuality and moral autonomy of the state, while at the same time they rejected contractarian arguments for its legitimacy. J. K. Bluntschli, for example, writing during the mid-nineteenth century, criticized Pufendorf, Locke and Kant (to a lesser extent) for failing to see that the will of the person of the state was not composed of the wills of each individual. For Bluntschli the social contract was both historically and logically absurd. There was no evidence of any such historical event, and a political contract, dealing as it did not with private but public goods, required the prior existence of the community whose common good it aimed to promote. He argued that the state was a developing maturing 'moral and spiritual organism' with 'a personality which, having spirit and body, possesses and manifests a will of its own'.[58]

It would be anachronistic to attribute to the contractarians who personified the state the totalitarian and militaristic implications that have become associated with the German realists Trietscke and Bernhardi. The person of the state for Pufendorf, to take just one instance, had the modest objective of ensuring the security of its citizens, and could have no justifiable expansionist ambitions. It was purportedly subject to natural law and should always be motivated by the general rule: 'Let the safety of the people be the supreme law'.[59]

ANTI-CONTRACTARIANISM

Given that almost every non-contractarian theory of political obligation, morality, justification and legitimation can be presented as *anti*-contractarian, we do not propose in this section to try to present a typology of all such arguments. That would be both impossible and fruitless. Instead the arguments and theories we review in this section are chosen for two reasons; first, they have a particular relevance to the forms of contractarianism discussed in these essays; second, and more importantly, a critical engagement with these arguments has formed an important part of the characterization and development of the varieties of contract theory we discuss. Thus Filmer's patriarchalism[60] is considered because, first, it forms part of the context out of which modern *civil* contractarianism emerged in the sixteenth and seventeenth centuries, second, it forms the immediate target of Locke's theory in the *Two Treatises*, and third, it has a renewed resonance in contemporary feminist critiques of contractarianism such as Carole Pateman's, which argue that *civil* contractarian arguments while dispensing with patriarchalism have merely replaced it with what she calls *fraternal* patriarchy, which continues to deny full equality and status to women.[61] If we turn to modern *civil* contractarians such as Rawls it is clear that his own argument is an attempt to salvage the Kantian project while at the same time answering or avoiding Hegel's critique of that Kantian enterprise. Much of the recent liberal contribution to the so-called liberal/communitarian debate has been at pains to emphasize the ways in which neo-Kantians can avoid the Hegelian inspired communitarian critique.[62] Indeed two recent commentators have argued that Rawls's most recent works take on a Hegelian character in response to communitarian criticisms.[63] Consequently, some anti-contractarian arguments form an integral part of the development of the varieties of contract theory discussed in the previous section.

The varieties of anti-contractarianism we will discuss in this section are patriarchalism and the critique of natural equality, Hume's account of political obligation and its utilitarian restatement, Hegel's critique of contractarianism and its contemporary restatement in communitarian theory and finally feminist responses to the social contract. Whilst feminist theories borrow much from these other forms of anti-contractarianism, there are nevertheless, distinctive perspectives which modern feminist theories highlight which merit treatment in their own right.

The use of contract and the concomitant idea of consent is, as we have seen, common currency among writers, many of whom invoked the language to legitimize political obligation and establish its limits. Such language was, however, in the view of most critics, singularly inappropriate because it suggested or implied that the obligation to obey authority, and even its very legitimacy, depended upon an original agreement by which succeeding generations were bound, or a continuously renewed agreement liable to be revoked if certain conditions were not met. There were numerous grounds upon which contractarianism was indicted, including its historical dubious-ness, impracticability, and flawed logic. The importance of denying the credibility of an original contract was of varying degrees of significance for the arguments of different critics. For Filmer it was crucial to show that the origin of society and government did not rest upon the agreement of naturally free and equal individuals, whereas for Hume it was a matter of indifference whether or not political society originated in a contract because its continuing legitimacy had nothing to do with its origin. For Hegel, however, it was important to show that the pre-civil state of nature assumed of its members characteristics that they could acquire only in society. The private rights of contract and property are used to legitimize the public rights produced by the legal and social institutions of the state, whereas in reality the opposite is the case, private rights are generated and legitimized by the sphere of public rights. A variation on this Hegelian argument is found in communitarian and Marxist critiques as well as in contemporary feminism.

Patriarchalism and the critique of natural equality

In order to understand Filmer's argument against the origin of government in the consent of the people, it is essential to grasp the importance he attached to the genesis of political obligation. In identifying the origin of government Filmer was asserting not only the form it first took, but also the form that it must always take.[64] The fact that God conferred upon Adam fatherly authority and dominion over the whole earth denies the contractarian origins of both political obligation and property. Fathers, or patriarchs and their successors, exercise a natural authority, that is inherent in the family, and command a natural obligation, that of children to their father. Fatherly authority, for Filmer, is at once real and abstract. It inheres in natural fathers, but it is not necessarily congenital: it is the authority that is natural, not the line of its descent.[65] Sons who are not themselves fathers, but who become heads of households or states exercise the authority attached to the office. Hence queens, in the absence of kings, exercise paternal rather than maternal authority.

Every child is born into a predetermined authority structure and naturally obligated to the father, there is no natural liberty and equality. The people cannot confer their authority upon a ruler, not because authority is inalienable, but because they have none. This is not to deny the existence of natural rights, they are simply not universal.[66] Fathers have natural rights and the power to consent to the transfer of their authority to another party. Such transfers are, however, unconditional because the power exercised is not derived from consenting heads of families, but merely substituted by God and acknowledged by them.

Filmer went to great pains to expose the absurdity of contractarian arguments, and it is this aspect of his thought that is widely considered the most penetrating.[67] If people are naturally free and equal, he argues, and if

God granted property in common, then it would require a unanimous agreement to take anything out of the common stock, or to institute an authority over them, a condition, in his view, that was simply impractical. Furthermore, Filmer like many of his contemporaries subscribed to the view that each individual is God's property and does not have a right to take his own life. It is therefore absurd to entertain the idea that consenting individuals could confer a power that they do not themselves have, namely that of life and death, upon a sovereign. Only God has this power and it is He who confers it upon kings. In addition, if God did not ordain natural liberty and property in common, it is gross impertinence and in violation of his will to destroy this condition by instituting a juridical inequality and private dominion. Such transformations of the original condition make natural law self-contradictory. Against Grotius Filmer argues that:

> Whereas Grotius saith that by the law of nature all things were at first common (Grotius I, i, x, 7), and yet teacheth that after property was brought in it was against the law of nature to use community (Grotius I, i, x, 4), he doth therby not only make the law of nature changeable, which he saith God cannot do, but he also makes the law of nature contrary to itself.[68]

A more extreme argument for natural authority and the rejection of the contractarian conception of man as a free and equal subject is offered by Joseph de Maistre.[69] His arguments are addressed at a general level to the pretensions of the European Enlightenment and the French Revolutionaries, but a particular target was also Rousseau's account of natural equality. For Maistre as for Filmer, man's natural condition was social. But whereas Filmer's patriarchal theory has some subtlety in exposing the logic of the contractarian position, Maistre's argument is primarily a scathing indictment of the presumption of man to challenge a Divine injunction. The contractarian enterprise was for him simply one further example of mankind's inherent wickedness and sinfulness in presuming to challenge the authoritative will of God. In effect his argument is that attempts to justify political obligation or political authority were further examples of man's sinful pride. And it is precisely this sin of pride which grounds the need for an unquestionable political authority in the person of the monarch. Consequently, attempts to circumscribe the authority of the monarch are also ruled out on the grounds of man's natural rebelliousness. Any attempt to assert equal civil or political rights would dissolve the possibility of an unquestionable and absolute authority without which barbarism, disorder and chaos would engulf the world. Maistre's account of man's natural condition as subject of a divinely instituted political and social order, is coloured by his deep pessimism about human nature and his extreme views about man's almost irredeemable sinfulness, views that were to get him into trouble with the Catholic Church. The curiosity of Maistre's argument is that his account of human nature is a caricature of Hobbes's account of the state of nature as a state of war, yet his argument differs from Hobbes's in that he sees society as man's natural state. Consequently, for Maistre political authority, while necessary for Hobbesian reasons, derives no justification from such contractarian arguments. Instead it is the Divinely instituted and authoritative will of God, and unlike Hobbes there is no residual right held against such an authority.

Maistre's arguments are not simply directed against the contractarian tradition but against any attempt to question, legitimize or circumscribe political authority and thus they form an important source for extreme anti-rationalist conservatism; however, they are also important in that they inspire one of the main strands of reaction to Rousseau's *The Social Contract*, and support the reassertion of political absolutism in the face of Rousseau's arguments for popular sovereignty. (On this see Jennings's Chapter 6.)

Whilst Maistre's heterodox theological opinions and Filmer's biblical literalism mean that both theories of absolute authority and Divine Right have very little impact on modern debates, other historical critiques of contractarian accounts of political obligation such as David Humes's, still have great power.

Humean anti-contractarianism and utilitarianism

Hume is generally taken as one of the most devastating critics of contractarianism. At the same time he provided no comfort for the Divine Right and patriarchal theorists of political obligation. In *A Treatise of Human Nature* Hume suggests that societies predate governments, and that the most likely cause of the establishment of the latter was not discord among members of the same society, but external threats and conflicts. The vulnerability of societies to sudden danger necessitated retaliatory and immediate authoritative responses which were most conveniently entrusted to a single individual. Hume argues that this natural origin of monarchy is far more plausible than the contention that it is derived from the natural right of patriarchy.[70] This is not incompatible with the view that he later expressed, which attributed a natural equality to men of 'rude' natures who most probably would have consented to the exercise of some form of authority over them. Because of insufficient sophistication to comprehend the complexity of the act, submission is unlikely to have been total:

> each exertion of authority in the chieftain must have been peculiar, and called forth by the present exigencies of the case: the sensible utility, resulting from his interposition, made these exertions become daily more frequent; and their frequency gradually produced an habitual, and, if you please to call it so, a voluntary, and therefore precarious, acquiescence in the people.[71]

Hume, then, did not wish to deny that the origin of government might have rested upon consent. What he wanted to insist upon was the disjunction between its origin and continuing legitimacy. He could admire Grotius and

Pufendorf for the emphasis they gave to self-interest in the formation of civil society, but deplored the road that they took in grounding political obligation in the natural law of keeping faith with one's promises.[72] Whereas consent could legitimize the origins of government, interests are served by the continuing existence of its authority. As governments secure peace and commodious living it is not the consent of our ancestors, not even our own tacit consent, but the fact that it is in our interests that we are obligated to give our allegiance.[73] The obligation to obey civil government is in order to sustain harmony and security. Keeping one's promises promotes reciprocal confidence and trust in social practices. They are distinct obligations with different ends and interests. Government in fact provides the authority to sustain a society in which promises are made and discharged with confidence, and if reneged upon capable of being enforced.[74] (See Castiglione's Chapter 5.)

Whereas Hume's arguments address the idea of political obligation being derived from a promise, or the idea that society might similarly have its origins in an agreement, to say nothing of his undermining of the epistemology of natural law, for later utilitarians who took their inspiration from Hume there is little or no discussion of contractarian arguments at all. Although Jeremy Bentham famously attacks the idea of society and political obligation being derived from a promise, he assumes that he is merely rehearsing the devastating and conclusive arguments of Hume. Bentham writes:

> As to the Original Contract . . . The stress laid on it formerly, and still, perhaps, by some, is such as renders it an object not undeserving of attention. I was in hopes, however, till I observed the notice taken of it by our author, that this chimera had been effectually demolished by Mr Hume. I think we hear not so much of it now as formerly. The indestructible prerogatives of mankind have no need to be supported upon the sandy foundation of a fiction.[75]

Bentham in attacking Sir William Blackstone's use of the idea of an original contract follows Hume in claiming that the social contract idea is actually redundant in explaining our obligations to government. This is because the institution of promise-keeping is itself not morally basic but instead conventional, therefore the appeal to an original promise cannot do any work unless we already have a prior reason to keep our promises. When a social contract theorist is asked why individuals should keep their promises, they can answer only in terms of utilitarian or consequentialist reasons. First, that individuals will suffer from the disapproval of others if they do not keep their word and this will make it more difficult for individual's to enjoy the benefits of social cooperation, so non-compliance results in punishment or mischief. Second, promise-keeping is a useful social practice which is to the advantage of all and it would be undermined if people did not keep to their word, so promise-keeping is to each person's long-term advantage or benefit. Thus individuals have a reason to keep promises in that the general interest is best served by their so doing. But if that is the case, why appeal to a promise or contract as the basis of political obligation, why not appeal directly to the general interest which is doing all the work in this argument? Bentham argues instead that political society does not emerge from an original contract but is merely the result or a habit of obedience. He writes:

> When a number of persons (whom we may style *subjects*) are supposed to be in the *habit* of paying *obedience* to a person, or an assemblage of persons, of a known and certain description (whom we may call *governor* or *governors*) such persons altogether (*subjects* and *governors*) are said to be in a state of *political* SOCIETY.[76]

This habit of obedience will continue as long as the governor or governors act in the interest of the governed, or more precisely endeavour as far as possible to maximize the greatest happiness of the greatest number. Thus neither is the origin of society to be explained by the original contract, nor is it the case that political obligations derive from an original promise; instead they are conventional and based upon consequentialist reasons. However, one might argue in favour of the contract theorists, that if the obligation to keep a promise cannot be morally basic, why should the obligation to maximize the general happiness or to act for the sake of public utility be any more morally basic?

What reason is offered by the utilitarians? Hume (though not strictly a utilitarian) offers as we have seen an account based on self-interest and natural sympathy for others. This recourse to naturalism is one of Hume's greatest legacies to utilitarianism and contemporary moral and political thought. Bentham, too, adopts naturalistic reasons for acting on utilitarian principles although he does not try to derive the obligation to maximize the greatest happiness of the greatest number from the fact that individuals attempt to maximize their own advantage, in the way that J. S. Mill does in his essay on *Utilitarianism*.[77]

The popularity of such naturalistic accounts of ethical first principles lead to a decline in the use of social contract arguments. The late nineteenth and early twentieth centuries see, with a few honourable exceptions, the disappearance of contractarianism from Anglo-American ethical debates, and an increasing dominance of utilitarian and consequentialist arguments or non-contractarian intuitionist critiques of utilitarianism.[78]

The attitude of contemporary utilitarianism towards contractarian arguments is more ambiguous. Some such as R. M. Hare have been particularly critical of Rawls's use of the device to support his conception of 'justice as fairness',[79] arguing that it is little more than a version of intuitionism. However, recently there has been a renewal of interest in contractarianism as a foundational strategy in the work of utilitarians such as John Harsanyi. Harsanyi uses the idea of a rational bargain as justification of a utilitarian principle. The bargain does not provide reasons independent of utility for obeying the law, or acknowledging political authority, but the rational agreement does ground the principles on which these obligations are indirectly based. Harsanyi's conception of the social contract places him in the *moral* contract tradition yet he is also one of the most significant modern defenders of utilitarianism, a tradition that at least with Hume, Bentham and Mill was inimical to contractarianism.

Whilst Hume's arguments appear conclusive against original contract justifications of political obligation and the origin of political society, other forms of contract argument have as we have seen proved attractive to modern rational choice utilitarians. This shows that the consequentialist tradition is not necessarily inimical to contractarian arguments. Other sources of anti-contractarian arguments have proved to be much more resilient in their hostility to all forms of contractarianism. Perhaps the most significant anti-contractarian arguments are those advanced by contemporary communitarians which derive their impetus from the philosophy of Hegel.

Hegel and the communitarians

Hegel, like Hume, rejects the Divine Right of kings as the basis of political obligation. Everything, even the most pernicious of things is ordained by God, and no special right can be claimed merely on this basis. Unlike Hume, however, Hegel also rejects utility as the basis of obligation. It is just as possible to point to the disadvantages as it is to the advantages of government.[80] The idea of an original contract, or a continuing contract between the people and the monarch, is anathema to Hegel's whole conception of philosophy because it assumes the separateness and autonomy of individuals rather than their unity. It conceives the state as a voluntary association with obligations freely chosen, and gives priority to private over public right, ignoring the fact that the former is dependent upon the latter, and not the other way around as contract theory claims. The language of contract transfers from civil society, the realm of capricious wills and individual interest, a relationship totally inappropriate for characterizing that which pertains between the individual and the state. The state is not, for Hegel, a contractual relation designed to protect the property rights of individuals, nor is it to be deemed the private property of the monarch. From early in his writings Hegel was contemptuous of 'the form of such an inferior relation as the contractual one [having] forced its way into the absolute majesty of the ethical totality'.[81] A contractual relationship, he later argues, 'is a casual tie arising from the subjective need and choice of the parties'.[82] The political relationship is qualitatively different in that it is absolutely necessary, objective and released from considerations of choice or caprice. In *Elements of the Philosophy of Right* Hegel argues that 'it is the rational destiny of human beings to live within a state, and even if no state is yet present, reason requires that one be established'.[83] The state is the ethical order in which individuals realize their capacities and potentialities, they do not choose it, they are born into it, not with natural rights, but with the capacity to acquire the rights and duties that have arisen as a result of human practices and which are sustained by the state. The right to exercise one's subjective conscience is possible only in such an ethical order, and in which one's obligations are prescribed by one's situation.[84] Or to put it in Bradley's famous characterization of the life of man: 'What he has to do depends on what his place is, what his function is, and that all comes from his station in the organism'.[85] (See Haddock's Chapter 8.)

Marx's critique of contractarianism and liberalism as bourgeois ideology builds upon Hegel's account of the individual as a social creation, although he gives this argument a materialist interpretation. Like Hegel he denies that individuals can have a pre-social existence or that their identities are given prior to social interaction. Whilst he devotes little attention directly to the idea of a social contract (see Wilde's Chapter 9) his critique of abstract individualism is by implication also an attack on Hobbesian contractarianism in which individuals are presented as naturally competitive and appetitive in an environment of scarcity. This Hobbesian situation is not for Marx, indicative of man's natural condition, rather it merely signifies his condition in one historical epoch which is shaped by the capitalist mode of production. The classic social contract theorists present a distillation of man's condition in the emerging capitalist mode of production as if it were the universal natural condition of mankind. Social contract arguments are therefore irrelevant from Marx's perspective for three reasons; first, because man's natural condition is not static as the contractarians assumed; second, because any political arrangements legitimized in a social contract agreement are merely going to reflect the imbalance of forces built into the capitalist mode of production, thus any agreement made is not going to have any moral force, so social contract arguments of the Kantian sort are also redundant; and third, because the nature of present politics is determined by the mode of production, any genuine attempt to secure human emancipation is possible only with the revolutionary overthrow of capitalism. Whereas Hegel uses the argument that individuals are situated in a social context to make man feel at home in the world, Marx subverts the enterprise by arguing that it is only by changing the world and overcoming alienation, exploitation and conflict that man can build a genuine community in which he can realize his full human potential.

Whereas Marx holds out the possibility of genuine 'community' only after the revolutionary transformation of society and the withering away of the very state that Hegel saw as fulfilling man's rational nature, a more recent strand of Hegelian inspired anti-contractarianism has resurrected the idea of community as a moral ideal or source, without placing this ideal either at the end of history or necessarily identifying it with the state. This communitarian strand of criticism includes contemporary philosophers such as Charles Taylor, Michael Sandel, Alisdair MacIntyre and Michael Walzer among others.[86] These various communitarians differ in significant respects.

MacIntyre, for example, presents his anti-contractarianism as part of a damning indictment of post-enlightenment culture, whereas Taylor and Walzer want to salvage key 'liberal' values but derive them from non-contractarian foundations. However, what they all share is a rejection of the resurrection of Kantian contractarianism inspired by Rawls's *A Theory of Justice*. Sandel's argument is presented as a direct communitarian critique of Rawls's liberal contractarian argument and therefore will be considered here as representative of the key aims of the other communitarians.

There are three key components to communitarian arguments which have their roots in Hegel's critique of social contract theory and Kantian moral philosophy; first, the 'embeddedness thesis', second, the social or 'cultural options thesis', and third, a positive account of the nature of an ideal community. On this last issue most communitarians have least to say and what they do say is usually either disappointing or implausible.

The 'embeddedness thesis' takes a variety of forms but in Sandel's case is directed against what he calls Rawls's use of an 'unencumbered self' in his account of the original position. Rawls argues that in order to prevent individuals adopting principles of justice that are in their own interest, they must be denied knowledge of key aspects of their personality. There are two points to be made here. First, Sandel claims that this is a metaphysically suspect account of personal identity for it assumes that individuals can distance themselves from all of their attributes in this way and yet remain significantly distinct individuals. Sandel, following Hegel, argues that this is implausible as our identities are constituted by our social attachments and our commitments to conceptions of the good. Without these, we are not merely left with an impoverished account of the individual but with no real individual at all: behind Rawls's 'veil of ignorance' the individual disappears altogether. The implication of this for social contract theory is that it undermines the possibility of any kind of bargain or interpersonal agreement. For if it is the case that behind the 'veil of ignorance' all the individuating factors of personality are excluded then the idea of separate individuals disappears. Thus instead of an agreement or an interpersonal choice we have a situation of recognition of validity on the part of an impersonal subject. This leads on to the second significant feature of the 'embeddedness thesis'.

Sandel's primary target is Rawls's reassertion of the Kantian idea of justice or morality as impartiality. This idea of justice as impartiality, it is argued, is unsustainable because it is unattainable; there is no Archimedean point from which we can adopt an impartial perspective that will at the same time provide individuals with a reason for suspending their partiality. The social contract device used by Rawls cannot provide such an Archimedean perspective because even if it were not flawed it cannot provide individuals with a reason for adopting the impartial perspective, as impartiality is already build into its structure. The communitarian's point is that social contract arguments cannot provide a moral motivation unless one is already inclined to accept a conception of the individual as a free and equal subject separable from his or her constitutive attachments, and if one already accepts such a view then the social contract serves no useful purpose in justifying justice. (See Kelly's Chapter 13.)

The social or 'cultural options thesis' is also developed from Hegel's own criticisms of Kant's conception of autonomy. Here the point being made is not that the conception of the autonomous subject is incoherent but rather that the exercise of genuine moral autonomy requires a particular social context. Autonomy cannot be exercised in abstraction from a social context. Genuine autonomy requires a rich and diverse culture in which autonomous individuals can make genuine and informed choices among realistic and valuable life options. Such a culture is corroded by the neutralist liberalism that follows from contemporary social contract theory and the atomistic individualism it is built upon. Any political authority which adopts strict neutrality towards the goods that individuals pursue is in danger of seeing the diversity of a plural culture disappear in the face of mass opinion. If, on the other hand, the state adopts a stance of protecting important components of a society's culture then it must necessarily abandon a strict impartiality between individual's choices and forms of life and assert grounds for preferring some ways of life above others. This cannot be done within the terms of contract arguments. Thus critics such as Taylor argue that even political liberalism needs more than the underpinnings of a neutralist contractarianism.[87]

A more radical version of this argument which sees the individualism of post-enlightenment culture as a threat to morality itself is offered by Alasdair MacIntyre. MacIntyre sees the individualist challenge to the idea of moral authority as the chief loss of modern culture. The primacy of the individual, and individual judgement and will, undermines the possibility of moral authority and the only way this can be rescued is by recovering a conception of community as a shared moral inheritance in which individuals can find objective moral criteria. MacIntyre is influenced by Aristotle and Aquinas as well as Hegel, in seeing community as a common life constructed around a shared conception of the Good. The problem for MacIntyre and other communitarians, is specifying what form that common life should take and how we get from our present situation of decline to this new moral ideal. Marx presents one answer, but it is not an answer that many feel compelling given the history of the twentieth century. If communitarians also put off the realization of community then we are left with the problem of what to do here and now. If, on the other hand, they attempt to recover a politics appropriate to our present circumstances then it is often the case that their conclusions are disappointingly similar to the abstract liberalism to which they take such exception. Whilst the communitarian critique poses difficulties for contractarian defences of liberal political principles, it is much less damaging to the liberal political theory than is often claimed. (See Chapters 8, 13 and 14 by Haddock, Kelly and Martin.)

Feminist objections

The last important category of anti-contractarian arguments to be considered are those derived from the feminist tradition. In recent years the growing literature on feminist political thought has encouraged a reconsideration of some of the fundamental categories of political theorizing, in its attempt to show not only that the canon of 'great' texts has systematically excluded women, but also that the very terms of modern political thought are not gender neutral, but support the gender structure of society and the perpetuation of male dominance. The concept of the social contract has particularly attracted the attention of feminist theorists because of its conception of the natural condition of man as being one of freedom and equality. It is in relation to the politics of the subject and individual identity that feminists have made the most significant and radical challenges to contractarian modes of thought.

For feminist critics of the contract tradition such as Carole Pateman, the whole conception of society as a contractual association between free and equal subjects is part of the problem that has to be addressed if women are to emancipate themselves from the male dominance of modern societies. The classic contractarians such as Locke, Kant and Rousseau are criticized not merely because they explicitly excluded women from the category of rational subjects who could consent to political rule. The idea of the individual as a free and equal subject is a peculiarly male category because it is conceptualized around a pre-existing sexual division of labour in which women are consigned to the tasks and responsibilities of the domestic sphere, thus freeing men to exercise their free wills in the public or political realm. It is only because of this pre-existing domestic subordination of women that male subjects could be free and equal subjects. Similarly when Rousseau claims in *The Social Contract* that 'Man is born free, but everywhere he is in chains',[88] he chooses to ignore the fact that no person is born free of authorities, duties or responsibilities, as all children male or female are born to parents, and these parents have natural obligations to them and are not therefore free to abandon them. That said the burden of these responsibilities and duties towards children has been unequally distributed as is illustrated by Rousseau's abandonment of his own children. Consequently, while 'men' might well be free and equal subjects, women certainly are not, and are rarely even considered equal bearers of rights because of their different, less rational natures.

Pateman continues her alternative account of the modern contract tradition by arguing it is based on the replacement of patriarchalism by fraternity, in which the dominance of the father is replaced by the sexual dominance of men over women. The unequal right of the patriarch to the bodies of women is replaced by the equal right of men to exercise sexual dominance over women. Pateman's argument has stimulated a heated debate within political theory and feminism (see Coole's Chapter 11), and whatever the overall merits of her argument it has proved to be an important motive for feminist theorists to return to the classical contract tradition and the reappraisal of the canon of 'great' texts.

A development of some of these strands of criticism is to be found in the 'different voice' feminism of Nancy Chodorow and Carol Gilligan.[89] These theorists challenge the idea of a universal moral psychology concerned with justice, rights and principles, offering instead an account of these categories as male and contrasting them with female 'ethic of care' based on the categories of empathy, proximity and relatedness. The male emphasis on rights, justice and principles is premised upon the separated and oppositional nature of males, which is reflected in the state of nature narratives of classic contract theory. This oppositional character of male moral theorizing has its origin in the developmental psychology of males with their need to separate and distance themselves from their mother, something that is far less important to female children.

Such 'psychological' theories have also prompted considerable debate among feminists, not least because the very differences that Gilligan and Chodorow discuss might well simply be reflections of the socialization processes of a male structured society. But also, these theories raise the possibility of essentialist theories that modern feminists have been at such pains to overcome in the search for genuine emancipation. If women are after all 'naturally' prone to exhibit what might uncharitably be called 'domestic' virtues then surely it could be argued they are best suited to the domestic realm, unlike men who are naturally suited to the public realm or politics. This is hardly the sort of conclusion even 'different voice' feminists wish to draw, though some not only have argued for the transformation of the public sphere by the 'ethic of care' but also have argued that the domestic realm ought to be given a higher status and be seen as a more attractive option by modern women.

The challenge posed by the questioning of identity has lead not only to the so-called 'ethic of care', but also to a much more radical challenge to the terms of liberal egalitarianism and its emphasis of impartiality and distributive justice. Difference feminists such as Iris Marion Young and Seyla Benhabib[90] have argued that in order to achieve genuine emancipation from the male dominant power structures of modern society, what is needed is not merely gender neutral policies of redistribution, but a rethinking of the goals of political theory addressed to the problems of institutional domination. This approach has taken many feminist theorists into the field of democratic theory and away from the terms of liberal political theory with its emphasis on contract and impartial agreement between equal subjects. Equal rights are of little value in a world where the exercise of those rights is itself frustrated by the structures of gender domination in modern society.

Not all contemporary feminists are as antipathetic to contractarian forms of argument, but even those who find something of value in the aspirations of the liberal emancipatory project, such as Susan Moller-Okin,[91] nevertheless recognize that the way contractarian arguments are used, even by writers like Rawls, needs significant revision if they are to accord men and *women* genuine equality of status as well as equality of right.

CONCLUSION

In this chapter we have presented an account of the diversity of uses to which the social contract may be put and provided a review of the most important strands of anti-contractarian argument. A critical review of such a vast literature can be only cursory, and we will have succeeded in our purpose if we have raised questions that others are stimulated to answer.

What should be clear from our account and the following chapters is the resourcefulness of the contractarian traditions in the face of fundamental criticisms of the sort posed by Hume, Hegel or modern feminism. However, it is also clear that the ideal of political life as an agreement on fair terms of association between individuals who have a recognized status as free and equal is a moral ideal that has a very deep resonance in modern culture, and it is one that has proved a great inspiration to those who do not enjoy the recognition of that status. Thus whilst Rawls may well have weakened his commitment to the 'original position' and Gauthier may also have retreated in the face of major criticisms, it would be foolishness indeed, to chose to write the obituary for contractarianism.

NOTES

1 Gierke, Gough and Barker are the obvious traditional examples, but see also the more recent examples of Patrick Riley, *Will and Political Legitimacy*, Cambridge, Mass., Harvard University Press, 1982, ch. 1; Michael Lessnoff, *Social Contract*, London, Macmillan, 1986, p. 2; Michael Lessnoff (ed.), Introduction, *Social Contract Theory*, Oxford, Basil Blackwell, 1990, p. 3; David Mapel, 'The Contractarian Tradition and International Ethics', in *Traditions of International Ethics*, Terry Nardin and David Mapel (eds), Cambridge, Cambridge University Press, 1992, p. 186; Robert Sugden, 'The Contractarian Enterprise', in *Rationality, Justice and the Social Contract*, David Gauthier and Robert Sugden (eds), Hemel Hempstead, Harvester Wheatsheaf, 1993, p. 1.
2 See, for example, J. W. Gough, *The Social Contract: A Critical Study of its Development*, 2nd edn, Oxford, Clarendon Press, 1957, ch. 2; D. G. Ritchie, 'Contributions to the History of the Social Contract Theory', in *Darwin and Hegel and Other Philosophical Studies*, London, Swan Sonnenschein, 1893; Vicente Medina, *Social Contract Theories: Political Obligation or Anarchy*, Savage, Md, Rowman & Littlefield, 1990, pp. 2–3; Lessnoff, *Social Contract*, ch. 1; Ernest Barker, *Greek Political Theory*, London, Methuen, 1977, p. 64; W. K. C. Gutherie, *A History of Greek Philosophy*, vol. 3, Cambridge, Cambridge University Press, 1969, ch. 5.
3 Plato, *The Republic*, Harmondsworth, Penguin, 1987, 358e–359. See Barker, *Greek Political Theory*, p. 142, where he emphasizes Plato's rejection of the social contract proper, that is the contract of political society.
4 John Harsanyi, 'Morality and the Theory of Rational Behaviour', in *Utilitarianism and Beyond*, A. Sen and B. Williams (eds), Cambridge, Cambridge University

Press, 1982; James Buchanan, *The Limits of Liberty: Between Anarchy and Leviathan*, Chicago, University of Chicago Press, 1975; John Mackie, *Ethics: Inventing Right and Wrong*, Harmondsworth, Penguin, 1977; David Gauthier, *Morals by Agreement*, Oxford, Oxford University Press, 1986.

5   Gauthier, *Morals by Agreement*, p. 6, suggests that he wants to show how principles for choice can be rationally generated 'without introducing prior moral assumptions'.

6   Aristotle, *Politics*, John Warrington (trans.), London, Heron, no date, p. 81. I use this earlier literal translation in preference to later value-loaded renditions that have Lycophron saying that the laws are the 'guarantor of men's reciprocal rights'. For an excellent discussion of these questions see R. G. Mulgan, 'Lycophron and Social Contract Issues', *Journal of the History of Ideas*, 1979, vol. XL.

7   The German Calvinist Althusius is generally credited with being the first to articulate the modern conception of the social contract because he incorporates a contract of society and of government. At all levels of society, including the family, Althusius suggested that the relations were contractual. See *The Politics of Althusius*, Frederick S. Carney (trans.), London, Eyre & Spottiswoode, 1965, p. 117. It is clear, however, that the holders of rights in Althusius's theory are groups and corporations and not individuals. He does not characterize the social contract as an agreement between bearers of natural rights which is the hallmark of the later classic theories. An extract from Althusius is reprinted in Lessnoff (ed.) *Social Contract Theory*, pp. 27–49.

8   Hugo Grotius, *On the Law of War and Peace*, Francis W. Kelsey (trans.), Oxford, Oxford University Press for the Carnegie Endowment for International Peace, 1925, Prolegomena, par. 15, book I, ch. 1, par. 14, and book III, ch. 19, par. 2.

9   Pufendorf argues that it is 'no more possible for civil sovereignty to create goodness and injustice by precept, than it is for it to command that poison lose its power to waste the human body': Samuel Pufendorf, *On the Law of Nature and Nations, Eight Books*, C. H. Oldfather and W. A. Oldfather (trans.), Oxford, Oxford University Press for the Carnegie Endowment for International Peace, 1934, book VIII, ch. i, par. 5.

10 Pufendorf, *Law of Nature and Nations*, book III, ch. iv, par. 6; Knud Haakonssen, 'Hugo Grotius and the History of Political Thought', *Political Theory*, 1985, vol. 13, p. 256.

11 See Samuel Pufendorf, *On the Duty of Man and Citizens According to Natural Law*, James Tully (ed.), Cambridge, Cambridge University Press, 1991, book I, 6.1, 6.2, 7.1, 8.1. The extent to which most of Locke's argument in the *Two Treatises* rests upon this *'first and fundamental natural law'* has been little noticed. John Locke, *Two Treatises of Government*, Peter Laslett (ed.), Cambridge, Cambridge University Press, 1988, I, §86 and §88, and II, §6, §8, §23, §123, §128, §129, §134, §159 and §220.

12 Locke, *Two Treatises*, I, §95, and II, §171.

13 For Locke it is the preservation of property that impels us to enter civil society (II, §138), but property is, of course, the 'Lives, Liberties and Estates' of the people (II, §123). As God's property we have an obligation to enter civil society to preserve it:

> For men being all the Workmanship of the one Omnipotent and infinitely wise Maker; All the Servants of the one Sovereign Master, sent into the World by his order and about his business, they are his Property. . . . Everyone as he is bound to preserve himself, and not to quit his station wilfully; so by the like reason when his own Preservation comes not into competition ought he, as much as he can, *to preserve the rest of Mankind* (II, §6)

14 R. Nozick, *Anarchy, State, and Utopia*, Oxford, Basil Blackwell, 1974.

15 In Jean-Jaques Rousseau, *The Basic Political Writings*, Donald A. Cress (ed.), Indianapolis, Ind., Hackett, 1987, p. 70.

16 See the famous chapter VII of Jean-Jacques Rousseau, *The Social Contract* in *Basic Political Writings*.

17 Rousseau, *Basic Political Writings*, p. 164.

18 Immanuel Kant, 'The Contest of the Faculties', in *Kant's Political Writings*, Hans Reiss (ed.), Cambridge, Cambridge University Press, 1991, p. 187.

19 Kant says, 'even if the power of the state or its agent, the head of state, has violated the original contract by authorising the government to act tyrannically and has thereby in the eyes of the subject, forfeited the right to legislate, the subject is still not entitled to offer counter-resistance': Kant, 'On the Common Saying: "This May Be True in Theory, But it Does Not Apply in Practice" ', in *Political Writings*, Reiss (ed.), p. 81.

20 Kant, *Perpetual Peace*, in *Political Writings*, Reiss (ed.), pp. 125 and 121. See also Patrick Riley, 'On Kant as the Most Adequate of the Social Contract Theorists', *Political Theory*, 1973, vol. I.

21 J. Rawls, *A Theory of Justice*, Oxford, Oxford University Press, 1971.

22 J. Rawls, *Political Liberalism*, New York, Columbia University Press, 1993.

23 T. M. Scanlon, 'Contractualism and Utilitarianism', in *Utilitarianism and Beyond*, pp. 103–28; B. Barry, *Theories of Justice*, Berkeley, Calif., University of California Press, 1989.

24 See F. Oakley, 'Disobedience, Consent, Political Obligation: The Witness of Wessel Gansfort (*c.* 1419–1489)', *History of Political Thought*, 1988, vol. IX; A. Black, 'The Juristic Origins of Social Contract Theory', *History of Political Thought*, 1993, vol. XIV; Harro Höpfl and Martyn P. Thompson, 'The History of Contract as a Motif in Political Thought', *American Historical Review*, 1979, vol. 84.

25 R. W. and A. J. Carlyle, *A History of Medieval Political Theory in the West*, Edinburgh, Blackwood, 1970, vol. III, p. 150.

26 St Thomas Aquinas, *On Law Morality and Politics*, Indianapolis, Ind., Hackett, 1988, p. 269.

27 Marsilius of Padua, *Defensor Pacis*, Alan Gerwith (trans.), Toronto, Toronto University Press, 1980, book I, iv, 4.

28 Cited in Lessnoff (ed.), Introduction, *Social Contract Theory*, p. 5.

29 James VI and I, *The Trew Law of Free Monarchies*, in *Divine Right and Democracy: An Anthology of Political Writing in Stuart England*, David Wootton (ed.), Harmondsworth, Penguin, 1986, p. 103.

30 Printed in *Divine Right of Kings*, Wootton (ed.), p. 109.

31 James I, *Trew Law*, pp. 103–4.

32 An example of which was M. Salamonio, *De Principatu* (1512–1514)

33 See Gough, *The Social Contract*, pp. 39–48; Otto Gierke, *Political Theories of the Middle Ages*, F. W. Maitland (trans.), Cambridge, Cambridge University Press, 1968, pp. 88–9.

34 Richard Hooker, *Of the Laws of Ecclesiastical Polity*, A. S. McGrade (ed.), Cambridge, Cambridge University Press, 1989, pp. 87–92. Cf. Höpfl and Thompson, 'Contract as a Motif in Political Thought', pp. 934–5.

35 Hooker, *Of the Laws*, p. 142.

36 For a discussion of these developments see Quentin Skinner, *The Foundations of Modern Political Thought*, vol. 2, *The Age of Reformation*, Cambridge, Cambridge University Press, 1978, chs 5 and 9.

37 Gough, for example, expresses disappointment that an explicit social contract theory is not to be found in Vitoria nor Molina, but is heartened by the fact that Suarez not only implies a social contract as the origin of the state, but also talks of a contract between the king and the people: *The Social Contract*, pp. 68–71.

Gough's interpretation is, however, misleading. As Skinner points out, Suarez is concerned to dispel the idea that the pre-civil condition implied a solitary existence, and that the power exercised over the community has its source in individuals. See Skinner, *The Foundations*, vol. II, p. 157. See also B. Hamilton, *Political Thought in Sixteenth-Century Spain*, Oxford, Clarendon Press, 1963, p. 3.

38   Plato, *Crito* in *The Last Days of Socrates*, Harmondsworth, Penguin, 1972, pp. 90 and 92.

39   Plato, *Crito*, pp. 90–1.

40   See Riley, *Will and Legitimacy*, ch. 1; Francis Oakley, 'Legitimation by Consent: The Question of the Medieval Roots', *Viator*, 1983, vol. XIV.

41   R. G. Collingwood, *The New Leviathan*, revised edn, David Boucher (ed.), Oxford, Clarendon Press, 1992.

42   See, for example, Locke, *Two Treatises*, II, §128:

> A man has two Powers. . . . The first is to do whatsoever he thinks fit for the preservation of himself and others within the permission of the *Law of Nature*: by which Law common to them all, he and all the rest of *Mankind are one Community*, make up one society distinct from all other Creatures. And were it not for the corruption, and vitiousness of degenerate Men, there would be no need of any other; no necessity that Men should separate from this great and natural Community, and by positive agreements combine into smaller and divided associations.

43   Even Kant rejects the idea of a world state on practical grounds in favour of a states-based pacific federation.

44   Francisco de Vitoria, 'On Civil Power', in *Political Writings*, Anthony Pagden and Jeremy Lawrence (eds), Cambridge, Cambridge University Press, 1991, pp. 10, 16 and 25.

45   Vitoria, 'On Civil Government', pp. 31 and 40.

46   Vitoria, 'On Civil Power', pp. 20 and 40.

47   Vitoria, 'On the American Indians', in *Political Writings*, Pagden and Lawrence (eds), pp. 246 and 250–1.

48   Hugo Grotius, *The Rights of War and Peace including the Law of Nature and Nations*, A. C. Campbell (trans.), Westport, Conn., Hyperion Press, 1993, book I, ch. 1, par. xiv. His theory of property, however, justified Dutch imperialism against barbarian communities.

49   Cited by Peter Pavel Remec, *The Position of the Individual in International Law According to Grotius and Vattel*, The Hague, Martinus Nijhoff, 1960, p. 71.

50   See Anthony Black, *Political Thought in Europe 1250–1450*, Cambridge, Cambridge University Press, 1992, ch. 1; Michael Oakeshott, 'On the Character of a Modern European State', in *On Human Conduct*, Oxford, Clarendon Press, 1975; Ernest Barker's introduction to Otto Gierke, *Natural Law and the Theory of Society*, Cambridge, Cambridge University Press, 1934; Maitland's introduction to Gierke's *Political Theories of the Middle Age*; Gough, *Social Contract*, pp. 44–6.

51   Thomas Hobbes, *Leviathan*, C.B. Macpherson (ed.), Harmondsworth, Penguin, 1968, pp. 81–2.

52   Hobbes, *Leviathan*, p. 220. In *De Cive* Hobbes says, 'cities once instituted do put on the personal proprieties of men': London, Harvester, 1972, ch. 14, sect. 4.

53   Pufendorf, *Law of Nature and Nations*, VII, ii, 13.

54   Pufendorf, *Law of Nature and Nations*, VII, ii, 5. See also I, i, 12–13.

55   Emer de Vattel, *The Law of Nations or the Principles of Natural Law*, Washington, DC, Carnegie Institution, 1916, I, introduction, 2.

56   Thomas Reid, *Practical Ethics: Being Lectures and Papers on Natural Religion,*

Self-Government, Natural Jurisprudence, and the Law of Nations, Knud Haakonssen (ed.), Princeton, NJ, Princeton University Press, 1990, p. 254.

57 Rousseau, *Basic Political Writings*, pp. 148–9.

58 J. K. Bluntschli, *The Theory of the State*, Oxford, Clarendon Press, 1898, pp. 22–3, 66–7, and 296–7.

59 Pufendorf, *Law of Nature and Nations*, VII, ix, 3.

60 See Filmer, *Patriarcha and Other Writings*. Johann P. Sommerville (ed.), Cambridge, Cambridge University Press, 1991,

61 Carole Pateman, *The Sexual Contract*, Cambridge, Polity Press, 1988.

62 See S. Caney, 'Liberalism and Communitarianism: A Misconceived Debate', *Political Studies*, 1992, vol. 40, pp. 273–89.

63 C. Kukathas and P. Pettit, *Rawls: A Theory of Justice and its Critics*, Cambridge, Polity Press, 1990, pp. 144–5.

64 See James Daly, *Sir Robert Filmer and English Political Thought*, Toronto, University of Toronto Press, 1979, pp. 57–8; John Dunn, *The Political Thought of John Locke*, Cambridge, Cambridge University Press, 1969, p. 60.

65 Filmer argues that kings are not now as they once were the natural fathers of the families over which they rule, but 'they all either are, or are to be reputed, the next heirs to the first progenitors': Sir Robert Filmer, *Patriarcha*, p. 10.

66 'There is, and always shall be continued to the end of the world, a natural right of a supreme father over every multitude': Filmer, *Patriarcha*, p. 11.

67 See, for example, John Plamenatz, *Man and Society*, new edn, London, Longman, 1992, vol. I, pp. 252–64.

68 Robert Filmer, *Observations Concerning the Originall of Government* in *Patriarcha and Other Writings*, p. 234.

69 Joseph de Maistre, *Étude sur la souveraineté, Oeuvres complètes*, vol. I, Lyon, 1884. For an account of Maistre as, an anti-liberal see S. Holmes, *The Anatomy of AntiLiberalism*, Cambridge Mass., Harvard University Press, 1993, pp. 13–36; for a more sympathetic account see R. Lebrun, *Throne and Altar: The Political and Religious Thought of Joseph de Maistre*, Ottawa, University of Ottawa Press, 1965.

70 David Hume, *A Treatise of Human Nature*, P. H. Nidditch (ed.), 2nd edn, Oxford, Oxford University Press, 1992, p. 541. In 'Of the Original Contract' Hume argues that if we admit that all authority is by Divine commission then no special claims to absoluteness can be pleaded over the most menial magistrate who similarly acts on God's commission. Reprinted in Barker, *Social Contract*, p. 148.

71 Hume, 'Of the Original Contract', p. 149.

72 *The Letters of David Hume*, J. Y. T. Greig (ed.), Oxford, Clarendon Press, 1932, vol. 1, p. 33.

73 Hume, 'Of the Original Contract', pp. 160–1. See also Duncan Forbes, *Hume's Philosophical Politics*, Cambridge, Cambridge University Press, 1975, p. 66.

74 Hume, *Treatise*, p. 544.

75 J. Bentham, *A Comment on the Commentaries and A Fragment on Government, Collected Works of Jeremy Bentham*, J. H. Burns and H. L. A. Hart (eds), London, Athlone Press, 1977, *A Fragment*, ch. 1, § 36.

76 J. Bentham, *A Fragment, Collected Works*, ch. I, § 10.

77 J. S. Mill, *On Liberty and Other Essays*, John Gray (ed.), Oxford, Oxford University Press, 1991, ch. 4. Strictly speaking Bentham thought no such proof of the principle of utility was either possible or necessary: see J. Bentham, *An Introduction to the Principles of Morals and Legislation, Collected Works of Jeremy Bentham*, J. H. Burns and H. L. A. Hart (eds), London, Athlone Press, 1970, p. 13.

78 R. G. Collingwood's resurrection of contractarianism as an attempt to find a way beyond utilitarianism and intuitionism in *The New Leviathan*.

79 R. M. Hare, 'Rawls' Theory of Justice', in *Reading Rawls*, N. Daniels (ed.), Oxford, Basil Blackwell, 1975, pp. 81–107.
80 G. W. F. Hegel, *Elements of the Philosophy of Right*, Allen W. Wood (ed.), Cambridge, Cambridge University Press, 1991, § 281 A (G).
81 G. W. F. Hegel, *Natural Law* (1802–3), T. M. Knox (trans.), Philadelphia, Pa, University of Pennsylvania Press, 1975, p. 133. For Hegel's criticisms of the abstraction of a state of nature see pp. 62 and 64–5.
82 G. W. F. Hegel, 'Proceedings of the Estates Assembly in the Kingdom of Wurtenburg (1815–16)' in *Hegel's Political Writings*, Z. A. Pelczynski (ed.), Oxford, Clarendon Press, 1964, p. 281.
83 Hegel, *Philosophy of Right*, §106.
84 Hegel, *Philosophy of Right*, §150 and §153.
85 F. H. Bradley, *Ethical Studies*, 2nd edn, Oxford, Clarendon Press, 1927, p. 173.
86 See C. Taylor, *Sources of the Self*, Cambridge, Cambridge University Press, 1989; M. Sandel, *Liberalism and the Limits of Justice*, Cambridge, Cambridge University Press, 1982; A. MacIntyre, *After Virtue*, London, Duckworth, 1981, and *Whose Justice? Which Rationality?*, London, Duckworth, 1988; M. Walzer, *Spheres of Justice*, Oxford, Basil Blackwell, 1983.
87 C. Taylor, *Multiculturalism and the Politics of Recognition*, Princeton, NJ, Princeton University Press, 1992.
88 Rousseau, *The Social Contract*, p. 141.
89 N. Chodorow, *The Reproduction of Mothering: Psychoanalysis and the Sociology of Gender*, Berkeley, Calif., University of California Press, 1978; Carol Gilligan, *In a Different Voice*, Cambridge Mass., Harvard University Press, 1982.
90 I. Marion Young, *Justice and the Politics of Difference*, Princeton, NJ, Princeton University Press, 1990; S. Benhabib, *Situating the Self*, Cambridge, Polity Press, 1992.
91 S. Moller-Okin, *Justice, Gender and the Family*, New York, Basic Books, 1990.

2 Hobbes's contractarianism

A comparative analysis

Murray Forsyth

Perhaps the most perplexing problem raised by the doctrine of the social contract that emerged and flourished in Europe in the seventeenth and eighteenth centuries is that it produced political prescriptions that were profoundly at variance with one another. Thomas Hobbes, John Locke and Jean-Jacques Rousseau, the three classical expositors of the doctrine, developed concepts of the state that were scarcely compatible. The first endorsed the absolute state, the second the provisional state, and the third the moral state, or the state-as-church. Are we to conclude that the notion of the social contract is like an empty bottle, capable of being filled with any content? Does it have any meaning in itself, underlying the different concepts of the state that it served to justify? Should we remain neutral between the different usages, or should we take sides in favour of the 'real' or 'true' doctrine of the social contract against its distorted or false forms? In the discussion that follows I shall focus on Hobbes's doctrine of the contract, but endeavour, in doing so, to answer these broader questions.

HOBBES AS 'NOT REALLY A CONTRACT THEORIST'

Perhaps the best place to start is by looking briefly at a book, by Jean Hampton, devoted entirely to *Hobbes and the Social Contract Tradition.*[1] Hampton 'takes up the cudgels' in no uncertain way. She maintains that there are two kinds of traditional social contract theories,

> the kind that explains the state's justification by saying that people *lend* their power to political rulers *on condition* that it be used to satisfy certain of their most important needs, and the kind that explains the state's justification by saying that people *alienate* or give up their power to political rulers in the (mere) *hope* that doing so will satisfy certain of their most important needs. Advocates of the first kind of argument are drawn to an agent/principal understanding of the ruler/subject relationship; advocates of the second kind of argument are espousing a master/slave interpretation of the ruler/subject relationship that precludes legitimate rebellion'.[2]

A little later she goes further and states that her analysis has revealed two forms of domination, 'the domination of a master and the domination of a "hired" protection agency'.[3] (The notion of a 'hired protection agency' is derived expressly from Robert Nozick.) What Hampton calls 'the contractarian story' can, in her view, produce only the second form of domination. In her own words: 'I have presented the contractarian's "hired-protection-agency" form of domination as the contractarian's only conception of political domination'.[4]

Hampton believes Hobbes 'put forward the finest statement ever' of the 'alienation' social contract theory,[5] and as the excerpts above make plain, her book is primarily concerned to demonstrate the invalidity of his theory: it is not, in her view, an authentic social contract theory at all; it does not require any reference to a social contract; and it leads to a master/slave concept of political rule. Hampton does not stop there, however. She also rearranges and reworks some of the elements in Hobbes's theory to show how it could, without too much difficulty, become an authentic or valid social contract theory in the sense that she has defined it. Hobbes is right, in her view, only to the extent that he can be 'salvaged' as Locke, or as a Nozickean variation of Locke.

Hampton's thesis is interesting because it reflects and expresses – in a highly sophisticated and intricate format – a common attitude or reaction to Hobbes. Although the latter was the first great theorist of the social contract, he is widely held to have used it in a cunning and illegitimate way to spike in advance the guns of the real theorists of the social contract who came later. Locke conversely is taken to be the authentic voice of the social contract, largely, one suspects, because he makes, in Hampton's words, rebellion legitimate, and thus makes the relationship of government and people appear heavily contractual, like a 'hiring and firing' arrangement. And Rousseau? He is usually suspected, by those who follow this line of thought, of not 'really' being a social contract theorist either. His talk of the 'alienation' of rights is seen as bringing him worryingly close to Hobbes, and in addition his concept of the 'general will' has 'organic' overtones at variance with what is held to be the essentially 'mechanical' theory of the social contract. Hampton is typically suspicious of Rousseau's contractarian credentials.[6]

I wish to question this whole interpretative tendency, and in particular the attitude towards Hobbes that it embodies. There are, as everyone agrees, profound differences between the ideas of the leading theorists of the social contract, but to divide them in such a way that Locke becomes the touchstone of the authentic social contract doctrine and Hobbes and Rousseau deviations from authenticity is to miss the deeper antithesis between the writers. The main line of distinction or differentiation does not, I will argue, coincide with that drawn by Hampton: it runs instead between Hobbes, on the one hand, and Locke and Rousseau on the other. The difference is not in the first place between doctrines of alienation and slavery, and doctrines of 'hiring', but between social contract theories of the state that give priority to the demands of the political order, and the 'earthly city', and those that give priority to the demands of the inner moral law, and the 'city of God'. To establish this contrast I shall first attempt to identify and explain the shared or general elements in the various notions of the social contract, and then to show where and why they diverge.

COMMON FEATURES OF SOCIAL CONTRACT DOCTRINES

The first and most obvious common element in the doctrine of the social contract is that the foundation of the true or authentic body politic is held to be a pact or agreement made by all the individuals who are to compose it. It is tempting to say that it is a pact *between* all the individuals who are to compose it, but this would disqualify Rousseau's contract. For Rousseau the original pact of association is not one between individuals, but rather 'a reciprocal commitment between society and the individual, so that each person, in making a contract, as it were, with himself, finds himself doubly committed'.[7] The phrase about each person 'making a contract, as it were, with himself' is of immense significance for understanding the essentially moral character of Rousseau's contract, a subject to which we shall return later, but can pass over here.

Let us return to the common features. The social pact is emphatically not a pact between rulers and ruled – a subject which has its own history – but a pact to *establish* rule. It marks the transition from the 'state of nature' to the 'civil state'. The leading theorists of the seventeenth and eighteenth centuries tended to equate the individuals who made the pact with 'men'. They probably meant by this 'adult males'. Some – Locke perhaps – may even have equated them with the male heads of households. Modern commentators may wish to rebuke and correct them for this narrowness; some have. But such criticism should not be allowed to obscure the main point, which is that the notion of a social contract implied and embodied a huge advance in the idea of human equality, and that the very ambiguity in the words 'men' and 'man', their simultaneous connotation of males and humanity, made it possible for the theory to be expanded beyond the limited assumptions of its founders.

The emergence of the notion of the social contract is hence linked intimately with the emergence of the idea of the equality of human beings. It is the political expression of this idea, developing alongside, and interweaving with, the religious and economic expressions of it. The notion of human equality did not, of course, originate in the seventeenth century. But the Protestant Reformation gave a vast impetus to the idea (all the classic exponents of the social contract were Protestant). The rapid expansion of a money economy, or market relationships, embodied it. And the furious civil and external wars that disrupted Europe in the century from 1560 to 1660 encouraged the idea politically. War and death are great levellers. Hobbes's rather grotesque idea that the principle of human equality is supported by the fact that men are equally capable of killing one another reflects this sombre fact.[8] So does his idea that all men without distinction fear violent death, which plays, of course, a pivotal role in his construction of the state.

The core of the idea of equality which is embodied in the contract theory is not, however, man's power to kill, but rather the principle that all men are equally free. While – as we shall see – not all the classical writers agreed exactly on the meaning of this principle, they did agree on this: that each man, by right of nature, that is, by right of his human character, rather than through the mediation of other men, possessed the quality of freedom. Even Hobbes, who spoke of equality in the grimly physical terms alluded to, also spoke of man's inherent right to 'use his own power, as he will himself, for the preservation of his own nature'.[9] More concisely and trenchantly, he wrote that 'all men equally, are by nature free'.[10]

The social contract doctrine expresses conversely the idea that there is no quality or attribute adhering to certain people which imposes naturally – that is to say, directly and without mediation, or through its mere existence – a duty on others to obey their commands. Rule upheld solely by right of birth, by divine right, by 'charisma', by physical force – these are all denied legitimacy. Most importantly, the doctrine denies the idea, that can be traced back to Plato, that insight or access to the 'truth', whether it be the revealed truth of religion or the supposedly scientific truth of ideology, qualifies certain people to exercise supreme sway over the rest.

More positively, the notion of a social contract expresses the idea that all rule – all just and legitimate rule – is made or established (in a word, constituted) by those who are ruled. Given that individuals are inherently free and equal, the first stage in the establishment of rule can only take the form of a contract, that is to say a simultaneous agreement in which, by definition, the wills of all the participants are expressed. Only such a foundation can create or constitute a form of rule that binds or obliges those who are naturally free.

Two further characteristics common to the various doctrines of the social contract need to be noted. First of all, the social contract is at heart a simultaneous agreement between or by a multitude of individuals, rather than a consecutive aggregation of bilateral agreements. It is a contract by which the many, the multitude, transform themselves or incorporate themselves into an acting unity – however much the nature of this acting unity may vary between the various writers – and not a succession of contracts that happen to overlap in terms of their participants and hence to create a purely external linkage between many people or 'peoples'. It is true that Hobbes, through his theory of the 'commonwealth by acquisition', does provide for this second, consecutive form of contract. So does Locke, with his doctrine of tacit consent, and indeed with his doctrine of the express consent of generations subsequent to the original contract. So does Rousseau with his notion of tacit consent. But none of these ideas represent the heart of the concept of the social pact, as developed by these writers. They are an alternative or supplement to it (Hobbes), or simply a supplement to it (Locke and Rousseau). The heart of Hobbes's contract is the act of generation described in Chapter XVII of *Leviathan*, and articulated at length by him in the two following chapters – an act by which a multitude simultaneously transforms itself into a unity.

Finally, and linked to this, the social contract is always a distinct and special contract, which cannot and must not be put on a par with the everyday contracts of buying and selling with which everyone is familiar. The form may be similar, but the content, the substance, is fundamentally different. Ordinary contracts leave the personality of the contractors intact. They are instruments for settling the way in which the contractors will henceforth act with regard to certain issues or things. The social contract aims always at creating a permanent union between the contractors themselves, and a union that will continue to bind the successors of the original contractors, with or without their express adhesion. It aims always at giving practical effectiveness to a common will regarding the fundamentals of human coexistence shared by the contractors. By common will here is meant a common determination to move 'away' from something and 'towards' something else. Hobbes, Locke and Rousseau all posited such a will. Those who – because of the exceptional significance with which Rousseau invested the term 'general will' – insist on separating the 'mechanical' idea of the social contract from the 'organic' idea of a general or common will are thus in danger of obscuring the nature of the doctrine.

This is perhaps as far as generalization about the doctrine of the social contract can go. Once we go beyond this and start to look closely at what each writer puts into the contract itself, then highly important differences begin to open up. As stated earlier, it is possible to distinguish two broad directions in which the basic idea of the social contract was developed. On the one hand, the social contract was seen primarily and exclusively as the stepping stone towards the creation of a political body capable of meeting man's practical, earthly, political needs. On the other, the social contract was seen as a means of creating a body politic, but simultaneously as a means of keeping the body politic subordinate to the realm of morality, or the 'kingdom of God'.

THE BASIC DIVERGENCE WITHIN SOCIAL CONTRACT DOCTRINE

Hobbes, of course, represents the first tendency. Locke and Rousseau, despite the manifest differences between them, belong to the second. The principle of distinction rests on the relationship that the various theorists establish between the direct commands of the inner individual conscience, and the humanly constituted political order of mankind. It is Hobbes's relentless secularism (not to be equated with atheism), his refusal to start from absolute moral presuppositions, that set him apart from the others. More precisely it is his notion that the human constitution of a secular or temporal power, concerned wholly with external peace, security and earthly felicity, is itself the fulfilment of God's purpose for man, is itself the implementation of morality, that marks off his doctrine of the social contract from that of Locke and Rousseau.

For Locke, the structure of civil government is a supplement to the kingdom of God portrayed in his state of nature. The 'society' or·'community' created by the Lockian social contract acts on the one hand to constitute civil government, but on the other to ensure the ultimate subordination of this government to the laws of the original and indestructible natural kingdom of God. It faces two ways simultaneously: it is the guard and shield of the heavenly city, and the basis of the earthly city. The latter is always, as it were, on probation.

Rousseau takes an important step beyond Locke, but one that is thoroughly in keeping with the spirit of Locke's doctrine. Rousseau does not envisage a naturally 'constituted' moral kingdom; to this extent he is like Hobbes. The existing world is, for Rousseau, thoroughly corrupt. Like Hobbes he sees the creation of the political order as absolutely necessary. But, unlike Hobbes, Rousseau sees the political kingdom as but the means, or more precisely, the vehicle, for the inner, moral regeneration of man, which is his primary goal. His very problematic – how to find a form of association in 'which each individual, while uniting himself with the others, obeys no one but himself, and remains as free as before' – reflects his moral presuppositions.[11] Rousseau thus makes the first step in the construction of the body politic – the social contract itself, whose peculiar nature was noted earlier – into an act by which men subordinate themselves directly to the sovereign moral law, named by him the general will. In the contract men in effect undertake to rule themselves henceforth through their reason or conscience – as they are ruled in Locke's state of nature. For Rousseau there could be no distinct representation of the common will – that would be an act of 'alienation'. By which he meant that it would amount to the destruction of man's essential character as an inwardly governed moral being. The only representation he allowed was in what he called the 'government', a paltry, provisional institution, wholly subordinate to the 'people' formed by the social contract. Rousseau's contract was hence akin to a joint 'confession' of 'conversion' to the moral life, or to the formation of an independent church or congregation in the Protestant tradition. Once again, but more thoroughly than in Locke, the outer, political realm was subordinated to the inner spiritual kingdom. For Rousseau, the governing principle of all states, whatever their form of 'government', was 'virtue'.

It is entirely in keeping with the general tendency of the doctrine of the social contract developed by Locke and Rousseau that they were both strong advocates of the separation of powers, in the sense of the *subordination* of powers. For both writers, the farther political power was from the people as a whole, and the more it was representative in character, the more it had to be subject to control. According to Locke's ideal scheme, the legislature, in the form of an elected assembly, was subordinate to the political community as a whole, while the executive was subordinate to both the legislative assembly and to the political community. According to Rousseau, as we have seen, the executive or 'government' was strictly subordinate to the popular assembly, which was the constituent assembly and the ordinary legislature combined. In each case emphasis was placed on the supreme power of the people as a whole, and this was linked to the idea that the people stand directly under the rule of the moral law.

For Hobbes, by contrast, the political order was granted full autonomy. It was not the pale offspring of a higher, spiritual kingdom. Nor was it itself the vehicle for the creation of a higher, spiritual kingdom. The political order, for Hobbes, had its own original roots in the perpetual tendency of human freedom to produce war. Politics, for Hobbes, was war, and the perpetual struggle to subdue, restrain and corral war. War was not an unfortunate and temporary side-product of human existence, nor was it to be explained as simply the product of the designs of certain wicked or evil men (which did not preclude the possibility that in certain instances it might be the work of such men). Nor, finally, was war due to the 'belligerent nature' of the human being. War, in other words, did not take place solely because individual human beings are inherently pugnacious. Hobbes certainly considers that some men were so constituted that they were naturally pugnacious – he described them as vain-glorious men, or men who use violence 'for trifles, as a word, a smile, a different opinion, and any sign of undervalue, either direct in their persons, or by reflection in their kindred, their friends, their nation, their profession, or their name'.[12] But Hobbes's theory of war was not based wholly or essentially on the existence amongst mankind of such men. It was based on broader factors, on the very nature of man, or, more precisely, on the nature of man when he comes into close proximity with his fellow men.

War, for Hobbes, was the product of a relationship, albeit a negative one, between the wills of two or more persons. A person adopts a posture of war when, in a given situation, his original right and capacity to decide what is good, desirable or reasonable for him comes into fundamental conflict with another person's identical right and capacity. War springs from the fact that 'all men are, by nature, equally free'. Individual conviction of the rightness of one's own conscience is just as capable of producing war as individual conviction that something external belongs to one. The ultimate cause of war is not a particular 'thing' or 'substance' – whether economic or religious – but the right possessed by each person, in an interacting group or 'multitude', to decide for himself over what is his and how it is to be preserved. We shall discuss this right more fully later on.

It was precisely because politics as war was so deeply rooted in human nature that, for Hobbes, the restraint of war – the formation of the state –

could not be likened to the 'hiring of an agent'. The formation of the state was rather a fundamental act of human creation, which instituted, not an 'agent' but an 'actor', that is to say, a distinct will equipped with the means and the power to hold at bay a permanent tendency amongst and between human beings towards violent conflict. (Slavery did not, *pace* Hampton, enter into the Hobbesian equation. It was significantly the moralist Locke, not the man of politics, Hobbes, who justified slavery.)

The Hobbesian social contract is thus wholly and unabashedly political. It is the only consistent and legitimate means of creating a power capable of holding war at bay. The contract forms initially a 'people' capable of deciding by a majority vote on a common representative authorized to preserve internal peace and external defence.[13] The mission of the 'people', in Hobbes's schema, is to create such a power swiftly and completely. In modern terminology, the function of a constituent assembly is precisely to constitute – not to rule, nor to sit permanently in judgment. For Hobbes the primary aim is not to control, but rather to *make* a body politic that accords with the logic of politics. While in Rousseau's doctrine the people as constituent power continue to meet at regular intervals, bringing the 'government' to heel each time they do – a system of permanent revolution – in Hobbes's system the people as constituent power are but a fleeting moment in the all-important process of establishing government.

Still less is the Hobbesian contract a joint pledge of moral self-discipline in the mode of Rousseau. It is an act of self-subjection, to be sure, but of self-subjection to an external, objectivized, representative will, not merely to one's own internal, spiritual, personal will. It was, for Hobbes, an illusion to think that common acknowledgement of a higher moral law was in itself enough to prevent war. Hobbes came perhaps closest to answering Rousseau directly when he wrote:

> For if we could suppose a great multitude of men to consent in the observation of justice, and other laws of nature, without a common power to keep them all in awe; we might as well suppose all mankind to do the same; and then there neither would be, nor need to be any civil government, or commonwealth at all; because there would be peace without subjection.[14]

For Hobbes equally there could be no sense in the doctrine of separating and subordinating political powers in the manner of Locke and Rousseau. He had no instinctive distrust of representation. On the contrary, the formation of the state was at heart an act of representation – in the sense of 'making present' or 'making public' the common will for peace. His whole emphasis, when it came to the structure and organization of public powers, was on the interrelatedness of such powers, on the need for a nerve of connection to run through them, allowing them to act effectively in pursuit of their authorized end. There had to be unity in the public will, and this unity was for him best effected by having one person at the heart of what today we call the 'decision-making process'. Doubtless he went too far in his advocacy of unity in government, but his conviction that a representative assembly requires leadership and direction, his profound scepticism about 'government by assembly', and his deeply ingrained sense that rule requires a single person at the centre, have surely been endorsed rather than refuted by subsequent history.

HOBBES'S CONTRACT EXAMINED MORE CLOSELY

Hobbes's social contract was the dramatic culmination of a step-by-step process of developing human rationality, which he described in Chapters XIII to XVII of *Leviathan*, and which is usually subsumed under the general name of the 'state of nature'. It was a complex process, not altogether free from obscurity. The interaction of naturally free human beings, the interplay of reason and passion, and the push and pull of efficient causes (fear of death) and final causes (desire for felicity, or a more contented life) combined to bring the 'state of nature' to the point at which the transformatory social contract was made.

In the course of this process men were driven to see that their original freedom, directed solely towards the satisfaction of their individual passions, must be guided, not merely by reason in the sense of self-concentrated calculation, but by 'right reason', in the form of the laws of nature, if it was not to destroy itself. The laws of nature were for Hobbes the only objective morality. They were, as he stressed again and again, eternal, God-given and immutable; not made, or agreed upon, by men, but discovered by reason, under the pressure of passion, and furthermore 'agreeable to the reason of all men'.[15] They prescribed the kind of action and the form of external behaviour that free individuals must adopt towards others if there was to be a minimum of social coexistence, a minimum of peace. Moreover they were not categorical but conditional – in the sense that they required external implementation on one's own side only when there was an indication on the side of the 'other' of a willingness to follow them too. They were hence moral laws of a very special nature, which marked a sharp break with traditional, conventional, classical and above all religious concepts of the subject and content of morality. They are best seen as a first attempt to distinguish clearly what were later to be termed the rules of 'right' *in contrast to the rules of 'morality'*, by writers such as Kant, Fichte and Hegel. Or, to put it a different way, they were the rules of *political* morality.

The third and final stage in the development of the state of nature – the stage at which it is transcended and abolished – comes when men, or rather, given groups of men, realize that it is not enough to rely on individual, conditional implementation of the laws of nature, but that there has to be a positive, collective act of creation, an act of state-building, by man himself if God's laws are to become fully binding.[16] For Hobbes the present kingdom of God on earth is in itself but a tenuous, insubstantial, partial order; an order that requires human action to acquire strength, solidity and completion. In other words, what God gives to man – the laws of nature – require and demand responsive human activity. This is a typically Protestant conception applied to the social and civil realm. In Lutheran terminology, God's gift or '*Gabe*' is at the same time '*Aufgabe*', a task laid upon mankind.[17] In making the state man fulfils the task that has been laid upon him by the Creator. The sovereign is literally God's 'lieutenant' on earth.[18]

There are two further aspects of Hobbes's contractarianism that deserve closer investigation. The first has already been touched upon; it is Hobbes's notion of natural right. The second is perhaps best termed the problem of the ontological status of the 'state of nature' and the contract which puts an end to it.

It has often been pointed out that Hobbes's theory of the social contract involves the 'alienation' of man's natural right, while Locke's theory involves the preservation of natural rights. As a first step in distinguishing between the two writers this contrast is unobjectionable. However, it can all too easily obscure the more important point that Hobbes's natural right is quite different in kind from Locke's natural rights. The difference, once again, is intimately linked to the relative significance accorded by the two thinkers to the spiritual, God-governed realm and to the political realm.

Hobbes conceived man's natural right not, like Locke, as an objective, spontaneously acknowledged status, but as a subjective freedom, the freedom to decide for oneself. For Hobbes, as for Locke, man was by nature a possessing animal, but for Hobbes man did not enjoy a natural right of ownership over what he possessed, or (to put it in different words) he did not naturally enjoy the respect of others for his possessions. What man had was a right unilaterally to judge or decide what was necessary to be done to secure his own preservation.[19] This meant he had the right to judge for himself what he needed for his preservation and when his preservation was being threatened or endangered by others, and to take whatever action he thought fit to secure his preservation and to remove threats or dangers to it. There was, for Hobbes, no firm, divinely established, status of security and property in the state of nature, such that a conflict there always took the form of a clash between objective 'wrong' and objective 'right', between the 'good' and the 'wicked', between the 'criminal' and the 'punisher'. Rather there was a constant interplay of rightful claims and rightful counter-claims, a constant clash of right. Moreover the right of nature included a right to wage war. 'It is lawful by the original right of nature to make war'.[20]

Once the distinctive feature of Hobbesian natural right is grasped, the fact that he called for the giving up or alienation of this right loses its seemingly servile connotation. Hobbes was in no sense opposed to the right of property in the sense of a mutually respected individual entitlement to 'life, liberty and estate'. It was one of the primary responsibilities of the Hobbesian commonwealth to establish this right. What he argued was that this right could not become a reality until a prior right – the right unilaterally to decide – was renounced in favour of the ruler, who thereby became 'sovereign'. It is because Hobbes accords the individual a more far-reaching original right in the state of nature than Locke that he demands a more far-reaching abnegation of individual right in the civil state. It is paradoxically because he is more of an 'individualist' that he is more of a 'statist'.

It is time to turn to the second, rather more general question of the ontological status of Hobbes's state of nature and the social contract. Clearly the Hobbesian state of nature is not the description of a particular historical development. Most commentators agree that it is also not an historical generalization of the type: 'this is how most states originate', however closely it may resemble certain historical realities. The usual conclusion is therefore that it is an 'hypothesis', in the sense of a mental construction that goes beyond a generalization. This conclusion, however, does not in itself resolve the most interesting question. The term 'hypothesis' is not free from ambiguity, as a glance at any history of scientific thought makes plain.[21] Mental constructions of this kind can take different forms. What kind of hypothesis, then, is Hobbes's state of nature?

A key criterion for distinguishing different kinds of hypotheses would seem to be the degree of 'necessity' accorded to them by those who construct them. This is not, of course, the only question that needs to be asked of a given hypothesis, but it is a highly important preliminary question, that helps to prevent misconceptions when examining the content of hypotheses. The kind of hypothesis which lays claim to the highest ontological status is that which is deemed to be a necessary stage or 'stepping-stone' (to use Plato's analogy) in the explanation of what is necessary – as distinct from contingent – in the working of the natural or moral worlds. This is what we mean when we say that we cannot explain phenomenon 'y' unless we posit 'z' – 'z' being the hypothesis. At the other extreme stand hypotheses that are made solely to indicate the range of the 'possible', of what 'might' or 'could' be, without laying any claim to be anything more than a speculative exercise, and having no determinate purchase on reality.

In between these two extremes come a range of different forms that are more difficult to categorize. There are, for example, hypotheses which are intended to be possible, probable or highly probable explanations of the necessary working of an aspect of the world, but for which no claim is made that they are the only or ultimate way by which the phenomenon is to be explained. This type abounds in natural science. Then there are hypotheses which are deemed to be 'useful' or 'helpful' for some practical rather than strictly theoretical purpose by those who make them. They are not claimed to be necessary or even possible steps in the explanation of the necessary, but useful instruments for achieving some desired result – for example, 'illuminating the problem' or 'aiding discussion'. The hypothesis is here adjusted to the particular practical objective that is desired; in this sense it is contingent.

This categorization of the different types of hypotheses – which is not intended to be exhaustive – may seem rather bloodless and formal. To bring out its significance, I wish to compare Hobbes's hypothesis or construction of the state of nature and the social contract with that of another thinker, not, this time, Locke or Rousseau, but someone from our own day, who, like Hobbes, is concerned with justice. John Rawls's hypothesis of an 'original position' and a 'contract', put forward in his well-known book *A Theory of Justice*, seems to bear, at first sight, some resemblance to that of Hobbes.[22] But what is the status of Rawls's hypothesis? Does he make the same ontological claim for it as Hobbes does for his? Is the resemblance real?

The place of hypothesis in Rawls's theory is described by him in the first chapter of his book and may be summarized as follows. Politically organized societies, in Rawls's view, are and should be regulated by principles of justice. The latter come first in order of priority; all forms of social cooperation must be judged and if necessary reformed or abolished in terms of prior principles of justice. However, principles of justice are chosen by individuals; they are 'conventional'. People can and do choose differently. The task of 'a theory of justice' is to present a conception of justice which is not mere description, but will provide 'in the first instance a standard whereby the distributive aspects of the basic structure of society are to be assessed'.[23] More precisely: 'our object should be to formulate a conception of justice which, however much it may call upon intuition, ethical or prudential, tends to make our considered judgments of justice converge'.[24]

Given the inherently conventional character of justice, how is this to be done? Rawls believes that it can be achieved by discovering what principles of justice individuals would choose if they were placed in a mentally constructed 'fair' condition. In other words, if the choice of principles of justice made by individuals were conceptually restricted by certain factors, then some kind of convergent, and hence theoretically acceptable, outcome might emerge. A 'fair' condition Rawls defines as one which is constructed according to notions of fairness that are either accepted by most people, or that may be considered as 'reasonable', and which is assumed to exist before any social cooperation between the individuals concerned has taken place.

Such is the overall context and rationale of Rawls's hypothesis of the 'original condition'. The bulk of his book is concerned with defining and redefining and adjusting the 'fair' conditions, and with seeking to calculate the convergence, i.e. the 'agreement' or 'contract' by individuals about principles of justice, that might emerge from these conditions.

What is the ontological status of Rawls's hypothesis? First, it is clear that his hypothesis lacks any direct connection with the necessity of the thing itself, namely justice. It is not seen by Rawls as a necessary stepping-stone for explaining what justice necessarily *is*. Rather it is part of a thought experiment designed for a practical purpose: the encouragement or inducement of convergence in people's subjective ideas about justice. It takes the form: 'if convergent ideas about fairness are fed into one end of a hypothetical situation, then convergent ideas on justice may emerge from the other end – let us see what these ideas might be'. Such convergence as is obtained is the product of a mental construction that is designed to produce convergence, and for this very reason, because it is not connected to the necessity of things, but dependent on a practical end, and hence contingent, it carries little theoretical conviction. As Rawls himself states: 'I do not claim for the principles of justice proposed that they are necessary truths or derivable from such truths'.[25] And again: 'Moral philosophy must be free to use contingent assumptions and general facts as it pleases'.[26] So we are left with little more than an interesting and sophisticated intellectual game.

Finally, and ironically, although Rawls himself eschews deduction from self-evident premises, he makes the general assumption, in elaborating his theory, that individuals can and should make some form of positive agreement amongst themselves on what is to count as 'justice', before they engage in 'social cooperation'. But is this assumption self-evident? Does it not make social cooperation (negotiations over the meaning of justice) precede social cooperation? Does it not make social cooperation precede any common notion of justice? Is the latter a soundly based supposition? Rawls does not seem to consider it necessary to address these issues.

In complete contrast, Hobbes's hypothesis of the state of nature is intended by him to be a necessary step in the explanation of the necessary working of the political world. His was an hypothesis in the ancient meaning of the term, namely that which 'stands under' that which appears, or is the 'sub-position' of a phenomenon. Suppositions of this kind were, in his system of thought, either revealed by an analysis of the phenomenon in question, or produced 'synthetically' by reasoning one's way forward from the 'very first principles of philosophy' to the phenomenon.[27] Hobbes believed that one could uncover the necessary features of the body politic by following either route. We will concentrate here on his account of the analytical method, as it provides the most revealing insight into the status of hypotheses in his system. Hobbes wrote:

> even they also that have not learned the first part of philosophy, namely, *geometry* and *physics*, may, notwithstanding, attain the principles of civil philosophy, by the *analytical method*. For if a question be propounded, as, *whether such action be just or unjust*; if that *unjust* be resolved into *fact against law*, and that notion *law* into the *command* of him or them that have *coercive power*; and that *power* be derived from the *wills* of men that constitute such power, to the end they may live in peace, they may at last come to this, that the appetites of men and the passions of their minds are such, that, unless they be restrained by some power, they will always be making war upon one another; which may be known to be so by any man's experience, that will but examine his own mind.[28]

The crux is that analysis and hypothesis are here correlative terms. Analysis is the taking apart conceptually of the phenomenon experienced to find its necessary causality. Hypothesis is that which is not immediately present or perceptible in the phenomenon experienced, but is required in order to explain its necessary rather than contingent character. As the passage indicates, such hypotheses require to be confirmed by constant reference back to experience – the latter must always, so to speak, be retained and consulted in the mind of the analyst as he proceeds with his work. It will be recalled that Hobbes, when he first describes the 'state of nature' in Chapter XIII of *Leviathan*, takes some pains to show the reader that his 'inference' is confirmed by experience. It would be a gross error to conclude from this that he saw his hypothesis as but a 'possible' explanation of the civil world that he was engaged in 'testing'. It was rather a link in a chain of reasoning from effect to first cause and back again.

It would also be a gross error to envisage Hobbes's hypothesis as a 'useful' mental detour to achieve a practical objective. To be sure, Hobbes hoped that his theory of the state would have a beneficial practical impact. But there is all the difference in the world between saying 'knowledge, or the intellectual grasp of what is true and necessary, is of practical value', and saying 'practical value, or usefulness, is the criterion of knowledge'. Hobbes agreed emphatically with the first principle, but not with the second.

It could be contended that Hobbes regarded his hypothesis only as a 'possible' explanation of the working of the real world. But he himself stated quite plainly that while in the natural sciences it was not possible to make final, categorical demonstrations of the causes of things, because the natural world was not made by man, it *was* possible to make final, categorical demonstrations of the causes of things in the science of geometry and the civil order, where the things under consideration where constructed by man.[29]

Hobbes's hypothesis – or hypotheses – of the state of nature and the social contract were hence framed by him as the absolutely indispensable links in a demonstration of the necessary or essential nature of the body politic, whatever the empirical or phenomenal characteristics of such bodies might be. They were parts of the definition of the noumenal state, the state in and for itself. This definition was simultaneously a guide to what the empirical state should become. Discussions of his hypotheses that detach them from their specific function within a specific argument, and treat them as, for example, contributions to the theory of rational choice, sidestep the central issue of their potency as illuminators of the enduring qualities of the state.

CONCLUSION

The paradox in the classical idea of the social contract is that it was used, on the one hand, as part of an endeavour to legitimize the state in and for itself, as a body with its own distinct, political logic, and used, on the other hand, as part of an endeavour to reassert the supremacy of the inner, spiritual kingdom over the state, over politics. Hobbes and Rousseau express the extremes. The one was concerned to rein back the extravagant claims of the inner individual conscience in the interests of external social peace, while the other was concerned precisely to assert the claims of the inner individual conscience against the interests of external social peace. Yet each argued that the foundation of the rightly ordered body politic was a social contract.

These two tendencies correspond to two tendencies in Protestantism. In part, Protestantism, as it developed during the early modern period, sought, in the same way as Roman Catholicism, though with a different theology, to subordinate the political to spiritual. In part, however, it sought to renounce this overweening aspiration, and to elevate the political as the best protector of the individual and his private faith. It is this second, more secular tendency, that Hobbes, above all, represents, and which his doctrine of the social contract exemplifies.

Both these broad tendencies can, moreover, be seen reappearing in the great political upheavals that took place in America and France at the end of the eighteenth century, when the doctrine of the social contract was transmuted into the concrete demand – that was always implicit in the theory – that the people should act as the 'constituent power'. In the writings and actions of Paine and Hamilton, and Sieyes and Robespierre, the same basic divergence of attitude towards the political can be discerned as in the writings of Hobbes, Locke and Rousseau.[30] It is not a divergence about which one can remain neutral.

NOTES

1 J. Hampton, *Hobbes and the Social Contract Tradition*, Cambridge, Cambridge University Press, 1986.
2 Hampton, *Hobbes*, p. 256.
3 Hampton, *Hobbes*, p. 278.
4 Hampton, *Hobbes*, p. 278.
5 Hampton, *Hobbes*, p. 3.
6 Hampton, *Hobbes*, p. 271.
7 Rousseau, *The Social Contract*, M. Cranston (trans.), Harmondsworth, Penguin, 1968, book 1, ch. 7, p. 62.
8 Hobbes, *Leviathan*, M. Oakeshott (ed.), Oxford, Basil Blackwell, 1960, part 1, ch. XIII, p. 80.
9 Hobbes, *Leviathan*, part 1, ch. XIV, p. 84.
10 Hobbes, *Leviathan*, part 2, ch. XXI, p. 141.
11 Rousseau, *Contract*, book 1, ch. 6, p. 60.
12 Hobbes, *Leviathan*, part 1, ch. XIII, pp. 81–2.
13 I have discussed more fully the role of the 'people' in Hobbes's doctrine of the formation of the state in M. Forsyth, 'Thomas Hobbes and the Constituent Power of the People', *Political Studies*, 1981, vol. XXIX, pp. 191–203.
14 Hobbes, *Leviathan*, part 2, ch. XVII, p. 110.
15 Hobbes, *Leviathan*, part 2, chap XXVI, p. 177.
16 For a fuller investigation of the 'three stages' in the evolution of the Hobbesian state of nature see M. Forsyth, 'Thomas Hobbes and the External Relations of States', *British Journal of International Studies*, 1979, vol. 3, pp. 196–209.
17 For a discussion of '*Gabe*' and '*Aufgabe*' see J. S. Whale, *The Protestant Tradition*, Cambridge, Cambridge University Press, 1955, pp. 92–102.

18 Hobbes, *Leviathan*, part 2, ch. XVIII, p. 114.
19 The 'right of nature' is defined by Hobbes at the start of ch. XIV of *Leviathan*.
20 Hobbes, *Leviathan*, part 2, ch. XXVIII, p. 208.
21 See, for example, the discussion of hypothesis in A. C. Crombie, *Augustine to Galileo*, Cambridge, Mass., Harvard University Press, 1979, *passim*.
22 J. Rawls, *A Theory of Justice*, Oxford, Oxford University Press, 1973.
23 Rawls, *A Theory of Justice*, p. 9.
24 Rawls, *A Theory of justice*, p. 45.
25 Rawls, *A Theory of Justice*, p. 21.
26 Rawls, *A Theory of Justice*, p. 51.
27 I have discussed Hobbes's method of analysis and synthesis more fully in 'Thomas Hobbes: *Leviathan*', in *A Guide to the Political Classics: Plato to Rousseau*, M. Forsyth and M. Keens-Soper (eds.), Oxford, Oxford UniversityPress, 1988, pp. 120–46.
28 Hobbes, *Elements of Philosophy*, part 1, ch. VI, in *The English Works*, W. Molesworth (ed.), vol. 1, p. 74.
29 Hobbes, *Six Letters to the Professors of Mathematics*, in *English Works*, W. Molesworth (ed.), vol. VII, pp. 183–4.
30 For this final stage in the evolution of the contract doctrine see the essays devoted to Hamilton and Sieyes in M. Forsyth, M. Keens-Soper and J. Hoffman, *The Political Classics: Hamilton to Mill*, Oxford, Oxford University Press, 1993.

3 John Locke

Social contract versus political anthropology

Jeremy Waldron

CONTRACTARIANISM

Modern contractarians accept without question that most of the social and political institutions which interest them are not in fact the upshot of any contract or agreement among those whose lives they affect. They are happy to repudiate ideas like the state of nature and the original contract as historical hypotheses, to regard them, in Robert Nozick's phrase, as 'fact-defective' characterizations, and to accept that the actual evolution of political society probably took an entirely different course from the one the contract image suggests.[1]

Many accept also that the legitimacy of the modern state and our obligations to it do not depend on the reality of our consent or voluntary submission. For example, John Rawls concedes, 'No society can . . . be a scheme of cooperation which men enter voluntarily in a literal sense; each finds himself placed at birth in some particular position in some particular society'.[2] To the extent that it is used at all, the social contract is understood as a purely hypothetical construction: not an assumption of fact but, as Kant described it, 'merely an *idea* of reason' that generates the basis of a normative standard for testing laws and social arrangements. We do not ask whether the arrangements were in fact agreed to; we ask instead whether they *could have been* agreed to by people working out the basis of a life together under conditions of initial freedom and equality. If the answer is 'No', then we have a basis for condemning the institutions in question as incompatible with the very ideas of freedom and equality, quite apart from their actual origin or purpose.[3]

Treating the social contract as a *purely* normative model is one way of responding to its evident implausibility as an historical hypothesis. But it may not be the only way. In this article I shall argue that the political theory of John Locke provides an example of a somewhat different approach to the issue of historicity or otherwise of the social contract idea.[4] Locke is sometimes regarded as someone who, naively, presented the social contract as a historical fact – someone, therefore, whose theory is discredited at least in part by David Hume's criticism that '[a]lmost all the governments which exist at present, or of which there remains any record in story, have been founded originally, either on usurpation or conquest, or both, without any pretence of a fair consent, or voluntary subjection of the people'.[5] Against this interpretation, I shall argue that Locke presented a much more realistic picture of social and political development than the one usually attributed to him. The picture he presented does not on the face of it have much in common with the social contract story. But, as we shall see, it is possible to discern in Locke's arguments a way of relating and interweaving the two which is much more complicated, and philosophically more challenging and interesting, than the modern deployment of contractarian ideas as purely normative devices.

LOCKE'S TWO STORIES

I start from the fact that in the *Second Treatise* Locke appears to tell not one but *two* stories – and two quite different stories – about the development of politics and civil society.

The first and most familiar is the classic story of the state of nature, the social contract, and the deliberate institution of political arrangements. This is a story which divides the history of each territorial society into two sharply distinguished eras. In the first era, men live together as free and equal individuals, without any relations of political authority, governed only by the rules and principles of natural law.[6] In the second era, the modern era, men relate to one another in a framework of political institutions – legislatures, courts, socially sanctioned property arrangements, and so on – institutions which articulate the natural rules and principles in the clear and determinate form of positive law.[7] The watershed between the eras is the two-step process of the Lockian social contract. Responding to certain difficulties in the state of nature, the free and equal members of natural society meet together and agree to constitute a new artificial community by pooling their powers and resolving to act jointly and collectively to uphold their respective rights and liberties.[8] Then, in the second step of the contract process, this newly constituted community – the people – by a majority decision sets up specialist agencies to which its power is entrusted for the purposes of legislation, the execution of laws, the promotion of the public good, and possible confederation with other groups.[9] These are the familiar institutions of contemporary government, and thus the second step ushers in the modern era of human history.

The other story has an utterly different shape. It is based on what we may term Locke's speculations in political anthropology. This is the story of the gradual and indiscernible growth of modern political institutions, modern political problems and modern political consciousness out of the simple tribal group. The story goes something like this. Since time immemorial, social groups have been under the authority of one man, usually a father-figure or patriarch. In the first instance, that authority consisted simply in the patriarch's informal ability to settle any disputes that sprang up between members of the group and occasionally to punish members for behaving in antisocial ways. As such, his authority was scarcely distinguishable from the natural rule of a parent over his children.[10] From time to time, his authority might take on a more determinate aspect of *leadership* when the group came into warlike conflict with other groups; but when that passed, the leader's authority would lapse back into its previous indeterminate state.[11] The main dynamic for the growth of political authority, Locke argues, was economic not military. As the natural economy developed and the use of money became widespread, the incidence of disputes and the temptation to antisocial behaviour increased, and the role of conciliatory, adjudicative and punitive authority became gradually more important within the social group.[12] With the increased frequency of its exercise, there was a tendency for authority to become less informal and gradually more institutionalized so that there developed recognizable procedures for resolving disputes and dealing with social infractions, and specialist officials to operate them. At the same time, however, the room for abuse and corruption also expanded.[13] Because the development of government was gradual and indiscernible, men could easily be mystified about its nature and justification; and Locke charts with the development of political institutions a concomitant growth in political ideology culminating in the fantasy of the divine right of kings.[14] The course of human political development, on this second story, has left men bewildered and mystified and it is now the task of true philosophy – the task Locke takes upon himself – to dispel some of that mystification.

The contrast between the two stories could hardly be greater. On the first account, government is explicitly conventional: its institution is the deliberate act of free and equal individuals acting consciously and rationally together in the pursuit of their goals. On the other account, the growth of government is largely unconscious – it develops by what Locke calls 'an insensible change'[15] – and retrospectively that development is a mystery to those involved in it.

Equally, the periodizations of history suggested by the two stories are utterly different. The first gives a clear division of history into political and pre-political periods separated by the dramatic events of the social contract; the second gives no distinct periodization of this sort at all, but only the growth of modern government 'by degrees'[16] out of the family or the tribe. If it suggests a division of history, it is the periodization of Locke's theory of property and natural economy – the gradual shift from poor and simple equality in the first ages of the world[17] to a radically unequal but immensely more productive economy organized around monetary exchange.[18] But since political authority (either in its embryonic patriarchal form or in the explicit institutions of civil society) is present in this story from start to finish, the economic periodization does not generate any clearly corresponding periodization of the political.

The first story, of course, is the locus of Locke's arguments about political morality. His normative theory of rights, his attack on absolutism, his views on representation and the separation of powers, and his vindication of resistance and revolution are all made intelligible and defensible in the *Second Treatise* primarily with reference to the story of the social contract.

There is no need to go into details; one example will do. Locke's opposition to absolutism is based on the idea that government is founded on individual consent and that there are clear limits on what individuals will or may give their consent to. 'A Rational Creature cannot be supposed, when free, to put himself into Subjection to another, for his own harm'.[19] Locke argues that the attributes of Hobbesian or *jure divino* absolutism are not what rational creatures can intelligibly be supposed to have consented to. Such an absolutism, leaving them worse off than they would have been in the state of nature, is not a possible subject for a deliberately conceived and explicitly set out charter of cooperation and trust formed by individuals bargaining together under conditions of juridical freedom and equality. Agreement to such terms could not be construed as genuine consent, but would have to be taken as a temporary act of insanity or irrationality from which no binding obligation could plausibly be inferred.

Now, as long as we stick with the social contract story this appears an important and compelling argument. It represents individual rights against the government in an attractive light as the limits on what could have been consented to coming out of the state of nature.[20] Rights against the government are not merely the rights that individuals start with in the state of nature (as they are, for example, in Nozick's account).[21] Rather, they are natural rights supported and bolstered by Locke's insistence that it is incredible to imagine their being traded away or alienated. The rational choice framework of the contract story provides a basis for Locke's claim that arbitrary or absolute government could not possibly have been legitimized by the consent of those subject to it.[22]

But if we shift our attention to the anthropological story, the argument hardly seems to get a grip at all. If authority as a fact of human life is immemorial, and if the development of modern government has been, not deliberate, but largely unconscious and indiscernible, then there seems little room for the considerations about the nature and reality of consent that the Lockian argument relies on. For reasons I shall outline later in this chapter, I think that conclusion may be premature. But certainly, as it stands, the anthropological account of political development appears to lend its weight more to something like the royalist patriarchialism of Robert Filmer – Locke's target in the *Two Treatises* – than to the constraints of the liberal theory of government by consent.[23] It looks then as though Locke needs to be able to rely on the social contract story to make the points he wants to make in liberal political morality.

PROBLEMS FOR THE CONTRACT STORY

The trouble is that the contract story as it stands is historically and sociologically implausible. The point is not simply that it used to be thought plausible, but now is not. We cannot say that Locke and his contemporaries believed naively in this account of the development of political society, but that we know better. Locke was perfectly well aware of the strain that the contract story placed on the credulity of his contemporaries. Twice in the *Second Treatise* he imagined an objection being put forward along these lines:

> Tis often asked as a mighty objection, where are, or ever were, there any men in such a State of Nature?[24]

> To this I find Objection made . . . that there are no instances to be found in Story of a Company of Men independent and equal one amongst another, that met together, and in this way began and set up a Government.[25]

Objections like these were put forward against natural law theory by Robert Filmer; indeed they were as commonly evoked in the seventeenth century by what John Dunn has called the expository feebleness of the social contract story as they have been ever since.[26] From the moment the theory of the social contract was invented, critics have ridiculed what they took to be its absurd historical pretensions. And of course, Locke's sensitivity to the objection would have been reinforced by the fact that he himself appears to have accepted, in parts of the *Second Treatise*, an alternative story about the development of political society in which the drama of the social contract plays no discernible role at all.

As if this were not enough, there is a further difficulty with the historical plausibility of the contractarian account. Not only is there evidence that political society evolved in a non-contractarian way, there is also none of the sort of evidence we should expect to find if contractarian events had been involved in its development. The point is stated clearly by David Hume:

> It is strange, that an act of mind, which every individual is supposed to have formed, and after he came to the use of reason too, otherwise it could have no authority; that this act, I say, should be so much unknown to all of them, that, over the face of the whole earth, there scarcely remain any traces or memory of it.[27]

The problem is hermeneutical. Given that the law of nature is plain and intelligible to all rational creatures,[28] and that civil society is the result of a deliberate agreement among its citizens, why do people need John Locke to instruct them in political theory? Surely if what he says is true, people would know all this already. If, on the other hand, people are ignorant of these points, and if they live relatively contented lives under irrational and tyrannical regimes, then what Locke says in the contract story about the political development of mankind must be mistaken. Indeed, one could say that Locke's own political concerns – his agitation against the spread of absolutism from continental Europe to England, and his worries about the prevalence and popularity of the Divine Right theory – themselves testify against the truth of his approach. How could politics be so corrupt and potentially oppressive if his theory about the deliberateness of its institution were true? If society is a result of human intention, how can it be at the same time so dark, so mystifying, and so obscure to those who are involved in it?

Fortunately, the contract story is not the only account Locke offers of political and social development. As we have seen, he presents also a gradualist, anthropological account, and that does not seem to be subject to anything like the same difficulties.

To begin with, it is much more plausible as a historical or prehistorical account. Though political anthropology was a young science when Locke was writing – indeed, he can claim to be one of its pathfinders[29] – his understanding of the processes of social and political growth is not spectacularly different from some of the more plausible theories put forward today. The gradualist idea of a shift from inchoate patriarchal authority to formal political institutionalization offers a much better account of the anthropological data than the idea of a dramatic shift from a pre-political state of nature to an explicitly political civil society. And the *dynamic* of political development in Locke's anthropology – economic growth and increase in economic contention – seems more plausible than the other idea of man's juridical aspirations in the state of nature.

Moreover, unlike the social contract story, the anthropological account is not discredited by any assumption than men are conscious of the growth of political institutions, still less that they are their deliberate creation. Instead, Locke offers a plausible account of the development of political ideology and of the emergence of an intellectual climate in politics in which a theory like his was called for. The account goes like this.

As political authority became more formal and, in particular, as it detached itself from other social roles and relationships, an art of specifically political flattery grew up in society.[30] Against a general background of historical and anthropological ignorance, 'Learning and Religion'[31] began to produce the most bizarre characterizations of the political, of which the idea of monarchy by Divine Right and the claim that Charles and James Stuart were heirs by primogeniture to the God-given authority of Adam were the most recent, the most alarming and the most absurd. The blossoming of royalist ideology, Locke believed, threatened to distort and perhaps subvert the course of political development, and to drive it into new channels of absolutism and oppression, with the misery and instability which that would generate. Against the background of this crisis in political legitimization, Locke claims that it has become necessary *for the first time* for men 'to examine more carefully the Original and Rights of Government and to find out ways to restrain the Exorbitances and prevent the Abuses of the Power'.[32] (This idea that the need for political self-consciousness is the novel feature of the modern age would sound almost Hegelian were it not for the fact that Locke seems to view it rather as a regrettable and contingent necessity than as the consummation of the growth of spirit in the world.) The *Second Treatise* – according to its author – is itself the theory that is called for by these circumstances.

Thus, instead of the paradoxes of the social contract, we have in Locke's anthropology a theory of the political which purports to have the remarkably modern ability to explain both the circumstances of its own production and the novelty and strangeness that would initially be attributed to it.

So the anthropological story cannot be faulted in the ways that the social contract story can be. But then Locke is in a difficulty. We have already seen that it is the contract story that packs the normative punch of his political philosophy. It gives us the theory of rights, representation, separation of powers, justified resistance, and so on. The anthropology, on its own, gives none of this. It seems, therefore, that the story Locke needs (for his moral and political purposes) he cannot have (for historical reasons), and the story that is consistent and historically plausible is not one that gets him anywhere near the normative conclusions he desires. To rescue Locke from this dilemma, we need to develop an account of the relation between the two stories which can explain the role and usefulness of the contract idea notwithstanding its defects as a developmental hypothesis. That is what I shall attempt in the rest of this chapter.

THE HISTORICITY OBJECTION

We have seen already how sensitive Locke was to the historical implausibility of the contract account, to the 'mighty objection' often raised that history reveals no instances of 'a Company of Men, independent and equal one amongst another, that met together, and in this way began and set up a government'.[33]

He responds to the difficulty in a number of ways. Sometimes he writes as though the challenge was purely and simply to produce 'instances' of people in the state of nature, or 'instances' of the explicit contractual founding of a political society. Thus, he writes sometimes as though the production of a single counter-example would suffice to refute the objection, as though he were trying to establish nothing more than the bare logical possibility of the contractarian hypothesis. 'To those that say there were never any men in the State of Nature', he responds by adducing Garcilaso de la Vega's account of the two men of different nationalities who found it necessary to bargain together for subsistence goods after they had been shipwrecked fortuitously on the same desert island.[34] But of course no example could be less apt if Locke's intention here is to offer a historical instance of what things were like in the first great era of human history or pre-history. Pedro Serrano and the other shipwreck victim are not merely stuck in the most bizarre and exceptional circumstances, but they are themselves castaways from civilization and their ability to contract with one another, as much as their ability to survive in these peculiar circumstances, arguably derives from their previous socialization. If anything, the Garcilaso case favours something like a Filmerian anthropology – as a classic example of the exception that proves the rule.[35]

Much the same is true of the instances that Locke cites of contractualist foundation. For the deliberate institution of government by free and equal individuals, we are given the classical stories of the origins of Rome and Venice, and the founding of the Italian city of Terentum by a group of Spartan exiles under Palantus in the eighth century BC.[36] And we are told that 'no Examples are so frequent in History. . . as those of Men withdrawing themselves . . . from the Jurisdiction they were born under, and the Family or Community they were bred up in, and setting up new Governments in other places'.[37] But these cases are just not particularly telling, since they involve, not the foundation of a state by people who till then had had no experience of the political, but the foundation of a *new* state by exiles from an old one.[38] As an account of the original development of the political, they tell us nothing at all.

Whether or not these are illuminating instances, there is a further point to be made about Locke's strategy. It cannot be enough for someone who takes contractualism seriously as a historical hypothesis to establish merely that *someone* once lived in what was recognizably a state of nature, or that *some* states were built on a contractual foundation. To do the work that it is supposed to do in this sort of theory, the contractualist claim has to be that, on the whole, *all* political development takes place in this way; the claim has to be that this is the way political societies are *normally* built up. That may be a little extreme: Locke certainly acknowledged that some kingdoms were established through conquest or usurpation.[39] But he denied they were entitled to be called 'political societies':

> Though governments can originally have no other rise than that before-mentioned, nor polities be founded on anything but the consent of the people, yet such has been the disorders ambition has filled the world with, that, in the noise of war, which makes so great a part of the history of mankind, this consent is little taken notice of; and therefore many have mistaken the force of arms for the consent of the people. But conquest is as far from setting up any government as demolishing a house is from building a new one in the place.[40]

The point is not merely verbal. Locke's theoretical position requires him to establish that a political society with any trace of legitimacy, or a political society to which any allegiance or obligation is owed, must have been set up by consent. He is required to say that it is legitimate only if and to the extent that its foundation is consensual. Even if we see the *Two Treatises* narrowly as a contribution to contemporary English politics, their author must be making that claim at least about the government of England: the rights he asserts and the complaints he lays against the Stuarts make sense only on the assumption that there was an original contract which has either been broken or is in danger of being broken. Since he adduces no specific evidence of an English contract, his only basis for that particular claim is the general, or more or less universal, hypothesis.

This is not to say that there is no place for argument by counter-example. At one point Locke responds to those who criticize the state of nature idea, by saying:

> It may suffice as an answer to the objection at present; that since all Princes and Rulers of Independent Governments all through the World, are in a State of Nature, 'tis plain the World never was, nor ever will be, without Numbers of Men in that State.[41]

The point is common enough in the natural law tradition – it is made in almost exactly similar terms by Hobbes.[42] But its effectiveness is primarily negative: it demolishes the patriarchialist claim that there is a seamless web of natural authority in the world, and it is deployed here with what John Dunn has described as devastating polemical force, attacking Filmer's theory of inescapable natural hierarchy and his theory of the Adamite succession at the point where they converge in manifest absurdity. But Dunn is quite right to note also that, for all its philosophical and rhetorical force, this example adds nothing to the case for a historical reading of the ideas of state of nature or social contract.[43]

Other responses which Locke makes do acknowledge the need to argue a broader case for the hypothesis. In a number of places, he attempts to draw on his own very considerable knowledge of anthropology to provide examples that might persuade us that the state of nature is 'typical' among primitive man. Thus we are given contemporary descriptions of the people of Brazil, Florida and Peru, who at least until recently lived not in kingdoms or commonwealths but like apes 'in Troops', without any political relationships.[44] And we are also offered one or two examples – some of them biblical, some of them anthropological – of men living in the state of nature in the earlier chapter on property.[45]

However, apart from the unhelpful cases mentioned earlier of people withdrawing from one political community to set up another, Locke is unable to make much of a case that explicit contract lies at the foundation of politics. He says of his opponents that 'They would do well not to search too much into the Original of Governments . . . lest they should find at the foundation of most of them, something very little favourable to the design they promote, and such a power as they contend for'.[46] But he fails to provide the evidence that is necessary to back up such a warning.

In fairness, we must add that Locke is well aware of the lack of evidence, and indeed that it is something which he takes time to explain. The explanation he offers is historiographical: 'Government is everywhere antecedent to Records, and Letters seldom come in amongst a People, till a long continuation of Civil Society has, by other more necessary Arts provided for their Safety, Ease and Plenty'.[47] The result is that civil societies, like human individuals, 'are commonly ignorant of their own Births and Infancies'[48] –

a dangerous point one would have thought for a contractarian to make. Therefore, he says 'it is not at all to be wondered that history [in the sense of historical records] gives us but little account of Men, that lived together in this State of Nature'.[49]

THE RELEVANCE OF HISTORY

The one other response Locke offers to the historicity objection reveals an intriguingly ambivalent attitude towards history, which, I think, helps to point us in the direction of a possible reconciliation between the contractarian and the anthropological accounts.

In the attempt to warn off his opponents that I mentioned a few paragraphs earlier, Locke suddenly interpolates a comment to the effect that 'at best, an Argument from what has been, to what should of right be, has no great force'.[50] The comment echoes several in the *First Treatise*, where Locke indicates that 'the Practice of Mankind'[51] is a dangerous premise on which to base moral and political doctrines, given the depths of depravity to which 'the busie mind of Man [can] carry him'.[52] The tone of these comments indicates his scepticism about the idea that 'the Example of what hath been done, be the Rule of what ought to be'.[53] All this is interesting, for it indicates considerable doubt on Locke's part about the significance of purely historical speculation about the origins and antecedents of government, and therefore about the necessity of treating the social contract as a historically credible idea.

We have to be careful, though, how we understand the point. There are two ways in which what happened in an earlier period may possibly be thought relevant to modern normative thinking.

It may be thought relevant, first, just because it is *earlier*, perhaps because we think that the earlier it is the more likely it antedates recent forms of corruption. This is the logic of 'the Ancient Constitution' – some aboriginal form of political organization which is normatively relevant for us simply on account of its pristine purity. I think John Dunn is absolutely right to insist that Locke is engaged in the task of disentangling liberal political thought from this sort of idea, and that he has reached the conclusion that no period of history can be normative for any other simply on account of its *date*.[54] That Locke has not torn himself away *entirely* from this mode of thinking is indicated perhaps by his continued insistence throughout the *Two Treatises* that human society has degenerated as history has gone on, and in his occasional almost Rousseauian references to the honesty and virtue of aboriginal man. But these references to aboriginal virtue are more than made up for by Locke's praise of progress and the increase of modern economy and population,[55] and are in any case seldom treated as vehicles for his main political ideas.

Historical speculations may have relevance of a rather different sort for political philosophy. If it is true that governments were set up in a consensual arrangement with the governed, then they are constrained morally by past events in the same way as a promise in the past constrains the person who made it or in the same way as someone's past act of kindness can place me under some obligation of gratitude towards him. In other words, there are certain moral principles which give past events present moral significance: the rule of promise-keeping, the principle of gratitude, the obligation to make good any damage one inflicts on others, and perhaps also the historical principles of acquisition and transfer of property entitlements. Finding out, therefore, whether governments are based on consent is certainly a historical exercise, but it is an exercise which is also important *now* because it will tell us, hopefully, what governments are morally bound by the terms of their institution to do. I do not think that Locke ever wanted to reject *this* mode of historical reasoning, and so the actual veracity of the social contract story remains an important problem for him.

In his essay 'Of the Original Contract', David Hume tries to argue that there is no real difference between these two modes of historical speculation. If, when we talk about the social contract, 'the agreement, by which savage men first associated and conjoined their force, be here meant, this is acknowledged to be real; but being so ancient, and being obliterated by a thousand changes of government and princes, it cannot now be supposed to retain any authority'.[56] In other words, even though the historical events of the social contract may have been morally relevant for the subsequent behaviour of the people who were parties to it, that by itself is not morally relevant for *our* behaviour *now*. The fact that our earliest ancestors set up consensual government and were bound morally by the terms of their consent does not show that *we* ought to do the same.

This, I take it, is a fair point as far as it goes. However, Locke's claim, I shall argue, is not that we should have government by consent just because our ancestors did, but rather that the history of human politics represents a framework and a continuum of consent given freely, though perhaps implicitly, down the ages by the members of succeeding generations, and broken only by occasional violations of consensual principles on the part of governments. Since an overlapping history of consensual government would retain direct moral significance for our practice today, it *is* important to find out what actually happened.

POLITICAL ANTHROPOLOGY AGAIN

We have concerned ourselves so far with Locke's response to the accusation that the story of the social contract is historically false. If we turn our attention now to what he says about the other story – the gradualist anthropology of government – we find a more sophisticated theory of historical relevance.

The anthropological account of the development of government looks convincing; it seems, as I have said, to be the more plausible of Locke's descriptions of the history of human politics. But as it stands, it certainly fails to represent that history as an overlapping continuum of consent down the ages. It looks instead, as Locke acknowledges, more congenial to Robert Filmer's theory of patriarchy.[57] Still, appearances can be deceptive in history, and Locke is adamant that historical facts do not speak for themselves. We need to *interpret* them, we need to look not only at the events which have happened but also at the reasons *why* they happened,[58] and we need to be able to locate those happenings and those reasons in an already-established framework of moral categories.

A mundane example will help here, to illustrate the approach Locke is taking. Not all cases of promising are marked out easily for us by somebody's uttering the explicit words 'I hereby promise to do such-and-such'. Often promising is implicit or even tacit, and the expectation which a person is obliged to fulfil arises from his actions and his perceived motivations rather than his words. To see whether or not a promise has been made and what our obligations are, it is important not merely to record a history of the facts, not merely to ask 'What happened?', but to subject the facts to moral scrutiny, to ask 'How are these events to be viewed? What are they to be understood *as?*'

It is clear from some of his other writings, that this is exactly the approach that Locke thinks should be taken to history. On the one hand, he is anxious to stress the moral importance of historical study. He says in the *Essay Concerning Human Understanding*:

> I would not be thought here to lessen the credit and use of history; it is all the light we have in many cases, and we receive from it a great part of the useful truths that we have . . . I think nothing more valuable than the records of antiquity; I wish we had more of them and more uncorrupted.[59]

On the other hand, he insists, in a *Journal* entry noted by Richard Ashcraft, that the study of history is useful only 'to one who hath well settled in his mind the principles of morality and knows how to make a judgment on the actions of men'.[60]

How, then, will one who is versed in ethics and the categories of morality view the events which go to make up the story of Locke's political anthropology? The answer depends – obviously – on what those ethics and categories of morality happen to be. And here at last we begin to get a sense of the relation between the two stories about the development of political society. For the principles of ethics and morality which Locke thinks we ought to bear in mind when we consider the history of political development are none other than the postulates and the dynamics of the social contract story.

Men are created free and equal by God and they are *ab initio* subject to the law of nature. Since they are created without manifest subordination one among another, nothing can put any of them under the authority of any other without his own consent. Parents, of course, have responsibility for the actions of their children and this constitutes a sort of authority; but in its very nature it is an authority limited in time and function. That apart, political arrangements must be either consensual or illegitimate; the moral premises allow no other alternative. So far as consent is concerned, there are both moral and rational limits on what may intelligibly be consented to, and these limits generate a moral doctrine of constrained and limited government, with individuals retaining natural rights against their rulers. And so on, and so on.

It is the same old story again, but this time presented in the moral not the historical mode, as the articulation of a framework of categories for interpreting and judging actual events. The contract story is not intended as a historical description; it is intended rather as a moral tool for historical understanding. It is the function of the political anthropology to offer us an account of what actually happened; while the contract story offers us the moral categories in terms of which what actually happened is to be understood.

I will not go into all the details of the way in which Locke applies these moral categories to his political anthropology. His general strategy is to suggest that, with the growth of political authority, those subject to it indicated by their implicit acquiescence at each step that it was made with their consent, and on conditions of trust rather than abject prostration. Of course the alternative accounts are limited; Locke gives us a very small menu of moral categories with which to approach the story. Either we are dealing with a case of parental authority, in which case the authority is strictly limited to the welfare and education of children, and limited in time as well;[61] or we are dealing with a case of political authority, in which case it must be based on implicit consent and limited by the rational and moral constraints on consent;[62] or else we are dealing with a case of violence and aggression in which case it involved no moral obligation at all, save perhaps for the obligation to resist.[63] Those are the only alternatives that a Lockian morality gives us. If a given historical event does not obviously fit one category or the other, then it is the task of historical *judgement*, judgement informed by moral sensitivity, to determine which one best applies. Locke does not pretend that this is an easy task. His theory of resistance and revolution – undoubtedly the cutting edge of his normative theory – is dominated by the warning that the gravity of the consequences of rebellion places a heavy and inescapable responsibility on those who make these judgements, a responsibility for which they will be answerable to heaven.[64]

Since the moral categories we have are necessary for the study of history, they cannot themselves be the product of historical study. Their basis lies in reason or, as Dunn puts it, in the *ahistorical* arguments of natural theology.[65] The point of the social contract story is to provide a moral template to be placed over historical events and over our present predicament, for the purpose of ascertaining what it is right and wrong for us and our political rulers to do. Locke's task in the body of the *Second Treatise* is to place that template over his political anthropology in such a way as to yield the moral description of our history as an overlapping continuum of political consent with the implications for contemporary political practice that such a characterization would generate.

CONTRACTUALISM AND INCREMENTALISM

With this apparatus in hand, we can see how to respond to the difficulty we noted earlier – the problem posed for contract theory by people's ignorance of the nature and function of the political institutions they were supposed themselves deliberately to have constituted.

The initial response to that difficulty was to concede the point. Locke's political anthropology charts a gradual growth in politicization against a background of ignorance and mystery. Unlike the social contract story, it does not assume that people can perceive the general tendency of what is going on, or that they can foresee the eventual upshot of the 'gradual' and 'insensible' development of specialized political authority. And this certainly means that the categories of *consent* and *contract*, and the rights and obligations that go with them, made available by the social contract story, cannot be applied to the political history of a society as a whole.

But it does not mean that the categories have no role at all to play. Even if the agents involved did not perceive the long-run tendency of politicization, still they may have been involved consciously and consensually in each step of that process, and that may be sufficient to warrant characterizing the individual steps in contractualist terms.

Consider, for example, the following series of events taking place and being repeated over a long period of time. A father disciplines his children; his children continue to respect him as they grow through adolescence to maturity; they continue to come to him for advice and conciliation; he forms the expectation that he will continue in this role; he insists that he alone should be the one to punish the crimes of, and resolve conflicts among, his adult children; he extends this authority to the case of visitors and strangers among them as well; that power is transferred from father to eldest son on the father's death; it becomes expected that this is the way things are done around here.[66]

Though with hindsight this series of events can be read as the establishment of a sort of hereditary monarchy, we may doubt whether it ever appeared in that light to the members of the family group concerned (at least not until its final stages). So we may not be able to say, in this case, that *hereditary monarchy* was set up by consent; that may not be a description that corresponds to anyone's sense of what he ever agreed to.

We may still be able to say, however, that *each step* in that process took place consciously and consensually: the children accepted their father as sole adviser; they accepted his exclusive right to punish; they accepted his right to punish strangers; and they acquiesced in the transfer of that right from father to eldest son; and so on. For each step we may be able to describe the reasons for the increase in confidence and trust. The grown children of a man would find it easy to accept that their adult differences should be referred to him as their childhood ones had been: 'where could they have had a fitter Umpire than he, by whose Care they had every one been sustain'd, and brought up, and who had a tenderness for them all?'.[67] The 'Dignity and Authority' which this conferred on him would make it easy for them to see him as the person to whom difficulties with outsiders should most appropriately be referred and to restrain themselves from exercising a right to punish on their own account.[68] Not only that, but also it would provide a salient point of coordination for the group in the face of any serious external threat. When the patriarch died and his property passed to 'able and worthy Heirs', it would also be easy to accept that the confidence that had been reposed in the father should pass with it unless there was overwhelming reason to vest it elsewhere.[69]

With this sort of background, the moral categories of contractualism became entirely appropriate. For each incremental step in the development of a political institution, the idea of the state of nature defines an initial moral baseline and hence the array of general moral categories that we have at our disposal. We can then explore the moral significance of what actually happened using these categories, locating the changes in a moral space which makes their practical implications clear. If the changes are describable in terms of consent, we can draw moral conclusions about obligations, rights and the limits of power. The reasons for each step being clear enough, we can see each participant responding to them, not necessarily in an express declaration of consent, but in the way consensual moves are usually made in everyday life – quietly, even tacitly, without any reason being seen to make a fuss. We can say then that the children acquire obligations to their father-ruler and rights against him, not because we have evidence of any explicit undertaking to this effect, but because that is the best moral understanding we can get of what has been going on in the development of this society.

The language Locke uses to describe the consent involved in this sort of example is interesting: 'Thus 'twas easie, and almost natural for Children by a tacit, and scarce avoidable consent to make way for the Father's Authority and Government'.[70] There was no song or dance about a precise age of majority – 'one and Twenty, or any other Age, that might make them free Disposers of themselves and Fortunes' – at which these obligations were assumed. The move was 'easie' and 'scarce avoidable' in the sense that no other solution to the problems of social order that they faced ever needed to be considered in the early ages of mankind. But still it was not natural in the sense of being explained independently of men's wills by the law of nature; it was, as Locke insists in a telling phrase, '*almost* natural', in the sense of being something that, human nature being what it is, people would decide to do without fuss or bother in most social circumstances.

Notice also how the term 'almost natural' indicates the difficulty of the historical judgments involved in our assessment of this case. Superficially, patriarchy looks like the upshot of natural processes: that was the appeal of Filmer's theory. Only the closest scrutiny of the facts, together with a sophisticated moral awareness, including a moral understanding of the respective functions and limits of political and parental authority, can reveal that it must really have been based, as much as the foundation of Venice and Rome, in human convention and decision.

I have stressed that, in Locke's theory, the moral categories of contract and consent apply to the incremental steps in the development of politics and not to the process as a whole. This explains why it is possible for that development to be both conventional and at the same time mystifying to those who were involved in it. Locke, as we have seen, accused the new breed of ideologists – the 'servile Flatterers'[71] of absolute power – of exploiting the resulting credulity, and of teaching 'princes to have distinct and separate Interests from their People'.[72] Though he is convinced that 'there cannot be done a greater Mischief to Prince and People, than the Propagating wrong Notions concerning Government' (*Two Treatises*, Preface), he is sure that in the end this propaganda will never be entirely successful. 'Whatever Flatters may talk to amuze Peoples Understandings,' he writes, 'it hinders not Men, from feeling'.[73] The political virtue that is the residue of the gradual consensual development of government will in the end assert itself, and people will have 'the sence of rational Creatures'[74] to resist the arrogance of power and to find for themselves more explicit ways of checking and limiting it. These are the circumstances in which Locke's theory was called for, and that political virtue provides a foothold for it in the understanding of those to whom it is addressed.

TACIT CONSENT AND MEMBERSHIP

There is one final complication to clear up. I have argued that contractarian categories can be applied to the events charted in Locke's political anthropology, meaning not that the whole sequence of events can be read as a single consensual exercise, but that each particular step in the anthropological development can be read as a consensual event. I have argued also that reading the particular events in that way is a matter of judgment. We are not dealing with one giant contract or agreement, nor are we dealing with a whole lot of little contracts, at least not at an explicit level. Locke's account asks us rather to accept that we are dealing with a series of events each of which can be read in terms of *tacit* consent or agreement on the part of those involved. If you like, the process I have described is doubly inexplicit: the particular events involve tacit rather than explicit consent; and the development of the whole series of events, considered as a single process, may not have been explicitly in anybody's mind.

Now towards the end of Chapter 8 of the *Second Treatise*, Locke develops a doctrine which we may call the doctrine of differential obligation. He suggests that a person whose obligation to a society stems only from tacit consent is not 'a member of that society' in a full-blooded sense. He has an obligation to obey its laws (unless they are unjust), but he is not obliged to remain 'a perpetual Subject of that Commonwealth'[75] in the way that a full member is. The tacit consenter is free at any stage 'to go and incorporate himself into any other commonwealth, or to agree with others to begin a new one, *in vacuis locis*, in any part of the world he can find free and unpossessed'.[76]

The grounds for the doctrine of differential obligation are far from clear; I shall not go in to that here. The question that we have to ask is this: does the anthropological account imply that when a political society has evolved tacitly in the way we have described, its inhabitants are not full members of that society for the purposes of the doctrine of differential obligation?[77]

It is hard to be confident about an answer, and any account we give will have to involve a charitable reconstruction of a difficult and obscure part of Locke's theory. The answer I want to suggest is negative: tacit consent for the purposes of the doctrine of differential obligation is not the same as tacit consent for the purposes of the interpretation of Locke's political anthropology. For the purposes of the doctrine of differential obligation, tacit consent is very much the consent imputed to a person simply in virtue of his possession or enjoyment of property in a country. As Locke puts it, 'the obligation any one is under, by virtue of such enjoyment, to submit to the government, begins and ends with the enjoyment'.[78] The point is one about the *basis* of the tacit consent, not the tacitness as such.

Locke does say that 'he that has once, by actual Agreement, and any express Declaration, given his Consent to be of any Commonweal, is perpetually and indispensably obliged to be and remain unalterably a Subject to it'[79] and he does insist that 'Nothing can make any Man so, but his actually entering into it by positive Engagement, and express Promise and Compact'.[80] The suggestion seems to be that full membership connotes obligations so burdensome that they could be assumed only explicitly, that a tacit assumption would never suffice. But that has the unwelcome consequence of implying that native-born inhabitants of a society are in exactly the same position as resident aliens unless and until they take an explicit oath of allegiance.[81]

The interpretation I prefer distinguishes potential subjects into three groups, not two. As well as (a) those who are subject to a society by virtue merely of their enjoyment of property and (b) those who are subject to it because they have given an express undertaking, there are also (c) those whose consent to a political arrangement is and has been 'almost natural',[82] in the sense that they have grown up with it and acquiesced in its development and in its authority over them at every stage. The threefold distinction is suggested by Locke's use of the analogy of a family in discussing tacit consent:

But submitting to the Laws of any Country, living quietly, and enjoying Priviledges and Protection under them . . . no more makes a Man a Member of that Society, a perpetual Subject of that Commonwealth, than it would make a Man a subject to another in whose Family he found it convenient to abide for some time; though whilst he continued in it, he were obliged to comply with the Laws, and submit to the Government he found there.[83]

A house guest owes a sort of tacit consent to the rules of a family by virtue of his temporary residence; but his situation *vis-à-vis* the family is different, not only from someone who has deliberately chosen to join the family (a new son-in-law, for example), but also from the children who have grown up into its structure. Of course, Locke is emphatically committed to deny the claim that people are naturally members of the society into which they are born, in any literal sense of 'naturally'.[84] But we have already seen that an adult child's consensual subjection to the political authority of a father-ruler would be 'easie and almost natural';[85] discussing the matter, Locke seems to imply that the distinction between 'the express or tacit Consent of the Children' makes no difference,[86] and he notes that it is 'no wonder, that they made no distinction betwixt Minority, and full age; nor looked after one and Twenty, or any other Age, that might make them the free Disposers of themselves and Fortunes'.[87] In societies whose political development has followed the path charted in Locke's anthropology, the line between the sort of membership that flows from the tacit consent of an alien, and the sort that flows from the words of one who undertakes express allegiance is simply blurred.

That blurring posed no difficulty in practice until rulers began to abuse their authority and to mystify those who were subject to it about its origins. Then, as we have seen, it became important to examine events more carefully to see how exactly moral categories like consent and obligation could be applied.[88] We have to examine events in which the consensual aspect is muted and scarcely discernible, and ask how they stand in regard to a moral that admits no other basis for political obligation. And we have to contemplate the possibility of a modern politics in which (regrettably) it becomes important for the issue of consent to be somewhat more explicit, and for there to be opportunities for its expression and presumptions of competence and majority to formally embody the principle that nothing can put a man 'into subjection to any Earthly Power, but only his own Consent'.[89]

If I am right about this, then the term 'tacit consent' is playing two quite different roles in Locke's political theory. On the one hand, it stands for a particular moral category: consent that consists in nothing but the enjoyment of property in a society binds a person no further than that enjoyment lasts. This is, if you like, an ideal type of tacit consent, and it is contrasted with the ideal type of explicit consent which brings full membership with it. It is one of the moral categories with which we approach the interpretation of history.

One the other hand, 'tacit consent' is also a way of characterizing a particular set of historical events, such as the gradual emergence of a polity out of a family. The 'tacitness' consists in the fact that the consensual aspect of those events is not evident on their face, that it requires judgment to discern it. And one of the things that judgment has to address is whether the consensual element of these events, such as it is, conforms more to the ideal of explicit consent or more to the ideal of tacit consent as categories in Locke's moral theory.

CONCLUSION

I said at the outset that I would use the *Second Treatise* to make points with more general applicability to political contractarianism. Contractarians have sometimes written as though we had to choose between regarding the social contract as an actual historical event and regarding it simply as a hypothetical idea to aid normative thinking. I hope I have shown that in Locke's political theory there is a third alternative.

We do not need to take contractarianism as the claim that political institutions were set up in a single dramatic event, or a small series of events, in order to take it seriously as a historical hypothesis. That some arrangement is a human invention or contrivance, answerable to human purposes, does not necessarily mean that it was invented *all at once*; human inventions (the arch, the water wheel) can be developed gradually over time, even over long periods of time, without losing their essentially artificial or conventional character. In a Darwinian age, we tend to associate evolutionary processes with natural processes, and to assume that that which has evolved cannot possibly be described as artificial. But again, that is a mistake. A set of institutional arrangements may evolve by gradual steps over a period of time; but if each step involves elements of choice, deliberation and purpose, then the whole process takes on an intentional flavour, becomes susceptible to intentionalist categories, and may be evaluated in terms of human purposes in the way that contract theory requires. This remains the case even if it is true – which it usually is – that *the whole process* was not the subject of anyone's intentions and that the overall direction of the development was unforeseen. That is not a reason to withhold intentional evaluation from each – and therefore all – of the steps in the process, since each step can at least be seen as the upshot of intentional human action, and all subsequent steps remain an open subject for our choice.

Let me finish on a more gloomy note. We all know that the history of each political society has been punctuated by events which have nothing in common with consensual or contractual moves. Suddenly a form of government is thrust on a people against their will, or suddenly changes are made in the way they are governed which are wholly oppressive and which influence the character and constrain the direction of even the consensual changes that follow them. All this is true, and of the classical contract theorists, only

Hobbes wanted to say that even the most oppressive changes still had to be understood as contractual events. For the others – and for Locke in particular – it is no part of contractarianism to be optimistic or idealistic about political history. Contractarianism has critical as well as legitimizing resources. The strength of the theory is that it provides a set of categories by which events like oppression and subjugation can be evaluated negatively, and with which attempts to draw doctrines of obligation, allegiance and legitimacy out of such a history can be resisted. It is explicit in the moral categories of contractarianism that, as Locke puts it, 'no-one can be . . . subjected to the Political Power of another, without his own Consent'.[90] The setting up of political institutions by force, or the setting up or altering of institutions in a way that everyone could not possibly agree to, has no effect whatever so far as the establishment of obligation or political legitimacy are concerned.

Thus, viewing events through the template of the social contract story does not mean that we must view every stage in the history of our political development as a legitimate contractual step. It means simply that we should view it using contractarian categories, and that means treating each step *either* as though it involved elements of choice, consent and obligation, *or* as though it were an incident of force, oppression and the persistence of a right to resist, and drawing the appropriate conclusions. That is the choice that the contract approach gives us for each stage in the process of our political development. We make judgments, and the upshot of those judgments will contribute towards an estimation of our moral position in relation to the political system which is currently claiming our allegiance. No doubt this estimation will be very complicated, but of course it is no part of the contractarian philosophy to commit us to the view that political obligation and political legitimacy are simple and straightforward issues.

NOTES

1 Robert Nozick, *Anarchy, State, and Utopia*, Oxford, Basil Blackwell, 1974, pp. 7–9.
2 John Rawls, *A Theory of Justice*, Oxford, Oxford University Press, 1971, p. 13.
3 See Immanuel Kant, 'On the Common Saying: "This May Be True in Theory, But It Does Not Apply in Practice" ', in *Kant's Political Writings*, Hans Reiss (ed.), Cambridge, Cambridge University Press, 1970, p. 78. See also Jeremy Waldron, 'Theoretical Foundations of Liberalism', *Philosophical Quarterly*, 1987, vol. 37, pp. 134ff.
4 John Locke, *Two Treatises of Government*, Peter Laslett (ed.), Cambridge, Cambridge University Press, 1988. Subsequent references in the notes to this work, are by treatise and paragraph number.
5 David Hume, 'Of the Original Contract', in his *Essays, Moral, Political and Literary*, Eugene F. Miller (ed.), Indianapolis, Ind., Liberty Classics, 1985, p. 471.
6 Locke, *Two Treatises*, II, 4–86.
7 II, 134–243.
8 II, 87–95 and 99–131.
9 II, 96–8 and 132–3.
10 II, 74–5 and 105–107.
11 II, 108–9.

12 II, 111.
13 II, 94.
14 II, 111–12.
15 II, 76.
16 II, 110.
17 II, 33–8, 75 and 107–8.
18 II, 44ff.
19 II, 164.
20 For other similar lines of argument, see Locke, *Two Treatises*, II, 23, 93, 131, 135–6, 138–9, 149, 163–4, 168 and 222.
21 Nozick, *Anarchy, State and Utopia*, p. ix.
22 For the importance of this theme in early modern political thought, see Richard Tuck, *Natural Rights Theories: Their Origin and Development*, Cambridge, Cambridge University Press, 1979, esp. chs. 7–8. See also Jeremy Waldron, *Nonsense Upon Stilts: Bentham, Burke and Marx on the Rights of Man*, London, Methuen, 1987, pp. 11–13.
23 This is recognized by Peter Laslett in the footnote to II, 74 of his edition of the *Two Treatises*. See also G. Schochet, 'The Family and the Origins of the State in Locke's Political Philosophy', in *John Locke: Problems and Perspectives*, J. W. Yolton (ed.), Cambridge, Cambridge University Press, 1969.
24 II, 15.
25 II, 100.
26 John Dunn, *The Political Thought of John Locke: An Historical Account of the Argument of the 'Two Treatises of Government'*, Cambridge, Cambridge University Press, 1969, p. 100. For Filmer's critique, see *Patriarcha and Other Political Works of Sir Robert Filmer*, P. Laslett (ed.), Oxford, Basil Blackwell, 1949.
27 Hume, 'Of the Original Contract', p. 470.
28 II, 12.
29 In the introduction to his edition of the *Two Treatises*, Peter Laslett remarks that 'Locke may be said to have done more than anyone else to found the study of comparative anthropology' (p. 98 n.); similarly Dunn, *Political Thought of John Locke*, p. 46 n., describes him as 'in fact one of the best-informed students in the Europe of his time of variations in the moral, social, political and religious practices of non-European countries'.
30 II, 111–12.
31 II, 92.
32 II, 111.
33 II, 15 and 100.
34 II, 14–15.
35 See R. H. Cox, *Locke on War and Peace*, Oxford, Clarendon Press, 1960, pp. 95ff. for a discussion of this example.
36 II, 102–3.
37 II, 115.
38 The same is true of the enterprise that Locke imagined colonists embarking on when he produced the 'Fundamental Constitutions of Carolina', in *The Works of John Locke*, 9th edn, London, T. Longman and others, 1794, vol. 9; and also of the examples of political 'beginnings' in Hannah Arendt's famous study of this issue in *On Revolution*, Harmondsworth, Penguin, 1973. See generally the useful discussion in D. J. O'Connor, *John Locke*, New York, Dover Books, 1967, pp. 206ff.
39 II, 175–98.
40 II, 175.
41 II, 14.
42 Thomas Hobbes, *Leviathan*, C.B. Macpherson (ed.), Harmondsworth, Penguin, 1968, ch. 13, pp. 187–8.

43   Dunn, *Political Thought of John Locke*, pp. 106–7.
44   II, 102.
45   II, 36, 38, 41 and 49.
46   II, 103.
47   II, 101.
48   II, 11 and 101.
49   II, 101.
50   II, 103.
51   I, 56.
52   I, 56.
53   I, 57.
54   Dunn, *Political Thought of John Locke*, pp. 106–7.
55   II, 37–44.
56   David Hume, 'Of the Original Contract,' in *Essays Moral, Political and Literary*,
     E. F. Miller (ed.), Indianapolis, Ind., Liberty Classics, 1985, pp. 470–1.
57   II, 75–6.
58   II, 106.
59   John Locke, *An Essay Concerning Human Understanding*, J. W. Yolton (ed.),
     London, Dent, 1961, 4. 16, §11, p. 258.
60   Richard Ashcraft, 'Locke's State of Nature: Historical Fact or Moral Fiction?',
     American Political Science Review, 1968, p. 899. Ashcraft's reference is to Locke's
     Journal for 6–10 April 1677.
61   II, 58 and 170.
62   II, 23 and 134–42.
63   II, 16–21 and 228–9.
64   II, 21, 168, 176, 204 and 232.
65   Dunn, *Political Thought of John Locke*, p. 97.
66   II, 76.
67   II, 75.
68   II, 74.
69   II, 76.
70   II, 75.
71   II, 239.
72   II, 111.
73   II, 94.
74   II, 230.
75   II, 122.
76   II, 121.
77   I am grateful to a referee for *The Review of Politics* for pressing this question.
78   II, 121.
79   II, 121.
80   II, 122.
81   Cf. II, 191. There is a discussion of Locke's 'hapless and clumsy treatment' of
     this issue in Dunn, *Political Thought of John Locke*, pp. 131–43.
82   II, 75.
83   II, 122.
84   II, 118.
85   II, 75.
86   II, 74.
87   II, 75.
88   II, 111–12.
89   II, 119.
90   II, 95.

4 Locke's contract in context

Martyn P. Thompson

The current revival of academic interest in contract theory has produced almost as many reinterpretations of Locke as of Kant.[1] Two aspects of these will occupy my attention here: the one general; the other much more specific. The first is the development of different classificatory schemes designed to highlight the variety of contractualist ideas and to organize historical understandings of past contractualist thinking. Of obvious relevance here are Michael Lessnoff's and Richard Saage's recent refinements to the distinction between governmental and social contracts, a distinction that served as the organizing idea behind J. W. Gough's standard history of the subject.[2] Jean Hampton has offered new insights by exploring a different classificatory pair: Hobbesian 'alienation' contract theory versus Lockian 'agency' contract theory.[3] Thomas P. Slaughter and John Millar have applied less formal distinctions between Hobbesian and Lockian contract theories in attempting to understand the contractualisms of the 1688 Revolution.[4] And, as a final example, David Gauthier has identified four different kinds of contract theories: original contractarianism, explicit contractarianism, tacit contractarianism and hypothetical contractarianism.[5] In each of these classifications, Locke's *Second Treatise* features prominently. But for all the differences in the interpretation of that work that arise from locating it within these various classificatory contexts, there is one point which these commentators have not challenged. This is that Locke's *Second Treatise* contains a relatively abstract logical theory of the origins, extent and end of civil government.

Yet precisely this point has been challenged recently by Richard Ashcraft. Ashcraft's challenge and the considerable impact it has made constitute the second aspect of current reinterpretations of Locke that I shall consider. In pursuing what he takes to be a historically accurate understanding of *Two Treatises*, Ashcraft claims that practically all of Locke's previous interpreters have been led astray by uncritically accepting the conventional wisdom that Locke's text contains in part, at least, a theoretically rigorous inquiry into the nature of the social bond and into the character and limits of political obligation. Having worked his way through the dense undergrowth of late-seventeenth-century pamphleteering, Ashcraft claims that Locke's *Second Treatise* was not intended to be a theoretically rigorous work at all.

Locke wrote it 'for a radical *minority* of individuals with whom he and Shaftesbury were associated'. Its main arguments and exactly the same phraseology are to be found in other, now utterly obscure, writers like Robert Ferguson 'the Plotter'. In short, Ashcraft concludes, Locke was '*not* engaged in constructing a formal logical theory' in *Two Treatises*. Rather, like others on the far left of the British political spectrum, he was 'addressing himself to the commission of a specific political act', he was providing 'a political declaration for the revolutionary movement' of the 1680s. That declaration, he further claims, was written in exactly the same language that the extremists were all using.[6]

If Ashcraft is right then we must completely rework our understandings of Locke's meanings in *Two Treatises*. If the proper context for interpreting Locke's contractualism is the perceived needs of a minority of British revolutionaries, then focusing upon Locke's supposed contributions to the theoretical concerns of natural jurisprudence is to misunderstand Locke's point. In what follows, I shall argue that Ashcraft certainly has a case but that it is vastly exaggerated. I shall suggest that Ashcraft is right to reject as inadequate the various classificatory schemes that have been proposed by those primarily interested in the theoretical analysis of the *Second Treatise*. But I shall also suggest that Ashcraft's alternative interpretation is itself one-sided. In doing all this, I shall be obliged to rehearse and refine arguments that I have developed elsewhere, arguments which Ashcraft has dismissed as 'simplistic and extreme'.[7]

Since my argument will be slightly complex, I shall sketch its stages before commencing. First, I shall review the evidence for believing that the classifications of ideas of contract noted above are inadequate for understanding the variety of contractualist arguments that were being deployed in England and elsewhere during the time that Locke composed and published *Two Treatises*. Second, I shall restate and refine the essential elements of an alternative context for understanding the meanings of appeals to contract in political debate that I have discussed elsewhere. This will involve comparing William Atwood's contractualism with Samuel Pufendorf's. Third, I shall illustrate the importance of this alternative context by comparing Locke's contractualism with Robert Ferguson's. This comparison is central to my argument since Ashcraft has asserted that Locke and Ferguson shared the same radical views and the same styles of argument. Finally, by reference both to Locke's own statements about the character of *Two Treatises* and to the evidence of the immediate reception of the work in Britain and Europe, I shall suggest a more appropriate way of understanding Locke's contractualism than that offered either by Ashcraft or by his main opponents.

SEVENTEENTH-CENTURY CONTRACTARIANISM: RECENT DEBATES

First, then, I shall note the inadequacies of recent typologies of contractualism to account for the evidence of deployments of ideas of contract in the late seventeenth century. It is self-evident that the immensely important House of Commons' resolution, accepted by the Convention Parliament on 7 February 1689, had nothing to do with either Hobbesian or Lockian ideas of contract. The resolution ran:

> That King *James* the Second, having endeavoured to subvert the Constitution of the Kingdom, by breaking the original Contract between King and People, and by the Advice of Jesuits and other wicked Persons, having violated the fundamental Laws, and having withdrawn Himself out of this Kingdom, has abdicated the Government; and that the Throne is thereby vacant.[8]

Neither for Hobbes nor for Locke were sovereigns a party to a contract with their subjects. In Hobbes, the sovereign was the beneficiary of contractual authorization. In Locke, the relations between sovereign and people were relations of trust, not contract.[9] Thus if such a crucial understanding of contract as that involved in the official interpretation of the 1688 Revolution slips through the net of Hobbesian versus Lockian contractualisms, then that particular net itself is clearly inadequate.

Certainly, the contract referred to in the Commons' resolution is an example of a contract of government. Certainly, too, at least some of the references to contract, compact and covenant in Hobbes and Locke are references to social as opposed to governmental contracts. And certainly, also, in the enormously influential works of Pufendorf published in the 1670s, we encounter clear examples of both social and governmental contracts. But the enormous variety of kinds of contracts referred to in the political literature of the late seventeenth century, the variety of synonyms offered for them, the different levels of analytical abstraction from day-to-day politics in which they occur, and the bewildering number of quite contradictory practical political lessons that were drawn from each, all cast doubt on the appropriateness of trying to elicit their meanings by reference to their being either governmental contracts or social contracts. A few examples must suffice.

As both the Commons' resolution and Pufendorf's theoretical works testify, some ideas of contract were central to both the theoreticians and the practitioners of late-seventeenth-century politics. There was, of course, nothing particularly novel in appealing to contracts in both practical political argument and theoretical inquiry by the late seventeenth century. But the vast majority of lawyers, politicians, divines, academics and journalistic pamphleteers who did so in Britain in the 1680s and 1690s were little interested in theoretical refinements to a traditional political concept. They were certainly not interested in any such theoretical refinements as those suggested by Gauthier in the move from original contractarianism to hypothetical contractarianism. The fact that arguments from contract were drawing upon a legal analogy was clearly not their concern. They freely used a wide variety of contractualist notions and frequently considered them in conjunction with, or as a substitute for, such other legalistic concepts as 'stipulation', 'trust', 'capitulation', 'covenant' and 'compact'. Very often, contract was simply equated with the coronation oath or with the laws of the land – as was the case in the Convention Parliament debates about the Commons' resolution. But just as often, as occasion appeared to suit, writers left the realm of legal analogy and considered the idea much more loosely as simply 'promises', 'bargains', 'compromises', 'barriers' and 'agreements'. Furthermore, the literature is strewn with many different sorts of contracts. A reader very soon encounters not just social contracts and contracts of government, not just original, explicit and implicit contracts, but also fundamental contracts, constitutional contracts, national contracts, political contracts, mutual contracts, a 'Popular Contract and rectoral Contract' and 'express Original and continuing' contracts. Finally, as is now perfectly clear, although in Britain Whig writers generally were much more likely to appeal to contracts in their political writings than people of other political persuasions, such appeals were far from uncommon in the arguments of Tories and Jacobites as well.[10]

In the face of this enormous variety, attempts to organize late-seventeenth-century appeals to contract into either Hobbesian or Lockian contractualisms or into references to either a contract of government or a contract of society or into increasingly theoretically refined distinctions between original, explicit, tacit and hypothetical contractarianisms are bound to break down. The main problem with these classifications is that they impose order on the historical evidence by reference either to supposedly dominant forms of contract theory or to the supposed logic of any appeal to contract in political argument. They break down when the supposedly dominant forms turn out not to have been dominant at all and when the supposed logic of contractualism turns out to be different from the logical implications that were, in the past, taken to follow from them. The late-seventeenth-century evidence clearly shows that neither Hobbes nor Locke was a dominant model and that the logical implications were almost as varied as the number of writers invoking ideas of contract.

But none of this need lead to the conclusion that we are confronted, then, by a hopeless confusion. I have suggested elsewhere an alternative way of understanding appeals to contract in late-seventeenth-century political argument and I propose to refine and illustrate that suggestion again. In all brevity, my suggestion is that we reject models and timeless logic as the organizing ideas behind histories of contractualisms and that we look instead at the specific questions that contractualist writers asked themselves and the ways in which they went about answering them. Three distinct patterns of question and answer emerge from doing so. And though they are no more than patterns or ideal types of question and answer (they are not some reification of 'concepts and language into exclusive paradigms', as Ashcraft claims), they are helpful in understanding particular contractualist texts. This, at least, I hope to show with respect to Locke's *Second Treatise*.[11]

THREE PATTERNS: CONSTITUTIONAL, PHILOSOPHICAL AND INTEGRATED

I have called the three patterns of contractualist thought constitutional contractarianism, philosophical contractarianism and integrated contractarianism. The third is by far the most common in the practical political literature of the late seventeenth century. It consists of various attempts to integrate into the same flow of argument the very different patterns that constitute the first two. So we must be clear about the differences between the first two before we can appreciate the character of the third. Now Locke revealed that he was aware of something of the distinction between philosophical and constitutional contractarianisms when he noted 'Some Thoughts concerning Reading and Study for a Gentleman' in 1703. 'Politicks', Locke wrote, 'contains two parts very different the one from the other. The one containing the Original of Societies, and the Rise and Extent of Political power, The Other, the Art of Governing men in Society'. For the first part Locke recommended

> the first Book of Mr. Hookers Ecclesiastical Polity, and Mr. Algernon Sydney's Book of Government; The latter of these I never read. (Let me here add, Two Treatises of Government, printed 1690. And a Treatise of Civil Polity [by Peter Paxton], printed this year) To these one may adde Puffendorfe *De Officio Hominis et Civis*, and *De Iure Naturali et Gentium*, which last, is the best book of that kinde.

As to the second, very different part of political studies, that was a question of experience and history. And Locke went on to recommend an English gentleman to read

> Mr. Tyrrel's History of England ... the Ancient Lawyers (such as are Bracton, ffleta, Henningham, Myrror of Justice, My Lord Coke on the Second Institutes, and Modus tenendi Parliamentum, and others of that kinde, whom He may finde quoted in the late controversies between Mr. Petit, Mr. Tyrrel, Mr. Atwood, &c. with Dr. Brady, as also I suppose in Sadler's Treatise of the Rights of the Kingdom, and Customs of our Ancestors ...) wherein He wil finde the Ancient Constitution of the Government of England. There are two volumes of state Tracts printed since the Revolution, in which there are many things relating to the Government of England.[12]

Locke's distinction here seems to reflect a traditional division between the theoretical and the practical study of politics. His claim that his own *Two Treatises* should be understood as contributing to the first and not the second is clearly important for any attempt to characterize its contractualism. But first it must be noted that ideas of contract are to be found playing very significant roles in much of the literature Locke recommends for *both* kinds of political study. Yet there is an obvious difference between the patterns of contractualist argumentation to be found in each of them. This emerges most clearly if we compare Pufendorf's arguments (as supposedly the best example of the first kind of literature) with Atwood's (as a representative of the second). I shall first sketch Atwood's theory as exhibiting the pattern of constitutional contractarianism and then look at Pufendorf as exemplifying the pattern of philosophical contractarianism.

According to Atwood, in his controversies with Dr Brady and beyond, questions about the requirements of the English constitution should be settled by reference to constitutional law alone. This apparently unobjectionable assertion was a pointed remark in terms of the contemporary disputes. It was aimed at the contributions both divines and laymen were making with supposedly constitutional arguments drawn from natural or divine law. Throughout his career, Atwood was thoroughly sceptical about abstract notions of natural law and natural rights. In 1682, he expressed his doubts about natural rights. These, he claimed, were 'thin and metaphysical Notions, which few are Masters or Judges of'. Again, in 1698, he attacked William Molyneux for his ''wheedling Notions of the *inherent*, and unalienable Rights of Mankind'. And in 1705, he reaffirmed his distaste for rhetorical 'Flourishes about the Law of God, of Nature, and of Nations' and insisted that 'nothing but the Law of *England* can settle Man's Judgements of the Nature of the English Monarchy'.[13]

Atwood's contract theory, then, made hardly any appeal to ideas of natural law, natural rights or states of nature. It instead purported to be a legally and historically valid account of the English constitution. In brief, his theory was the following. At the time of the Saxon Heptarchy, our Saxon ancestors contracted together and set up fundamental laws to secure their liberty and property. At the same time, they agreed to institute a monarchy which would execute these and subsequent laws made by King, Lords and Commons assembled in Parliament. The prospective king was made to swear in his coronation oath that he would act only accordingly to law, and the people – understood as 'every proprietor (of land especially)' – promised to obey him if he kept within the law. Thus, Atwood argued: 'The King's [Coronation] Oath is the real Contract on his side, and his accepting the Government as a Legal King the virtual one; and so it is *vice versa*, in relation to the Allegiance due from the subject'.[14]

The coronation oath was the original contract or at least a representation of it. This led to several interesting results. It provided a way of relating the ancient original contract constitution to the contemporary, seventeenth-century constitution, since all monarchs were required by their oaths to swear to keep the laws of their predecessors, and so on back to the original laws. Furthermore, the original contract – evidenced in 'history' books like the *Mirror of Justices* – was not simply a past event which had created the ancient constitution. It was also, and much more importantly, the 'express Original and continuing' contract, the process whereby the consent of the governed was made a legal requirement for legitimate governmental action. The theory also allowed considerable flexibility in interpreting what the fundamental laws enjoined, since (in the absence of any historical records) it was considered acceptable to argue from the supposed intentions of the original contractors. The fundamental laws designed by our ancestors guaranteed certain fundamental rights and fundamental liberties. According to Atwood, the whole system of those laws and liberties constituted the 'Fundamental Constitution' of England.[15]

The interesting thing about this fundamental constitution was not so much the particular provisions that it was supposed to have contained (for these varied according to the particular cause which Atwood was promoting) but rather that it provided an extraordinary legal principle of constitutional interpretation. Since the constitution was the product of the design of our ancestors, and since our ancestors were rational men, it followed, Atwood argued, that they would never have designed anything that could be harmful to their descendants. He admitted that they would not have been able to foresee the several turns of state that occurred in later ages, but he argued that they did make constitutional provisions for them. Again, they must have done so because they were rational men. They neither insisted that all the laws they made should be accounted fundamental, nor that all fundamental laws should remain unalterable. He thought it was certainly true that 'They that lay the first foundation of a Commonwealth, have Authority to make Laws that cannot be altered by Posterity. . . For Foundations cannot be removed without the Ruin and Subversion of the whole Building'. But this he considered only, in the last resort, applied to what he called the 'chief Fundamental Law', the law that *salus populi suprema lex esto*. This law, the 'chief constitutional law', the 'Foundation of the Agreement' as he called it, was 'the scope and end of all other laws', the test through which all laws and public actions must pass before they could be accepted as valid according to the constitution. This, indeed, was an extraordinary principle of constitutional interpretation. Law books, records and history were all ultimately subordinate to the fundamental law of *salus populi*.[16]

If pressed, Atwood was prepared to argue that 'by the Law of Nature, Salus Populi *is both the Supream, and the first Law in Government: and the scope and end of all other Laws, and of Government itself*'. But he never confused the moral law with the positive law of the land, as so many of his contemporaries did. All laws ultimately derived their authority from God, he asserted (following Fortescue), but human laws (unlike God's law or the law of nature) might change yet remain authoritative. The primacy of rights at positive law in Atwood's constitutional contractarianism is nowhere more apparent than in his terse comments about James I's title to the English throne. James, he asserted, 'having, upon an undoubted legal right, been recognized *King of England* . . . thereby the Right became Divine'. The same priority is to be found throughout Atwood's writings. He always insisted that he wrote in accordance with the constitutional law of the land. He insisted that he could justify the various causes he believed in by reference to historical and legal testimony alone. In all this, his constitutional contractarianism aided him enormously. For as a last resort, if law books, cases, commentaries and histories failed him, he could still appeal to the chief fundamental law of the ancient and continuing original contract constitution, a constitutional law which declared that it was only by being in accordance with *salus populi* that a rule or action could properly be described as constitutionally valid.[17]

Atwood articulated his constitutional contractarianism in the context of the increasing polarization and radicalization of the British political public in the 1680s.[18] The theory was developed, then, during exactly the same period as witnessed the writing and publication of *Two Treatises*. But Atwood's theory welded together inquiries into the ancient English constitution and contractualist inquiries into the constitutional arrangements of the various European polities. It was certainly, like Locke's theory, a response to the adoption of Filmerian arguments by several leading royalists. But it was a very different response from Locke's, even though it appealed centrally to contract. Its main notions were legal. Atwood's arguments revolved around a register of fundamentals – fundamental law, fundamental rights, fundamental liberties, fundamental contracts and the fundamental constitution of England. His questions were of the kind; how did the English constitution originate, what sort of constitution was it, what specific rights and duties did its laws define and guarantee, and what did all this imply for practical political activity in the present? His answers were ostensibly gathered from law books and constitutional history. Thus when Atwood published his defence of the 1688 Revolution in 1690 (at the same time as Locke), he was adamant that only his legalistic arguments were appropriate for the task:

> All the Opposers of our present Settlement, who pretend to talk Sense, when press'd home, grant that the Constitution of the English Government must be the Guide to their Consciences in this matter . . . and thus Lawyers are *the best Directors of Conscience* in this case . . . The great Unhappiness of this Nation is, that *Divines* not only set up for the greatest States-Men, but will pretend to be the best Lawyers and Casuists in these points.[19]

Small wonder, then, that Atwood's defence of the legitimacy of the Revolution makes no significant reference to those notions so prominent in Locke, notions of natural law, natural rights, states of nature, social contract and appeals to heaven. Such notions were alien to English law, whereas the register of fundamentals was not.

Let me now turn to Pufendorf and the pattern of philosophical contractarianism. We should expect to find in Pufendorf at least what Locke found there. And we do. We find contractualist answers to the question 'What is "the Original of Societies, and the Rise and Extent of Political power"?' Or, in Locke's slightly different formulation in 1699, we find answers to the question 'What are "the natural Rights of Men, and the Original and

Foundations of Society, and the Duties resulting from thence"?'[20] We certainly find discussions of the character of natural and civil law. But we find nothing about the contractual inheritancies or contractualist constitutions of specific polities. In short, there is nothing even remotely resembling Atwood's constitutional contractarianism in Pufendorf.

Nor should we expect there to be. For Pufendorf's major works – the *Elementorum jurisprudentiae universalis* (1660), *De jure naturae et gentium* (1672) and *De officio hominis et civis* (1673) – addressed the same kinds of questions as had occupied Grotius and Hobbes, not the kinds of questions that Atwood addressed. Indeed, one of Pufendorf's main tasks was to reconcile the insights of Hobbes and Grotius. Grotius appeared as the culmination of the Aristotelian-Christian tradition, Hobbes as the exponent of a new rationalist-individualist critique of that tradition. Hence in exploring the logic of modern social and political relations, Pufendorf attempted to reconcile the Hobbesian idea that community and sovereignty can be explained only by reference to individual willing with the Aristotelian-Christian notion that community and sovereignty were natural phenomena deriving from the condition of mankind or the will of God.[21] Grotius had been correct to ground his account of civil society upon 'the Aristotelian dictum that man is by nature sociable'. But his account was defective largely because it underrated the great force of self-interest in human affairs and also because it perpetuated traditional confusions by upholding the doctrines of divided sovereignty and natural, pre-contractual, property rights. Hobbes, on the other hand, had overplayed the importance of selfishness and egocentricity. Thus both his portrayal of the state of nature and his rigorously logical account of political obligation were one-sided.

In all this, Pufendorf was very clear about the kind of inquiry in which he was engaged. His first major work began with the assertion that he was writing about the 'science of law and equity, which is not comprehended in the laws of any single state, but by virtue of which the duties of all men whatsoever toward one another' are determined. He was inquiring into 'matters of morality', not questions of specific constitutional arrangements.[22] This science of morality concerned 'juridical demonstrations' and these, in turn, involved appeal to two kinds of principles: rational and experimental. Pufendorf explained the difference between them. The first he called 'axioms' and their 'certainty and necessity' flowed from 'reason itself, without the perception of individual details, or without instituting a discussion, merely from the bare intuition of the mind'. The second he called 'observations' and their 'certainty . . . is perceived from the comparison and perception of individual details uniformly corresponding to one another'. Among his axioms, Pufendorf included such principles as that man is rational, that he is created by God and that he has a moral law to guide him. Observation, however, led to such experimental principles as that man is naturally selfish but with a lesser, though nonetheless natural, inclination to live in association with others of his kind.[23]

The appeal to both axioms and observations in part accounts for the complexity of Pufendorf's analysis of the state of nature. He has several, different accounts of the state of nature. But two, in particular, serve him in his endeavour to portray the logical necessity for the modern state. He distinguishes between the 'purely natural state' and the 'modified' or 'mixed' state of nature. The relationship between them was one of increasing correspondence to the complexities of the real world. The purely natural state was the state of individuals abstracted from all social and divine relationships. It was an entirely rational construction, explicitly acknowledged never to have existed. Purely natural man was characterized by 'weakness and natural helplessness' and by 'self-love'. The mixed state of nature was the state of mankind living in societies but in the absence of political arrangements. This state, Pufendorf believed, had once existed and still did exist in the relations between independent political communities. The pure state of nature was inhabited by naturally free and equal moral persons. Natural equality consisted in the absence of authority relationships and natural liberty was expressed in the natural right of self-preservation. The mixed state of nature introduced the authority relationships involved in social institutions like marriage, the family and property but they did not compromise natural liberty. For the governing rules of the mixed state of nature were the universal laws of nature – moral laws which Pufendorf, following Grotius, declared could be rationally demonstrated with near mathematical certainty and which 'would have had a perfect force to obligate man, even if God had never set them forth also in His revealed word'. In elaborating on Hobbes's first law of nature, Pufendorf identified the fundamental prescription of natural law as that 'Every man, so far as in him lies, should cultivate and preserve towards others peaceful sociability, which is suitable to the nature and goal of universal humanity'. This fundamental prescription was the source of many less fundamental dictates which were, similarly, all derivable by 'sound reason alone'. They were rational axioms, then, not observations and they could be classified under three heads: rules governing man's conduct towards God, towards himself, and towards other men.[24]

The last of these are of most relevance here. The duties of man towards his fellows were subdivided into 'absolute duties' (of anyone to anyone) and 'conditional duties' (those owed 'only towards certain persons, a certain condition or status being assumed'). Absolute duties consisted of not injuring others, recognizing and treating all men as naturally equal, and promoting the advantage of others as far as possible. Conditional duties comprised all the other obligations that a man might enter into with others. And in all cases these duties 'presuppose an express or tacit agreement'. The foundation of all conditional duties, then, was 'the general duty which we owe under natural law . . . that a man . . . fulfil his promises and agreements'. This postulate of a natural law duty to keep promises was crucial to the logic of Pufendorf's account of the mixed state of nature and the rise of civil society.[25]

'Natural reason' alone could be counted on to discover that the obligation to obey natural law rested on God's will and rulership of all things.[26] Hence the mixed state of nature would be a very social state. Pufendorf located the institutions of property, marriage, the family and slavery (the extreme form of master–servant relationships) in the mixed state of nature. These institutions were contractual in nature. They originated in and embodied the mutual consent of individuals, consent which was conditional upon the fulfilment of the ends for which the institutions were established. They were natural institutions in the sense that they did not depend for their existence and right on civil law and nor, therefore, could they be abolished by civil authorities. The function of civil law was simply to protect these natural institutions and to specify the practical rules necessary for their conduct.

The primary distinction between institutions lay in their different 'ends'. The end of property was the satisfaction of physical needs. Hence *private* property was necessary 'to avoid quarrels and to introduce good order'. The end of marriage was the procreation of children. The end of the family was the care and education of those children. The end of slavery was the mutual advantage to be gained from 'exchanging material necessities for material conveniences'. Political society, too, had a distinctive end – 'mutual defence'. It was this which all the pre-political institutions were incapable of securing but upon which their continuing existence depended. Pufendorf's problem was to prove this last point having rejected both Hobbes's account of the state of nature and the Aristotelian-Christian notion that human nature itself compels the formation of civil societies. Given his conviction that the state was something artificial (resulting from human willing), he had to show that states arose because of some 'utility' which individuals would derive from them. That utility, furthermore, had to be sufficiently great to outweigh the considerable costs to natural liberty which modern citizenship undoubtedly involved.[27]

His solution emphasized those characteristics of natural man that Hobbes had exclusively considered. Selfishness all too easily dominated the natural inclination towards sociability. And excessively selfish conduct gave rise to the principle which explained the necessity for the state. It showed that 'no animal is fiercer or more untameable than man, and more prone to vices capable of disturbing the peace of society'. None of this, however, meant contradicting his previous arguments about natural sociability. Natural law was still law in the state of nature and social life of a kind was still possible (indeed, necessary) in the absence of civil arrangements. What it meant was that the laws of nature would, as a matter of fact, be sometimes broken and that social life outside civil society would be precarious. This was so because 'with many, through defect of training and habit, the force of reason grows deaf as it were. The result is that they aim at things present only, indifferent to the future, and are moved only by what strikes upon the senses'. Thus the search for security gives rise to the state.[28]

In order to show how these short-sighted, self-seeking individuals might become integrated into the moral and political community of the state,

Pufendorf elaborated perhaps the most complex series of contracts since Althusius. But he explicitly denied that he was concerned with either the historical or the 'imagined' origins of states. Rather, he was concerned with the 'necessary' origins of the state: necessary for a proper understanding of the nature of civil society and political obligation. The contracts he elaborated, then, were necessary truths known 'by reasoning' about the origins of civil societies from the existing fact of them.[29]

Thus 'for a state to coalesce regularly', Pufendorf argued, 'two compacts and one decree are necessary'. The first compact was a unanimous agreement of each of the future citizens (understood as the 'fathers and masters of families') with each other 'to enter into a permanent community'. This had to be followed by a decree stating the form of government which the permanent community was to have. And finally, 'another compact is needed, when the person, or persons, upon whom the government of the nascent state is conferred are established in authority'. This second compact consisted of the mutual exchange of promises – the future governors binding themselves to 'care for the common security and safety, the rest to yield them their obedience'. The state thus created united the individual wills of each citizen by subordinating them to the single will of the sovereign authority. The state, then, was 'defined as a composite moral person, whose will, intertwined and united by virtue of the compacts of the many, is regarded as the will of all, so that it can use the powers and resources of all for the common peace and security'.[30]

The implications that Pufendorf drew from this contractualist account of the state were not favourable to rights of resistance. Considerations of interest and convenience led heads of households to enter civil societies. Consent was essential for particular persons to incur obligations to particular societies but the obligation to continue obeying civil authorities was rooted in conscience conforming to God's will. Civil authority was 'from God' and God was 'understood antecedently to have enjoined upon the now numerous human race to establish states, which are animated, so to speak, by their highest authority'. Civil authority was 'supreme' and unaccountable 'to any human being'. It was 'absolute'. The holder of civil authority 'can neither be judged nor punished' in a human court and no matter what specific 'obligation he has contracted towards his subjects, provided only that he has preserved the right of supreme authority unimpaired', subjects have no right to try him for violations nor to 'apply force to him'. Doctrines of popular sovereignty and tyrannicide were 'an extremely perilous error'.[31]

But all this meant neither that government was necessarily unlimited nor that all sovereign commands must be obeyed. *Salus populi* was still the 'general law of rulers' since 'authority was conferred upon them, with the intention that the end for which states have been established, should be ensured'. Experience had shown that absolute monarchs might pervert that end. Hence 'some nations' have circumscribed supreme authority with limits like coronation oaths, parliaments and fundamental laws. Furthermore, natural law and the divine will provide limits to what any sovereign might legitimately command. Indeed, a sovereign who persistently demanded actions which were contrary to divine, natural law 'treats me no longer as a subject but as an enemy, and he himself is understood to have remitted the obligation by which I was bound to his authority'. The result was a matter of definition. By being forced to do wrong, 'I pass from being a subject into being a free enemy' and can then 'rightly employ against him also the means customarily used against an enemy'. For all this, however, Pufendorf argued against individual rights of resistance. Individual citizens, as with Hobbes, might rightfully resist only when faced by imminent death. In all other cases, he counselled passive obedience. But there were occasions when a whole people might legitimately resist. The logic of his argument required him to accept the proposition that 'A people properly has the right, in case of extreme necessity, namely, when the prince has become an enemy, to defend its safety against him'. For in this case, the people are no longer citizens or subjects but have been restored to their rights of self-defence by the very actions of their ex-sovereign.[32]

In all these inquiries, Pufendorf's arguments explore the implications of a conceptual register composed of naturals and civils: natural law, natural rights, states of nature, civil society and civil law. Nowhere does he tie his inquiries to any analysis of the particular state of political affairs in any part of the world. His 'universal jurisprudence' required asking about the nature of man, the social bond, the moral law and civil society. His answers appealed exclusively to rational and empirical principles. His ideas of contract were generated within an inquiry pitched at a far higher level of abstraction than those of any constitutional contractarians and their character and implications were, accordingly, different. Pufendorf's philosophical contractualism was part of an inquiry designed to understand the logic of social and political relationships. Atwood's constitutional contractarianism was part of a practical engagement designed as an intervention in the constitutional struggles of his day. Locke, then, was right. Pufendorf's theoretical inquiry into the contractual logic of human institutions was, indeed, very different from the constitutional contractualisms generated in the practical study of the history and experience of particular polities.

LOCKE'S CONTRACTUALISM RECOVERED

But Ashcraft, too, is right to insist that we do not stop here. If constitutional and philosophical contractarianisms constituted the opposite ends of late-seventeenth-century horizons of contractualist expectations, there was still no legislating for what any particular reader or writer might make of them. It is, in fact, very common to find amongst Locke's friends and contemporaries attempts to integrate the two contractualist patterns into the same flow of argument.[33] Two of the most self-conscious in doing so were Algernon Sidney and James Tyrrell. But it is also the case, as Ashcraft notes, that many others, like Robert Ferguson and John Wildman, on occasion did the same. However, whereas Ashcraft takes this evidence to prove that the distinction between constitutional and philosophical contractarianisms is thus unhelpful, my point is that the evidence reveals something interesting about prevalent (but confused) ideas of law, equity and history in late-seventeenth-century England.[34]

It will serve my purposes just to illustrate some of the odd doctrines that emerged from attempts to integrate the two contractualisms. John Tutchin in 1704 asserted that Englishmen's rights were the natural rights of mankind and English law was natural law. He did not shrink from the absurd conclusion:

> And consequently as all Mankind have *ab Origine* the same Rights with Englishmen: so ought they to have the same sort of King with Us: They ought to have the same Currency of *Law* as now we have in *England*, they ought to have a Prince on their several Thrones as is our Queen *Anne*.

Lord John Somers in 1701 insisted that the right to petition the House of Commons was a 'Natural Right of Mankind'. The anonymous author of *A Brief Account of the Nullity of King James's Title* (1689?) declared that 'It is a Maxim of our Law, That the Laws of God and Nature should take place before all other Laws'. And Sir James Tyrrell, Locke's friend, provided an elaborate account of the state of nature, social contracts after the Flood, and the contractual origins of Gothic constitutions (including the English) which allowed him to assert that the laws 'of Nature and right Reason' were part of English constitutional law.[35] At the very least, all this involved confusing ethical with civil rights.

I shall not pursue the complexities of integrated contractarianism any further here. Rather, in the light of what still seems to me a useful distinction between philosophical, constitutional and integrated contractarianisms, I shall turn to consider Ashcraft's contention that Ferguson and Locke shared the same radical views and styles of argument. They supposedly shared a coded language for discussing English politics consisting of key words and phrases like 'invasion of rights', 'usurpation', 'betrayal of trust', 'social contract', 'mutual covenant', 'state of nature' and the 'dissolution of government'. They also supposedly shared a radically democratic understanding of 'the people' which for them included artisans and tradesmen.[36]

A first point to note is that Locke certainly did use many of these phrases but he did so in a work which, in retrospect at least, he regarded as an example of (in my terms, not his) philosophical contractariansm. And certainly, a glance at the structure of the *Second Treatise* – with its argument proceeding from a number of assumptions about the nature of man as God's workmanship, to an analysis of the state of nature, to the generation of civil society in contract, to the trust of government, and on to the dissolution of government – lends superficial plausibility to this contention. In this argument, the supposition of a social contract is necessary for an understanding of the nature of the social bond. But that contract is in no way tied to historical evidence.[37] The relationships between government and governed are not contractual. They are rather relationships of trust. If rulers break their trust, then government is dissolved and the people may erect whatever form of government they please. This is the argument Locke developed sometime between 1680 and 1683 and published as a defence of the 1688 Revolution. But what of Ferguson in his defence of the Revolution?

Ferguson's title is *A Brief Justification of the Prince of Orange's Descent into England And of the Kingdom's Late Recourse to Arms. With a Modest Disquisition of what may Become the Wisdom and Justice of the Ensuing Convention in their Disposal of the Crown* (1689).[38] His exclusively practical aim is clear from the start. His argument is divided into four parts: a consideration of government in general; an account of the English constitution; an argument for the legality of the 1688 Revolution; and a suggestion that the Convention Parliament offer the crown to William of Orange. Ferguson begins the first part by asserting that the

> Consideration of Government in general, is none of my Province at this time; further than to observe, that as it derives its Ordination and Institution from God, so it is circumscribed, and limited by Him, to be exercised according to the Laws of Nature, (and of plain Revelation where vouchsafed) in subserviency, to the glory of the Creator, and the benefit of Mankind.

Obviously, Ferguson could not resist an appeal to handy higher principles to make a point about the moral obligations of rulers. The principles were contractualist. Rulers were 'under Pact and Confinement' to God to govern according to the law of nature. They were also contractually obliged to their subjects to govern according to the rules which the people decide shall 'define what shall be the measures and boundaries of the publick Good, and unto what Rules and Standards the Magistrate shall be restrained'.[39]

These contractualist principles were very familiar to seventeenth-century audiences. They had received classic expression in the French Wars of Religion of the previous century. They were the principles of the *Vindiciae contra tyrannos* (1579), a work republished in England in 1689. But Ferguson analysed neither the pre-political state into which God had at sometime intervened, nor the relationship between a ruler's moral and legal obligations. He was not concerned to specify exactly who the parties were to the two contracts. His principles were merely asserted. Their rhetorical function was to underpin his second main contention that the English constitution was contractual.

His argument to this point was, first,

> no Government is lawful, but what is founded upon Compact and agreement, between those chosen to govern, and them who condescend to be governed; so the Articles upon which they stipulate the one with the other, become the Fundamentals of the respective Constitutions of

Nations, and together with superadded positive Laws, are both the limits of the Rulers Authority, and the Measures of the Subjects Obedience.

Second, he drew the usual lesson from this central proposition of constitutional contractarianism: if rulers break their constitutional obligations then their subjects are no longer contractually obliged to obey them but may resist and replace them.[40] Third, he set about showing that England had just such a constitution historically founded upon, and continuing to embody, a contract: '*England* has been the most provident and careful of all Nations, in reserving unto itself, upon the first Institution of, and its submission unto Regal Government, all such Rights, Privileges and Liberties, as were necessary . . .; so it hath with a Courage . . . peculiar unto it, maintained its Privileges and Liberties through a large and numerous Series of Ages.' As a result, the rights of both the English king and people rested on 'fundamental and positive Laws'. All these, including *Magna Carta*, were merely declarative of 'the Original Institution of our Government'. But the 'most Fundamental and essential' law guaranteed the rights of parliament, precisely those rights which James II had infringed. For parliament was supposed to be the overseer of the executive power, the judge of constitutionality.[41] The scene was now set for the third part of Ferguson's argument.

I shall justify our 'Resisting and Abdicating of his late Majesty', he declared, 'from Principles which our Constitution and Laws do Administer'. Four acts in particular had 'unqualified' James: dispensing with the oath of supremacy; attacking the corporations; overthrowing 'the whole Legislative part of the Government'; and reducing the courts to 'Ministers of his Will, Pleasure, and unruly Lusts; instead of their being, Assertors and Vindicators of our National Rights'. James had broken his contract and, in these circumstances, had there been no resistance to him, the English would have denied their own heritage.[42]

In the final part of the pamphlet, Ferguson revealed much more than just his own political preferences. It becomes clear, for example, that he did not believe that James II's unconstitutional actions had 'dissolved' the government and that Englishmen had been returned to a 'state of nature', although he had argued exactly this some two years earlier.[43] Instead, he now argued that in the absence of a monarch and hence of a regular parliament, power had certainly devolved to the people. But the 'people' were not the artisans and tradesmen that Ashcraft insists both Ferguson and Locke took them to be. Rather, they were the people represented in the 'great Council', the Convention Parliament.[44] And his analysis of the political options available to the Convention was the following:

> But though *James* the Second stand unqualified, and morally disabled from being any more King, yet it is indispensably necessary we should have One, a King being no less essential in the Body Politick of *England*, than the Head is in the Body Natural. To dream of reducing *England* to a Democratical Republick, is incident only to persons of shallow Capacities, and such as are

acquainted with the Nature Government, and the Genius of Nations. For as the Mercurial and Masculine Temper of the English people, is not to be moulded and accommodated to a Democracy; so it is impracticable to establish such a Common-wealth, where there is a numerous Nobility and Gentry, unless we should first destroy and extirpate them.[45]

Nothing was further from Ferguson's mind. Rather, his advice to the Convention was simply 'to declare the Prince of Orange *King*', for this 'we owe him in point of Gratitude'.[46]

Ferguson's argument, despite Ashcraft, is constitutional contractarianism, prefaced by a bit of high-flown rhetoric. And the same applies to his earlier pamphlets. His main focus was always that of constitutionality, even when he dramatically converted to Jacobitism soon after the Revolution. He made the point himself in 1694:

whatever there was of an *Original Contract* between former Kings and the free People of these Kingdoms, yet it is undeniable, there is a very *formal* and *explicite One* between K. *William* and them. And, to declare my Opinion freely, without Reserve or Disguise, I do know of none before, besides that which was couched and implied in the *Constitution*. And as it is impossible to produce or shew any other, so the very Supposition of one, is not only inconsistent with the Doctrine both of our Churchmen and Lawyers, but repugnant to the Drift and Tenure of all our Laws.[47]

So Ferguson does, indeed, employ some, though not all, of Ashcraft's coded language. But, by 1689, that language was part of a far from radical revolutionary version of constitutional contractarianism.

Locke, as we have seen, also employs much of Ashcraft's language. But for the most part, the argument of the *Second Treatise* is pitched at a far higher level of generality than any version of constitutional contractarianism, including Ferguson's. Locke has next to nothing to say directly about the English constitution and he never engages in any of the questions and answers typical of constitutional contractarianism. Rather, his argument superficially follows the course implicit in its title, the course of an inquiry in the manner of philosophical contractarianism. Yet Locke does not sustain Pufendorf's level of inquiry throughout the work. An unmistakable practical political interest underpins the direction Locke takes. Quite explicitly, his aim is to undermine the arguments of Sir Robert Filmer (as the chief ideological authority of many Tory defenders of Charles II) and to offer an alternative account of the nature and limits of political power. This last (as we know since Laslett's superb reworking of Locke's text and historical contexts) was itself intended to serve the cause of the Shaftesbury Whigs.[48] The work, then, was at least in part a propaganda piece, written sometime between 1680 and 1683 and intended as a call for a revolution that had not yet occurred, rather than as a justification for 1688. It was published with small insertions and rewrites in different circumstances from those in which it was written. But as a defence of 1688 it remained a far more radical text than any other defences. It proved too radical to attract the support of the Revolutionary Whigs.[49] For in the circumstances of its publication, the *Second Treatise* declared in barely veiled generalities that James II's activities had 'dissolved' the government, that the people had a right to take up arms and then reconstitute the government anew in whichever form they pleased. This, quite clearly, was a far more radical view (and one quite at variance with the actual course of events) than Ferguson's.[50]

So Ashcraft is right in emphasizing Locke's radicalism but wrong in equating Locke's language and style with Ferguson's. Ferguson does say many things which Locke says, but he also says many things which Locke did not. Locke does use some of the key words and phrases that Ferguson uses. But in Ferguson those words and phrases are embedded in a theory of constitutional contractarianism; in Locke they are embedded in a theory which superficially, at least, follows the course of philosophical contractarianism. Yet both were engaged in writing and publishing propaganda. So where does this leave an interpretation of the character of Locke's contractualism?

According to Ashcraft, *Two Treatises* was nothing but propaganda. But the matter is not so simple. The best discussion of the relationship between philosophy and propaganda in the *Second Treatise* is still Laslett's. By looking at the discrepancies between the works in Locke's *corpus*, by contrasting Locke's own views about the character of philosophical inquiry with the argument of the *Second Treatise*, and by comparing Locke's work with Hobbes's *Leviathan*, Laslett concluded that the *Second Treatise* could on no account be considered a work of political philosophy. But nor was it simply propaganda. Rather, Laslett suggested, the work hovers between the universal systematizing impulse of philosophical inquiry and the practical political engagement of propaganda. It is a work of political theory – a work which, in its ambivalences and incoherencies, corresponded exactly to that liberal attitude which is suspicious of 'total, holistic' views of the world but which nonetheless has faith in a number of political doctrines designed to have an impact on practical policy.[51]

This seems to me the best way to characterize the *Second Treatise*. If the *Second Treatise* were just propaganda, it would have been very bad propaganda, as Locke himself could hardly have escaped noticing. It would have been bad when Locke wrote it and bad when he published it. For, at the very least, on both occasions he failed to address questions of constitutionality which were ever-present in the minds of the would-be revolutionaries. Their concerns with the constitutionality of resistance led some, like Ferguson, to pattern their own arguments along constitutional contractarian lines. It led others, like Algernon Sidney, to pattern theirs along integrated contractarian lines. None of them pursued exclusively the pattern of philosophical contractarianism, save Locke himself.

Yet the *Second Treatise* did *not* contain a philosophical inquiry. It contained an argument which climbed to certain theoretical heights and then dipped back down again, especially at the end, to the specifics of English constitutional conflicts. The conclusion, then, seems inescapable that the work mixes the modes of theoretical and practical inquiry. And without some such mixture, the evidence of the initial reception of the work would be incomprehensible. Let me glance at this evidence.

Quite clearly, the similarity between the *Second Treatise* and Pufendorf's philosophical contractarianism was sufficiently great for Locke himself to bracket his work alongside the *De officio hominis et civis* and *De jure naturae et gentium*. It was a theoretical study of politics. Locke was not alone in reading the *Second Treatise* this way. Its theoretical achievements were sufficiently great for Gershom Carmichael to use it, in his moral philosophy courses at Glasgow University from 1702–3, 'as a corrective to Pufendorf's more comprehensive but occasionally misguided system of natural jurisprudence'.[52] Jean Barbeyrac made similar use of it from at least 1706 onwards.[53] From a very different perspective, William Atwood made the same connection to Pufendorf's contractualism. *Two Treatises*, he declared in 1690, were 'the best Treatises of Civil Polity which I have met with in the *English Tongue*'. They successfully refuted Filmer and established government 'upon the only true Foundation, the Choice of the People'. They were relevant to Atwood's constitutional contractarian defence of 1688 because their 'Scheme of Government is not erected as the most perfect, but seems designedly adapted to what (their author) takes our Government to be, tho not expressly named'. In this respect, however, Locke's references to the dissolution of government and constitution anew were clearly unacceptable. If Locke had only attended better to Pufendorf, he would have avoided these errors. He would have seen that although James II had broken one contract 'there plainly was a farther contract . . . to prevent *Anarchy* and, Confusion, at any time the *Throne* might be *vacant*'.[54]

These responses are revealing. They confirm that Locke's text invited readers to locate its arguments within two, quite different interpretative contexts: that of English constitutional conflicts of the 1680s; and that of theoretical inquiries into the nature of civil society and the limits of political power. It is not that the first merely occasioned the second. This is the assumption behind the traditional view of Locke as a political philosopher. But nor is it that the second was merely the vehicle through which Locke addressed the first. This is the assumption behind Ashcraft's view of Locke as a propagandist. Rather, the text is located in both and hence its fruitful tensions as well as its obvious inadequacies. If read exclusively within the first context, the work was bad propaganda and an inappropriate defence of 1688. Its arguments were pitched at far too high a level of abstraction and they failed to address the issue of constitutional rights of resistance. When applied to 1688, the text failed because there had been no dissolution of government, no civil war and no constitution anew. If read exclusively as a theoretical inquiry, the work came off much better. But here, too, there were obvious problems. The work did not fulfil all the expectations arising from its form as philosophical contractarianism. From this perspective, its arguments were compromised by being unmistakably tied to merely English affairs. This is how Locke's European readers seem to have read the text. The most favourable commentators chose to emphasize its virtues of theoretical penetration, novelty and economy of argument.[55] But the most perceptive comment was that of the reviewer in Henri Basnage's journal, *Histoire des ouvrages des scavans*. The *Second Treatise* had considerable theoretical potential, it appeared. But, the review concluded, 'it is a shame that the author has not always managed to disengage his thoughts (from local politics), nor always fully developed his sentiments'.[56] For all that has happened to Locke's text in the intervening period, this judgement still has resonance. Locke's contractualism is developed in a text with theoretical ambitions, but those ambitions are curtailed in the interests of practical political engagements.

NOTES

1 See, for example, the literature discussed in *John Locke and Immanuel Kant: Historische Rezeption und gegenwärtige Relevanz*, Martyn P. Thompson (ed.), Berlin, Duncker & Humblot, 1991.

2 Michael Lessnoff, *The Social Contract*, London, Macmillan, 1986; Richard Saage, *Vertragsdenken und Utopie*, Frankfurt am Main, Suhrkamp, 1989; J. W. Gough, *The Social Contract*, Oxford, Clarendon Press, 1936.

3 Jean Hampton, *Hobbes and the Social Contract Tradition*, Cambridge, Cambridge University Press, 1986.

4 Thomas P. Slaughter, ' "Abdication" and "Contract" in the Glorious Revolution', *Historical Journal*, 1981, vol. 24, pp. 323–37; John Millar, 'The Glorious Revolution: "Contract" and "Abdication" Reconsidered', *Historical Journal*, 1982, vol. 25, pp. 541–55; Thomas P. Slaughter, ' "Abdicate" and "Contract" Restored', *Historical Journal*, 1985, vol. 28, pp. 399–403; Martyn P. Thompson, 'Significant Silences in Locke's *Two Treatises of Government*: Constitutional History Contract and Law', *Historical Journal*, 1988, vol. 31, pp. 275–94.

5 David Gauthier, *Moral Dealing: Contract, Ethics and Reason*, Ithaca, NY, and London, Cornell University Press, 1990, pp. 52–4.

6 Richard Ashcraft, *Revolutionary Politics and Locke's 'Two Treatises of Government'*, Princeton, NJ, Princeton University Press, 1986, pp. 327, 333, 392, 576 n. 223.

7 Thompson, 'Significant Silences', pp. 278–88; Martyn P. Thompson, *Ideas of Contract in English Political Thought in the Age of John Locke*, New York and London, Garland, 1987; Martyn P. Thompson, 'The Language of Contract in Modern European Political Thought', in *Language et Politique*, M. Cranston and P. Mair (eds), Bruxelles, Bruylant, 1982, pp. 171–81; Martyn P. Thompson, 'The History Of Fundamental Law in Political Thought from the French Wars of Religion to the American Revolution', *American Historical Review*, 1986, vol. 91, pp. 1,103–28; Harro Höpfl and Martyn P. Thompson, 'The History of Contract as a Motif in Political Thought', *American Historical Review*, 1979, vol. 84, pp. 919–44; Richard Ashcraft, 'Simple Objections and Complex Reality: Theorizing Political Radicalism in Seventeenth-century England', *Political Studies*, 1992, vol. 40, pp. 103ff.

8 *Journal of the House of Lords*, 1688–9, p. 110.

9 On Hobbes and Contract, see M. M. Goldsmith, 'The Hobbes Industry', *Political Studies*, 1991, vol. 39, pp. 143–5. On Locke and Contract, see John Locke, *Two Treatises of Government*, Peter Laslett (ed.), Cambridge, Cambridge University Press, 1988, pp. 113–15.
10 For a detailed discussion of the sources summarized here, see my *Ideas of Contract*, esp. pp. 18–125.
11 Ashcraft, 'Simple Objections and Complex Reality', p. 103. For a fuller discussion of Locke in these terms, see my *Ideas of Contract*, pp. 126–84.
12 John Locke, *Some Thoughts Concerning Education*, J. W. Yolton, and J. S. Yolton (eds), Oxford, Clarendon Press, 1989, pp. 321–3.
13 William Atwood, *Lord Hollis his Remains*, London, 1682, p. 293; William Atwood, *The History and Reasons of the Dependency of Ireland upon the Imperial Crown of the Kingdom of England*, London, 1698, p. 211; William Atwood, *The Superiority and Direct Dominion of England over Scotland*, London, 1704, p. 392.
14 William Atwood, *The Fundamental Constitution of the English Government*, London, 1690, p. 2.
15 See the discussion of Atwood in my *Ideas of Contract*, pp. 75–103.
16 Atwood, *The Fundamental Constitution*, pp. 59, 50, 78–9 and 12.
17 Atwood, *The Fundamental Constitution*, pp. 78 and 81; Atwood, *The Superiority and Direct Dominion*, p. 524; Atwood, *The Fundamental Constitution*, pp. 78–9.
18 See my *Ideas of Contract*, pp. 48–74.
19 Atwood, *The Fundamental Constitution*, pp. 2–3.
20 John Locke, *Some Thoughts Concerning Education*, pp. 321 and 329.
21 See, for example, A. P. d'Entrèves, *Natural Law*, London, Hutchinson, 1951, pp. 48–62.
22 Samuel von Pufendorf, *Elementorum Jurisprudendentiae Universalis*, C. H. Oldfather and W. A. Oldfather (eds), Oxford and London, Carnegie, 1934, vol. II, pp. xxx and xxviii.
23 Pufendorf, *Elementorum*, vol. II, pp. 209 and 233–4.
24 Pufendorf, *Elementorum*, vol. II, p. 241. Samuel von Pufendorf, *De Officio Hominis et Civis*, F. G. Moore (ed.), Oxford and London, Carnegie, 1926, vol. II, book 1, ch. 3, sect. 13. On the complexities of states of nature in Pufendorf see *Samuel Pufendorf's 'On the Natural State of Men'*, M. Seidler (ed.), Lewiston, Queenston, Lampeter, Edwin Mellen Press, 1990, pp. 25–53 and 112–20.
25 Pufendorf, *De Officio Homis et Civis*, vol. II, book 1, ch. 6, sects 1–2; ch. 9, sect. 1; ch. 9, sect. 3.
26 Pufendorf, *De Officio Hominis et Civis*, vol. II, book 1, ch. 3, sect. 10.
27 See L. Krieger, *The Politics of Discretion: Pufendorf and the Acceptance of Natural Law*, Chicago, University of Chicago Press, 1965, pp. 107–8 and 112–17; Pufendorf, *De Officio Hominis et Civis*, vol. II, book 2, ch. 5, sects, 1, 2 and 4.
28 Pufendorf, *De Officio Hominis et Civis*, vol. II, book 2, ch. 5, sects 8, 6–7 and 9.
29 Krieger, *The Politics of Discretion*, pp. 120–1.
30 Pufendorf, *De Officio Hominis et Civis*, vol. II, book 2, ch. 6, sects 7–9 and 10.
31 Pufendorf, *De Officio Homis et Civis*, vol. II, book 2, ch. 6, sect. 13; ch. 9, sects 1–2; Pufendorf, *Elementorum*, vol. II, pp. 284, 288–9, 291 and 292.
32 Pufendorf, *De Officio Hominis et Civis*, vol. II, book 2, ch. 11, sect. 3; ch. 9, sect. 6; Pufendorf, *De Jure Naturae et Gentium*, C. W. Olfather and W. A. Oldfather (eds), Oxford and London, Carnegie, 1934, vol. II, book 7, ch. 8, sect. 5; Pufendorf, *Elementorum*, vol. II, pp. 287, 288, 292–3, and 293–4; Pufendorf, *De Jure Naturae et Gentium*, vol. II, book 7, ch. 8, sect. 5.
33 Ashcraft, 'Simple Objections and Complex Reality', p. 103; Thompson, 'Significant Silences', pp. 285–8; Thompson, *Ideas of Contract*, pp. 185–253.
34 Thompson, *Ideas of Contract*, pp. 185–96.
35 John Tutchin, *The Observator*, 99, 3 April 1703; J. Somers, *Jura Populi Anglicani*,

London, 1701, p. 31; Anon, *A Brief Account of the Nullity of King James's Title*, 1689?, in *State Tracts*, I, p. 284. For similar doctrines and an account of Tyrrell, see Thompson, *Ideas of Contract*, pp. 185–96 and 226–47.

36 Ashcraft, *Revolutionary Politics*, pp. 392–405.
37 Thompson, *Ideas of Contract*, pp. 158–60.
38 My discussion of Ferguson is based on notes taken many years ago. I have not had the opportunity to check them against the original.
39 Robert Ferguson, *A Brief Justification of the Prince of Orange's Descent into England*, London, 1689, pp. 5 and 6.
40 Ferguson, *A Brief Justification*, pp. 7–8, 8–9 and 10–11.
41 Ferguson, *A Brief Justification*, pp. 12, 13, 13–14 and 17.
42 Ferguson, *A Brief Justification*, pp. 18, 19, 20 and 20–1.
43 Ferguson, *A Representation of the Threatning Dangers, Impending Over Protestants in Great Britain*, London, 1687, p. 31. But even here Ferguson is exclusively concerned with the restoration of the ancient contract constitution and the constitutionality of resistance.
44 Ferguson, *A Brief Justification*, pp. 31–2.
45 Ferguson, *A Brief Justification*, p. 23. Ashcraft is, of course, perfectly clear that Ferguson was never a republican: Ashcraft, *Revolution Politics*, p. 394.
46 Ferguson, *A Brief Justification*, p. 36.
47 Robert Ferguson, *A Letter to Mr. Secretary Tenchard*, London, 1694, p. 4. Ashcraft's argument about Locke and Ferguson sharing the same views and political language turns on his interpretation of one main pamphlet which he alone has attributed to Ferguson: Anon, *An Impartial Enquiry into the Administration of Affairs in England, 1684*. The attribution may be correct. But even from Ashcraft's own description (I have been unable to consult a copy), it is clear that the author was concerned primarily with both moral and constitutional rights to resist tyranny. It may well, then, be an example of integrated contractarianism. But, as the analysis of Ferguson's published defence of 1688 shows, his argument then was couched almost exclusively in constitutional contractarian terms. See Ashcraft, *Revolutionary Politics*, pp. 333–7.
48 John Locke, *Two Treatises of Government*, Peter Laslett (ed.), Cambridge, Cambridge University Press, 1960. Laslett's revised student edition of 1988 is now the only edition of *Two Treatises* worth consulting.
49 Locke, *Two Treatises*, Laslett (ed.), pp. 45–6; Martyn P. Thompson, 'The Reception of Locke's *Two Treatises of Government*'", *Political Studies*, 1976, vol. 24, pp. 184–91.
50 Locke, *Two Treatises*, Laslett (ed.), II, ch. xix. See J. G. A. Pocock, 'The Fourth English Civil War: Dissolution, Desertion and Alternative Histories of the Glorious Revolution', *Government and Opposition*, 1988, vol. 23, esp. pp. 157–66.
51 Locke, *Two Treatises*, Laslett (ed.), pp. 79–92, esp. 90.
52 James Moore, 'Theological Politics: A Study of the Reception of Locke's *Two Treatises of Government* in England and Scotland in the Early Eighteenth Century', in *Locke und Kant*, pp. 77. See also James Moore and Michael Silverthorne, 'Gershom Carmichael and the Natural Jurisprudence Tradition in Eighteenth-Century Scotland', in *Wealth and Virtue: The Shaping of Political Economy in the Scottish Enlightenment*, I. Hont and M. Ignatieff (eds), Cambridge, Cambridge University Press, 1983. pp. 80–7.
53 Moore and Silverthorne, 'Gershom Carmichael', p. 81.
54 Atwood, *The Fundamental Constitution*, pp. 101–2.
55 *Du Gouvernement civil*, David Mazel (?) (transl.) Amsterdam, 1691, Advertisement. Cf. *Bibliothèque universelle et historique*, Amsterdam, 1686ff, octobre 1690, avril 1691.
56 *Histoire des ouvrages des scavans*, Rotterdam, 1687ff, juin 1691.

5 History, reason and experience

Hume's arguments against contract theories

Dario Castiglione

If there is such a thing, the history of social contract theory and of its critics needs to be rewritten.[1] The re-emergence of the 'contract argument' as a central element in one of the most influential tendencies in contemporary political philosophy requires a change in our view of the earlier chapters of that history, which many thought had definitively come to an end with David Hume's devastating critique.

Bentham, of course, was crucial in spreading the conviction that the very idea of the social contract was nonsense – or as nonsensical as natural law and natural rights were – and in identifying Hume as the author who had convincingly demonstrated it. But Bentham was not the only one who, at the close of the eighteenth century, thought so. In the *Enquiry concerning Political Justice*, Godwin, for instance, could do neither more nor better than to reproduce the main reasons advanced by Hume in his *Essays* and in the *Treatise*,[2] where he had set out to undermine the position he attributed to Locke and to the Whigs of his time.

With the reawakening of interest in the social contract, Hume's position and arguments need to be reassessed in terms of both their historical and their general philosophical value. This has already partly been done by a number of recent works on Hume's political theory and, to a more limited extent, by a few studies of contractarianism at large.[3] There remains, however, a certain ambiguity on the exact import of Hume's position, and on the nature of his criticisms. What follows is intended as an attempt to put forward a general interpretation of Hume's critique by first clarifying the meaning of his discussion of contemporary contract theories, and by then briefly addressing the rather different question of the philosophical value which some of his arguments maintain in the face of a trans-historical model of social contract arguments.

TWO KINDS OF PACT

Broadly speaking, seventeenth- and eighteenth-century contract theories fall into two distinct groupings, which can be identified by asking the two different questions of 'What are the bases for social cooperation?' and 'What are the reasons for political obligation?' By excluding the simple proposition that social and political relationships are the outgrowth of natural, mainly familial, relationships and patterns of behaviour, contract theories clearly implied an *artificial* conception of the forces which hold the social fabric together and which establish and reinforce political obligation.

The artificiality of such relationships was not uncontroversial amongst authors who subscribed to a contractarian view, being largely dependent on each author's particular conception of the natural condition of humanity, on the logical status which he (it was almost invariably a 'he') attributed to the laws of nature, and on how he conceptualized ideas of rights and duties. On the whole, the main contractarian theories of the time should also be understood within the more general language of modern natural law,[4] and distinguished from other uses of the idea of contract, such as those to be found in the literature on the Ancient Constitution and similar modes of argument,[5] which clearly rejected the strongly philosophical and fundamentally problematic attitude which prevailed in truly contractarian views of society and politics.

Traditionally, the two questions of social cooperation and political obligation were addressed by imagining two different kinds of pacts. The *pactum societatis*, between individuals or families living separately in a natural condition, was meant to have formed civil society itself. The *pactum subjectionis*, of the people with a ruler, was understood as the crucial moment in which political authority was established. The latter passage was sometimes conceived as a two-stage process, in which members of an already established society would first give themselves a *form* of government, and only at a later stage would transfer their power and swear their allegiance to a particular ruler. The exact number of pacts involved in the passage from the savage condition, where separate individuals naturally related to each other, to the complex set of relationships of equality and subordination characterizing the state of civil society is, however, largely irrelevant. Hobbes envisaged a single pact of transference of rights and power from natural individuals to the sovereign; Pufendorf insisted instead on the historical separation between three contractual moments.[6] Nonetheless, the idea of two pacts seems to be the most adequate, since, as has already been suggested, it graphically captures the main conceptual distinction between the establishment of social order and that of government.

Critics of contractarian theories could therefore direct their arguments against either or both of these two *original* moments in the organization of collective life, and indeed they did so, though often without distinguishing between them with precision. The 'fiction' of the state of nature, for instance, which in the two-pact scheme is strictly speaking relevant only in the formation of society, was also rejected as part of the account of the origin of government. Such a confusion, although not to be found in Hume's position, has however crept into some of the commentaries on Hume's criticism of contract theories, so that it seems worthwhile to begin with an account of the different targets of Hume's critique and of the kinds of arguments which he employed against contract theories.

THE ORIGIN OF SOCIAL INSTITUTIONS

Perhaps we should make clear from the beginning that when Hume referred to the 'original contract' he meant an historically specific theory, establishing the origin of government on a consensual act.[7] This has nothing to do with his discussion of the way in which society itself and other institutions originate, although clearly there are points of contact between the two sets of problems. In fact, Hume, and after him Smith, put forward the curious view that the theory of the 'original contract' was to be found only in England, a consideration which was simply preposterous when referred to social contract theories in general, but which contained some truth when more narrowly applied to theories of *political* contract.[8]

That Hume was self-consciously dealing with two separate theories is evident from the organization of the material in his various works. Both theories come within his treatment of morals; but while his discussion of the 'fiction' of the state of nature, and his hypothesis of the gradual and piecemeal passage from family relationships to a more developed network of societal relationships, are dealt with in his theory of the origin of justice and property; the discussion of government as a cure for the 'narrowness' and 'infirmity' of the human soul, incapable as this is, when not forced by external authority or by self-imposed devices, of choosing its long-term interests over what it perceives as its more pressing, immediate ones, is broached within the context of more directly political considerations. In the *Treatise* the discussion of the two issues form the central part of the closely argued sequence from the origin of morals and the natural virtues, regulating the more immediate relationships between individuals, to the laws of nations. In his later works, the two arguments, although still linked, are discussed at length in separate texts. The origin of social institutions is still treated as one of the main sections of Hume's theory of morals, as put forward in the *Enquiry concerning the Principles of Morals*; while the question of government, only briefly touched upon in that text, is given greater attention in a number of political *Essays*, where references to his ethics are only implicit.[9]

As is well known, Hume's moral theory was largely intended as a compromise between those who adhered to a system of morals founded upon reason, and those who adhered to one founded on sentiment. The first part of Book III of the *Treatise* is, indeed, organized into two sections: first, 'Moral Distinctions not deriv'd from Reason', where it is duly shown that reason is not the first principle on which the sense of approbation and disapprobation is founded, in so far as actions may be laudable and blameable, but not reasonable and unreasonable; and second, 'Moral Distinctions deriv'd from a moral sense', this latter hypothesis being substantially accepted by Hume, with the corrective rider that reason be allowed a prominent role in determining the means most apt to achieve those moral goals decided by the sentiments – at least where certain virtues are concerned.

Hobbes, and the kind of social contractarianism normally associated with him, was not Hume's main target in this section of his work. Nevertheless, Hume's vision of sympathy and sociability, of the natural way in which human beings form their moral ideas, and of human actions as mainly characterized by a limited form of benevolence, greatly distance him from the Hobbesian conception of natural man and of the relationship between morality and self-interest. This latter was also associated with the work of Mandeville, generally regarded as a true Hobbesian, who had taken to its paradoxical conclusions the system of morals based on self-love, and whose insights in human psychology are aired and partly refuted by Hume in this very part of his work[10]

Hobbes's theories play a more significant part in the next section of the *Treatise*, where Hume tackled the more controversial issue – more controversial at least for his fellow Scots moralists – of justice, and of whether this should be considered a natural or an artificial virtue. In brief, Hume maintained that the feeling of pleasure normally associated with virtuous actions could not be derived from a consideration of its very virtuousness. This would imply circular reasoning, since the definition of virtue would then depend on its unexplained ability to elicit a sense of pleasure, while for Hume the source of the ethical categories of good and bad must be found in some motive of human nature 'distinct from the sense of its morality'.[11] Now, justice presented a peculiar problem: What is the natural motive, asked Hume, which compels us, for instance, to restore a borrowed sum of money to the lender? According to Hume, it is neither public nor private interest, neither public nor private benevolence. None of them, Hume insisted, is in fact capable of that universal and unconditional application which justice requires: 'from all this it follows, that we have no real or universal motive for observing the laws of equity, but the very equity and merit of that observance'.[12] The need for moral actions to be originally elicited by a motive distinct from the very sense of duty seems therefore not to apply in the case of justice, unless, as Hume suggested, 'we must allow that a sense of justice and injustice is not derived from nature, but arises artificially, tho' necessarily, from education, and human *convention*'.[13]

This is an important point in Hume's moral theory, and one where he clearly disagrees with mainstream natural jurisprudence,[14] and with most of his fellow Scots who had established the revised natural jurisprudence of Grotius and Pufendorf as the central plank of the teaching of morals in the Scottish universities.[15] His insistence that justice is an artificial virtue, the product of human convention, reminded many of the Hobbesian view that where there are no covenants there is no justice. But this was very far from Hume's intention, and, clearly foreseeing the possibility of the 'invidious constructions' which could be made of his theory, he several times insisted that, although he considered justice to be *artificial*, he did not regard it and its rules as *arbitrary*. Justice, property and the 'natural laws' regulating the distribution of property itself were the products of human belief, forethought and action; but, at the same time, the material circumstances in which they arose and the purposes to which they were institutionally directed implied definite and recognizable ('natural' in one specific sense of the word) patterns of behaviour.

Moreover, according to Hume, convention was not another word for pact or contract. He was keen to elaborate on this question:

> It has been observed by some, that justice arises from human conventions, and proceeds from the voluntary choice, consent, or combination of mankind. If by *convention* be here meant a *promise* (which is the most usual sense of the word) nothing can be more absurd than this position . . . But if by convention be meant a sense of common interest . . . it must be owned, that, in this sense, justice arises from human conventions.[16]

Convention, according to Hume, was a kind of unstated agreement arising from the perception that it may be mutually advantageous to either perform or avoid certain actions. The undefined nature of this act of agreement, as described by Hume, has the double function of denying that social cooperation is the product of contractual dealings, and that the obligation underscoring it is wholly justified by the kind of selfish rationality which prompts us to engage in such dealings;[17] but also of rejecting the view that there is something 'natural' and pre-social in one's adherence to the laws of justice or to one's promises, which as Hume suggested are conceptually and anthropologically unintelligible outside some form of civil association. Humean 'conventions' are neither strict contracts nor *nuda pacta* in the sense of the natural jurists; they are meant instead to convey the essentially non-legal idea that there are forms and principles of coordination which human beings hit upon in the course of pursuing their own interests. The trial-and-error form that such attempts take characterizes the essentially evolutionary process through which social institutions originate and are ultimately justified, bearing in mind that their shape and scope depends on the social conditions in which such institutions are formed and on how human imagination construes such conditions.

The artificiality of social institutions on which Hume insisted was not therefore meant as a recognition of the validity of contractarian intuitions as elaborated by Hobbes, but it rested on Hume's conviction that the traditional categories of both the theorists of the 'selfish system' and the Grotius and Pufendorf natural law school were largely inadequate to capture the complexities of the evolutionary process which gave rise to language, money, justice and society at large.

FROM SOCIAL TO POLITICAL CONTRACTARIANISM

So far, I have suggested that Hume rejected what may be called *social* contractarianism. I shall now discuss his attitude towards *political* contractarianism, or what he refers to as the idea of the 'original contract', meant as the contract which establishes government.

Two preliminary, and not often fully appreciated, points should be made to clarify the relationship between the two parts of Hume's critique. In discussing *political* contractarianism, it is on the whole irrelevant whether or not Hume's conjectural account of the beginning of society and government alludes to some kind of pre-political state,[18] where families and small groups live without much need for social, and particularly for political, institutions. More crucially, Hume rejected the idea, implicit in the works of Hobbes and Locke, but explicitly stated by Pufendorf, that the state of nature (and the consequent contracts between individuals or families) represents what Pufendorf called the *architectonic* of political discourse – that is, the logical structure through which political relationships can be understood and conceptualized. Conjectural accounts of the beginning of civil society can be found as early as Plato, Aristotle, Polybius, Cicero, Aquinas and Machiavelli, to name only a few amongst the many original political thinkers writing before Hume who cannot be said to have subscribed to contractarianism in any meaningful form. As we shall see, Hume's acknowledgement that some government may indeed have come about as the result of a contract between individuals already living together, was no concession to contract arguments.

The second point is of a subtler nature. It is often remarked that the thrust of Hume's discussion of political obligation and his rejection of the 'original contract' rest on an account of the historical implausibility of such a contract having taken place, or at least on the simple, but powerful, observation that none of the current governments can be said to have been founded in such a way. It is also said that Hume strengthened his historical argument by elaborating upon two supporting sets of observations, one mainly concerned with received opinion, or what people actually believe, as opposed to what the theory of the 'original contract' presumes that people ought to believe;[19] and the other of a more *philosophical* nature, purporting to show that there is no such thing as a natural obligation to keep promises. As David Miller has put it:

> Deriving our obligations to government from a contract would make sense if the obligation to keep promises were self-evident or had a rational justification. In that case the contract theory would be pinning a conventional obligation on to a natural. But ... the obligation to keep promises is itself artificial, and therefore as much in need of explanation as the political obligation it is being used to underpin [...]. In other words the contract theory introduces a needless circuit into the argument about government ... We see here how Hume's view of moral judgement supports his position in political theory.[20]

The contention that there is a strong link between Hume's conception of political obligation and his 'anti-rationalist' view of moral judgement is correct as far as it goes. As for the suggestion that this is Hume's *philosophical* trump card against the social contract, this needs some essential qualification.

Hume's discussion of promise-keeping in the *Treatise* appears as part of his general argument that justice, property and the other so-called 'laws of nature' – truthfulness to one's word being one of them – are really not natural at all. They are, as has already been said, *artificial* and the result of human conventions. The whole argument precedes the discussion of the origin of government and of the source of allegiance, where Hume is attempting not only to make a similar point, but also, as will be presently shown, to distance his position from those who believe that consent is at the root of political institutions. In support of this view, Hume emphasizes that both the obligations of allegiance and promise-keeping are ultimately founded upon their utility, since they enhance the strong interests we have respectively in 'peace and public order' and against the 'dissolution of society'.[21] As Miller remarked, Hume ruled out the appeal to the principle of fidelity, since this is a 'needless circuit' which leads back to the very same natural motive of interest. Consider, however, that Hume has already argued that justice and the other laws of nature were in place *before* a pressing need for government was clearly felt and forms of political rule were established. In principle, there would be no contradiction in arguing that an *artificial* obligation is established on another *artificial* obligation, provided that the latter can sustain the former. So, the argument that both are conventional, and both ultimately rest on an appeal to private and public utility, cannot be a complete *philosophical* refutation of the alleged contractual obligation to governments.

Two qualifications of Hume's position need to be taken into consideration here. Hume was indeed convinced that fidelity, like the other 'laws of nature', cannot sustain itself. He believed that a little reflection and experience convince people that it is not to their advantage to indulge their selfish inclinations, as when they feel 'naturally impelled to extend [their] acquisitions as much as possible',[22] disregarding the consequences of collective interaction. However, in the heat of action, reflection seems incapable of harnessing human 'original inclinations'. This is the rationale for government, whose main purpose is to ensure that citizens follow their reflective selves. It would therefore be paradoxical that an 'invention' intended to correct the deficiency of a principle which is incapable of regular enforcement of its own accord should depend for its obligation on that very principle.

The second qualification is, if possible, even more crucial. Besides pointing at the identity of the original principle on which both fidelity and allegiance rest, Hume stressed that their obligations are distinct:

> Tho' the object of our civil duties be the enforcing of our natural, yet the *first* motive of the invention, as well as performance of both, is nothing but self-interest: And since there is a separate interest in the obedience to

government, from that in the performance of promises, we must also allow of a separate obligation. To obey the civil magistrate is requisite to preserve order and concord in society. To perform promises is requisite to beget mutual trust and confidence in the common offices of life. The ends, as well as the means, are perfectly distinct; nor is the one subordinate to the other.[23]

Although both civil and natural obligations can be reduced to self-interest, the particular interest which they support is different. This distinction between the two obligations is underscored by their belonging to the separate spheres of public and private life respectively. Hume was convinced that actions done in one's public or private capacity, and the principles underlying them should be kept apart, and that, contrary to what was often believed, private duties were 'more dependent' on public duties than vice versa.[24]

This point can hardly be overestimated, since it shows that Hume rejected one of the fundamental tenets of both natural jurisprudence and contract theories in particular, both of which made extensive use of private law categories and modes of discourse as paradigms for political arguments. Moreover, contract itself was one of the central, if not *the* central idea of private law, and theories of social contract were very much dependent on the civil lawyers' systematization of contract-making practices.[25] Hume, on the other hand, tended to invert the relationship between private and public law. The moral obligations dictated by the former are indeed established on the basis of 'natural obligations' (i.e. obligations based on 'natural' motives), and perceived more immediately by reflective beings; but the moral and natural obligations of civil justice, although obviously slower to be formed, in so far as they are intended to reinforce private justice, take precedence over the latter, since they are the condition for the 'laws of nature' to be exactly formulated and have proper enforcement. So, in the case of allegiance and promise-keeping, the latter's 'exact observance is to be consider'd as an effect of the institution of government, and not the obedience to government as an effect of the obligation of a promise'.[26]

HISTORY, REASON AND EXPERIENCE

The preliminary points I have just made question the traditional image of Hume's critique of contractarian theories of political obligation in important respects. I have argued that Hume could not rest his case on the 'historical fallacy' argument, since he himself recognized that governments may have arisen out of original contracts. I have also questioned whether the philosophical kernel of his critique lies in his discussion of promise-keeping, which is certainly crucial for his rejection of *social* contractarianism, but only indirectly relevant to his critique of *political* contractarianism. I intend now to sketch the relevant contexts within which we should read Hume's critique of the 'original contract', in order to define its underlying arguments with greater precision.

Hume's account of government is characterized by his conviction that, however imperfect, the protection and security that political society offers is far superior to that which can be attained in a state of perfect freedom and independence. Political disorder is the proof, *a contrario*, of such a simple truth:

> In reality, there is not a more terrible event, than a total dissolution of government, which gives liberty to the multitude, and makes the determination or choice of a new establishment depend upon a number, which nearly approaches to that of the body of the people.[27]

Hume then went on to say that in such circumstances wise men even prefer absolute government, backed and established by military power, to disorder and the power of the multitude, which, he believed to be 'unfit to choose for themselves'. This fear of popular government and disorder was nothing new, and certainly was in keeping with the moderate thrust of Hume's politics. But the more immediate preoccupation which can be read in Hume's texts, written between 1739 and 1752, were those concerning the 'philosophical' dispute between the parties in mid-eighteenth-century Britain, and the Jacobite question.[28]

Hume recognized that a general agreement on the necessity of government is not, in itself, a good reason for obeying a particular government. He pointed out, however, that there are great difficulties in establishing the rightful person, or corporate body, to whom allegiance is due, so that, in his view, 'present possession' is an argument of great *authority* in settling such issues, even greater, he maintained, than in the case of private property. Considering Hume's own theory of property and justice, this was a very strong claim to make, undermining, as Hume himself intended it to do, both the Whig theory of resistance, based on the assumption that legitimate sovereignty rests on an 'original contract' with the people, and Jacobite propaganda against the Hanoverian regime and against the settlement which had followed from the events of 1688.

Hume's emphasis on the authority of 'present possession' was not couched in the traditional language of 'passive obedience' used by Tory and High Church propagandists in direct opposition to the idea of an 'original contract'. If considered as a justification of allegiance to government, Hume regarded 'passive obedience' as an absurdity, with no foundation in either human nature or moral reasonings. Against the idea of 'passive obedience', Hume maintained that, since the duty of allegiance ultimately depends on public and private utility, and since the safety of the people is the only supreme law of government (*salus populi suprema lex*), in extreme circumstances 'passive obedience' would have neither rational nor natural justification, and 'present possession' itself would count for nothing.

Hume's criticism of current political views of the duty of allegiance are an indication that he did not consider the actual origin of government as being relevant to matters of legitimacy. Whether a particular government is established by force, or consent, or other connections of the imagination, what really matters is its ability to perform its main functions in the defence of peace and tranquillity. The right of resistance, although real and inalienable, needs careful hedging, and, in Hume's view, would need to be concealed from the public at large. Indeed Hume considered the 'fury and justice' of the people to be a greater threat to the benefits provided by government than the sovereign's encroaching powers, even more threatening than royal aspirations to absolute government, and in extreme circumstances worse than tyranny itself.[29]

From this it followed that theories founded on principles prone to undermine the security and stability of government were to be rejected as theories incapable of explaining both the very existence of government and the sense of allegiance from which government draws its support, and which it in turn tries to engender and reinforce. 'Original contract' theories were this kind of theory, giving, in Hume's view, too much prominence to the right of resistance, and investing the people with a reserve power over the established government, a power whose exercise they also prescribed whenever governments deviated from their appointed course. Political contractarianism, as a theory of political obligation, seemed to Hume to fail two important tests, by contributing to undermine the action of government over its subjects, and by failing to provide explanations for the motivational processes which established and sustained the action of government.[30]

In its outline, Hume's rejection of the 'original contract' seems mainly to rest on narrow political arguments and on a fundamental confusion between facts and values. Moreover, some modern commentators have argued that Hume failed to make clear the exact identity of the kind of contract theory he wanted to refute, since Locke's theory of political obligation, which Hume seems to suggest is the philosophically sophisticated basis for the 'fashionable' (i.e. Whig) theory of the 'original contract', is very different from the one Hume himself attacked.[31] In order fully to address both charges – that Hume contradicted his own predicament about the incommensurability of 'is' and 'ought' statements, and that he misunderstood Locke – another chapter would be needed, dealing with, among other things, the question of Hume's exact position on the ought–is problem[32] – which will be only implicitly touched upon here – and Locke's reception in the first half of the eighteenth century.[33] On the latter issue, I take it for granted that, if not against the true Locke, Hume directed his criticism against the popularized version of Locke's theory, which was mainly interpreted as a theory of consent, and which, in Hume's own words, maintained that the subjects have tacitly reserved the power of resisting their sovereign, whenever they find themselves aggrieved by that authority, with which they have, for certain purposes, voluntarily entrusted him.[34]

On a more constructive line, let me suggest that in eighteenth-century public discourse the 'original contract' theory was identified with a number of abstract principles, some of whose formulation was traditionally associated with Locke's work. In brief: first, men are naturally free, and civil subordination without consent gives rise to an illegitimate, and ultimately despotic, form of power; second, people are the real source of both political power and legitimate government (with a Brechtian formula, Algernon Sidney and Samuel Johnson intimated that since kings cannot form nations, it is better for nations to establish kings);[35] third, government is in the interest of the people, and the people – both as individuals and as a collective – are the ultimate judge of their own interests; fourth, power is ultimately revocable. This is a very crude description of the kind of philosophical kernel of the 'fashionable' theory which Hume sought to attack. Hume suggested that such a theory was untenable on account of 'history, reason and experience'. I believe that commentators have not taken Hume's tripartion of what he considered to be contract theory's failings seriously, and that by doing so have missed the true nature of Hume's objections against the theory itself. On the contrary, I submit that by distinguishing between these three levels of criticism one can make better sense of the philosophical import of Hume's position.

According to Hume, history, or the conjectural reconstruction of 'uncultivated societies', shows that the consensual establishment of government is a very rare occurrence, which however, as Hume admits in most of his writings dealing with the origin of government, probably gave rise to the first forms of political rule, on account of the degree of equality to be found in primitive societies and of their peacefulness. But as societies have progressed, and the records of history become more certain, there is little evidence that governments have originated in such a way. History therefore undermines the idea that the great majority of historical governments rest on historically recognizable pacts. This, of course, is no compelling argument against political contractarianism in general, but, in Hume's time it weakened the foundation of the kind of historical prescriptivism underlying some versions of contractarianism.[36] In any case, the argument from history cut both ways; if there was no reason why the establishment of governments on grounds other than consent could be taken as an objection to contractarian thinking, similarly, the allegedly contractual origins of early forms of government were no grounds for a consensual theory of political obligation.

The arguments which, according to Hume, reason contributes against the 'original contract' are rather complex and varied. On the whole, what Hume means by 'arguments of reason' is the kind of contradictions which can be detected between a truly consistent theory of political obligation founded on consent and the general experience of mankind concerning those institutes and practices also embraced by the supporters of political contractarianism. The argument about promise-keeping which I have already discussed is certainly a way in which reason questions the logical credentials of contractarianism; but the central issue raised by Hume is the nature and implications of the very act of consent. Take for example the question of people living in a foreign country, who, Hume argued, on the basis of a consensual theory of political obligation, should be entitled to full citizenship before and above everyone else. Consider the instance of 'a man' who, having come to the age of maturity and full rational control of his capacities, 'show'd plainly, by the first act he perform'd, that he had no design to impose on himself any obligation to obedience'.[37] What then of a 'poor peasant or artizan' whose consensual participation to life in a polity is thoroughly undermined by his destitute condition, preventing him from seriously considering the possibility of abandoning one country for another; and even when he does so, his action is motivated by crude necessity rather than being the result of free choice. 'We may as well assert', Hume wrote, 'that a man, by remaining in a vessel, freely consents to the dominion of the master; though he was carried on board while asleep, and must leap into the ocean, and perish, the moment he leaves her'.[38]

This raises the issue of tacit consent and acquiescence to law and government, an issue which Hume pressed against the 'original contract' theorists, particularly in relation to posterity's duty of allegiance. The volatility of the mechanisms through which tacit consent was meant to be given and the artificiality superimposed by the contrivance of contract on the socio-biological processes characterizing the passing of generations were cited as fundamental weaknesses in the contractarian argument. At the end of the day, Hume's 'arguments of reason' are intended as a true sceptic's rebuttal of a philosophical system incapable of squaring its own rational principles with reality.[39]

The third set of arguments which Hume advances against political contract is that of experience, which must be carefully distinguished from the arguments of history. This is an important distinction within Hume's philosophical system, even though history itself provides material for experience. In a sense, the arguments of experience are the reverse of those of reason. Where reason shows that the 'very subtle invention' of the contract cannot make sense of common reality;[40] experience proves that the underlying principles of reality are of a grosser nature and conform much better to the commonsensical appreciation of the fact that 'people are born to obedience'.[41] Interest, habit and imagination – the same kind of imagination which establishes the vital connection between causes and effects – are at work in the establishment of the duty of allegiance. According to Hume, the consensual theory of political obligation makes nonsense of people's own perception of the relationships in which they engage. What Hume referred to as the 'authority' of received opinion was in his view a forceful argument, not so much because these opinions matter in the courts of reason or philosophy, but because in common life received opinion is part of the very reality which needs to be explained. The apparent prescriptive value which Hume attributes to experience is not absolute, in the sense that there is no fixed record of experience which ought to be applied to our system of values; on the other hand, experience represents the limit of general philosophizing, because philosophy cannot overturn human nature. This kind of argument was of extreme importance in Hume's political philosophy, since he maintained that all sciences dealing with matters of fact – politics being one of them – are entirely based on experience. So, in rejecting experience, contract theorists were doing bad metaphysics. Moreover, by failing to recognize that some form of political obligation was at work in all of those instances where the consent of the people played no part – and, of course, these were by far the greatest number – they were unwittingly maintaining that political experience is only the product of unreason.

HUME'S ENDURING CONTRIBUTION?

I hope that I have thus far indicated some of the complexity of Hume's arguments against social contract ideas, as he perceived them to have been formulated in his own time. I started by distinguishing between Hume's criticism of *social* and *political* contracts, contending that the arguments he used against them were similar, but independent from each other. This has led me to remark upon the importance which Hume attributed to the separation to be made between obligations arising from private and from public law, a point which distances him from the modern natural law tradition. I have also stressed the moderate and more immediately political nature of his criticism of the 'original contract' theory, a criticism only partly based on historical arguments. Hume's discussion of the origin of government and of political obligation was instead aimed at showing that the formation and legitimacy of political institutions is directly related to the actual and efficient execution of its function in support of public and private utility. Consequently, Hume considered the right of resistance as a *de facto* right, to be treated with caution for its potentially destabilizing effects on the body politic, and certainly to be excluded from political education.

The crux of Hume's argument is, however, that a contractarian theory of political obligation must give a consistent account of how its own emphasis on the exercise of the individual will can be reconciled with the general aims and regular functioning of government. The series of perplexities he raised represented a philosophically minded attempt at embarrassing the contractarians by drawing out the full consequences from their own principles. He backed up this scepticism of reason with a more positive, experiential account of political institutions and obligation. As already suggested, he explained the emergence of both societal and political institutions as part of an evolutionary process, taking place through the casual and often piecemeal formation of conventional practices (distinguished from covenants, promises, and definite acts of agreement) founded on a progressively discovered sense of mutual advantage, sharpened by the intervention of reason and forethought, and cemented by the imagination and by other natural qualities of human nature, thus producing the necessary security, regularity and stability required for social dealings in large societies.

The second fundamental principle which Hume developed in order to explain the actual working of government was that of opinion. Hume referred to opinion neither as a fully legitimizing principle nor in the narrower sense, used by earlier writers like William Temple,[42] of 'custom' and 'reputation'. Opinion was not considered as a passive principle of acquiescence, but endowed with the more dynamic function of cementing the relationship between governors and governed. It is true that Hume held force to be the most usual way in which government commenced, but force, like consent, worked only sporadically and for a limited period. Neither force nor consent could guarantee the smooth running of government and its stabilizing role within society at large. In this sense, Hume's treatment of opinion assumed a more specific meaning, anticipating more modern theories of legitimacy, which stress how power and authority cannot work in a vacuum, but require some disposition to obedience founded on natural motives.

For all that, Hume's criticism of contract theories did not amount to their complete philosophical rejection, as Bentham and others thought, but rather to an alternative explanation of political institutions. It may be argued that Hume could not offer such a rejection, because this would presuppose a complete philosophical argument *for* contractarianism. Recent developments in contractarian theory have shown that there are unsuspected resources in philosophical arguments, which can be put to use in different contexts and with new preoccupations. Naturally, it would be rash to assume that Hume's arguments can be meaningfully deployed within the current debate without allowing for changes of context and preoccupations. As remarked at the beginning of this chapter, seventeenth- and eighteenth-century theories of contract were mainly intended to address questions of political obligation and social cooperation. Post-Rawlsian theories are addressing similar questions, but focusing on the related problems of the nature of social justice and of why we ought to act morally. Cutting and chopping Hume's reasonings on contract theories is not the best way of asking whether he has anything to contribute to the current debate. Something, however, may be gained by considering Hume's general objections against the contractarian approach and by translating them within the modern debate. This is what I intend to do in the concluding remarks of this chapter.

In discussing Hume's attitude towards moral contractarianism, Gauthier's well-known claim that Hume is a contractarian at bottom must be considered.[43] In a nutshell, Gauthier's argument is that, although Hume's moral theory is founded on moral sentiments, his theory of property, justice and government is contractarian in its rationale, since mutual advantage is its only condition. Gauthier's own presentation of Hume's theory does not raise particular problems of interpretation; the controversial conclusion at which he arrives, however, is entirely founded on the supposition that a clear separation can be made between Hume's sentimentalist theory of morals and his contractarian position on justice and the other social conventions. Gauthier admits that, since Hume treats justice as a moral virtue, there must be some connection between the two theories; but he insists that 'connection is not identification'.[44] The question is, however, whether Gauthier has confused the part with the whole. Hume's theory of morals comprises two distinct, but inextricably connected, parts. On the one hand, Hume argued that natural virtues are entirely based on sentiments, and that they give rise to our sense of morality; on the other, he insisted that many social virtues are artificial, and cannot be explained by simply making reference to the natural sense of approbation or disapprobation. In a world dominated by conditions of relative scarcity and the presence of agents motivated by limited generosity, morality *is* a mixture of natural and artificial virtues. Neither can completely prevail because it is only their combination which constitutes morality *as we know it*. In Hume's view, a world where everyone is motivated only by artificial virtues is not a *moral* world; and a world dominated only by natural virtues is not a *viable* world. Attempts to construct systems of morality on a contractarian basis would probably be considered by Hume as purely speculative exercises with no anthropological foundation.[45]

The other question I want to raise, in the attempt to establish some meaningful connections between Hume's theory and the current debate, is that of the hypothetical contract. It has been argued that Hume's criticism discredits only classical formulations of the contract theory, but not hypothetical contractarianism.[46] This opinion partly rests on the misconception that Hume's main argument is of the 'historical fallacy' type. I have already shown that this is not the case. The reason why Hume's argument cannot be considered an implicit refutation of the hypothetical contract is different, and has to do with the fact that Hume would probably argue that hypothetical contractarianism is not contractarian at all. In order to show this, we must turn back to some of the issues already discussed in connection with Hume's 'arguments of reason'.

Arguably, Hume's sceptical objections against the idea that tacit consent was the foundation of the political obligation of generations which had taken no part in the 'original contract' made the greatest impact on the eighteenth-century debate. Both supporters and critics of the Whig theory recognized that the whole theory may stand or fall on this very point. It has already been noticed that Hume considered the theory to imply a number of consequences in contrast with the general practice of mankind. If followed through, the contractarian theory of political obligation seemed to be both extremely volatile and unworkable. But one crucial objection raised by Hume was that political obligation founded on consent was contradicted by the 'authority' of received opinion. Earlier on, I noticed that this argument should be included amongst those from experience, but it must now be added that it has some bearing on the arguments of reason. According to Hume, people's lack of awareness, particularly in the case of posterity, cuts at the root of consensual theories of political obligation because it amounts to a clear proof that no act of the will has taken place: 'A tacit promise is, where the will is signified by other more diffuse signs than those of speech; but a will there must certainly be in the case, and that can never escape the person's notice, who exerted it, however silent or tacit'.[47] Since a necessary condition for an act of the will is to be known to the person who exercises it, according to Hume, people's lack of awareness of having engaged in a covenant is conclusive proof that such an unknown promise is no promise at all.

The difficulty raised by Hume struck a chord particularly with some of the Scottish supporters of Locke's theory, who tried to find a way out by introducing an interesting conceptual innovation in the form of the juridical fiction of the quasi-contract.[48] In modern positive jurisprudence the idea of quasi-contract is a sort of aberration, because its obligation does not fit within any of the classical categories of obligation: from generation (like family obligations), from the violation of law (reparation of an injury), or from a proper contract.

The appeal of the quasi-contract theory for authors like Hutcheson and Reid consisted in the fact that it did not require a specific act of consent. Indeed, quasi-contract excludes consent *a priori*, since a definite consent expressed by the parties would transform it into a normal form of contract or promise. The obligation from quasi-contract derives from a benefit already incurred (as in relationships of tutelage), where the beneficiary's consent is not required for the simple reason that it cannot be obtained, if not, perhaps, *a posteriori*. The obligation to compensate the benefactor is however established by a principle of justice, which, and this is the crucial element, not only does not require a previous consent, but also overrules the contrary will of the parties. Things are distinctly different when considering tacit consent. As Hutcheson himself noticed when discussing private contracts, an explicit declaration to the contrary invalidates actions, or signs, which could be interpreted (or misconstrued) as expressing 'tacit consent'. But our obligation from quasi-contract does not depend on consent; nor can it be made void by an act of the will. Its obligation is considered quasi-contractual because it is imagined that if the beneficiary were able to express consent at the time when he or she were in need, they would have certainly consented to take a particular obligation. This, according to Hutcheson, is the kind of obligation under which future generations fall, and which establishes their allegiance without recourse to tacit consent. To have accrued the benefits of security and social peace constitutes a bond to the community and to its political institutions, so that the passage from childhood to full participation in civil life happens with no solution of continuity, and requires neither explicit nor tacit consent.

Hume's answer to the quasi-contract argument was formulated in a letter to Hutcheson himself,[49] where it is said that this interpretation of the nature of political obligation amounts to a *de facto* rejection of Locke's theory. Indeed, in his letter, Hume regretted that Hutcheson had not made this point 'more express'. The reason underlying Hume's reading is easy to see and follows from what has already been said about Hume's conviction that the presence of some form of actual consent is an intrinsic part of contract making. Hutcheson's quasi-contract has no contractarian force, or so Hume believed, because it is entirely founded on interest. Hutcheson thought differently, for he considered the obligation of quasi-contract to derive from the 'natural' sense of justice. Moreover, he considered quasi-contract obligations to hold in the same way in private and public law. Both conceptual moves were, of course, incompatible with Hume's own understanding of natural and moral obligations. But the relevant point within the context of the post-Rawlsian debate (or the post-Kantian, for that matter) is that in Hume's view hypothetical contracts beg the very question they are meant to answer, for they seem ultimately to rest on non-contractarian principles of obligations. This is, after all, a very much disputed point in the current literature.[50]

I do not think that on the two general issues which I have here briefly raised – of whether a contractarian moral theory is feasible and whether it can establish autonomous principles of obligation – either the *historical* Hume of the first section of this chapter or the *hypothetical* Hume of the concluding section offer definitive, or even fully convincing answers. Something more positive can instead be said on the political import of Hume's arguments against social contract theories. Although, as I hope to have shown, his criticisms were always insightful and often compelling, on the whole, they proved somewhat unimaginative. Hume did not see, or perhaps only partially understood and rejected as a threatening development, modern politics' trend towards democratization and popular sovereignty. It is significant that, when he was told that amongst Rousseau's works the one for which Rousseau himself expressed a particular predilection was the *Social Contract*, he said that this was a 'preposterous' idea.[51] How wrong he was.

NOTES

1 In an article written together with Stephen Buckle we expressed some doubts about the possibility of writing a meaningful history of social contract theories: S. Buckle and D. Castiglione, 'Hume's Critique of the Contract Theory', *History of Political Thought*, 1991, vol. XIII, pp. 457–80. This chapter is a development of some of the ideas already discussed in that article, so I would like to acknowledge my indebtedness to Stephen for having contributed to my own understanding of Hume.

2 William Godwin, *Enquiry Concerning Political Justice*, Isaac Kramnick (ed.), Harmondsworth, Penguin, 1976, pp. 212–16. In the course of this chapter Hume's works, *Essays Moral, Political and Literary*, E. F. Miller (ed.), Indianapolis, Ind., Liberty Classics, 1985; *A Treatise of Human Nature*, L. A. Selby-Bigge (ed.), 2nd edn revised by P. H. Nidditch, Oxford, Clarendon Press, 1978; and *Enquiries Concerning Human Understanding and Concerning the Principles of Morals*,

Selby-Bigge (ed.), 3rd edn revised by P. H. Nidditch, Oxford, Clarendon Press, 1975, will be cited respectively as *Essays, Treatise* and *Enquiries*.

3   Amongst the many, D. Forbes, *Hume's Philosophical Politics*, Cambridge, Cambridge University Press, 1975; D. Miller, *Philosophy and Ideology in Hume's Political Thought*, Oxford, Clarendon Press, 1981; M. Geuna, 'Aspetti della critica di Adam Ferguson al Contrattualismo', in *Passioni, Interessi, Convenzioni*, M. Geuna, and M. L. Pesante (eds), Torino, Angeli, 1992; N. Phillipson, 'Propriety, Property and Prudence: David Hume and the Defence of the Revolution', in *Political Discourse in Early Modern Britain*, N. Phillipson and Q. Skinner (eds), Cambridge, Cambridge University Press, 1993; M. Lesnoff, *Social Contract*, London, Macmillan, 1986; R. Hardin, 'From Power to Order, from Hobbes to Hume', *Journal of Political Philosophy*, 1993, vol. 1, pp. 69–81; D. Gauthier, 'David Hume, Contractarian', *Philosophical Review*, 1979, vol. 88, pp. 3–38; 'The Social Contract Ideology', *Philosophy & Public Affairs*, 1977, vol. 6, pp. 130–64.

4   For recent historically minded assessments of the natural law tradition, see R. Tuck, *Philosophy and Government 1572–1651*, Cambridge, Cambridge University Press, 1993; R. Tuck, 'The "Modern" School of Natural Law', in *The Languages of Political Theory in Early-Modern Europe*, A. Pagden (ed.), Cambridge, Cambridge University Press, 1987; K. Haakonssen, *The Science of a Legislator*, Cambridge, Cambridge University Press, 1981; K. Haakonssen, 'What Might Be Properly Called Natural Jurisprudence', in *Origins and Nature of the Scottish Enlightenment*, R. H. Campbell and A. S. Skinner (eds), Edinburgh, John Donald, 1982. For a more philosophical interpretation, see M. Riedel, *Metaphysik und Metapolitik: Studien zu Aristoteles und zur politischen Sprache der neuzeitlichen Philosophie*, Frankfurt am Main, Suhrkamp Verlag, 1975, ch. 6; N. Bobbio, 'Il Modello Giusnaturalista', in N. Bobbio and M. Bovero, *Societa' e Stato nella Filosofia Politica Moderna*, Milano, Il Saggiatore, 1979. For a summary of my position, see D. Castiglione, 'I Paradigmi nella Storiografia Politica: Il caso dell'Illuminismo Scozzese', *Teoria Politica*, 1988, vol. 4, pp. 89–106.

5   M. Thompson, *Ideas of Contract in English Political Thought in the Age of Locke*, New York and London, Garland, 1987.

6   T. Hobbes, *Leviathan*, R. Tuck (ed.), Cambridge, Cambridge University Press, 1991, p. 120; S. Pufendorf, *On the Duties of Man and Citizen*, J. Tully (ed.), M. Silverthone (trans.), Cambridge, Cambridge University Press, 1991, p. 136.

7   M. Thompson, 'Hume's Critique of Locke and the "Original Contract"', *Il Pensiero Politico*, 1987, vol. 10, pp. 189–201; Geuna, 'Aspetti della Critica', pp. 154–7; Buckle and Castiglione, 'Hume's Critique', pp. 470–5.

8   Hume, *Essays*, p. 487; A. Smith, *Lectures on Jurisprudence*, R. L. Meek, D. D. Raphael and P. G. Stein (eds), Oxford Clarendon Press, 1978, p. 316.

9   Hume's main essays dealing with the question of the 'original contract' are 'Of the Origin of Government'; 'Of the Original Contract'; 'Of Passive Obedience'.

10 On the relationship between Mandeville and Hume in moral theory, see M. M. Goldsmith, 'Liberty, Luxury, and the Pursuit of Happiness', in *Languages of Political Theory*, Pagden (ed.); D. Castiglione, 'Considering Things Minutely: Reflections on Mandeville and the Eighteenth-Century Science of Man', *History of Political Thought*, 1986, vol. 7, pp. 463–88.

11 Hume, *Treatise*, p. 479.

12 Hume, *Treatise*, p. 483.

13 Hume, *Treatise*, p. 483.

14 J. Moore, 'Hume's Theory of Justice and Property', *Political Studies*, 1976, vol. 24, p. 2; I have developed the discussion of 'convention' in D. Castiglione, 'Hume's Conventionalist Analysis of Justice', *Annali della Fondazione Luigi Einaudi*, 1987, vol. XXI, pp. 139–73.

15 See J. Moore and M. Silverthone, 'Gershom Carmichael and the Natural

Jurisprudence Tradition in Eighteenth-Century Scotland', in *Wealth and Virtue: The Shaping of Political Economy in the Scottish Enlightenment*, I. Hont and M. Ignatieff (eds), Cambridge, Cambridge University Press, 1983; Moore and Silverthone, 'Natural Sociability and Natural Rights in the Moral Philosophy of Gershom Carmichael', in *Philosophers of the Scottish Enlightenment*, V. Hope (ed.), Edinburgh, Edinburgh University Press, 1992.

16 Hume, *Enquiries*, p. 306.
17 See *Treatise*: 'Upon the whole, then, we are to consider this distinction betwixt justice and injustice, as having two different foundations, viz. that of *self – interest* . . . and that of *morality*', p. 533.
18 Miller, *Philosophy and Ideology*, pp. 84–5; Hardin, 'From Power to Order', pp. 60–73.
19 For a discussion of this point see pp. 109–11.
20 Miller, *Philosophy and Ideology*, pp. 79–80.
21 Hume, *Essays*, p. 480.
22 Hume, *Essays*, p. 480.
23 Hume, *Treatise*, pp. 543–4
24 Hume, *Treatise*, p. 546.
25 P. S. Atiyah, *The Rise and Fall of the Freedom of Contract*, Oxford, Clarendon Press, 1979, ch. 6.
26 Hume, *Treatise*, p. 543.
27 Hume, *Essays*, p. 472.
28 See Hume's essays: 'Of the Original Contract'; 'Of Passive Obedience'; 'Of the Coalition of Parties'; 'Of the Protestant Succession'.
29 Phillipson, 'Propriety, Property and Prudence'; Buckle and Castiglione, 'Hume's Critique', pp. 470–5 and notes to the text.
30 D. Forbes, 'Hume's Science of Politics', in *David Hume Bicentinary Papers*, G. P. Morice (ed.), Edinburgh, Edinburgh University Press, 1977.
31 M. Thompson, 'Hume's Critique'.
32 A. C. MacIntyre, 'Hume on "Is" and "Ought"', *Philosophy*, 1962, vol. 37, pp. 148–52; E. Sapadin, 'Hume's Law, Hume's Way', in *David Hume*, Morice (ed.).
33 R. Ashcraft and M.M. Goldsmith, 'Locke, Revolution Principles, and the Formation of Whig Ideology', *Historical Journal*, 1983, vol. 26, pp. 773–800; M. M. Goldsmith, '"Our Great Oracle, Mr Lock": Locke's Political Theory in the Early Eighteenth Century', *Studies in the Eighteenth Century*, 1992, vol. 16, n.s., 1, pp. 60–75.
34 Hume, *Essays*, p. 466.
35 A. Sidney, *Discourses Concerning Government*, London, 1698, p. 8; S. Johnson, *An Argument Proving . . .*, London, 1692, p. 30.
36 Buckle and Castiglione, 'Hume's Critique', pp. 464–5 and n. 24.
37 Hume, *Treatise*, p. 548.
38 Hume, *Essays*, p. 475.
39 The opposition of reason to common experience was a typically sceptical strategy. Hume, of course, used it with great subtlety throughout his philosophical works.
40 Hume, *Treatise*, p. 549.
41 Hume, *Treatise*, p. 548.
42 W. Temple, *An Essay upon the Original and Nature of Government*, repr. Los Angeles, 1964, *passim*. I have discussed the relationship between Hume's and Temple's conceptions of 'opinion' in *Dell'Opinione*, Palermo–Sao Paolo, Ila Palma, pp. 23–7. For a slightly different interpretation of the understanding of 'opinion' in eighteenth-century Britain, see J.A.W. Gunn, *Beyond Liberty and Property*, Montreal, 1983.
43 D. Gauthier, 'David Hume', *Philosophical Review*, 1979, vol. LXXXVIII.
44 Gauthier, 'David Hume', p. 3.

45 This point seems to me to be closely related to the dispute between liberals and communitarians on the embeddedness of the self.
46 Michael Lesnoff, *Social Contract*, London, Macmillan, 1986, pp. 83–96.
47 Hume, *Treatise*, pp. 547–8.
48 F. Hutcheson, *A Short Introduction to Moral Philosophy*, Glasgow, 1747; T. Reid, *Practical Ethics, Being Lectures and Papers on Natural Religion, Self-government, Natural Jurisprudence, and the Law of Nations*, K. Haakonssen (ed.), Princeton, NJ, Princeton University Press, 1990. I have discussed the Scottish context of this debate in Dario Castiglione, 'Variazioni Scozzesi su Contratto and Opinione', in *Passioni, Interessi, Convenzioni*, Geuna and Pesante (eds). Other interesting discussions of the same topic are in K. Haakonssen, 'Introduction' to Reid, *Practical Ethics*; Geuna, 'La Critica', pp. 149–53; P. Birks and G. McLeod, 'The Implied Contract Theory of Quasi-Contract: Civilian Opinion Current in the Century before Blackstone', *Oxford Journal of Legal Studies*, 1986, vol. 6, pp. 46–85.
49 D. Hume, *The Letters*, J. Y. T. Grieg (ed.), Oxford, Clarendon Press, 1932, vol. 1, p. 1,948.
50 The literature on this topic is vast. Two works which question the philosophical coherence of Rawls's contractarianism by raising problems similar to the ones here discussed are M. Sandel, *Liberalism and the Limits of Justice*, Cambridge, Cambridge University Press, 1982, pp. 104–32; J. Gray, 'Social Contract, Community and Ideology', in *Liberalisms. Essays in Political Philosophy*, London, Routledge, 1989.
51 Hume's letter to Hugh Blair, in Hume, *Letters*, vol. II, p. 28.

6 Rousseau, social contract and the modern Leviathan

Jeremy Jennings

Political thought in nineteenth-century France was haunted by the excesses and disorder of the Revolution and in all of this Rousseau occupied centre stage. The political literature of the period – and especially up to around 1850 – was in fact almost one long consideration of Rousseau's own person and character and of the consequences of *The Social Contract*.[1] Whether loved or loathed, Rousseau came to be seen not only as a contract theorist but also as the prophet of popular sovereignty, as the patron of a modern Leviathan that had swept away all before it. To show how this was the case and what it meant for the development of political thought in France the core of this chapter will seek to examine three strands of political opinion, each of which in its day exercised considerable influence and (in two cases) power: that associated with Catholic Reaction and the post-Napoleonic Restoration; the liberalism of Benjamin Constant and the writer-politician François Guizot; and finally the anarchism of Pierre-Joseph Proudhon. For all their profound ideological differences each shared a horror for what they saw as the Rousseau-inspired radical political and social change of Robespierre's Jacobin dictatorship and each saw an intimate connection between this project and the theoretical presuppositions of Rousseau's contract theory. First, however, I intend to say something about the very French context in which Rousseau's theory of social contract had its origin and then look at what I take to be the significance of his ideas and the innovations they entail.

Writing in *Philosophy and the State in France*,[2] Nannerl Keohane has argued that, in the context of the absolutist theory of the *ancien régime*, 'Frenchmen who welcomed consolidation of power in the monarchy were ... not unconcerned with the securities and liberties of subjects. They believed that concentrated power provides more effective protection for all the members of a community than divided power'. The point is a simple one. The Anglo-American liberal tradition has taken it to be axiomatic both that power must be checked and divided if it is not to be abused and that the protection of the rights of individuals by the state is of fundamental importance. It is only thus that freedom can be said to exist. Yet, as Keohane points out, in France from the sixteenth century until well into the eighteenth century the first of these key conditions for a liberal polity was 'rejected outright' whilst the second was 'commonly ignored'. This, it is further argued, made sense in the context of a society which was both divided and parcelled and in which therefore not only was a strong state necessary but also that state – in the form of an absolute monarchy – came to embody claims to represent the generality, as opposed to the partiality and particularity, of society's interests. As Ellen Meiksins Wood has commented: 'The king embodied the *public* aspect of the State as against the private character of his subjects'.[3] In this situation the key contemporary political question was that of rendering royal power 'more truly public', of cleansing it of particularistic influences, of ensuring that *la monarchie absolue* – whether real or imagined – did not decline into a *monarchie arbitraire*. The moral prescription was that the monarch should work for the greater good of the kingdom.

The idea therefore of a single superior and sovereign will capable of expressing the permanent and common interests of the entire nation was, in the French context, very much a response to the specific historical conditions of institutional and societal instability and was, furthermore, designed to enhance, rather than to diminish, the freedom enjoyed by the individual. It was moreover a widely- and long-held belief. Classically it is to be found in Bodin's concept of the indivisibility of sovereignty but so too, as J. H. Shennan has shown, by contrast it appears in the political vocabulary of the Parlement of Paris in the eighteenth century.[4] The same political disposition also brought with it a pervasive distrust of those intermediary powers and voluntary associations that later French liberal writers were to consider as one of the all-important guarantees of English liberty. Estates, parlements, the Church and other similar bodies, all were seen as feudal remnants voicing private (and therefore selfish) corporate concerns and even when defended by Montesquieu came to be conflated with aristocratic power and what was known as the *thèse nobiliare*. But this was not all. To quote Ellen Meiksins Wood again:

> Even in more radical attacks on royal absolutism, the public will of the state was not generally opposed, as in England, by asserting private interests or individual rights against it. Nor was the common good redefined as a public interest essentially constituted by private interests.[5]

Rather what tended to happen was that the precise location of the source and principle of generality was transferred away from the monarch towards some other institution deemed capable of expressing its superior claims. The complaint, in other words, was not so much that the sovereign might have said 'L'Etat c'est moi' but that he acted as if he believed that 'L'Etat c'est à moi'.[6]

The conclusion drawn by Keohane is therefore unambiguous. 'Many of Rousseau's authoritarian passages', she writes, 'were restatements of hoary arguments in French absolutist thought'.[7] And nowhere was this more so than with the concept of the general will, replete with the injunction that sovereignty could be neither divided nor restricted coupled with the total alienation of each individual and of all his rights to the community. Rousseau's innovation was to deny that this sovereign will could be indefinitely identified with one individual, thus opening up the way for its all-important redescription as the real will of all those citizens who made up the membership of the political body. In this fashion was the theory of absolute monarchy transformed into the radically democratic alternative of absolute popular sovereignty. The misunderstanding is to believe that in either case a concern for the liberty of the individual was absent.

Here again it would be wrong to overstate Rousseau's originality. Long before him those not prepared to accept that sovereignty had its origin in either paternal power or divine right had been ready to concede that its source was to be found in the people. What marked Rousseau out from his predecessors was that they, unlike him, saw active sovereignty as being only the people's temporary possession, as something that was to be handed over to the appropriate authority as soon as possible, only rarely (and in some cases never) to be reclaimed. Pufendorf, for example, even went so far as to define the handing over of the right to govern by a defeated people as a meaningful form of consent. Not only was Rousseau unwilling to grant that sovereignty could be given away either under duress or by tacit agreement but also he even opposed its voluntary and unforced transfer. Sovereignty, in short, was not like a piece of property that could be freely disposed of: it was an inalienable possession, part of the individual's very humanity. Rousseau's contribution, as Robert Derathé has argued,[8] was therefore to attribute not only the origin but also the exercise of sovereignty to the people.

The implications of these ideas upon Rousseau's conception of contract were necessarily profound, and this because the 'fundamental problem' he thus set himself was nothing less than that of squaring the circle:

> how to find a form of association which will defend the person and goods of each member with the collective force of all and under which each individual, while uniting himself with the others, obeys no one but himself and remains as free as before.[9]

The contrast with the position endorsed by Hobbes could not have been more stark. As Hobbes perceived it, the human condition was so bleak that men could escape from the war of all against all only by agreeing to transfer lock, stock and barrel their natural right to govern and to arbitrate in disputes to the single sovereign power of Leviathan, preserving only their right to self-preservation. The trade-off was a straightforward one: life and an element of liberty in exchange for obedience to the sword. For Rousseau there was to be no trade-off, there were to be no losses, only gains. Men, he believed, could have both liberty and law if they were able to construct a society where they ruled themselves.

For Rousseau then there was to be only one contract of association and no pact of submission. 'Each individual', he writes, 'recovers the equivalent of everything he loses'. But something 'remarkable' takes place when the contract is signed. The individual, in Rousseau's phrase, is 'doubly committed': first to his fellow contractees and second as a member of the state in relation to the sovereign. The individual thus finds himself to have entered into a reciprocal agreement not only with the body of which they were to become members but also with a sovereign which henceforth is deemed to possess a moral personality. The latter point is fundamental. Rousseau, as much as Hobbes, was aware that a contract where everyone was free to decide upon its terms and when it was to be observed was a recipe for disaster. To prevent the inevitable descent into a 'state of nature' where the association would be 'either tyrannical or void' Rousseau therefore has resort to what amounts to a fiction: the general will. Its existence as something which 'is always rightful and always tends to the public good' is sufficient to allow Rousseau to stipulate that it is the sovereign and the sovereign alone who is the sole judge of the contract's implementation. The state as such is viable only upon this condition.

Rousseau's contract is thus in one sense anything but contractual. Postulated is a pact between a collectivity considered as a single moral person and each of its members taken individually. From this it follows that of the two contracting parties it is only one – the individuals concerned – who could be in breach of the agreement entered into. By an altogether different route we arrive therefore at a conclusion that at one level is similar to that of Hobbes: the social contract gives 'absolute power' to the sovereign over his subjects.

If this is so it is in part because Rousseau, unlike for example Locke, did not view the foundational contract as a means of regulating the required balance between rights bearing individuals and government or of securing the liberal functioning of institutions. For him, as for Hobbes, the contract was constitutive of society itself. Where, however, Rousseau diverged from Hobbes was in the ends envisaged. For Hobbes it was civil peace and commodious living, for Rousseau it was ensuring that men could unite without giving up any of their liberty and the moral improvement of the constituent parts of civil society.

The argument here is sufficiently well known as not to need explanation. As Rousseau puts it:

> What man loses by the social contract is his natural liberty and the absolute right to anything that tempts him and that he can take: what he gains by the social contract is civil liberty and the legal right of property in what he possesses.

Expressed differently, there is no other solution to our problems than the substitution of the arbitrary relations that exist between men for the obedience of the citizen to the law. To that end, however, it is necessary that the members of the association transform themselves from a group of isolated individuals with many different wills into a community with a common will or interest. As we pass from the state of nature into civil society, justice is to replace instinct as a rule of conduct and in this way we obey only rules that we have prescribed to ourselves and thus enjoy untrammelled 'moral freedom'.

Given the controversy caused by this proposition it is interesting to note that it is precisely at this stage of the argument that Rousseau chooses to declare that 'the philosophical meaning of the word "freedom" is no part of my subject'. In a way his concerns were more mundane and straightforward. What he, unlike so many of his predecessors ('Grotius and the rest' as Rousseau describes them), was eager to reject was the idea that the individual could contract into anything and under any circumstances and that in this way the rights of slavery, conquest and despotism could be justified. Rousseau always opposed such a conception of contract and he did so for the good reason that 'to renounce freedom is to renounce one's humanity'.

Of course, what the reader was to make of this has been open to a wide range of interpretation. Rousseau himself, given his belief that sovereignty could not be subject to the procedure of representation, was convinced that his ideas could be applied, if at all, only to states whose geographical area did not exceed that of a small city. Political simplicity was to be the preferred model and it was only later (in his reflections upon the projected governments of Corsica and Poland) that these strictures were to be relaxed. More profoundly Rousseau's musings upon the social contract and the society to which it was to give rise tied in with the broader Rousseauian theme of how both individuals and peoples could be structured for virtue.

To Rousseau's contemporaries it was precisely this preoccupation with virtue that struck the deepest chord. 'Jean-Jacques', Robert Darnton writes in *The Great Cat Massacre*,[10] 'opened up his soul to those who could read him right, and his readers felt their own souls elevated above the imperfections of their ordinary existence'. Here the key texts were the *Confessions* (nothing quite like its intimate and often sordid self-examination had been seen before) and the *Nouvelle Héloïse* (which had run to some seventy editions by 1800) and not *The Social Contract*. 'Almost single-handedly', Emmet Kennedy has written, 'Rousseau precipitated an affective revolution'.[11] It was moreover this sensibility, the intense longing for moral elevation and purity, that was to be magnified out of all proportion in the Revolution that began in 1789.

The question of Rousseau's (and more broadly the Enlightenment's) connection with the French Revolution has long been the cause of controversy. Indeed, the debate sprang out of the Revolution itself, as a text such as Mounier's *Recherches sur les causes qui ont empêche les français de devenir libres et sur les moyens qui leur restent pour acquérir la liberté*,[12] first published in 1792, clearly illustrates. Cast as 'the worst book ever written on government', *The Social Contract* was taken to be the handbook of 'our modern legislators'. By the time that the liberal Amable de Barante published his *De la littérature française pendant le dix-huitième siècle*[13] in 1809 the connection between the Revolution and the *philosophes* of the eighteenth century, and specifically Rousseau, was taken to be beyond doubt. Rousseau, de Barante contended, by belittling 'the sentiment of duty' had done more than anyone else to undermine the moral foundations of the *ancien régime.* This was the principal 'vice of his philosophy'.

But stated in this way we have no sense of the emotional (and frequently tearful) frenzy that Rousseau induced amongst his disciples. The community born out of the social contract was to be frugal, hard working, virtuous, distrustful of wealth, free of corruption, trusting to the simple qualities of the people cast as the repositories of all that was good in society. Armed thus men such as Robespierre and Saint-Just had little difficulty affirming their own rhetorical and moral ascendancy over opponents that bore the mark of absolute evil. What happened when the people were found to be unworthy of the love that had been invested in them was the recourse to an ever-extensive dictatorship, the combination of virtue and terror, with the general will of society supposedly articulated by a twelve-man Committee of Public Safety.

The revolutionaries then were not just millenarians: they were, as Norman Hampson remarked, 'Rousseauist millenarians'.[14] Moreover the hypnotic effect of their actions was such as to bequeath to France a living tradition and style of politics that was deeply imbued with Rousseauian notions. The bare bones of what virtually amounted to a revolutionary catechism can be easily sketched out.[15] Sovereignty belonged to the people. There were no limits to its sovereignty because the field of politics was itself without limits. It was the task of the community to ensure that the general will was respected and it alone had the right to decide upon the sacrifices that were to be demanded of each individual. The role of government was limited to the execution of the general will as expressed by the people as sovereign. Man was naturally good: it was society that made him bad. Money and the activities it engendered were the source of corruption. The role of society therefore was to transform and to create a new man. Its political expression was to be the Republic.

Here, in effect, was a pattern of discourse which in Rousseauian terms, as should be clear, switched the emphasis towards popular sovereignty and the reign of virtue. But underpinning this vision there remained a heavy reliance upon Rousseauian contract theory. The manner in which this was expressed can be seen by examining the ideas of the Christian socialist Pierre Leroux.[16] Like many writers of his generation Leroux was convinced that the French Revolution had produced 'societal anarchy' and what he described as 'anarchy at the bottom of the heart of every man'. The end of politics, he therefore believed, was to proclaim those truths that would restore 'harmony to the human soul'. In this Rousseau was to occupy a central role. The force of Rousseau's argument, Leroux contended, was first to destroy the false bases upon which previous claims to sovereignty had rested (monarchy, aristocracy and theocracy) and then to show where properly it resided (within each and every person). From this it followed that human society must rest upon a contract through which each individual would hand over his sovereignty to the community at large but whose terms would ensure that he obeyed only himself. The individual, Leroux argued,

> will remain sovereign, and society will be legitimate, if social power having been given over to the whole there is an identity of interests and of views between each person and the community, between the sovereign as everyone and the sovereign as individual.[17]

Such a system of government, he claimed, would be a democracy and its guiding principle would be the sovereignty of the people. Rousseau's 'greatness' therefore lay in his advocacy of liberty and in his recognition that this would demand the destruction of all past forms of tyranny. Rousseau thus figured as 'the philosopher of fraternity'.

Leroux, however, was not blind to the difficulties posed by Rousseau's ideas, not least in the shape of the contract, but his principal concern – as befitted anyone who believed that Robespierre was Rousseau in action – was to allay fears that the premised popular sovereignty would produce nothing but 'tyranny' and 'demagogy'. It would not, Leroux believed, for the good Rousseauian reasons that the 'true sovereign' would emerge only with the aid of the Legislator and because the required harmony between the will of each and the will of all would not be possible unless democracy and fraternity were accepted as a religion and as a 'common faith'.

In Leroux, therefore, we have an example of how Rousseau was re-read in the light of the experience of the Revolution of 1789 and of how the idea of contract was crucial to his interpretation as a proponent of popular sovereignty, a doctrine perceived as the dominant faith and political force of the future. Many in France on both the democratic and revolutionary Left were to agree. So too did this perception of Rousseau find assent elsewhere on the political spectrum. Two minor texts typical of this view are Pierre Landes's *Principes du droit politique, mis en opposition avec ceux de J.J.Rousseau sur le Contrat social* and Gabriel-Jacques Dageville's *De la propriété politique et civile, ou du vrai contrat social*,[18] the former being a chapter by chapter commentary on Rousseau's text running to almost three hundred pages. The difference is that here Rousseau and the doctrines he had apparently espoused were viewed with deep foreboding and resentment.

Nowhere was this hostile reaction more evident than amongst those writers who, like Rousseau, believed that sovereignty was one and absolute but who saw the origin of that sovereignty to be found not amongst the people but in God. Of these no one put the case more succinctly than Joseph de Maistre.[19] The core of the theocratic argument directed specifically at Rousseau lay in the assertion that man was by nature 'sociable' and therefore that it made no sense to speak of man existing prior to the existence of society. The latter, de Maistre argued, was 'the direct result of the will of the Creator who wanted that man should be what he had always and everywhere been'. It followed that it was 'a major error' to conceive society as a 'choice' based upon either human consent, deliberation or what de Maistre described as 'a primitive contract'. The confusion, he believed, derived in part from a misunderstanding about what was meant by the word nature and in this context he was in no doubt that such 'anomalous' examples as the 'American savage' had little to teach us. It was absurd to seek the character of a being in its most undeveloped and untypical form. Moreover by the same token a people could not be said to predate the existence of sovereignty. A sovereign, in de Maistre's view, was necessary to make a people and therefore society and sovereignty both appeared at precisely the same time. 'There was', de Maistre writes, 'a people, some kind of civilization and a sovereign as soon as men came into contact with each other'. The same logic also told de Maistre that the very power which had decreed the existence of the social order and of sovereignty had also willed 'modifications to sovereignty according to the different character of nations'. Nations, de Maistre believed, quite definitely had different characters and from this different types of government were derived that in each case were best suited to the conditions. Thus to ask in the abstract, as Rousseau had done, what was the best possible form of government was to pose an insoluble question. 'From these incontestable principles', de Maistre went on,

> derives a conclusion which is no less so: that the social contract is a chimaera. Because if there are as many governments as there are different peoples, if the various forms of these governments are perforce prescribed by the power which has given to each nation its moral, physical, geographical and commercial qualities, then it is no longer possible to speak of a pact.[20]

In short, each people had the type of government that suited it and none of them had been either chosen or self-consciously created.

As such Rousseau was cast as 'the mortal enemy of experience'. If history taught that monarchy was the most natural and universal form of government and that no pure form of democracy had ever existed this in no way prevented Rousseau from proclaiming that the 'sole legitimate government' was one that he himself acknowledged was made for Gods, was suitable only for small states and for a people with a simplicity of morals. So too Rousseau judged democracy not by how it actually worked – 'Of all the monarchs', de Maistre wrote, 'the hardest, the most despotic, the most intolerable, is the monarch people' – but in terms of its theoretical perfection, hence the general will was by definition always right. The whole thing, from the idea of the social contract upwards, was nothing more than 'un rêve de collège'.

Just as importantly there lay beneath this critique of Rousseau an alternative (and perhaps more compelling) account of the origin of society and of the nature of government. De Maistre's 'general thesis' was that human beings were relatively powerless and therefore were incapable of any significant level of creative activity. They were also tainted by original sin and hence were not, as Rousseau believed, potentially perfect. From this de Maistre found himself in agreement with Hobbes. 'Society', he wrote,

> is in reality a state of war and here is to be found the necessity of government: given that man is evil he must be governed: wherever several people want the same thing there must be a superior power over everyone who can adjudicate and who can prevent them from fighting each other . . . a being who is both social and evil must be put under the yoke.[21]

Government was not therefore a vehicle for human liberation but was rather a remedy for the consequences of original sin. If there was a difficulty it was not that the sovereign should not exercise his will 'invincibly' but that he should be prevented from exercising it 'unjustly' and this was to be avoided by dispensing power to the Papacy rather than to Rousseau's 'blind multitude'. How then was the legitimacy of government to be assessed? For de Maistre all governments – given their divine source – were in a sense good governments but the best were those that provided the greatest sum of happiness to the greatest number of people over the longest period of time. And ultimately that could be measured by the simple criterion of their longevity or duration.

The import of de Maistre's argument as a whole was, of course, that the French Revolution, directly inspired by Rousseau's 'disastrous principles', had been a frontal assault upon what he chose to describe as 'the eternal laws of nature'. This was to be a refrain taken up by the ideologists of Catholic counter-revolution on a regular basis and it might therefore be worthwhile momentarily to glance at two other examples of how the presuppositions of Rousseau's theory of social contract were dismissed and challenged. The writings of Louis de Bonald have neither the brilliance nor the trenchancy of those of de Maistre but nevertheless they provide a good example of how Rousseau's own arguments were used to subvert the very ideas for which he was taken to stand. Bonald's overall assessment of Rousseau's achievement, articulated in his magisterial *Théorie du pouvoir politique et religieux dans la société civile, démontrée par le raisonnement et par l'histoire*,[22] was disarmingly straightforward. He had, Bonald declared,'sacrificed society for man, history for his own opinions and the universe for Geneva'. Society became nothing more than a collection of individuals and accordingly the general will was dissolved into the sum of individual and particular wills, with individual pleasure and happiness, not general well-being, becoming its goal. This, Bonald argued, represented 'the most complete refutation of his work'.

Writing around the same time the young Félicité de Lamennais was to adopt a strikingly similar attitude to the man he contemptuously referred to the 'Genevan sophist'. This might be surprising simply because if Lamennais is now remembered it is almost always as the disciple of democracy and the oppressed, as the ex-communicated priest whose radicalism was voiced under the banner of 'Dieu et la liberté'. Yet for the royalist Lamennais, of the *Essai sur l'indifférence en matière de la religion*,[23] everything was clear: the Reformation had given birth to Descartes who himself had given birth to the philosophy of the eighteenth century which in turn had produced 1789, 1793 and its catalogue of crimes. In all of this, he believed, the atheistic implications of Rousseau's doctrines had played a significant role.

There were two sides to Lamennais's argument. First, Rousseau the deist led us unerringly towards uncertainty and indifference and thence to the destruction of society itself. But the same results were also obtained by another dimension of Rousseau's philosophy: contract theory. The starting-point here was a set of assumptions with which we are now familiar: society itself was natural; it had not been constituted by men but by God; radical change was not a possibility. Rousseau, on the other hand, believed that a 'primitive pact' formed 'the true basis' of the social order. 'Never', Lamennais commented, 'was there a doctrine so absurd, so deadly and so degrading as this'.[24] What then were his grounds for dissent? In the first instance no society had been seen to originate in this way and in any case it was a ridiculous idea to imagine that a society could owe its existence to a random collection of individuals meeting by chance in the woods! Second, every pact implied sanctions to ensure that it was observed but where in Rousseau were these sanctions to be found? Nothing, Lamennais argued, was there to stop people reclaiming their sovereignty. Nor was Lamennais convinced that anything changed with the signing of the social contract. Each individual remained as he was before, sovereign of himself, and therefore subject to nothing else but the will of the strongest. Moreover Rousseau could come up with no better reason for adhering to the contract than self-interest. On this fragile basis did philosophy wish to ground society.

The criticism did not stop there, however. Once the doctrine of the social contract had been accepted by the people, it had turned society into one vast arena where only private interests dominated. Governments acted solely upon the basis of self-preservation and self-aggrandizement and much the same was true of the masses. 'If', Lamennais wrote, the latter 'are allowed for one minute to sense their power they will abuse it in order to destroy everything and will run headlong towards anarchy believing all the time that they are marching towards liberty'.[25] Because something had been willed by the people and clothed in the garment of the general will did not always make it right. The same doctrine, in short, which had dethroned God, had dethroned kings, had in turn dethroned man and reduced him to the level of an animal. Turmoil followed turmoil, revolution followed revolution.

Lamennais's conclusion was unambiguous and placed Rousseau at the heart of the century's ills. Once man was told that his reason was the source of truth and his will was the source of power then truth became nothing more than what appealed to his inclinations and power was reduced to naked force. The members of society, with their equal rights and their contrary interests, would destroy themselves down to the last man were it not for the fact that the strongest would enslave the weakest and would make his will the sole law and the sole standard of justice. 'Such', Lamennais wrote, 'is the necessary result of the absurd social contract'.

The irony in all of this was that as the Papacy remained true to its conception of the unity of throne and altar, Lamennais found himself increasingly drawn to the sufferings of Europe's Catholic peoples and from this on to a liberal defence of liberty of conscience, liberty of the press and liberty of education. It is to this strand of political opinion that I now want briefly to turn. Liberalism in France, as elsewhere, was multifaceted but, stated simply, with the outbreak of the Revolution there were those who were prepared to clothe their calls for reform within the doctrine of natural rights and with this came a willingness to speak of a pact or contract as the origin of civil society. One example of this was Pierre Daunou's *Essai sur la constitution*,[26] published in 1793; another was Pierre Louis Roederer's *Cours d'organisation sociale*,[27] published in the same year. If anything, however, the influence in both cases was Lockian rather than Rousseauian, the emphasis falling upon the contract as a means of protecting pre-existing rights (and especially the right to property). Moreover, as events unfolded – and specifically with the radicalization of the language of rights that accompanied the rise of the Jacobins – the enthusiasm amongst liberals for such a style of political argument waned considerably. As I have shown elsewhere,[28] when in 1819 Daunou published his *Essai sur les garanties individuelles que réclame l'Etat actuel de la société*,[29] he began by proudly proclaiming: 'Nowhere will I have resort to abstract principles, to the hypothesis of a social pact, to a discussion of its clauses, or to the anterior or natural rights it presupposes'. For men such as these – the *idéologues* – utility was now taken to be a far sounder guide.

This is not to say that Rousseau now ceased to trouble the consciences of French liberals. He continued to do so and this primarily because of the principal theoretical presupposition upon which the social contract was thought to rest: popular sovereignty. The best example that can be provided here is that of Rousseau's fellow Swiss Protestant Benjamin Constant.[30] Constant's attitude towards Rousseau was nothing if not ambiguous. Writing in *The Spirit of Conquest and Usurpation*,[31] published in 1814, he commented: 'It will be apparent, I believe, that the subtle metaphysics of *The Social Contract* can only serve today to supply weapons and pretexts to all kinds of tyranny, that of one man, that of several and that of all, to oppression either organized under legal forms or exercised through popular violence'. This was to be one of the central themes of Constant's most famous essay, *The Liberty of the Ancients compared with that of the Moderns*. But in a footnote to his remark in the 1814 text he added: 'I do not wish to join Rousseau's detractors. . . . He was the first to make a sense of our rights popular; his voice has awakened generous hearts and independent minds'. The same ambivalence is to be found in the extensive discussion of Rousseau's ideas that begins Constant's *Principles of Politics*.[32] Where Constant found himself in agreement with Rousseau was in an acceptance that 'there are only two sorts of power in the world: one, illegitimate, is force; the other, legitimate, is the general will'.[33] Where he diverged from Rousseau was in his understanding of the precise nature and extent of that will. As perceived by Rousseau the general will was translated into the unlimited sovereignty of the people and for Constant it was precisely the absence of limits that posed the gravest threat to liberty. 'When', he wrote,

> you establish that the sovereignty of the people is unlimited, you create and toss at random into society a degree of power which is too large in itself, and which is bound to constitute an evil, in whatever hands it is placed.[34]

Constant, like Mill after him, was eager to establish that there was a part of human existence which 'by necessity remains individual and independent' and which therefore was properly beyond social control. Rousseau, he remarked, 'overlooked this truth', thus providing theoretical support for despotism. And here was the heart of the problem. Rousseau, Constant argued,

> defined the contract struck between society and its members as the complete alienation of each individual with all his rights, without any reservations, to the community. In order to reassure us about the consequences of such an absolute renunciation of all parts of our existence for the benefit of an abstract being, he tells us that the sovereign, that is the social body, can neither harm the totality of its members, nor any of them in particular. Since everyone gives himself entirely, all share the same condition, and nobody is interested in making the condition onerous to others. Because every individual gives himself entirely to all, he does not give himself to anyone in particular. Everybody acquires over his associates the same rights as he surrenders in their favour. Thus he gains the equivalent of all that he loses together with the greater strength to preserve what he has.[35]

In this what Rousseau forgot was that as soon as the sovereign sought to make use of his power, as soon as the practical organization of authority was begun, the sovereign had to delegate it, thus destroying the very qualities the sovereign was said to embody. Whether we liked it or not we were, in other words, not giving ourselves to nobody but were submitting ourselves to those who acted in the name of all. We were not entering into a condition equal for all but one in which certain individuals derived exclusive advantage and were above the common condition. Not everyone would gain the equivalent of what they would lose because the result of the contract was 'the establishment of a power which takes away from them whatever they have'. If there was a parallel to be drawn it was with what Constant described as 'Hobbes' whole dreadful system'. The 'absolute' character of the contract envisaged in each case was such as to ensure the continuous violation of individual liberty irrespective of whether sovereignty was exercised in the name of the monarch or of democracy.

Rousseau, Constant wrote, was appalled by the consequences of his argument and by the 'monstrous force' he had created. So appalled, in fact, that he set out a series of conditions that destroyed the principle he had just proclaimed. By announcing that sovereignty could be neither delegated, alienated nor represented he was, in other words, declaring that it could never be exercised at all. Constant's own answer to these issues was to define a conception of liberty thought appropriate to the modern age and to recommend a set of political institutions based upon the English model so despised by Rousseau. Other liberals adopted a different strategy in their attempts to restore political stability to post-revolutionary France but invariably a place for Rousseau was found in the debate. One such case was François Guizot.

The crucial factor here was Guizot's conviction that power should reside in the hands of those who had the 'capacity' to govern properly.[36] To attain that end he had in part to challenge the most fundamental of Rousseau's assumptions: namely that the will of the individual was the source of the sovereign's legitimacy. 'It is not true', Guizot proclaimed, 'that man should be absolute master of himself, that his will should be his legitimate sovereign, that at no time and by no right does anyone have power over him if he does not consent'.[37] Beyond the will of the individual, Guizot wanted to argue, lay a law that was called reason, that embodied wisdom, morality and truth and unless it was followed the use we made of our liberty was absurd and reprehensible. This was not a law made by men and therefore could not be changed or abolished by men: it was rather a question of discovering what this law was. Existing independently of our will we were free to obey or disobey the dictates of our reason but it was reason alone that constituted the 'sole source of all legitimate power'.

Stated thus it might be argued that Guizot's position was closer to Rousseau's than he realized but the intended force of his argument was that the sovereignty of the people was to be contrasted to the sovereignty of reason and with this that the claims of democracy were to be rejected in favour of those of a new political elite drawn primarily from the bourgeoisie. In the process, moreover, Guizot hit upon a criticism of Rousseau that was to be taken up by people with far more radical intentions: any form of contract which bound our will in the future was a restriction of our individual liberty. 'What does it matter', Guizot pointed out, 'if a law should have emanated from my will yesterday if today my will has changed? Can I only will once? Does my will exhaust its rights in one single act?'[38] In England this objection had first been voiced by William Godwin in his *Enquiry Concerning Political Justice*; in France it was taken up by the first self-proclaimed anarchist, Pierre-Joseph Proudhon.[39]

Proudhon was a man not known for being moderate towards those he disagreed with and his attitude towards Rousseau was no exception. First of all Proudhon was in no doubt that Rousseau was directly responsible for what he described as 'the great deviation of "93"' and for the society of 'frightful chaos and demoralisation' that it had produced. Rousseau, in short, was unambiguously identified with a tradition that, in Proudhon's eyes, had been 'bewitched by politics', Jacobinism. Furthermore, it was within this tradition that Rousseau's concept of social contract was to be located. Rousseau, he argued, understood 'nothing of the social contract' and because this was so he had articulated 'an offensive and defensive alliance of those who possess against those who do not possess'. It was 'a contract of hatred', a 'monument of incurable misanthropy', a 'coalition of the barons of property, commerce and industry against the disinherited proletariat', an 'oath of war'.[40] The fundamental error, as Proudhon saw it, was to see only the political relations that existed between men and therefore to see the contract as an agreement between citizen and government. In such an agreement there was

> necessarily alienation of a part of the liberty and of the wealth of the citizen . . . it is an act of appointment of arbiters, chosen by the citizens without any preliminary agreement . . . the said arbiters being clothed with sufficient force to put their decisions into practice and to collect their salaries.[41]

The force of Proudhon's argument was that Rousseau had provided a spurious, if brilliantly oratorical, defence of the domination of the state, in this case the one and indivisible Jacobin Republic. Yet Proudhon, unlike other of Rousseau's critics, did not want to abandon the idea of contract. Far from it: it was precisely the idea of what Proudhon termed the 'free contract' that would lead to the dissolution and ultimate disappearance of the state. The key here was what Proudhon saw as the transition from distributive justice, defined as the reign of law and as feudal, governmental and military rule, to commutative justice, the dominance of the economic and industrial system. It was by moving away from politics to economics that his preferred model of decentralized and pluralistic self-government – mutualism – would come into existence.

A proper contract, Proudhon argues, is not one between governed and governing (as, he contended, Rousseau believed) but excluded government and was between individuals as individuals. What characterizes this contract is that it is an agreement for equal exchange, in which several individuals organize themselves for a definite purpose and time. Each contractee is therefore mutually obliged to provide a certain amount of goods, services and work in exchange for other goods, services and work of equal value. Beyond this each of the contractees was perfectly independent. The contract therefore is 'essentially reciprocal': it implied no obligation upon the parties concerned except that which resulted from their personal promise of reciprocal delivery. Just as importantly, it was not subject to any external authority. 'When I agree with one or more of my fellow citizens', Proudhon wrote, 'it is clear that my own will is my law; it is myself who, in fulfilling my obligation, am my own government'.[42] Likewise, by agreeing upon a contract individuals indicated their willingness to 'abdicate all pretension to govern each other'. More than this, Proudhon envisaged that this system of contract could be extended indefinitely throughout society, producing a community that would be composed of an intricate web of contracts freely agreed upon by the individuals concerned. 'It implies', Proudhon wrote, 'that a man bargains with the aim of securing his liberty and his well-being without any personal loss'.[43]

Seen in this light it was what Proudhon described as 'the constitution of value' that was 'the contract of contracts'.[44] Each contract was to be based upon a 'just price' for the goods and services exchanged and this, in Proudhonian terms, made possible the realization of what he regarded as a pattern of justice that was 'totally human and nothing but human'. All conflicting interests were reconciled and all divergences were unified. 'Everything else', he wrote, 'is war, the rule of authority'.

Proudhon's case against Rousseau therefore was that he had fundamentally misinterpreted the idea of the social contract as it had emerged out of the sixteenth century. This 'revolutionary tradition', born in the quarrel between Bossuet and Jurieu, had given us 'the idea of the social contract as an antithesis of government': under the guise of eloquence and paradox Rousseau had turned it into its opposite. This itself might appear surprising and paradoxical but it does perhaps lead us to a conclusion.

A contemporary writer as perceptive and gifted as Carole Pateman has drawn attention to Rousseau as a critic of what she describes as 'the fraudulent liberal social contract'.[45] The liberal contract, she argues, serves to justify social relationships and political institutions that already exist whilst Rousseau's contract provides 'an actual foundation for a participatory political order of the future'. The latter's democratic social contract, she goes on, is one of association based on self-assumed obligation and of substantive equality between 'active citizens who are political decision-makers'. From our brief survey of political thought in the first half of the nineteenth century it is clear that there were few in France who saw it that way. The republicans, with their passion for the one and indivisible Republic, would perhaps have been able to make sense of this description but for the rest the experience of the French Revolution had been such as to convince them that Rousseau and his idea of social contract had merely transposed the absolutism of government on to another plane. Sovereignty was presumed to reside in the people, the state had been left intact, and thus the modern Leviathan had been created. This, Rousseau's critics concurred, had been a catastrophe without precedent. For them it was quite definitely a case of *la faute à Rousseau*.

NOTES

1 See J. Roussel, *Jean-Jacques Rousseau en France après la Révolution, 1795–1830*, Paris, Armand Colin, 1972.
2 N. Keohane, *Philosophy and the State in France*, Princeton, NJ, Princeton University Press, 1980, p. 7.
3 E. Meiksins Wood, 'The State and Popular Sovereignty in French Political

Thought: A Genealogy of Rousseau's General Will', *History of Political Thought*, 1983, vol. IV, p. 287.
4   J. H. Shennan, 'The Political Vocabulary of the Parlement of Paris in the Eighteenth Century', *Società Italiana di storia del diritto: atti del Iv congresso internationale*, Florence, 1982, pp. 951–64.
5   Meiksins Wood, 'The State and Popular Sovereignty', p. 309.
6   See H. H. Rowen, *The King's State*, New Brunswick, NJ, Rutgers University Press, 1980.
7   Keohane, *Philosophy and the State*, p. 442.
8   R. Derathé, *Jean-Jacques Rousseau et la science politique de son temps*, Paris, Vrin, 1970.
9   J.-J. Rousseau, *The Social Contract*, Harmondsworth, Penguin, 1971, p. 60.
10   R. Darnton, *The Great Cat Massacre*, New York, Basic Books, 1984, p. 249.
11   E. Kennedy, *A Cultural History of the French Revolution*, New Haven, Conn., Yale University Press, 1989, p. 112.
12   J. J. Mounier, *Recherches sur les causes qui ont empêche les français de devenir libres et sur les moyens qui leur restent pour acquérir la liberté*, Paris, Gattey, 1792.
13   A. de Barante, *De la littérature française pendant le dix-huitième siècle*, Paris, Colin, 1809.
14   N. Hampson, 'The Heavenly City of the French Revolutionaries', in *Rewriting the French Revolution*, C. Lucas (ed), Oxford, Clarendon Press, 1991, p. 53.
15   See J. Julliard, *La Faute à Rousseau*, Paris, Seuil, 1985, p. 46.
16   P. Leroux, 'Aux Politiques', in *Oeuvres de Pierre Leroux (1825–1850)*, vol. I, Paris, Lesourd, 1850, pp. 89–288.
17   Leroux, 'Aux Politiques', p. 154.
18   P. Landes, *Principes du droit politique, mis en opposition avec ceux de J.-J. Rousseau sur le Contrat social*, Paris, Maradan, 1801; G.-J. Dageville, *De la propriété politique et civile*, Paris, Delauney, 1813.
19   See especially J. de Maistre, 'Etude sur la souveraineté', *Oeuvres complètes*, vol. I, Lyons, Ville et Perrussel, 1884, pp. 309–554 and 'Examen d'un écrit de J.-J. Rousseau sur l'inégalité des conditions', *Oevres complètes*, vol. VII, pp. 507–66. On de Maistre see R. A. Lebrun, *Throne and Altar: The Political and Religious Thought of Joseph de Maistre*, Ottawa, University of Ottawa Press, 1965.
20   J. de Maistre, 'Etude sur la souveraineté', *Oeuvres complètes*, vol. I, p. 329.
21   J. de Maistre, 'Examen d'un écrit de J.-J. Rousseau', *Oeuvres complètes*, vol. VII, p. 563.
22   L. de Bonald, 'Théorie du pouvoir politique et religieux dans la société civile démontrée par la raisonnement et par l'histoire', *Oeuvres de M. de Bonald*, xii, Paris, Le Clere, 1843.
23   F. de Lamennais, *Essai sur l'indifférence en matière de la religion*, Paris, Tournachon-Molin et H. Seguin, 1817.
24   Lamennais, *Essai sur l'indifférence*, p. 328.
25   Lamennais, *Essai sur l'indifférence*, p. 336.
26   P. Daunou, *Essai sur la constitution*, Paris, Imprimerie Nationale, 1793.
27   P.-L. Roederer, *Cours d'organisation sociale* (1793), in *Oeuvres complètes*, Paris, Firmin Didot, 1859.
28   See my 'The *Déclaration des droits de l'homme et du citoyen* and its critics in France: Reaction and *Idéologie*', *Historical Journal*, 1992, vol. 35, pp. 839–59.
29   P. Daunou, *Essai sur les garanties que réclame l'Etat actuel de la société*, Paris, Foulon, 1819.
30   On Constant see S. Holmes, *Benjamin Constant and the Making of Modern Liberalism*, New Haven, Conn., Yale University Press, 1984; B. Fontana, *Benjamin Constant and the Post-Revolutionary Mind*, New Haven, Conn., Yale University Press, 1991.

31 B. Constant, 'The Spirit of Conquest and Usurpation and their Relation to European Civilization', *Political Writings*, Cambridge, Cambridge University Press, 1988, pp. 51–167.
32 B. Constant, 'Principles of Politics Applicable to all Representative Governments', *Political Writings*, pp. 169–305.
33 Constant, 'Principles of Politics', p. 175.
34 Constant, 'Principles of Politics', p. 176.
35 Constant, 'Principles of Politics', p. 177.
36 See F. Guizot, 'Philosophie politique: de la souveraineté', in F. Guizot, *Histoire de la civilisation en Europe*, Paris, Pluriel, 1985. Similar ideas are also to be found in F. Guizot, *Histoire des origines du gouvernement réprésentatif en Europe*, 2 vols, Paris, Didier, 1822.
37 Guizot, 'Philosophie politique', p. 366.
38 Guizot, 'Philosophie politique', pp. 363–4.
39 See P.-J Proudhon, *General Idea of the Revolution in the Nineteenth Century*, London, Pluto, 1989. On Proudhon see A. Noland, 'Proudhon and Rousseau', *Journal of the History of Ideas*, 1967, vol. XXVII, pp. 33–54.
40 Proudhon, *General Idea of the Revolution*, p. 118.
41 Proudhon, *General Idea of the Revolution*, p. 115.
42 Proudhon, *General Idea of the Revolution*, p. 205.
43 Proudhon, *General Idea of the Revolution*, p. 113.
44 Proudhon, *General Idea of the Revolution*, p. 237.
45 C. Pateman, *The Problem of Political Obligation: A Critique of Liberal Theory*, Oxford, Polity Press, 1985, pp. 142–62.

7 Kant on the social contract

Howard Williams

There are four distinctive aspects to Kant's theory of the social contract. The first (and perhaps the most well known) is that Kant entirely does away with any supposition that a social contract has actually been concluded by the members of any particular society. He sees the social contract as an intellectual construct with moral and practical significance. It is a notion that should affect our motives and intentions in acting rather than one which arises in observing the world. Second, the notion of a social contract is connected to a programme of political reform which it is incumbent upon the rulers and the subjects of a state to try to implement. In Kant's view there is a certain kind of political system which fits best with the idea of a social contract and as rational beings we have a duty to work peacefully to bring such a system into being.

Third, Kant's notion of the social contract does not stop at the boundaries of nations. He believes that the idea of the state which underlies the social contract has cosmopolitan implications. In founding a successful domestic order you cannot overlook the international context into which the state falls. Kant unusually therefore tries to operate the idea of the social contract at an international level. He has work for the idea of the social contract in the relations among states as well as in the relations among individuals. A fourth and final feature of Kant's theory of the social contract is that it is forward looking. In his use of the theory Kant tries to transcend his own time. As well as taking into account many previous social contract theories Kant in some respects anticipates contemporary developments in social contract theory, particularly in the writings of John Rawls. We might then regard Kant's theory as providing a useful point of entry to social contract theory as a whole.[1]

The object of this chapter is to highlight the uniqueness and continued relevance of Kant's account of the social contract. This uniqueness and relevance stem from the fact that Kant deals with the social contract within the context of his critical philosophy as a whole. In his critical philosophy Kant attempts to place moral philosophy (of which political philosophy is a part) upon a firm foundation. Kant believes our intentions in actions can be made rational. In other words, he believes the rules which guide our behaviour can be made internally consistent and universally applicable. This applies both to legal rules and rules of virtue which externally and internally respectively restrict our actions. In making these rules rational Kant thinks we can enjoy peaceful and productive relations with one another at the personal and social level, and between societies. Kant is therefore unique in the faith he has in reason and relevant because now, more than ever, when we embark on a new era in world history, such faith seems necessary.

Kant's style of philosophizing was to immerse himself in contemporary and classic literature in order to acquaint himself with the problems associated with an area of interest. Only then would he seek to construct his own solution to the problems. Consequently he never simply took over the arguments of others, rather he sought to shape those arguments according to his own view of the subject. Kant saw himself as a philosopher who was concerned to develop his own distinctive approach and to demonstrate its plausibility in relation to alternatives. This naturally coloured his attitude to social contract theory. Although deeply influenced by the classical writings of Hobbes, Locke and his contemporaries Rousseau and Hume, Kant nevertheless sought to modify their conclusions on the social contract in the light of his own critical philosophy. Looking at Kant's attitude to these writers helps therefore to situate his theory.

Kant follows Thomas Hobbes closely in his understanding of the pre-societal stage or the state of nature. But there are aspects of Hobbes's account of our emergence from the state of nature that Kant amends and refines. Hobbes's picture of the state of nature is one of a hostile and harsh condition. He equates the state of nature with the state of war. Kant is less inclined to present the individual state of nature as an observed reality but he does, like Hobbes, equate the state of war with the state of nature.[2] Kant took the state of war to be the usual relation among states in his time. In such a natural condition uncertainty prevails, in particular about justice and right. Kant regards it as an obligation upon states and individuals to try to leave such a lawless condition because neither states nor individuals would conform to their idea in this situation. From the moral viewpoint the state of nature (wherever it occurs) is an inferior condition and has to be surpassed. Like Hobbes, Kant sees this coming about in the domestic sphere through the submission of individuals to an absolute authority. Individuals submit through a notional covenant in order to bring law into being. Any legal authority is for Kant also a legitimate authority because through legal punishment it can secure the implementation of some moral rules. But we are not bound to this authority (as with Hobbes) uncritically. We have the right of publicity in order to air our grievances about the way in which our necessarily fallible leaders exercise their authority. Just as the social contract sets up an ideal of behaviour for the subject, so also in Kant's view it does for the sovereign.

Kant appears to find acceptable John Locke's view of the role of the social contract in establishing citizenship, but Kant finds less attractive the theory of resistance that Locke derives from a strongly voluntarist view of the contract. Kant's political theory allows no scope for violent resistance to an established sovereign. The sovereign does not incur any perfect or enforceable duties from the social contract. Rather the sovereign incurs an imperfect (not legally enforceable) duty to exercise rule as though a social contract were in force. When a sovereign body fails to act in accordance with the spirit of the social contract, subjects are in no position to remove it. They may criticize through public utterances in writing or in print but they have nonetheless to obey. Kant also distances himself from Locke in his treatment of property under the social contract. For Locke property rights exist prior to any acceptance of the social contract.[3] For Kant property rights become possible only through the acceptance of a social contract within a civil society.

Rousseau is perhaps Kant's favourite social contract theorist. Kant finds particularly persuasive Rousseau's account of the role played by the general will in the social contract and the united general will figures prominently in Kant's version.[4] However, the final interpretation given of the united general will in Kant's social contract theory would be unacceptable to Rousseau. Kant believes the sovereignty of the general will has to be alienable and must be seen by those who see themselves participating in the general will as residing in the legitimate government. Rousseau made Kant think carefully about the rational origins of civil society but Kant differs profoundly in his understanding of human nature and the function of government. For Rousseau we are by nature innocent and it is society which corrupts us. Kant believes that human beings have the potential for both good and evil. We can allow ourselves to be seduced by nature and do the wrong thing or we can assert our wills and do what is right. As Kant sees it, we are both phenomenal beings (determined by nature) and noumenal or intelligent beings (determined by choice or will). Our natural, pre-societal freedom does not appeal to Kant in the way it does to Rousseau. Kant agrees with Rousseau that we have come to enjoy a moral freedom in civil society, but with Kant (unlike Rousseau) this is the only freedom which counts. With Rousseau the individual always remains sovereign both in the state of nature and, through the general will, in civil society. But Kant does not accord actual sovereignty to the individual in this way. Since Kant sees freedom as deriving from an externally imposed sovereign in the form of political authority, our participation in the sovereign's power is always notional rather than actual. In Kant's view each individual requires a master, no one can rule her or himself.

Probably another decisive influence upon Kant's appreciation of the social contract – and equally upon his critical philosophy as a whole – was David Hume. In his critical philosophy Kant modelled himself on John Locke and David Hume. He agreed with the view of these British philosophers that no absolute certainty could be attached to the knowledge we derive from observation. And he concluded with Hume that we could not appeal to our past experience, based upon observation, to establish the reality of the social contract. Yet unlike Hume, Kant believes the notion of the social contract still has a central role to play in political philosophy.[5] Kant does not accept Hume's reliance upon custom in the theory of knowledge and ethics. On the contrary, Kant believes that both our knowledge and political philosophy can be rationally grounded.

Classical social contract thinking was at its most influential arguably just at the point when the modern nation-state was emerging. We might then think that it was too tarred with the brush of national politics to serve as a tool either of understanding or recommendation in the present age. The process of globalization appears to threaten the notion of a national or domestic social contract. But the national state is not set to disappear. Individuals still see citizenship primarily in national terms. The subjection of the contemporary state to international influences may mean, however, that in certain key respects contract theory has to be modernized. Some method may have to be devised to take the theory beyond the nation-state context. I suggest that if this is the case then Kant's account of the social contract might be a most useful starting-point.

Kant's account of the social contract fits into the framework of his philosophy as a whole. Kant's political philosophy is a part of his practical (or moral) philosophy which emerges from his *Critique of Pure Reason* and *Critique of Practical Reason*.[6] His political philosophy is presented systematically in the first part of the *Metaphysics of Morals*, which deals with the *Metaphysical First Principles of the Doctrine of Right* (1797). Many of his political ideas had been elaborated earlier in essays such as 'What is Enlightenment?'(1784) and *Perpetual Peace* (1795). In the *Metaphysics of Morals* Kant provides us with a social contract theory shorn of all its empirical trimmings. His social contract theory provides no reference to history nor to any actual conditions where a contract might be taken to be effective. Kant sees the social contract as an exciting but entirely rational concept. The concept fits into our framework of motivation as rational individuals. It is not supposed to describe any existing state of affairs. The concept of the social contract complies with the limits set upon reason in Kant's critique of theoretical knowledge and with the positive value given to our ethical ideals outlined in the *Critique of Practical Reason*.

Kant has his own terminology in accounting for the significance of a concept like the social contract. He regards the social contract as an *a priori idea of pure practical reason*. *A priori* ideas of reason are ideas we have to possess in order to make experience possible. In an empirical sense space and time are such essential ideas which make it possible for us to know objects. In terms of civil society the idea of the social contract is also such an essential idea for without it, it would be impossible for us to experience civil society. The idea of the social contract and the idea of the state go together in Kant's political philosophy. There can be no actual state without the idea of the state being accepted:

> A state (civitas) is a union of a multitude of men under laws of Right. Insofar as these are a priori necessary as laws, that is, insofar as they follow of themselves from concepts of external right as such (are not statutory), its form is the form of a state as such, that is, of the *state as idea*, as it ought to be in accordance with pure principles of right. This idea serves as a norm for every actual union into a commonwealth and as a guiding thread for its inner constitution.⁻

So however we might view the historical origins of an existing state we have to see it as being rationally based upon a set of logically connected concepts. For instance, we might in our picture of the British state give emphasis to its feudal and monarchical origins, perhaps taking a short detour to explain the Civil War, and perhaps the reform of the franchise in the nineteenth century, but this, in Kantian terms, would not be sufficient to justify the state, nor to ground any sense of citizenship on our part. For Kant social cooperation cannot be based solely on matters of fact, even impressive historical matters of fact. Our cooperation has to be founded on some notion of consent.

This is where the social contract comes in:

> The act by which a people forms itself into a state is the original contract. Properly speaking, the original contract is only the idea of this act, in terms of which alone we can think of the legitimacy of a state. In accordance with the original contract, everyone within a people gives up his external freedom in order to take it up again immediately as a member of a commonwealth, that is, of a people considered as a state.[8]

Here we can see the separation between the empirical and the rational coming in again. Whatever the appearance, be it a monarchy, an aristocracy or a democracy, the sensible and persuasive basis of the state is a social contract. If a state is going to work for beings who are both intelligent and physical beings then it has to be seen as rooted in an agreement among equal and free individuals who are able to dispose over their independence in the way they see fit.

From the standpoint of individual freedom the necessity for a social contract becomes apparent to Kant when he is discussing property. Kant is not able to accept a theory of property which relies wholly upon empirical conditions. In keeping with his general philosophy he distinguishes between intelligible and physical possession.[9] All that we can empirically guarantee is the maintenance of our physical possession of an object. Taken solely from the standpoint of observation, an object belongs exclusively to me when I have it on my person or in my grasp. John Locke's theory of property has strongly empirical features of this kind.[10] In John Locke's view, we establish our entitlement to a thing through transforming it with our labour. Agriculturalists demonstrate their ownership over a strip of territory by enclosing it, ploughing it, seeding the land or allowing it to be grazed. Others have then to respect this ownership as the land cannot be regarded as the product of their labour. But such a historical or empirical view of the origins of ownership will not do for Kant. In his view, all that is established by prior labour is physical possession. Property for Kant involves interpersonal recognition and the acceptance of a similar moral and intellectual framework for acting. In short, for there to be property there has first to be intelligible possession.

The notion of intelligible possession is an *a priori* idea of reason. Kant thinks it is impossible to found property solely on observation or understanding: we need also to refer to reason. Reason is a form of thinking which is universal, interpersonal and impartial. Reason is not the reason of one or other individual; Kant sees it as the basis of our collective thinking. Rules of collective thinking and action have to exist for individual thought and action to be possible. For Kant the existence of property is tied to the possibility of action based upon reason. We cannot will that we possess something without at the same time accepting that others may possess objects:

> the rational title of acquisition can lie only in the idea of a will of all united a priori (necessarily to be united) which is here tacitly assumed as a necessary condition; for a unilateral will cannot put others under an obligation they would not otherwise have.[11]

The notion of a social contract underlines the rational basis of property. We have to will that property exists with others in a properly constituted civil society. A united general will has to be assumed for this purpose and we conceive of this general will coming into being through a social contract.

In normative terms Kant presents a very powerful version of the social contract. It is true that in terms of domestic civil society we cannot with Kant enforce the social contract as individuals in the way that Rousseau suggests. Rousseau puts individuals in such a powerful position that they can as part of the general will dissolve the domestic social contract if they feel its conditions are being undermined.[12] Kant will have none of this because he puts the stress as much on the duties that the sovereign incurs from the social contract as upon any rights that might accrue to individuals. But the normative picture is still a powerful one. Both ruler and the subject are bound by a vision of the social contract if they are to see a state realized in practice. Thus, the social contract represents for Kant not an optional way of looking upon political institutions. The idea is just as necessary to our social experience as the representations of time and space are necessary to our life experience. Both the members of the state and individuals who are its sovereign or part of its sovereign body are encouraged by Kant to regard the state as though it were founded upon a social contract. This social contract binds and creates a united general will which makes possible the use of legal coercion. For Kant freedom and the citizenship which arises from it are tied up with the possibility of legal coercion. Because we are limited and fallible creatures Kant believes that we must be subject to the possibility of restraint. If we fail to behave in a way which accords with the liberty of others then we can be legitimately punished by a publicly created authority.

Kant's conception of freedom in a political context accords with the notion of social freedom developed by Rousseau in the *Social Contract*. Rousseau contrasts a primitive pre-social freedom in which we are free in the most unrestricted of senses with a restricted social freedom brought about by the social contract.[13] The first, primitive or natural freedom, may be freedom as it is popularly conceived, as freedom from constraint, but the second is the only possible freedom in a civilized society. And this second kind of freedom is unavoidably connected with the notion of punishment – where we fail to comply with the requirements of peaceful social cooperation. As Rousseau puts it,

> in order that the social compact may not be an empty formula, it tacitly includes the undertaking, which alone can give force to the rest, that whoever refuses to obey the general will shall be compelled to do so by the whole body.[14]

But if the individual member of the state is constrained by the possibility of coercion the sovereign or participants in the sovereign body, such as rulers and ministers, must envisage themselves as limited in their powers by the general will. They should conceive of themselves as rulers and ministers through the general will. They are its agents and for that reason subordinate to it. They are the agents of the general will because they take into account the freedom of all others who are bound by the social contract. So the task of rulers and ministers should not be dictated simply by considerations of enhancing or holding on to their power, rather their focus should be primarily upon their obligations to the society they represent.

One of the main obligations of rulers, as Kant conceives it, is to move their society as rapidly as is possible towards the ideal of a republican government. Where members of the sovereign body are fortunate enough to live in a society which already approximates to the ideal (such as the United States) they are, of course, to strive as far as is possible to maintain the republican form of government. In most societies (as in Britain, for example) the obligation is more one of reform, where the leaders of the governing party should feel it their duty to encourage the division between legislative and executive powers and also to enhance the functioning of legislation. The three authorities of a state for Kant are the legislative power, the executive power and the juridical power. The courts, the government and the legislators should bear a proper relation to one another. As Kant sees it, they are

> subordinate to one another, so that one of them, in assisting another cannot also usurp its function; instead each has its own principle, that is, it indeed commands in its capacity as a particular person, but still under the condition of the will of a superior.[15]

Legislators should not seek to implement the law nor should members of the executive seek to make the law. Rulers should seek to coordinate the society's activities under the law and judges should administer the law in particular instances.

Subjects of the British state would be encouraged by Kant to support their ministers in the work of reform. Where the government seemingly shows little interest in reform enlightened individuals may encourage an interest in the public in republican ideals. This can be done by addressing the public in speeches and publications. But change should not be brought about forcibly. In a legally founded state illegal means of achieving political reform are wholly ruled out by Kant. The participation that a member of a state enjoys in the united general will which maintains the society's solidarity is ideal. The general will cannot be turned into a positive political power separate and hostile to the government. This would imply that the government had ceased to function on behalf of the general will. To try to make it reform by taking violent action would lead to a futile and dangerous confrontation. A bad government has to be persuaded of its duties.

Michael Lessnoff provides a very useful summary of Kant's conception of the social contract. As he says:

> In one way, Kant's conception of the social contract as nothing but an idea of reason considerably weakens its impact; but on the other hand, it greatly broadens its scope. Kant's idea of reason. . . is not a criterion of political obligation. Kant recoils from Rousseau's bold dictum that only derivation from, or conformity to, the (ideal) social contract makes man's political 'chains' legitimate, and still more from his implicit conclusion that we have no obligation to obey powers not legitimate in this sense. Rather, for Kant the idea of the possible social contract is to be taken as a guide by legislators and rulers; it is certainly not to be used by subjects as an excuse for resistance or disobedience. But if Kant's application of the contractarian idea is in this way relatively timid, in another way it is markedly ambitious. The idea of testing political institutions by their conformity to a possible contract of all those subject to them can be very widely applied; and Kant applied it in a considerable variety of ways.[16]

But I have to disagree with Lessnoff's view that Kant fails to see the social contract in terms of political obligation. Kant does see it as part of political obligation but in a novel way. We are obligated both as subjects and rulers to regard our society as though it was established by a social contract no matter how unfair or harsh it appears at a particular time. For Kant we are obligated to any state that appears to be able to maintain law. The grip on law may be tenuous and possibly in some instances the laws themselves might be seen as lacking in justice, nonetheless if there is a reasonable prospect of law being enforced we have to support the legitimacy of that state. But we support its actual legitimacy in terms of the ideal norm of the social contract.

Our obligation is to an ideal which we have to realize in the world and Kant is aware that this can occur under the most difficult of circumstances. The obligation is not to any existing state but rather to an idea of the state. So there is no chance of the one letting the other down, as there is in other theories of political obligation.

There is one other respect in which I should like to modify Lessnoff's account. He argues that Kant sees the social contract as an idea by which to test political institutions. This rather makes the conditions of the social contract sound like the ideal set of examination questions set for candidates for political union. But, according to Kant, neither are citizens nor rulers in a position to set examination questions for the state to pass. Rather the conditions of the social contract represent goals that good rulers and good citizens will seek to achieve. The result of failure to progress along these lines is not punishment for the state and its rulers but punishment for everyone. The task of putting a bad state in order is one for both citizens and rulers. As Kant puts it, 'Therefore a people cannot offer any resistance to the legislative head of a state that would be consistent with right, since a rightful condition is possible only by submission to its general legislative will'.[17]

We are bound by the social contract and the idea of a general will even if we think the state is corrupt. To loosen ourselves as citizens from the ties of such an idea can only make the problems of political legitimacy and social order worse. Rather than lend aid to disruption we should throw in our hand behind a reforming sovereign. As Lessnoff astutely notes, for Kant this conclusion follows naturally from the idea of the social contract.

In comparison with Hobbes, Locke and Rousseau, Kant goes further, for Lessnoff, 'by also using the idea of the social contract as a test of the justice of laws. Laws are to be framed in such a way that they could be consented to by every subject or, rather, citizen'.[18] Indeed for Kant the social contract is the measure of the modern state. All rulers of modern states have to conceive their actions as though they were consented to by their citizens in a common and equal voice. In order to do this rulers should ensure that there is the widest possible public discussion of policies and new laws. Rulers should also encourage the greatest enlightenment of their people and allow academic learning to flourish. The existence of an independent academic or philosophical realm is vital to Kant's conception of the state. If a state is to live up to the ideal of the social contract a critical vigilance has to be maintained. And only by preserving an independent class of learned individuals can such a vigilance be fostered.[19]

So much of Kant's political philosophy is in the categorical mood. This is no accident. It both flows from his critical philosophy and coincides with his view of the role of political thought. The categorical imperative is the key message of Kant's moral philosophy. According to the formulation of this categorical imperative I most favour we are never to treat others solely as means but always also as ends. But this imperative is not a mere accidental or voluntary feature of the human condition. For Kant it is an unavoidable and necessary feature of humanity. This is why he regards it as a categorical imperative. He thinks as a rational being you can no more avoid it than you can avoid breathing. And this categorical imperative structures Kant's moral philosophy just as it structures his political philosophy (of which he sees it a part). Political philosophy has to do with the realization of the categorical imperative in society at large.

The idea of the state which derives from the categorical imperative has not though to be pushed through violently or dogmatically:

> The different forms of states are only the letter of the original legislation in the civil state, and they may therefore remain as long as they are taken, by old and long-standing custom (and so only subjectively), to belong necessarily to the essential machinery of the constitution.[20]

To ensure stability a state may adhere outwardly to its inherited structure. For instance, the people of Britain might quite legitimately maintain for the present a monarchical element within their constitution. However, from the standpoint of political philosophy this ought not permanently to be the case. For, 'the spirit of the original contract involves an obligation on the part of the constituting authority to make the kind of government suited to the idea of the social contract'.[21] And the kind of government which conforms with the social contract is a very specific type, namely, a republic.

> Accordingly, even if this cannot be done at once, [the constituting authority] is under obligation to change the kind of government gradually and continually so that it harmonizes in its effect with the only constitution that accords with right, that of a pure republic, in such a way that the old empirical (statutory) forms, which served merely to bring about the submission of the people, are replaced by the original (rational), the only form that makes freedom the principle and indeed the condition for any exercise of coercion, as is required by a rightful constitution of a state in the strict sense of the word. Only it will lead to what literally is a state.[22]

Thus in terms of our motivation as citizens and the motivation of rulers, the social contract is an unavoidable ideal to which our political actions ought to conform. Whatever the empirical conditions of the state, policy measures should be seen in the light of a possible consensual agreement among citizens about the laws to be passed and enforced.[23]

One unique and final feature of Kant's concept of the social contract is that he extends it beyond the boundaries of states into international relations. This is in keeping with his idea of right which cannot be founded in isolation within one state:

> A league of nations in accordance with the idea of an original social contract is necessary, not in order to meddle in one another's internal

dissensions but to protect against attacks from without. This alliance must, however, involve no sovereign authority (as in a civil constitution), but only an association (federation); it must be an alliance that can be renounced at any time and so must be renewed from time to time.[24]

In Kant's terms no social contract is entirely actual in the sense that its agreement can be empirically observed. It is only effects which can be observed such as legal punishment and property ownership. With the international social contract there is more to observe in terms of agreement, as more and more states join a peaceful federation, but the international contract becomes actual only when we can observe effects such as respect for international law and the ending of war. This raises the possibility that states can participate in the international social contract without formally agreeing to join a peaceful federation. Since what is most important about a social contract are its effects, from Kant's perspective states that add to the effects or benefits of the international social contract might be regarded as making as useful a contribution as those who join the peaceful federation.

Rousseau develops the idea of the social contract in a most sophisticated form but does not at any length attempt to apply it to international society. In his writings on international politics Rousseau seems to think that any association amongst states is bound to break up damagingly because it is not in the self-interest of leaders. Rousseau's conclusions on the prospects for world peace are negative. The goal of a confederation of states is an entirely rational one when looked at from the standpoint of all concerned; however, when viewed from the standpoint of one state in particular, improvement may seem more possible though by a more individualistic route.[25]

Kant does try to extend the idea of an original social contract to international politics. Kant agrees with Hobbes that states in their relations with one another are in a condition of nature. Because they refuse to enter into juridically regulated relations with one another, such states are a standing offence to their fellow states. Kant sees this as a warlike condition which the leaders of states are duty bound to try to overcome. States have to be brought out of their state of nature.

It may seem that this application of the social contract at the international level is highly unrealistic. It is certainly a good deal different from the application of the social contract at the domestic level. But we have to bear in mind that Kant is not looking for an immediate cessation of hostilities and concord. He conceives his plan for *Perpetual Peace* as an inter-generational process. At the domestic level the idea of the social contract denotes a hypothetical state of affairs, suggesting an ideal of how relations among individuals should be ordered. In so far as possible Kant suggests legislation which makes people comply with the ideal of the social contract. Property laws, for instance, ensure you are punished if you steal or remove another's property. But not everything can be legislated for; we can abuse the property of others without having committed a criminal offence. Legally we can be punished for the gross abuse of public property (such as library books or park benches) but we cannot legislate against the simply casual or indifferent treatment of such property which may lead to more rapid wear and tear. Such bad treatment is wrong because it does not concur with the ideal of the social contract which regards us as having originally held everything in common. In this respect we rely on the good will of other individuals to ensure the conditions of the original contract are met. This provides the cement of civil society and backs up the law.

Kant thinks a similar spirit should underlie the attitude of the leaders of states to international politics. Just as the ideal of the social contract underpins social solidarity in domestic society (the reality of this solidarity is strengthened of course by the possibility of punishment) so the ideal of the social contract amongst states should guide action in international politics. As Kant sees it, the domestic contract itself requires the international sphere to be seen in this way. When Kant derives property with the help of the notion of a social contract he regards the title he establishes in a civil society as provisional only. It is provisional until such time as all human society is established under a civil union. Some states approximate to this civil union through having republican constitutions, but not even they found property in a wholly secure way because even republican states find themselves in a state of nature in relation to other states. Thus property right 'even if it is solved through the original contract, such acquisition will remain only provisional unless this contract extends to the entire human race'.[26]

The requirements of this international social contract would be similar to those of the domestic social contract. In the first place, states would be required to respect one another's property as though it had been shared out according to right on the basis of an original common ownership. Property in this context would imply not only the state's territory but also its resources, treasures and historic monuments and buildings. Second, just as citizens living under a domestic social contract are expected to respect the sovereignty of the state standing over them so the member states of the international society are expected to respect the moral authority of the international community. Since no actual international community exists, the leaders of states would be expected to join with others in a peaceful federation to work towards such a mutual international authority. Here, then, something different is being done with the idea of contract. But the international social contract authority would never be complete and therefore never be entirely analogous with domestic sovereignty. We might see the contract in the international sphere as more of an actual historical event, unlike in the domestic sphere. But it is not an event that occurs once and is over and done with. In contrast to the domestic social contract the international social contract can always be dissolved by its members and, if necessary, be reconstituted. However, it cannot be dissolved indefinitely because a measure of agreement on an international social contract, as outlined in Kant's conditions for *Perpetual Peace*, remains the foundation for a flourishing domestic society.

Kant has a well-deserved place in the history of social contract theory and in its present revival. But his attitude to the social contract is, in one key respect, somewhat different from most other thinkers belonging to the tradition and those seeking now to continue it. For the contemporary representative of the tradition, like John Rawls, the contract has to be viewed hypothetically as the tacit basis for social cooperation whereas for Kant we have to view the contract both hypothetically and categorically. Classical social contract thinkers like Locke and Rousseau do not distinguish very carefully between the historical origin of civil society and the hypothetical origin they deduce in the social contract. Part of the advantage of this was that a greater necessity might possibly cling to the contract if it might be seen (however tentatively) as belonging to the actual origins of a society. In his account of the social contract Kant removes this empirical foundation and distinguishes clearly between our rational grounding of society in the contract and its factual origins.

But Kant does not want to consign the contract to the pure realm of hypothesis. It is indeed an imaginative construct, much as is John Rawls's theory of justice, but it is not an imaginative construct that is simply a programme for society. With Kant the notion of a social contract is in moral terms constructive of a civil society because a civil society comes into being for Kant only in so far as we act as moral (or rational) agents. So for Kant it is not a question of our happily imagining a social contract as taking place if we want best to feel at home in civil society, rather we can belong to a civil society only in so far as we conceive ourselves as being bound by an original contract. In empirical terms it is not necessary for individuals to adhere to the idea of the social contract, but in moral terms it is absolutely necessary they do so. A civil society will in practice dissolve where its members cease to regard themselves as being bound by an original contract.

I will illuminate this distinction between the social contract being merely hypothetically necessary and its being categorically necessary by looking at the distinction Kant makes between hypothetical and categorical imperatives in the *Groundwork of the Metaphysics of Morals*. Here, he says,

> hypothetical imperatives declare a possible action to be practically necessary as a means to the attainment of something else one wills (or that one may will). A categorical imperative would be one which represented an action as objectively necessary in itself apart from its relation to a further end.[27]

Just as Kant regards the categorical imperative as a condition of willing in general so the recognition of the the social contract may be regarded not only as a means to the end of enjoying the advantages of civil society but also as a precondition for acting in a properly constituted society. As Kant sees it, the acceptance by the citizen of the idea of the social contract is no mere act of prudence. It may indeed enhance the individual's happiness to behave in a manner conditioned by the notion of a social contract. But the attainment of happiness is here subordinate to the more basic objective which is the possibility of any settled social life for all concerned. In his own terms Kant would see the notion of a social contract not as 'an assertoric practical principle' but as an 'apodeictic practical principle'.[28] The notion is not simply one that it is desirable for us to hold concerning civil society, it is its absolutely necessary foundation.

NOTES

1 Cf. P. Riley, 'On Kant as the Most Adequate of the Social Contract Theorists', *Political Theory*, 1973, vol. 1, pp. 450–71

2 *Metaphysics of Morals*, M. Gregor (trans.), Cambridge, Cambridge University Press, 1992, p. 152; *Akademie Ausgabe*, (hereafter *AA*) Berlin, 1901–68, vol. 6, p. 346.

3 J. Locke, *Two Treatises of Government*, London, Dent, 1977, p. 130:

> Though the earth and all inferior creatures be common to all men, yet every man has a 'property' in his own 'person'. This nobody has any right to but himself. The 'labour' of his body and the 'work' of his hands, we may say are properly his. Whatsoever, then, he removes out of the state that Nature hath provided and left it in, he hath mixed his labour with it, and joined it to something that is his own, and thereby makes it his property.

4 *Metaphysics of Morals*, p. 125; *AA*, vol. 6, p. 313. Cf. Howard Williams, *Kant's Political Philosophy*, Oxford, Basil Blackwell, 1983, p. 172.

5 Cf. D. Miller, *Philosophy and Ideology: Hume's Political Thought*, Oxford, Oxford University Press, 1981, pp. 78–80; Williams, *Kant's Political Philosophy*, pp. 167–9.

6 W. Kersting, 'Politics, Freedom, and Order: Kant's Political Philosophy', *Cambridge Companion to Kant*, P. Guyer (ed.), Cambridge, Cambridge University Press, 1992, pp. 342–3

7 *Metaphysics of Morals*, p. 125; *AA*, vol. 6, p. 313.

8 *Metaphysics of Morals*, p. 131; *AA*, vol. 6, p. 315.

9 *Metaphysics of Morals*, pp. 73–4; *AA*, vol. 6, pp. 251–2.

10 J. Locke, 'He that is nourished by the acorns he picked up under an oak, or the apples he gathered from the trees in the wood, has certainly appropriated them to himself . . . . And it is plain, if the first gathering made them not his, nothing else could': *Two Treatises of Government*, p. 130

11 *Metaphysics of Morals*, p. 85; *AA*, vol. 6, p. 264.

12 *Social Contract*, ch. 2, book 2, 'That sovereignty is inalienable', London, Dent, 1968, pp. 20–1.

13 *Social Contract*, p. 16.

14 *Social Contract*, p. 15.

15 *Metaphysics of Morals*, p. 127; *AA*, vol. 6, p. 316.

16 M. Lessnoff, *Social Contract*, London, Macmillan, 1986, p. 13.

17 *Metaphysics of Morals*, p. 131; *AA*, vol. 6, p. 131.

18 Lessnoff, *Social Contract*, p. 92. Cf. W. Kersting, *Wohlgeordnete Freiheit*, Frankfurt am Main, Suhrkamp, 1993, pp. 23–46.

19 *Perpetual Peace* in *Kant Selections*, L.W. Beck (ed.), London, Macmillan, 1988, p. 445; *AA*, vol. 8, p. 368.

20 *Metaphysics of Morals*, p. 148; *AA*, vol. 6, p. 340.
21 *Metaphysics of Morals*, p. 148; *AA*, vol. 6, p. 340.
22 *Metaphysics of Morals*, p. 148; *AA*, vol. 6, p. 340.
23 'Finally, we may remind ourselves that the hypothetical nature of the original position invites the question: why should we take any interest in it, moral or otherwise? Recall the answer: the conditions embodied in the description of this situation are ones that we do in fact accept': J. Rawls, *A Theory of Justice*, Oxford, Oxford University Press, 1972, p. 587.
24 *Metaphysics of Morals*, p. 151; *AA*, vol. 6, p. 344.
25 Cf. H. Williams, *International Relations in Political Theory*, Buckingham, Open University Press, 1991, p. 78.
26 *Metaphysics of Morals*, p. 87; *AA*, vol. 6, p. 266.
27 *Groundwork of the Metaphysics of Morals*, H. J. Paton, (trans.) New York, Harper, 1964, p. 82; *AA*, vol. 4, p. 414.
28 Groundwork, p. 82; *AA*, vol. 4, p. 415.

8   Hegel's critique of the theory of social contract

Bruce Haddock

That Hegel was in some sense a critic of social contract theory is beyond dispute. Indeed he was widely regarded, especially by an earlier generation of political theorists, as the philosopher who had most effectively undermined the doctrine's credibility. Gough, for example, in his classic study of the different guises assumed by the social contract from antiquity to modern times, admits that Hegel's 'portrait of human life is closer to history and reality than the abstractions of the contractarian school' and that he had 'enunciated a political philosophy totally at variance with everything' the social contract tradition had stood for.[1] Lessnoff has reiterated the point, arguing that, in Hegel's view, contract 'fails to do justice to the grandeur and majesty of the state, and the obligations it is thereby entitled to impose on the individual'.[2] The claim is that the community, and the state which expresses the identity of that community, logically and actually precedes the individual constituents of the community. It may be possible to regard individuals in some aspects of their lives as narrowly self-interested calculators of advantage; and in these spheres it might be proper to invoke the image of contract as a means of rendering their mutual relations intelligible. But contractual relations at the micro-level presuppose wider bonds which are not themselves contractual. To treat the state itself as the product of an actual or even hypothetical contract would thus invert the logical relationship which obtains between contractual and other obligations. Far from helping to clarify our understanding of political obligation, contractual language would actually muddy the issue, confusing our duty to fulfil voluntarily incurred commitments with the grounds for the fulfilment of our duties. Taken in conjunction with Hegel's more general insistence that cultures, practices, institutions, and so on should be seen as products of a progressively emerging historical process, these theoretical arguments would seem to make the idea of contract redundant. It could serve neither as a historical explanation of the establishment of states nor as a hypothetical explanation of the basis of obligation to the state.

Such is the received wisdom on Hegel's view of social contract theory. And it is certainly the case that arguments along these lines can be found in the *Philosophy of Right*. But there is another side to the story which is less often noticed. Despite his objections to full-blown contract theory, Hegel retains some contractualist language in his depiction of the necessity of the state. I am not thinking here exclusively of the section devoted to contract in the *Philosophy of Right*, where Hegel's attention is focused largely on contract in relation to property and day-to-day dealings.[3] The more interesting issue concerns the significance of mutual recognition in Hegel's theory of the state. The sort of relationship that Hegel wants to defend between the individual and the state depends upon the individual seeing the state as somehow an expression of his nature. The state must be regarded as the conceptual embodiment of the many ties that bind us to our communities. And a crucial dimension in the genesis of this awareness stems from recognition of a common social identity and interest in situations which are potentially unstable and threatening. My principal concern in this chapter, accordingly, is to explain not only why Hegel rejected contractual theories of the state but also why he retained some of the language and assumptions of social contract theory.

Before looking at Hegel's response to social contract theory, however, it is as well to characterize more precisely the nature of the beast he was confronting. If the idea of contract is treated elastically, it can be stretched to embrace a bewildering array of consensual theories of obligation. Ritchie, for example, in his excellent survey, begins with Socrates' refusal in the *Crito* to breach the tacit understanding (the Jowett translation gives 'implied contract') which binds individuals to the state, and proceeds to trace the fortune of different forms of contract, pact or consent through the Bible, Roman law and medieval controversies on the proper limits and authority of *imperium* and *sacerdotium*, to the more familiar contractual arguments of Hobbes, Locke and Rousseau.[4] Clearly the sorts of understandings which are being highlighted in these many and varied formulations are markedly diverse. It might be argued that what we are dealing with here is not different versions of one theory but a series of discrete theoretical positions which happen to deploy a number of common terms. It would surely be extending interpretative indulgence too far to equate Socrates' claim that we incur obligations through the continued enjoyment of public benefits with Rousseau's insistence that we could properly be under obligation only to a virtuous community.[5] Augustine may have been going too far when he likened 'petty kingdoms' to 'criminal gangs'; but his characterization of what constitutes a gang invoked orthodox contractualist assumptions ('a gang is a group of men under the command of a leader, bound by a compact of association, in which the plunder is divided according to an agreed convention').[6] Was the agreement struck between the elders of Israel to constitute David their king of a similar kind?[7] And what of God's promise to Noah not to destroy the world if certain conditions were fulfilled?[8] If this is to be construed as a contractual agreement, it is an agreement of a remarkable kind. The inequality of the contracting parties rules out any notion of reciprocity. Yet Noah and his progeny do receive benefits in return for proper conduct. And though God may no more be a fit and proper person to be a party to a contract than Hobbes's sovereign, the latter is nevertheless constituted by a contract and the former voluntarily incurs obligations.[9]

Social contract theory is thus a hydra-headed monster. Just as it is impossible to treat different versions of the theory as variations on a common theme, so specific objections will not be equally telling against each formulation. The problem is complicated in Hegel's case because he seldom dismisses an argument in straightforward fashion. His tactic is generally to treat particular positions as one-sided expressions of truths which are more adequately handled in more developed theoretical contexts. With this proviso in mind, however, it is nevertheless clear that his reservations about contractual theories of the state would not necessarily apply to the idea of tacit consent, though he nowhere uses that term. What he specifically objects to is the contention that obligation to the state should be regarded as similar in kind to obligation to a voluntary association, where we may (or may not) agree to set up or join an association to secure limited advantages. Our commitment to an association, in this scheme of things, would extend no further than our narrowly defined interest. A change of heart or predilection would simply lead us to focus our efforts and resources elsewhere. We would refuse to renew our subscriptions. Our (limited) commitments could be transferred to other associations. And so we would continue, until infirmity or death put an end to the pursuit of any satisfactions whatever.

In the passages of the *Philosophy of Right* where Hegel focuses directly on social contract theory, he emphasizes the arbitrariness of contractual decisions. In his fullest discussion of contract in the conventional legal sense, he highlights the contingent identity of the wills of two contracting parties, expressed in a common interest in a particular object.[10] The contracting parties happen to agree on the value of an object. In all other respects they are utterly indifferent to one another.

Can such a relationship be seen as the hypothetical archetype depicting a modern citizen's relationship with the state? Hegel's answer is emphatically no. He sees contractual relationships as specifically private. In the feudal period, Hegel grants, 'political rights and duties were regarded as, and declared to be, the immediate private property of particular individuals in opposition to the right of the sovereign and the state'.[11] But he denies categorically that the 'rights of the sovereign and the state' should be regarded as the product of 'the arbitrary will of those who have combined to form a state'.[12] In this respect, it makes no difference 'whether it is assumed that the state is a contract of all with all, or a contract of all with the sovereign and government'.[13] In each case, the presuppositions of the sphere of private property would have been transferred to the qualitatively distinct realm of ethical life and the state.

Why should the presuppositions of private engagements be inapplicable in relation to the state? Orthodox opponents of social contract, for whom the state is a *datum* from which our moral and political thinking begins, have no problem with the question. Filmer and Burke, for example, in their different ways, treat the rights and advantages that we enjoy in civil society as a product of the political order which is imposed upon us.[14] In this view, we do not choose to be members of a state and can do little or nothing, as individuals, to alter the configuration of relations within it. Hence it makes no sense to invoke a conception of arbitrary agreement in order to explain political obligation.

Hegel's position, however, is much more complex. He accepts that the state is a *factum*, a product of human endeavour and in some sense an expression of human nature. What he is unhappy with is the kind of willing involved in the making of contracts. The identity of interest between contracting parties extends no further than the object at the centre of their transaction. In Hegel's terminology, derived from Roman law, this is merely a 'common will'.[15] The state, however, in his view, is a genuine unity, embracing an entire institutional and cultural context. Haphazard agreement on specific ends cannot create this sort of unity but rather depends upon it. As Hegel puts the point, 'the individual is already by nature a citizen' of the state.[16] It is thus absurd to suppose 'that the arbitrary will of everyone is capable of founding a state' since 'it is absolutely necessary for each individual to live within the state'.[17] The necessity in question here is both logical and actual. And relationships based upon necessity cannot be explained in terms of the happenchance of individual decision.

But if it is wrong to base the state on the contingent wills of individuals, will in a different sense is nevertheless the basis of the state. Individuals acquire self-awareness in an institutional framework and, by degrees, recognize that institutional framework as the public face of their personal identities. Hegel describes the state as 'the actuality of the substantial will, an actuality which it possesses in the particular self-consciousness when this has been raised to its universality'.[18] Crucially, however, the will in question here is 'rational in and for itself' and the state which embodies it is an 'absolute and unmoved end in itself'.[19] What Hegel cannot allow is that an unmoved end in itself, the necessary condition for the fulfilment of individuals, should be dependent upon individual caprice.

Rousseau is singled out as the most influential modern propagator of this fundamental misconception of the relationship between state and individual. In Hegel's account, Rousseau is said to base the state upon the 'will and spirit' of the 'particular individual. . . in his distinctive arbitrariness', rather than on the 'rational will which has being in and for itself'.[20] Hegel grants that Rousseau has 'put forward the will as the principle of the state'; but while Rousseau's perspective is limited to the 'determinate form of the individual will', his argument is vulnerable to the objections which Hegel had previously advanced against contractual theories of the state.[21] The agreement of individuals, even the unanimous agreement of all members of a community, would still be an entirely contingent affair. A state so constituted might be regarded as authorized to proceed no further than the opinions of its members in its institutions and policies. And if these opinions should prove to be fickle, the state itself would be as insubstantial as a passing fancy. Any government-imposed limitation could be treated as illegitimate. A political form constituted by arbitrary agreement would thus be inherently unstable. Successive attempts in the French revolutionary period to erect a state on the sort of foundation proposed by Rousseau had issued in nothing but a 'fury of destruction'.[22] Failure in these cases Hegel interpreted as a direct consequence of theoretical error.

Whether or not Hegel's interpretation of Rousseau is defensible is quite another question. He consistently disregards Rousseau's crucial distinction between the general will and the will of all.[23] And though it may be the case that Rousseau's characterization of the general will fails to meet Hegel's stringent requirements (Rousseau does, after all, equate the general will with the common interest of the community, where Hegel insists that unity in the state must transcend the accidental coincidence of shared interests), it is nevertheless misleading to claim that the general will is arbitrary and capricious. It was precisely the capriciousness of individual willing that Rousseau had sought to overcome with his distinction. His insistence, indeed, 'that the general will is always rightful and always tends to the public good' might have been supposed to have gone at least some of the way towards meeting Hegel's requirements.[24]

Hegel, however, both in the *Philosophy of Right* and in the much fuller statement in his *Lectures on the History of Philosophy*, misses the point.[25] He welcomes Rousseau's attempt to portray the state as the realization of freedom, but denies that freedom can be properly discussed without invoking a notion of rationality. He insists, for example, 'that the notion of freedom must not be taken in the sense of the arbitrary caprice of an individual, but in the sense of the rational will, of the will in and for itself'.[26] But this is precisely what Rousseau himself had argued when he contrasted civil and natural liberty. To rest content with natural liberty, in Rousseau's scheme of things, is to remain a creature 'governed by appetite alone' and hence a slave to one's passions, while moral freedom in a properly constituted community 'makes man the master of himself' by introducing the idea of obedience to a self-prescribed law.[27]

That Hegel is guilty of a serious misreading of Rousseau is evident. But he does still have some textual justification for his charge that Rousseau's conception is too narrowly individualistic in form. Rousseau had characterized his task as the pursuit of 'a form of association which will defend the person and goods of each member with the collective force of all, and under which each individual, while uniting himself with the others, obeys no one but himself, and remains as free as before'.[28] Hegel reads this section as if Rousseau were arguing that the protection of property and personal security are the primary goals of the state. In other words, 'the interest of individuals as such' would be regarded as 'the ultimate end for which they are uniting', while the stress on 'uniting' for such specific ends suggests 'that membership of the state is an optional matter'.[29] Hegel denies both propositions. He contends that 'it is only through being a member of the state that the individual' could lead what he calls a 'universal life'.[30] Far from the state existing simply to further the mundane ends of practical life, Hegel argues that the state confers moral significance on pursuits which would otherwise be ephemeral. The real paradox is that Rousseau himself might very well have assented to Hegel's corrective reading of the proper relationship between state and individual, though one suspects he would not have been happy with the language in which the argument is expressed.[31]

So far we have been on fairly familiar ground. Given Hegel's basic assumptions about human agency and development, it could not be expected that he would endorse even a modified version of the social contract model in his account of political obligation. But having rejected what might be termed 'arbitrary consent', Hegel is left with a problem in finding a theoretical framework which is sufficiently flexible to embrace both the community and human agency as mutually supportive dimensions of a theory of politics. Where conservative or reactionary theorists had responded to the challenge of the French Revolution by reasserting the logical and historical priority of the state and the community, Hegel sought to show that the distinctive form of the modern state depended upon a tight relationship between the conceptions we form of ourselves as individuals and the conceptions we form of the public life of our communities. How this (essentially symbiotic) relationship is characterized is crucial to Hegel's theory. He had rejected Rousseau and the contractualists because their stress on individual choice made the state accidental. But it is equally the case that the claims of the community and the state can be exaggerated, leaving individuals as accidents in relation to the state's massive historical substance. In the text of the *Philosophy of Right* Hegel is at pains to guard against the latter tendency quite as much as the former. The residual contractual language which is evident in the text should be read in the light of this concern.

What must be stressed is that Hegel's case against contract is based upon a reworking, rather than a straightforward dismissal, of the currently available theories of political artifice. He did not treat the state as a natural phenomenon, nor our obligation to the state as a simple extension of the bonds of affection which tie us to our families, friends, localities, and so on. This is not to say that he regarded such bonds as altogether irrelevant to discussions of political obligation, only that he found the image of natural obligation inadequate in relation to the gamut of our public roles, rights, responsibilities and duties.

Hegel's specific discussions of natural obligation are instructive. In the *Lectures on the History of Philosophy* and the *Lectures on the Philosophy of History* he considers at some length the original harmony of early Greek culture, wherein an individual could envisage no other life for himself than that specified by the customs and traditions of the community.[32] A citizen's identification with the community as an Athenian was complete. The accident of birth distinguished Greeks from one another and from the wider barbarian world. Religious, moral and political obligations were handed down within the community and accepted unquestioningly. With the rise of philosophical criticism, however, a new and destructive spirit had emerged, epitomized for Hegel in the sophist school. It represented a challenge not simply to the state but also to the wider conception of what it means to be a human being. Ultimately the new spirit of criticism and individual judgement would undermine the *polis* as a form of association. People were enabled to think of their lives in terms of a potentially universal religious fellowship, buttressed by a legal framework that facilitated practical engagements between individuals and communities which might be utterly indifferent to one another.

Hegel's response to this new phenomenon is subtle and distinctive. He saw Plato's *Republic* as an attempt to restore the *status quo ante*. Plato, argues Hegel, was 'aware that the ethics of his time were being penetrated by a deeper principle which, within this context, could appear immediately only as an as yet unsatisfied longing and hence only as a destructive force'.[33] As a self-conscious attempt to restore the earlier integral community, it had necessarily to assume an authoritarian form. Even Socrates' death was seen in a positive light by Hegel. It highlighted a crucial point in the demise of a way of life. The political and moral implications of the Socratic revolution would not yet be clear; but the Athenian community could nevertheless deplore the critical assault on its culture and identity.[34]

Looking back on the Socratic crisis, Hegel recognized both the folly and necessity of Plato's reaction. He saw that Plato's attempt to extirpate criticism from the community had 'inflicted the gravest damage on the deeper drive behind it', namely the emergence of 'free infinite personality'.[35] But the principles he focused on proved to be 'the pivot on which the impending world revolution turned'.[36] When he responded to the dangerously subjective political currents in his own day, Hegel adopted the same balanced view. He accepted that the craving for individual satisfaction was a necessary feature of the modern state, though left to itself it could be endlessly destructive. But denying the right of individuals to fashion the state anew on the merest fancy did not involve an unthinking acceptance of the *status quo*. The passage in the *Philosophy of Right* where Hegel dismisses von Haller's attempt to portray the state as a simple natural fact is among the sharpest and most vehement in the text.[37] For Hegel the state is the product of human endeavour, though that endeavour is mediated in complex institutional channels. Individuals will demand fulfilment from the state. The task for philosophy is to explain what that fulfilment essentially involves.

In the modern context natural obligation retains its significance in family life.[38] Here, again, Hegel is careful to balance apparently contrasting sides to the argument. Though he sees the state as the apex of a network of institutional relationships, he is anxious not to reduce it to any of the subordinate institutions which sustain it. Marriage and family life are thus crucial to our development as human beings; but they do not exhaust our potential and sometimes need to be set on one side as we engage in wider economic, social and political pursuits. Hegel cannot follow Adam Müller, for example, who explains our obligation to the state in terms of an intricate web of family relationships which extend outward as the organization of civil life becomes more complex.[39] But neither can he accept Kant's interpretation of marriage as a civil contract designed to secure for men and women 'the reciprocal enjoyment of one another's sexual attributes'.[40] Granting that the origin of marriage is to be sought in the 'free consent of the persons concerned', Hegel argues that it must be seen as a special sort of agreement in which individuals 'give up their natural and individual personalities' within the union.[41] Love, we might say, transcends contract. And while Hegel admits that some of the feelings we have for our communities might be akin to love in certain respects, we cannot suspend our critical judgement and seal ourselves in an emotional cocoon. As lovers we can forgive the petty failings and peccadilloes of our partners. But as children we grow up and learn to see our parents in critical perspective. So it is with the state. We might first encounter organized institutional life in the family but we cannot remain bound by its perspective.

It is clear, then, that Hegel had fundamental objections to the two dominant conceptions of the state current in his day. He equated the contractarian view with endemic institutional instability. But the alternative account, which saw the state as the natural ground of all our strivings and enjoyments, placed insufficient emphasis on an individual's self-conscious identification with an institutionally differentiated community. Hegel wants us to accept that we cannot see ourselves as other than the products of established communities; but at the same time he insists that our institutions are artefacts rather than natural facts. The way we make institutions is, of course, very different from the way we make other artefacts. I may decide to make a table or pot as I please. Our institutional life is a much more complex affair. We learn to find our way around a world of practices and procedures. In confronting established practices, however, we both adapt ourselves and (subtly) mould our institutions. The fact that so many of us are involved in a bewildering network of engagements means that the institutional 'product' of our efforts will never be quite what we might have anticipated. But we remain the makers of our institutions, even if we do not make them exactly as we choose.

The significance of contract in this context should be evident. As a conceptual device it enables Hegel to set self-interested individual pursuits in a social framework without departing too far from the accepted legal understanding of the term. His larger concern is to show how the familiar institutions and conventions of our society are no more separable from us than our personal characteristics. But he builds his argument up from an analysis of the presuppositions of the notions of will and agency. If we are to think in terms of human beings making choices or doing things, for example, and Hegel argues that we find it very hard not to, then what sorts of institutional and cultural assumptions need to be invoked? The point can be put somewhat differently if we ask how we can possibly see ourselves as individuals. Hegel's response is emphatic. To see ourselves as individuals presupposes that we exist in a world of other individuals. At the very least, we must see ourselves as 'persons', that is, as potential bearers of rights. This is the sphere of what Hegel calls 'abstract right'.[42] It is a sphere characterized by legal or social recognition rather than developed relationships. Hegel sums up the 'commandment of right' as: 'Be a person and respect others as persons'.[43] We remain mutually indifferent at this level but cannot do without one another if we are to have any conception of ourselves at all.

But it is not enough to be simply potential bearers of rights. Recognition requires a public identity. As Hegel puts the point, a 'person must give himself an external sphere of freedom in order to have being as Idea'.[44] This external sphere is the realm of private property. We each have an 'absolute right of appropriation. . . over all things' which we express by a manifest act of will.[45] What we gain through property, however, is not merely the use and enjoyment of things but an 'embodiment of personality'.[46]

Yet we cannot identify our personalities unconditionally with the things we happen to own. Ownership, as an expression of will, presupposes a capacity to sell or transfer possession of a thing where that thing no longer reflects the identity of its owner. Divesting ourselves of things thus involves us in relationships with others. In contracting to buy or sell, for example, we necessarily recognize others as 'persons and owners of property'.[47] Hegel describes 'this relation of will to will' as 'the true distinctive ground in which freedom has its existence'.[48] In place of the straightforward relation between ourselves and the things we use and enjoy, we now have a complex relationship between agents who have chosen to 'embody' their personalities in particular ways.

What should be noticed here is that the conventional legal sense of contract can carry a heavier philosophical burden. Hegel's primary concern, after all, is not to propose a legal framework which might facilitate buying and selling but rather to analyse what we need to presuppose about other people in order to understand ourselves. The crucial requirement he comes up with is mutual recognition. The passages on property and contract in the *Philosophy of Right* should, in fact, be read in conjunction with his discussion of the emergence of self-consciousness in the *Phenomenology of Spirit.*[49] Hegel posits an initial situation in which men are aware of themselves only in contrast to nature. Nature is potentially hostile but they are able to transform it to satisfy (at least) some of their needs. But nature lacks any intrinsic significance beyond its capacity as a means to fulfil men's ends. It is only when we find our awareness of our own independence recognized by another individual with similar aspirations that we can attain self-consciousness. But this need for recognition involves inevitable conflict because individuals regard themselves as (in principle) unlimited. We want to describe our relations with one another in the same instrumental terms which we use to describe our relations with nature. The upshot is a conflict which can be resolved only when an individual asserts his independence to the extent of risking his life in order to subordinate another to his own desires.

This, essentially, is how Hegel sees the origin of lordship and bondage in the ancient world. The vanquished party in the struggle becomes a slave ministering to the capricious whims of his master. Such a relationship, however, cannot satisfy the master's initial yearning for recognition. By reducing the slave to the status of an instrument the master is denied the respect of an equal. The slave, on the other hand, though his condition is abject, has at least the satisfaction of working for a master whose moral superiority he implicitly acknowledged in the initial struggle. Yet the discipline of work, imposed on the slave against his wishes, proves to be an educational (and finally liberating) experience. In seeking to meet the demands of his master, the slave learns to transform nature. Though he is restrained, the slave continues to assert his independence of nature. The master, on the other hand, finds that he has become completely dependent on the slave's skill to satisfy his appetite. Neither party to the relationship can be called free because each manifests only an aspect of self-conscious freedom. But the self-understanding of both master and slave has been generated by the peculiar terms of their mutual recognition.

The relationship between master and slave cannot be described as contractual in the narrow sense. But it does rest upon a shared understanding. Whether or not it would be helpful to invoke a notion of tacit consent in this context is beyond my present concern. It is important to stress, however, that the slave's subordination to the master depends upon his acceptance of the relationship which obtains between them. Hegel explains in detail in the *Phenomenology* how the terms of reference of ancient culture collapsed and generated alternative ways of conceiving social and political relationships. Stoic and Christian ideas, for example, stressed a universal humanity which transcended community or status distinctions. These new ideas enabled people not only to respond differently to one another but also to see themselves in a new light. Mutual recognition retains its significance, though a developing cultural context furnishes previously inconceivable possibilities for conduct and understanding.

In the *Encyclopaedia of the Philosophical Sciences* Hegel describes the struggle between master and slave as the source of a specifically political relationship. He accepts that the form in which the struggle manifested itself could 'only occur in the natural state'.[50] In a developed state, 'the spirit of the people, custom and law' confer recognition on individuals in their various guises.[51] But a presupposition of that diversity is that individuals should at least recognize each other as rational, free persons, in other words, as potential bearers of rights. What master and slave had sought in their initial confrontation was the recognition of equals. The terms on which they resolved their differences could not satisfy that aspiration. But 'although the state may originate in violence', Hegel contends that 'it does not rest on it'.[52] What might have been murky in its beginnings is later justified in terms of wider possibilities for the fulfilment of human potential. The point to emphasize here, however, is that even in its violent foundations, the state is still the product of agreement and (limited) understanding. The state develops progressively as an ever more complex work of artifice. It serves not only as a practical means for satisfying various needs but also as a necessary condition for self-understanding. It thus constitutes 'the shape of reciprocity' in which individuals can recognize their freedom, individuality and mutual involvement.[53]

Citizens in the modern state contracting to buy and sell are thus the beneficiaries of a complex philosophical and moral tradition. What at first glance seems to be an engagement to transfer the ownership of an object on mutually agreeable terms turns out on closer inspection to be an indispensable dimension in the fashioning of personal and social identity. We cannot do without one another in this larger engagement; but neither can we accept any longer the wilful subordination that characterized slavery in the ancient world. Confronting each other as indifferent bearers of legal rights is a necessary condition for the emergence of the complex characters we are, settled in relation to the very many possibilities open to us yet flexible as we respond to specific situations. Contract, in this scheme of things, must be seen as an enabling device. It leaves the future notionally open ended, while tying us down to specific social procedures and practices. Procedures and practices may themselves change as societies develop. As Hegelian philosophers, however, we are limited to an understanding of the here and now. How we might see ourselves in a radically different world is a question philosophy cannot answer.[54]

When Hegel rejects, then, social contract as the grounding principle of the state, it should not be supposed that he is confining contract to the narrow economic sphere. His concern, rather, is to link individual striving with the wider community framework. Within the social contract tradition, especially in its seventeenth- and eighteenth-century forms, contract was often invoked as a means of distinguishing legitimate from illegitimate polities. Hegel approaches contract from a different angle. He is anxious not so much to defend individuals from the incursions of a legally limitless state as to examine the institutional conditions which enable individuals to flourish. His conception of institutions is so broad that he ranges across a wealth of administrative, sociological and economic material that would not normally find a place in a work of political philosophy. Within this context, contract performs a subordinate but significant role. It enables him to portray the state as an artefact without reducing it to the terms of an arbitrary consensus.

What needs to be emphasized, however, is that Hegel's rejection of an atomistic theory of politics should not be read as an unqualified rejection of individualism. Hegel's discussions of abstract right, morality and civil society were certainly designed to highlight the limitations of narrowly individualistic theoretical frameworks. But he was not arguing for anything like the restoration of the pre-Socratic community. His concern was to stress the social sources of a certain conception of individuality rather than to dismiss individual identity as a misleading theoretical fiction. It is surely significant that he did not endorse the integral communitarian critique of the French Revolution, despite his deep misgivings about the political instability unleashed by untrammelled individualism.

Nor has Hegel's position lost any of its relevance today. His arguments have often been invoked, along with Aristotle's, in communitarian critiques of liberal individualism. And, within the terms of this chapter, we can easily see why this might be so. A radically disembodied self is no more intelligible to Hegel than it is to (say) MacIntyre or Sandel.[55] Hegel accepts (with modern communitarians) that the self is a social product. But he argues vigorously that the individuality of a self is one of its principal guises in modern times. His case is thus that the philosophical grounds advanced by Hobbes, Locke and their progeny in defence of individualism are mistaken, not that a differently conceived individualism cannot be defended.

Hegel thus occupies a distinctive position within the gamut of communitarian arguments. While in broad terms he resurrects a teleological (neo-Aristotelian) account of human conduct, he does not go so far as to explain individual identity exclusively in relation to the performance of social functions. He insists that agents are the makers of the social world (albeit in complex and largely indirect ways) and not simply its products or vehicles. The contention is that we cannot conceive of agents outside a social context, not that we have to treat agency within the exclusive terms of reference of particular communities.

This modification of the communitarian position has far-reaching evaluative implications. Modern communitarians (MacIntyre and Sandel may again be taken as examples) have largely endorsed the view that particular community-based conceptions of the good are incommensurable. If, in Sandel's terms, a conception of the good is constitutive of my identity, it is simply not available to me to rank alternative conceptions of the good as possible options for me. I may well be able to learn something about myself from other conceptions of the good. But conceptions of the good are not preferences. Within a given conception of the good I will have various priorities. In another evaluative framework, however, these priorities may be meaningless.[56]

MacIntyre broadens the context to embrace not simply particular community-based conceptions of the good but larger traditions of moral understanding. He does not contend that each identifiable tradition constitutes a completely sealed universe of discourse. A commitment to logical argument within traditions will enable moral protagonists to understand one another even if incompatible grounding assumptions prevent moral agreement. Traditions can also be tentatively ranked in terms of their scope, durability and flexibility. MacIntyre consistently champions the Aristotelian/Thomist tradition against all versions of individualism. The Enlightenment tradition is rejected not simply because he happens not to like it but also because it is built upon an impoverished account of individual identity. In the last resort, however, argument between traditions is illustrative rather than logically compelling. MacIntyre may think less of me if I fail to recognize the moral riches of Thomism but he cannot convict me of making a logical error. His contention is that 'there are no tradition-independent standards of argument by appeal to which' rival traditions of moral inquiry 'can be shown to be in error'.[57] We are thus left without the sort of evaluative framework that Hegel sought to articulate in the *Philosophy of Right*.

It may be, of course, that Hegel's solution to the evaluative dilemma will be deemed to be incomplete or inadequate. MacIntyre specifically distances himself from Hegel when he moves beyond a conception of political philosophy as an expression of the guiding principles of particular communities to a transcendental view of absolute knowledge.[58] My point, however, is that it is misleading to construe Hegel's account of objective mind in narrow terms. Hegel insists that the ideal is immanent in the real, not that it furnishes merely an interpretative gloss on the real.

Political philosophers of a deontological cast of mind will still find Hegel's position unacceptable. Evaluative judgements are given force from his philosophy of history. He can talk about the shortcomings of particular communities or civilizations because of his view of the fulfilment of human potential in the course of history. The philosophy of history, in other words, provides him with a moral teleology. It may not suffice to silence his deontological critics. Indeed it is likely to be regarded as more vulnerable to objection even than the misinterpretation of his political philosophy along integral communitarian lines. But it does highlight the significance of the individual for Hegel. It is individual fulfilment and freedom which culminate in the modern state. Individuals need a certain sort of state in order to flourish. That state is itself the product of a tortuous history. But at its apogee it serves as a necessary means for the satisfaction of individuals and not as an end in itself.

The real problem for Hegel lies not so much in justifying a particular form of state from the perspective of his philosophy of history but in giving a defensible account of the moral decision and deliberation of individuals. For we cannot, of course, invoke a theoretical framework of which individuals may well be ignorant in order to explain their particular agonizing in response to taxing moral circumstances. Rawls focuses on precisely this dimension in his reformulated account of the original position. He insists that the original position is not a hypothetical meeting of interested parties but is 'characterized so that it establishes a fair agreement situation between free and equal moral persons and one in which they can reach a rational agreement'.[59] In Rawls's account we do not picture disembodied selves but selves with a very specific social and cultural inheritance. It is just this inheritance that obliges them to treat one another as free and equal persons. We can easily envisage circumstances in which this assumption would not be made. But in such circumstances rational agreement would have a quite different connotation and may not be morally relevant.

Rawls thus feels that he has answered (at least some of) the objections raised by Hegel against classical formulations of social contract theory.[60] He specifically endorses a fully social conception of human beings and does not reduce fundamental political agreement to arbitrary brokerage. What distinguishes him from Hegel, however, is his persistent commitment to reasonable agreement rather than mutual recognition. The commitment to reasonableness depends upon a prior commitment to persons as free and equal in relevant respects. But he cannot give us independent grounds for regarding persons as free and equal. Indeed reasonable agreement in the original position is essentially an elaboration of the implications of free and equal status rather than a compromise between different perspectives or points of view. In the strict sense it should not be regarded as an agreement at all but as an acceptance of logical necessity. Hegel, on the other hand, tries to take the argument several stages further back. He asks what we need to presuppose in order to have a conception of persons, not what follows from the particular conception of persons we happen to have. His concern is to explain the necessity of a social framework for the emergence of human qualities. As individuals we can recognize that necessity; but it does not help to picture us in any sense agreeing to it. Even as a metaphor agreement is illuminating only if it can in fact be withheld.

It should not surprise us that Rawls's attempt to meet some of the communitarian objections to his original formulation should have brought him closer to Hegel in certain respects.[61] My point, however, is that the conventional assimilation of Hegel to the communitarian position can, in fact, be misleading. Hegel's was not so much a rejection of individualism as an elaboration of its social presuppositions. Within these terms of reference, his response to contract is especially instructive. He seeks to extract a kernel of sense from traditional contract theory by detaching mutual recognition from its familiar atomistic framework. He is thus enabled to do justice to the ordinary business of practical life (involving individuals formulating plans and objectives, variously cooperating and colliding with one another) without reducing the state to the status of a contrivance to further the pursuit of individual advantage. This, to be sure, does not make him a social contract theorist, no matter how far the terms of the doctrine might be stretched. It does highlight, however, the danger of accepting at face value his sweeping dismissal of some of the more obvious shortcomings of the theory. He is content to treat social contract as a misleading philosophical fiction; but he does not deny that it has a significant point to make. His contention is that the point can be better made in a rather different narrative.

NOTES

1 J. W. Gough, *The Social Contract: A Critical Study of its Development*, Oxford, Oxford University Press, 1957, pp. 185, 186.
2 Michael Lessnoff (ed.), *Social Contract Theory*, Oxford, Basil Blackwell, 1990, p. 15. See also Michel Rosenfeld, 'Hegel and the Dialectics of Contract', in *Hegel and Legal Theory*, Drucilla Cornell, Michel Rosenfeld and David Gray Carlson (eds), New York, Routledge, 1991, pp. 228–57, who argues (p. 234) that 'Hegel rejects the social contract as the source of legitimacy for the state'; Patrick Riley, *Will and Political Legitimacy: A Critical Exposition of Social Contract Theory in Hobbes, Locke, Rousseau, Kant, and Hegel*, Cambridge, Mass., Harvard University Press, 1982, pp. 163–99.
3 G. W. F. Hegel, *Elements of the Philosophy of Right*, Allen W. Wood (ed.), H. B. Nisbet (trans.), Cambridge, Cambridge University Press, 1991, §72–81.
4 David G. Ritchie, 'Contributions to the History of the Social Contract Theory', in his *Darwin and Hegel and Other Philosophical Studies*, London, Swan Sonnenschein, 1893, pp. 196–226; Plato, 'Crito', in *Dialogues of Plato*, B. Jowett (ed.), Oxford, Oxford University Press, 1875, vol. I, p. 393.
5 Plato, 'Crito', in *The Last Days of Socrates*, Hugh Tredennick (ed.), Harmondsworth, Penguin, 1969, pp. 91–3; Jean-Jacques Rousseau, *The Social Contract*, Maurice Cranston (ed.), Harmondsworth, Penguin, 1968, pp. 49–50.
6 St Augustine, *City of God*, David Knowles (ed.), Henry Bettenson, (trans.) Harmondsworth, Penguin, 1972, p. 139.
7 2 Samuel, v, 3.
8 Genesis, ix, 1–29.
9 Thomas Hobbes, *Leviathan*, C. B. Macpherson (ed.), Harmondsworth, Penguin, 1968, pp. 223–8.
10 *Philosophy of Right*, §75.
11 *Philosophy of Right*, §75.
12 *Philosophy of Right*, §75.
13 *Philosophy of Right*, §75.
14 Sir Robert Filmer, *Patriarcha and Other Writings*, Johann P. Sommerville (ed.), Cambridge, Cambridge University Press, 1991; Edmund Burke, *Reflections on the Revolution in France*, Conor Cruise O'Brien (ed.), Harmondsworth, Penguin, 1968.
15 *Philosophy of Right*, §75.
16 *Philosophy of Right*, §75A.
17 *Philosophy of Right*, §75A.
18 *Philosophy of Right*, §258.

19 *Philosophy of Right*, §258.
20 *Philosophy of Right*, §29.
21 *Philosophy of Right*, §258.
22 *Philosophy of Right*, §5.
23 Rousseau, *The Social Contract*, p. 72.
24 Rousseau, *The Social Contract*, p. 72.
25 G. W. F. Hegel, *Lectures on the History of Philosophy*, E. S. Haldane (trans.) London, Kegan Paul, Trench, Trübner, 1892–6, vol. 3, pp. 400–2.
26 Hegel, *Lectures on the History of Philosophy*, p. 402.
27 Rousseau, *The Social Contract*, p. 65.
28 Rousseau, *The Social Contract*, p. 60.
29 *Philosophy of Right*, §258.
30 *Philosophy of Right*, §258.
31 See Ritchie, 'Contributions to the History of the Social Contract Theory', p. 226, for a hint that the relationship between Rousseau and Hegel should be reconsidered. The point is argued more fully in Bernard Bosanquet, *The Philosophical Theory of the State*, London, Macmillan, 1965; pp. 218–37.
32 Hegel, *Lectures on the History of Philosophy*, vol. 1, pp. 425–48; G. W. F. Hegel, *The Philosophy of History*, J. Sibree (trans.), New York, Dover, 1956, pp. 225–74.
33 *Philosophy of Right*, p. 20.
34 Hegel, *Lectures on the History of Philosophy*, vol. 1, pp. 425–48; Knox's footnote 26 to p. 10 of his edition of the *Philosophy of Right*, Oxford, Oxford University Press, 1952, pp. 301–2.
35 *Philosophy of Right*, p. 20.
36 *Philosophy of Right*, p. 20.
37 *Philosophy of Right*, §258.
38 *Philosophy of Right*, §158–81.
39 Adam Müller, 'Elements of Politics', in *Political Thought of the German Romantics*, H. S. Reiss (ed.), Oxford, Basil Blackwell, 1955, pp. 154–5.
40 See Wood's footnote 2 to §75 of his edition of the *Philosophy of Right*, p. 413; Immanuel Kant, *The Metaphysics of Morals*, Mary Gregor (ed.), Cambridge, Cambridge University Press, 1991, p. 96. I have followed Wood's translation.
41 *Philosophy of Right*, §162.
42 *Philosophy of Right*, §34–104.
43 *Philosophy of Right*, §36.
44 *Philosophy of Right*, §41.
45 *Philosophy of Right*, §44.
46 *Philosophy of Right*, §51. I have preferred Knox's translation here.
47 *Philosophy of Right*, §71.
48 *Philosophy of Right*, §71.
49 G. W. F. Hegel, *Phenomenology of Spirit*, A. V. Miller, (trans.) Oxford, Clarendon Press, 1977, pp. 104–38.
50 G. W. F. Hegel, *Philosophy of Mind*, part three of the *Encyclopaedia of the Philosophical Sciences*, A. V. Miller (trans.), Oxford, Oxford University Press, 1971, p. 172.
51 Hegel, *Philosophy of Mind*, p. 172.
52 Hegel, *Philosophy of Mind*, p. 172.
53 Hegel, *Philosophy of Mind*, p. 176.
54 *Philosophy of Right*, p. 23.
55 Alasdair MacIntyre, *A Short History of Ethics*, London, Routledge, 1967; Alasdair MacIntyre, *After Virtue: A Study in Moral Theory*, London, Duckworth, 1985, 2nd edn; Alasdair MacIntyre, *Whose Justice? Which Rationality?*, London, Duckworth, 1988; Michael J. Sandel, *Liberalism and the Limits of Justice*, Cambridge, Cambridge University Press, 1982. Note that among contemporary

theorists customarily described as communitarians, Charles Taylor offers a perspective closer to the interpretative position of this chapter. See especially his 'Cross-Purposes: The Liberal-Communitarian Debate', in *Liberalism and the Moral Life*, Nancy L. Rosenblum (ed.), Cambridge, Mass., Harvard University Press, 1991, pp. 159–82.

56 Michael J. Sandel, *Liberalism and the Limits of Justice*, pp. 133–74.
57 MacIntyre, *Whose Justice? Which Rationality?*, p. 403.
58 MacIntyre, *A Short History of Ethics*, p. 209.
59 John Rawls, *Political Liberalism*, New York, Columbia University Press, 1993, p. 286.
60 Rawls, *Political Liberalism*, pp. 285–8.
61 John Rawls, *A Theory of Justice*, Cambridge, Mass., Harvard University Press, 1971.

9 Marx against the social contract

Lawrence Wilde

The classical age of social contract theory had drawn to a close half a century before Marx embarked on his career as a social theorist. From Salomonio in the early sixteenth century to Kant at the end of the eighteenth century, it had served as a justificatory foundation for liberal theory. Although the bulk of Marx's theoretical critiques were directed against liberal political economy rather than liberal political theory, it is evident that his whole approach to social theory was incompatible with the assumptions of the social contract theorists. A closer comparison of their opposed assumptions is revealing in two important respects. First, it poses some fundamental criticisms of the contractarian tradition which go beyond those raised within the liberal tradition. Second, it reveals the self-imposed limitations of Marx's political theory which flowed from his eschewal of the normative approach associated with the contractarians. It leaves us to ponder whether his unwillingness to give careful consideration to the principles of political association in future socialist societies constitutes a serious hiatus in his emancipatory project.

Three main aspects of Marx's method clashed with the assumptions of the social contract tradition. The first was his opposition to the individualist premises employed in contract theory. Marx considered that the function of this individualism was to universalize and de-historicize a conception of human nature which was in fact a product of the market society which it served to justify. He considered the idea of the atomized individual coming into society as a contracting agent to be an ideological fiction. The second aspect is closely related, for he believed that the formal freedom postulated in liberal theory provided the framework of a society in which the majority of people enjoyed little substantive freedom. In contrast to the idealization of the abstract individual, Marx held to the view that the market societies based on this individualism necessarily denied the possibility of a truly human existence to the people who brought only their own labour power to the market. The alienation theme in Marx's writings implied a conception of what it was that made us essentially human, namely, our capacity to create according to a plan. Our creative capacity as social beings was evident in the productive achievements of humankind, but the compulsive processes of production deprived the producers of any experience of creativity. The human essence was in contradiction with human existence in capitalism, and this contradiction could be resolved only by the abolition of capitalism and its replacement by communism. Under capitalism, legally 'free' individuals were free 'like someone who has brought his own hide to the market and now has nothing else to expect but a tanning'.[1] In other words, the formal freedoms of liberal society masked the denial of human freedom for the mass of workers; there was only a semblance of human freedom. Against this Marx posited the grand but always vague ideal of 'the true realm of freedom'.[2] The third point on which Marx's method radically departed from social contract theory was his commitment to empirically grounded research and his distrust of the high level of abstraction at which so much previous political theory had been couched. It is quite clear that Marx was not interested in doing political theory in the same way as Hobbes, Locke or Rousseau, or, for that matter, most of the writers in the established canon of political thought. Let us examine these three points of difference more closely.

INDIVIDUALISM

In the introduction to the *Grundrisse* Marx condemned the liberal theoretical practice of treating historically detached and isolated individuals as the starting-point for scientific work. Referring to this facet of the methodologies employed by Adam Smith and David Ricardo, he dismissed it as originating in one of 'the unimaginative fancies of the eighteenth century'. He argued that these writers were not simply trying to recapture what was deemed to be natural, they were pushing a view of the individual as an 'anticipation of bourgeois society'. Even Rousseau was merely using the fiction of the natural in *The Social Contract* to justify his own view of the ideal society.[3] Bourgeois society had its origins in the sixteenth century and was maturing in the eighteenth, and Marx considered that the idealized view of the individual was a product of this development of free competition. The early individualists were guilty of taking relationships between abstract free individuals as the ideal form, and projecting them into the past as something natural. They saw the individual 'not as an historical result, but as the starting point of history'.[4] In seeing these writers as representative of particular interests and values which needed to be universalized in the process of ideological struggle, Marx introduced a very assertive sociology of knowledge. The individualists wittingly or unwittingly imposed their own interests and fears on an imagined history, and presented them as part of the natural order. Marx did not simply reject the idea of natural egoism as fictional, but alleged that this fiction reflected particular economic, social and political interests.

Let us pause to examine this argument. It does not necessarily impute a conscious decision by the liberal writers to devise a ploy to justify the free play of market forces in civil society. Taking free and equal individuals as the starting-point for political theory could be a sincerely held view, and, furthermore, the liberal politics with which it became associated after Locke might open the way for a political challenge from those groups who did not feel themselves to be quite so free and equal in liberal society. Marx considered that the political emancipation which developed as part of the liberal revolutions was 'a big step forward',[5] and he appreciated Locke as a progressive thinker.[6] This discourse of 'steps' and 'progress' was typical of Marx's developmental perspective, in which the world of the competitive individual and the market was regarded as being both an improvement on its predecessors in important respects and at the same time an alienated and self-destructive reality for the mass of the people. For Marx there was nothing 'natural' about the abstract, isolated individual described in liberal theory. But even if these early theorists of individual rights were implicitly promoting the development of a market society, might it not be the case that their views on the nature of human beings were valid? This point has been raised by Michael Lessnoff in response to C. B. Macpherson, whose influential work, *The Political Theory of Possessive Individualism*, criticizes the human nature premises of Hobbes from within a Marxist analytical framework. Does not the history of wars suggest that the Hobbesian conception of natural man as a competitive power seeker has a core of truth?[7] The problem with this appeal to intuitive truth is that no account of human existence in society can be taken to affirm or deny a notion of essential human nature which is allegedly present prior to society. Wars cannot be taken to evidence the view that humans are essentially and naturally motivated primarily by greed and fear; they demonstrate only that humans are capable of making war. Taking this propensity to be stipulative of what it is to be human is arbitrary and highly ideological, for its pervasive insinuation in the popular consciousness has supported both the liberal view of the primacy of the individual over society and the conservative view that humans need to be controlled if order is to be maintained. Marx recognized these dangerous implications and devoted great energy to combating this narrow individualism. He consistently rejected attempts to promote the individual as the primary unit of analysis in social investigation.

Let us now turn to Marx's treatment of rights in liberal theory. In his 1843 article *On the Jewish Question*, Marx outlined the limited nature of the rights gained in the evolution of liberal society. Although Marx endorsed Rousseau's abstract idea of 'political man' as a truly socialized individual,[8] he argued that this ideal was unrealizable as long as political society was separated from civil society. In civil society, egoistic individuals pursued their goals without regard for the social consequences, a situation which Marx described with Hobbes's famous phrase about the 'war of each against all', the *bellum omnium contra omnes*.[9] The establishment of the political state as a conscious act created the impression that civil society, standing 'outside' politics, was 'natural'.[10] Marx urged his readers to have 'no illusion about the limits of political emancipation', which, at that time, was considered by most radical thinkers to hold the key to human emancipation. In liberal states the citizen was divided into the public person and the private person, and political emancipation consolidated the development of a civil society in which each member 'acts as a private individual, regards other men as means, degrades himself into a means, and becomes the plaything of alien powers'.[11] Marx argued that 'political emancipation was at the same time the emancipation of civil society from politics, from having even the semblance of a universal content'.[12] So despite his acknowledgement that the emergence of representative democracy was the best we could hope for 'within the hitherto existing world order',[13] political freedom was not to be confused with human freedom.[14] He repeats this argument in *The Holy Family*, written in the following year.[15] As for human emancipation, in his early writings Marx spoke vaguely of the need for the individual to 're-absorb in himself the abstract citizen' and become, in effect, a true social being,[16] and in support of this that he quoted approvingly from Rousseau's *The Social Contract*.

HUMAN FREEDOM

The abstract individualism which irritated Marx was a necessary component of a conception of social life which endorsed private property as constitutive of human liberty. This was most explicit in Locke, for whom property was a natural right. Rousseau was well aware of the socially destructive consequences of wide discrepancies in the distribution of wealth, but against this he was able to counterpose only a romantic ideal of a community of small producers, showing no appreciation of the historical dynamic of capitalist production.[17] Marx, of course, considered that human emancipation could be achieved only through the abolition of capitalism. However, Marx shared one of the concerns of earlier contract theorists, the consideration of what it is to be essentially human. It is common for commentators on Marx to argue that he rejected any notion of an 'essential' human nature, for he regarded humans as social beings who could not be understood apart from their social and historical situation. While it is indisputable that Marx maintained that human nature changed in response to changing conditions, it is not readily appreciated that he also adhered to a philosophy of humanity, that is, an abstract view of what it was that made us distinctly human. Most of the textual evidence has been presented in Norman Geras's notable contribution, *Marx and Human Nature*, in which he refuted the widely held view that Marx had spurned the idea of a human nature.[18] While there can be no doubt that Marx was anxious to avoid developing a social theory which rested on moral appeals, the humanist premises are explicit in the early writings, and later in the *Grundrisse*. They are implicit in the theory of exploitation, particularly in the concept of commodity fetishism. In his view, what made us distinctly human was our ability to engage in creative social activity. Under capitalism this distinctly human power was simultaneously demonstrated by prodigious feats of production and denied by the deprivation of the producers in the labour process. There is a strong ethical dimension in Marx's social theory which enabled him to inveigh against the system and to talk freely of the dehumanization of the worker under capitalism.[19]

Marx did not begin his work from abstract philosophical premises, but from a desire to understand the material problems which he confronted as a newspaper editor shortly after leaving academic life. However, as a trained philosopher it was not surprising that he turned to study Hegel in order to clarify his own views on politics and law and point the way forward for further research. Marx emerged from this study as a communist. In the first place he rejected Hegel's idealist resolution of differences between interests in society, claiming that these differences were beyond resolution in reality.[20] Second, he recognized as Hegel's 'outstanding achievement' the centrality of the historical process of cooperative labour in constituting the 'essence of man'.[21] The study of Hegel inspired Marx to seek the 'anatomy of civil society' in political economy.[22] The key concept in his first forays was alienation, and implicit in this was the idea that workers under capitalism were denied the fulfilment of their essence of creative social activity. This view was not abandoned, but served as a foundation for both his theory of history ('historical materialism') and his theory of exploitation ('surplus value'). In *Capital*, Marx made the distinction between human nature in general and human nature as historically modified, when berating Bentham's utilitarianism precisely because it lacked a conception of what it was to be human.[23] However, Marxists who have wanted to emphasize the extent to which human behaviour is the product of social conditions have been loath to acknowledge that he did have a view of human nature 'in general'. 'Human essence' here refers to the 'general' view of what it is to be human, and in particular what distinguishes humans from other animals. 'Creative activity' refers to the preconceived modification of external nature; Marx and Engels at various times refer to this as 'labour' or 'work'.[24]

In *On the Jewish Question*, Marx argued that the community from which the worker was isolated by labour itself was 'life itself, physical and mental life, human morality, human activity, human enjoyment, human nature', and that this human nature was 'the true community of men'.[25] Later in the year, in his *Introduction to Hegel's Theory of the State*, Marx identified the proletariat as a class which could liberate not simply itself but the whole of society; in modern society it represented 'the complete loss of man', and it could liberate itself only through the 'complete rewinning of man'.[26] In the *Comments on James Mill* and the *Economic and Philosophical Manuscripts*, the alienation theme contained a clear idea of what it was that essentially constituted our humanity. Marx argued that humans were distinctive from other animals because they engaged in 'conscious life activity':

> In creating a world of objects by his practical activity, in his work upon inorganic nature, man proves himself a conscious species being. . . animals

also produce. . . but an animal only produces what it immediately needs for itself or its young. It produces one-sidedly, whilst man produces universally.[27]

Animals, he argued, produced only for the immediate physical needs of themselves and their young, while humans produced even when they are free from physical need and indeed only 'truly produce' in this state. Estranged labour, however, turned conscious life activity, 'his essential being', into 'a mere means to his existence'.[28] Marx regarded industry as the 'open book of man's essential powers', but it was a book presented to us 'in the form of estrangement'. He thought that the development of technology opened the way for human emancipation, 'although its immediate effect had to be the furthering of the dehumanisation of man'.[29]

Like Rousseau, Marx maintained that the individual was also a social being, and that it was unrealistic and unhelpful to conceive of individuals in abstraction from their social context.[30] He argued that 'human nature is the true community of men'.[31] Much later, in the introduction to the *Grundrisse*, he wrote that humans are naturally social animals who can isolate themselves only within society, and the idea of producing in complete isolation is as 'preposterous' as the idea that language could develop without individuals who live together.[32] In performing alienated labour, workers were estranged not only from their essentially human capacity, or species being (the phrase borrowed from Feuerbach), but also from each other. In capitalism they were not producing for one another but for money – their sociality was therefore incidental and instrumental rather being a conscious end in itself. This was illustrated by Marx in the passages concluding his *Comments on James Mill*, where he lamented that we speak to each other through the 'estranged language of material values'.[33] He then considered what it would look like if 'we carried out production as human beings', that is, producing for use rather than for profit. The products would be 'so many mirrors in which we saw reflected our essential nature', a reciprocal relationship in which work would be a 'free manifestation of life'.[34]

The most frequently cited statement in support of Marx's rejection of human essence is the sixth of the *Theses on Feuerbach*, written in 1845. Geras has provided a meticulous rebuttal of such an interpretation, and has forcefully argued that it is more reasonable to represent the thesis as an indication that Marx's view of human essence is an integral part of his theory of history.[35] Marx wrote that 'the essence of man is no abstraction inherent in each single individual', but that 'in its reality it is the ensemble of the social relations'.[36] He arrived at his conception of human essence from the real achievements of humans in their social relations, despite the fact that those relations were alienated. The achievements of modern production testified to human creative capability and provided the material possibility for a life without scarcity. But for those who lived by the sale of labour power there was no experience of creativity and a complete absence of control over the productive process. The process of this alienation in the organization and development of the productive system was the subject of his later political economy.

The conception of human essence was explicitly reaffirmed in 1862 in *Theories of Surplus Value* when he decried the 'sentimental' opponents of Ricardo for opposing the objective of production, thereby forgetting that 'production for its own sake means nothing but the development of human productive forces, in other words the development of the richness of human nature as an end in itself'.[37] Marx added immediately that under capitalism this 'development of the capacities of the human species takes place at the cost of the majority of human individuals and whole human classes', until in the end it 'breaks through this contradiction and coincides with the development of the individual'. He was here displaying an impatience with those who did not understand the 'scientific honesty' behind Ricardo's 'ruthlessness', for without this understanding of the dynamics of capitalist production the emancipatory forces could not identify its inner contradictions.

In the first volume of *Capital*, Marx returned to the theme of comparing human activity with the activity of other animals. He introduced his discussion of the labour process by arguing that although humans initially laboured instinctively at the animal level, they later developed the exclusively human characteristic of planning their work. Spiders produced rather like weavers, and bees built cells with greater skill than many architects, but 'what distinguishes the worst architect from the best of bees is that the architect builds the cell in his mind before he constructs it in wax'.[38] This emphasis on the constitutive role of creative social activity for human development was reiterated in one of his final works, *Comments on Adolph Wagner* (1879–80). Here he criticized Wagner for failing to treat the relation between 'man' and nature as a practical, social relation, rather in the way that he had criticized Feuerbach in 1845. Marx added that at a certain stage in the development of their productive activity humans 'christened' and 'denoted' their world linguistically.[39]

So Marx, like the social contract theorists, had a theory of human nature. But whereas they used their conceptions to justify various forms of market society, Marx developed his as part of his theoretical unmasking of the exploitative nature of the free play of market forces. He accused the political and economic theorists of drawing an elaborate ideological veil to suggest harmony where there could be none, a veil which 'is not removed from the countenance of the social life process. . . until it becomes production by freely-associated men, and stands under their conscious and planned control'.[40] The human emancipation which he sought was enunciated only in the most general terms, as, for example, when he wrote in the *Critique of the Gotha Programme* of a society which would operate according to the slogan 'from each according to his abilities, to each according to his needs'.[41] It presupposed the abolition of private productive property and production for profit, and it is clear that it involved a radical democratic control over the levers of power. This community, in which the human essence was realized in existence, was posited as an abstract ideal society, but without the futuristic specification of social arrangements which Marx and Engels had dismissed in their discussion of utopian socialism in the *Manifesto of the Communist Party*.[42] As Selucky has pointed out, there is an extremely important conception of community in Marx's work, but it remains largely implicit.[43] Marx makes out a strong case for questioning the liberal association of private property and freedom, but he is reluctant to outline how substantive freedom would be realized in communism.

FORMAL ABSTRACTION

At an early stage in his career Marx expressed impatience with the level of abstraction which Hegel and the Young Hegelians brought to their discussions of political issues. In the *Critique of Hegel's Philosophy of Right* he argued that Hegel's idealist method of reducing real interests to relationships between concepts caused him to fudge the genuine antagonisms in society. In this way Hegel held out the possibility of harmony within the existing framework of German society, a conclusion which Marx scorned.[44] Throughout *The Holy Family* he criticized the writers of the Young Hegelian school for engaging in conceptual sophistry and failing to grasp the interplay of specific interests in specific historical situations.[45] In *The German Ideology* Marx first set down his own theoretical framework, later known as historical materialism or the materialist conception of history, and he contrasted his own realism, historicism and materialism with the abstract idealism of his predecessors. His own method started from 'real premises', that is, 'men, not in any fantastic isolation and fixity, but in their actual, empirically perceptible process of development under definite conditions'.[46] Despite a reluctance to elaborate his own theoretical framework for fear that it would be used for 'neatly trimming the epochs of history', Marx set down the principles of historical materialism and declared the 'material production of life itself. . . as the basis of all history'.[47] He then made the bold but not so exaggerated claim that 'in the whole conception of history up to the present this real basis of history has either been totally disregarded or else considered as a minor matter quite irrelevant to the course of history'.[48]

Given the thrust of his methodological statements in *The German Ideology* we should not be surprised that Marx did not proceed to discuss the principles or processes which might be adopted in communist society. Yet Marx had no doubt about his communal goal, for 'only in the community has each individual the means of cultivating his gifts in all directions; hence personal freedom becomes possible only within the community'. This community was evidently to be free from the tutelage of a state standing above it, for the state was regarded as a 'substitute for community' or an 'illusory community' which in reality served the interests of the ruling class.[49] The communist society was conceived as one in which the 'association of individuals. . . puts the conditions for the free development and movement of individuals under their control'. This was contrasted to association under capitalism which was enforced by the division of labour and had become an 'alien bond'. However, even though these statements were couched at a high level of generality, Marx could not resist denigrating Rousseau's ideas of association in *The Social Contract* on the grounds that they were 'arbitrary'.[50] On the one hand, the philosophical premises and the whole emancipatory thrust of his social theory begged an ontology of the good society; on the other, Marx the social scientist was dismissive of approaches which might be regarded as speculative or utopian.

CONCLUSION

The only opportunity given to Marx to analyse a society in which the mass of the people held political power came in 1871 with the brief and tragic experience of the Paris Commune. It is interesting that Marxists who have wished to emphasize the libertarian strain in his thought have seized on his endorsement of the radical democratic practices of the Commune, set down in part three of *The Civil War in France* and in some of the preparatory materials. He supported the free election and recallability of all officials, including judges, and their payment at workmen's wages, as well as the abolition of the standing army and its replacement by a militia. In this way the Commune protected its popular power against usurpation by a new elite. The nation-state was to be preserved by a central government with limited functions, to be elected by the various communes in the country.[51] These passages contain no great detail about the workings of the Commune, but they have been frequently cited because they are Marx's only specification of political arrangements which might serve the emancipation of society following a successful workers' revolution.

The calamity of the Commune and the pressing need for its public defence by socialists precluded more detailed discussion of the problems (actual or potential) involved in accommodating differences and regulating social and economic life. However, these issues might have been dealt with in more general fashion, in a way which could have added a constructive dimension to socialist political theory. It would have entailed making explicit and systematic the ideas on human servitude and human potential which Marx worked on for forty years. However, in waging a successful battle of ideas within the revolutionary world against utopians and anarchists, Marx rejected normative approaches which might have resembled Rousseau-style contractarianism.[52] Furthermore, the subsequent emergence of mass political movements paying explicit adherence to Marx's ideas helped to marginalize alternative approaches which might have armed the movements with clearer institutional goals.[53]

In the absence of a theory enlarging on the principles of some sort of 'agreement of the people' for the future socialist society, a crucial tension remained between Marx's political and economic writings. The political theory implied a decentralized radical democracy, while the economic theory implied the necessity of a centralized planning mechanism to administer the market-less society.[54] The self-imposed limitations of Marxist political theory were thrown into stark relief by the success of the Bolsheviks in holding on to state power in Russia. The debates between Lenin and Kautsky reveal fundamental differences of interpretation and disposition on the key question of democracy.[55] We can only speculate whether it would have been quite so easy for Stalin to portray Soviet society as 'socialist' had Marx written more about the kind of democratic principles and processes which would serve as the *sine qua non* of an emancipated society.

NOTES

1   Karl Marx, *Capital*, vol. 3, Harmondsworth, Penguin, 1981, p. 959.
2   Marx, *Capital*, vol. 1, Harmondsworth, Penguin, 1976, p. 280.
3   Marx, *Karl Marx and Frederick Engels: Collected Works*, (hereafter *CW*) vol. 28, London, Lawrence & Wishart, 1986, p. 17.
4   Marx, *CW*, vol. 28, p. 17.
5   Marx, *CW*, vol. 3, p. 155.
6   Marx, *CW*, vol. 11, p. 105; *CW*, vol. 10, p. 253.
7   Michael Lessnoff, *Social Contract*, London, Macmillan, 1986, p. 109; cf. C. B. Macpherson, *The Political Theory of Possessive Individualism: From Hobbes to Locke*, Oxford, Oxford University Press, 1979, ch. 2.
8   Marx, *CW*, vol. 3, p. 167.
9   Marx, *CW*, vol. 3, p. 155.
10 Marx, *CW*, vol. 3, p. 167.
11 Marx, *CW*, vol. 3, pp. 154–5.
12 Marx, *CW*, vol. 3, p. 166.
13 Marx, *CW*, vol. 3, p. 155.
14 Marx, *CW*, vol. 3, p. 160.
15 Marx, *CW*, vol. 4, p. 144.
16 Marx, *CW*, vol. 3, p. 168.
17 Lucio Colletti, *From Rousseau to Lenin*, London, New Left Books, 1972, p. 157.
18 Norman Geras, *Marx and Human Nature*, London, Verso, 1983.
19 See Eugene Kamenka, *Marxism and Ethics*, London, Macmillan, 1969; George Brenkert, *Marx's Ethics of Freedom*, London, Routledge, 1983; Philip Kain, *Marx and Ethics*, Oxford, Clarendon Press, 1991.
20 Lawrence Wilde, *Marx and Contradicition*, Aldershot, Avebury, 1989, pp. 20–2.
21 This is contained in the passages on Hegel in the *Economic and Philosophical Manuscripts*, *CW*, vol. 3, pp. 332–3.
22 Marx describes his intellectual development in the introduction to the *Contribution to the Critique of Political Economy*, *CW*, vol. 29, pp. 262–5.
23 Marx, *Capital*, vol. 1, p. 759.
24 C. J. Arthur has pointed out that Marx used 'labour' to denote general creative activity in his later writings, whereas in the 1844 writings, Marx used it to denote productive activity under private property. Engels tried to distinguish between 'work' and 'labour', but the distinction does not really 'work' in linguistic terms: C. J. Arthur, *Dialectics of Labour: Marx and his Relation to Hegel*, Oxford, Basil Blackwell, 1986, ch. 1.
25 Marx, *CW*, vol. 3, p. 204.

26 Marx, *CW*, vol. 3, p. 186.
27 Marx, *CW*, vol. 3, p. 276.
28 Marx, *CW*, vol. 3, p. 276.
29 Marx, *CW*, vol. 3, pp. 302–3.
30 Marx, *CW*, vol. 3, p. 299.
31 Marx, *CW*, vol. 3, p. 204.
32 Marx, *CW*, vol. 28, p. 18.
33 Marx, *CW*, vol. 3, p. 227.
34 Marx, *CW*, vol. 3, p. 228.
35 Geras, *Marx and Human Nature*, ch. 2.
36 Marx, *CW*, vol. 5, p. 7.
37 Marx, *CW*, vol. 31, pp. 247–8.
38 Marx, *Capital*, vol. 1, pp. 283–4.
39 Marx, *CW*, vol. 24, pp. 538–9.
40 Marx, *Capital*, vol. 1, p. 173.
41 Marx, *The First International and After*, Harmondsworth, Penguin, 1974, p. 347.
42 Marx, *CW*, vol. 6, pp. 516–7.
43 Radoslav Selucky, *Marxism, Socialism, Freedom*, London, Macmillan, 1979, pp. 81–8.
44 Marx, *CW*, vol. 3, pp. 91ff.
45 As, for example, in the discussion of the French Revolution: Marx, *CW*, vol. 4, pp. 118–24.
46 Marx, *CW*, vol. 5, p. 37.
47 Marx, *CW*, vol. 5, p. 53.
48 Marx, *CW*, vol. 5, p. 55.
49 Marx, *CW*, vol. 5, p. 78.
50 Marx, *CW*, vol. 5, p. 80.
51 Marx, *The First International and After*, pp. 209–10.
52 Lucio Colletti has been foremost among Marxists in suggesting that Marx had much to learn from Rousseau's approach to political theory, e.g. *From Rousseau to Lenin*, part 3.
53 This theoretical deficit was highlighted by Karl Korsch in the aftermath of the German Revolution of 1918–19. See Douglas Kellner's introduction to Karl Korsch, *Revolutionary Theory*, Austin, Tex., University of Texas Press, 1977, p. 21.
54 Selucky, *Marxism, Socialism, Freedom*, pp. 86–7.
55 See Karl Kautsky, *Selected Political Writings*, London, Macmillan, 1983, chs 6 and 7; V. I. Lenin, 'The Proletarian Revolution and the Renegade Kautsky', in Lenin, *Selected Works*, vol. 3, Moscow, Progress, 1977.

10 Contractarianism and international political theory

John Charvet

The idea of a world ethical order may be conceived in terms of a basic structure, the fundamental or ethically primary units of which are either individual human beings, or individual states. However, whether we start, ethically speaking, from individuals or states, there may still be an important, if subordinate place, for the other type of ethical entity. Thus in a world ethical order composed primarily of individual human beings, states and states' rights may be thought to be necessary forms through which the ends of that order have the best chance of being approached; while in a states-based order individual humans may nevertheless come to be recognized in international law as being the bearers of legitimate claims in their own person.

My ultimate object in this chapter is with the possible choice between these approaches to the world ethical idea. However, which conception we adopt will depend entirely on how we understand an ethical order to arise in the first place. So I must begin with this issue, and will indeed be occupied by it for the most part. I shall pay special attention to the contractarian theory of such an order in both its classical and contemporary forms. I emphasize contractarianism, not because I believe that we can arrive at the best theory of these matters by learning from its errors, but because I believe that, properly understood, it is an essential part of the best theory.

In order to get anything out of contractarianism we must be able to interpret the idea of a state of nature, or that of an original position, in a way which makes them intelligible and plausible procedures for theorizing this subject matter. So I treat these ideas, following the contemporary theorists, as hypothetical conditions we can imagine ourselves to be in when we abstract ourselves from the details of our social and individual particularities and consider ourselves from a general point of view. This process of abstraction to the general features of human being or agency may, however, be present in theories which make no mention of a contract or ideal agreement. Theories of human rights which, like that of Alan Gewirth, move immediately from the general characteristics of agency to the positive equal value of such agents, and hence their rights, purport to find the structure of ethical order in reason itself.[1] But there are many, besides myself, who think that there is a blatant *non sequitur* in all such rationalist claims[2] and the presence of this gap between the initial general description of rational agency and its supposedly implicit ethical form is necessary if there is going to be room for a contractarian understanding of the ethical idea. (The fallacy lies in the Kantian-type universalization claim that the person who accepts the general description of himself as a rational agent that necessarily desires its own freedom and well-being is implicitly committed by that very description to desiring everyone else's freedom and well-being.)

SEPARATE INDIVIDUALITIES

Contractarianism evidently requires more than mere abstraction to general features of human agency. It involves the idea that we need to imagine ourselves as individuals, characterized only by this general nature, considering together, and agreeing on, at least some of the terms of 'social cooperation'. If all the terms of a just social order are given to the contractors prior to their contracting by God or Transcendental Reason, there will be nothing for them to do and the idea of an ideal agreement will have no role to play in the argument. This procedure of thinking of ourselves as purely general individuals making an agreement may be objected to on the grounds that if we are all supposed to have the same nature and the same interests, then each person's reasoning will be the same as every other person's and hence one person can decide for all. Such a decision could not be thought of as an agreement, since the latter requires at least two persons with different standpoints.[3] This objection is misconceived. There are a multiplicity of persons with different standpoints in the original position or state of nature. Each person has a different standpoint by virtue of being an individual subject with his own separate interest in the world. The nature of his subjectivity and interest is described in terms common to all, but this does not mean that the description is of only one individual. The need for, and possibility of, agreement, then, arises out of separate individuality.

To think of ourselves in this abstract, general way is not to deny that we are socially formed individualities. It is taken for granted that we are. But it is assumed that we can distance ourselves from our particular individuality and communality, and reflect on them from a point of view which sees them as just one way of being human among others, as particular determinations of human nature. (Of course, we can do this only by developing the appropriate concepts of human being, human society and so on, and these concepts have a history.)

What I mean by saying that we are socially formed individualities is first, that separate individuality is a capacity we develop through our powers of self-conscious reason, and these powers cannot be supposed to unfold in us apart from our participation in a social life; and second, that the conditions of social life are such that we necessarily begin to develop our capacity for self-conscious self-direction through the identification of ourselves and our good with a life lived in accordance with the values of our society. The process of abstraction to a conception of our general nature is then also a process of liberation from a narrow parochialism in which our society's way of life appears as the only conceivable way of being.

However, once we have come to think of our separate individuality from the general point of view and thereby to distance ourselves from our particular social origins, our concern must be to theorize the general communal form that is appropriate to or right for persons who understand themselves in this way; and it looks as though such theorizing will be impossible unless we can attribute to separate individuality in general some ends or interests that it has in respect of that separateness – in other words, ends or interests that are independent of social cooperation. For if the interests of persons were socially determined all the way down, then the general notion of separate individuality would collapse. We would seem to have the idea of such a perspective on the world, but we could give it no content.

Although self-conscious separate individuality is developed in persons through their social formation and arises in the first instance in a subordinate place to communal norms in their hierarchy of reasons for action, yet when such persons engage in the process of abstraction from the concrete integration of their interests with the values of their moral community, and think of their separate individuality from the general point of view, they must form the idea of interests that separate individuals as such have. There could not be interests of this type unless they can be attributed to persons independently of their being given any particular social form in this or that society. The interests must be present in every society whatever the specific stamp they receive in different social environments.

INDIVIDUALITY AND SOCIAL COOPERATION

Does this mean that they really are independent of all social cooperation in the sense that a person would have them even if he were an independent, non-social atom? Of course, such a being would not possess self-conscious reason-following individuality. Yet a person who has developed this self-understanding can from the reflective standpoint of his general agency think of himself as having these interests whatever society he belonged to, and even if he lost, as it were, his community through its disintegration, and had to act as an independent. He can even say that he would have had these interests in a sense even if he had never been a rational social being. For they are the interests of animal individuals also, although of course as such they cannot be the object of self-conscious concern. These natural interests are those of life and its reproduction, liberty and access to resources. They must be compatible with all social forms. But this is hardly controversial except in the case of liberty. For it may be thought that our natural interest in liberty requires the particular social equivalent of liberal-individual rights, and there clearly are social forms which do not recognize such rights. By liberty here I mean not being obstructed in the attainment of one's ends. In respect of our natural ends liberty will be relative to our concern for life and access to resources. So the required social equivalent of our natural interest in liberty will be the existence of entitlements through which the members of society can satisfy their interest in life and resources. The entitlement to participate in the collective organization of their satisfaction would meet this demand.

Let us suppose, then, that after entering upon the process of abstraction through which we arrive at the idea of our general human interests we also come to hold that we possess natural or human rights in respect of them; in other words, that persons as such, in virtue of being ends in themselves independently of their membership of particular communities, can claim rights to life and liberty and rights of access to resources. In that case we must believe ourselves to be immediately part of a universal ethical order the basic units of which are individual human beings with rights. The idea of such a universal order is given an initial elaboration in classic contractarian theory in the form of the notion of a state of nature.[4] This notion has subsequently been much ridiculed, not least by those writers in the communitarian tradition. But it has been given powerful contemporary reformulations by Nozick[5] and Gauthier,[6] and can, I think, be shown to be a necessary implication of the idea of a world of natural or human rights.

The idea of a state of nature is that of a world of human interactions in which the rules that all are capable of grasping and following involve mutual respect for persons' natural or human rights. It is said to be a state of nature by contrast with a political condition in which persons are members of territorially based formal complete associations or states. We might then be able to understand it as what I call an informal complete association[7] that is potentially world-wide, in the manner for example of the international informal community of chess-players. The idea of a world-wide state of nature would be that of an international informal community of natural or human rights-holders who pursue their good in interaction with others in accordance with the rules of natural right. It would, of course, be an anarchical world in which each right-holder would be entitled to interpret the rules for himself.

The concept of a state of nature is standardly criticized for its assumption of an asocial atomism, by which is meant the view that individual human beings can develop fully their human capacities as independent atoms outside society. In other words the concept is held to be incompatible with the idea of our necessary social formation as members of some community. But there is little warrant for this criticism. Asocial atomism is certainly not a necessary part of the concept. There is nothing in the idea of a state of nature which conflicts with the belief that persons need to develop their human nature through being formed in families and wider informal linguistically and culturally uniform 'neighbourhoods'. All that is required is that the reasons for action that persons acquire through membership of such groups be based on the fundamental principles of natural right and be translatable from one group to another to permit of universal interaction on common rules. Understood in this way, what I call, following Chris Brown,[8] cosmopolitanism, doesn't assert that persons at one time in the past lived independently and asocially, and yet possessed a set of natural or human rights. It can perfectly well acknowledge that the world has hitherto been divided into distinct formal complete associations each with its own set of reasons for believing and acting, which are not obviously mutually compatible. It needs to claim only that when the members of such communities come to reflect on their traditional beliefs and practices from the point of view of their general character as human individuals, they will independently arrive at the same fundamental conception of the principles of just interaction between persons – namely a set of universal individual rights. From the standpoint of these principles a cosmopolitan will then have to hold that a just world is one in which all human interactions are governed by mutual respect for rights, and that the existing territorially based formal complete associations must either be abolished or reconstituted in accordance with the new principles.

The idea of a state of nature is the attempt to conceive a world of just interaction encompassing all human beings without the existence of any politically based divisions among them. Of course, the early modern rights theorists who began with the idea of a state of nature standardly argued from its inadequacies to the justification of states once more, albeit states that conform to the rules of natural right. Nevertheless, given the cosmopolitan's adherence to a system of universal individual rights the idea of the state of nature without political divisions must have logical priority over the reconstitution of the state within cosmopolitan theory. This does not involve the belief that the state of nature ever existed, or even could exist without complete disaster for the human race. Yet it is necessary to entertain this idea in its social form as described above in order to see whether the system of universal rights is compatible with the existence of a world divided into formal complete associations. We may immediately conclude from the contemplation of the idea that such associations are justified.

I have discussed the logical necessity and priority of the idea of a state of nature in cosmopolitan theory without saying how we are to move from the understanding of the general character of individuality achieved from the reflective standpoint to the attribution to such individuals of rights; nor shall I now do so. If we reject the appeal to God or to a similar intuition to ground such rights, we can always address ourselves to pure reason or the general utility. However, I do not believe that either of these latter accounts of the ground of individual rights can be sustained, but shall not undertake to rehearse the reasons for this belief here. I shall show rather that valid arguments for believing that the state of nature is not a practicable form of moral association, and that formal complete associations are justified, at the same time call in question the cosmopolitan belief in the very idea of natural or human rights.

These arguments can be called the assurance and indeterminacy arguments. According to the former, although everyone has rights and consequently each person ought to respect the rights of others, yet no one can reasonably be required to constrain his pursuit of his good by regard to the rights of others in universal society without the assurance that the others will reciprocate. To suppose otherwise would expose the conscientious to exploitation and destruction by the unjust. The standard rights-based cosmopolitan argument for a territorially based formal complete association is then that it is only under the conditions of membership of such an entity that persons can obtain the desired reciprocal assurance. These conditions require, from the perspective of the assurance problem, primarily that those who do not respect others' rights will be effectively coerced, and so cannot enjoy the benefits of being free riders. Under such conditions the conscientious can have the confidence to live in accordance with their disposition, knowing that this disposition will not be a handicap to them in their pursuit of their natural interests as human individuals.

However, the above argument presupposes that what persons are entitled to in a state of nature is non-controversial, so that the only problem is that of securing a sufficient degree of law-abidingness among a population. The second argument from indeterminacy denies that there can be clear rules of interaction for all human beings in the absence of a communal decision procedure for determining their content. The standard formula for such rules consists in a set of equal rights of the Lockian type: life, liberty, health and possessions. It might be thought that life and health offer clear enough constraints on legitimate action if the duty to respect them is understood negatively. But in the absence of determinate rules regulating conflicts of liberty and access to resources, this certainty must disappear. For anyone may defend his liberty and possessions if necessary by injuring or killing another. As for the right to liberty, it obviously needs priority rules for establishing when one liberty is to be given precedence over another, since the undifferentiated liberties of each person will be in constant conflict with those of others. For the right to liberty means here not being made worse off in respect of one's opportunities to realize one's rightful aims by the actions of others. But one person's rightful aims are defined relatively to the liberty of others, and hence their rightful aims. So an equal right to an undifferentiated liberty is in itself quite empty. Are there any natural priority rules in respect of different liberties – that is to say priority rules that all would accept in a state of nature? Determinate property rules would be a great help, since they would establish the wrongfulness of many aims directed at, or on, to things owned by others. Furthermore there are obvious natural principles here – first occupancy and acquisition by labour, but their application is equally obviously constrained by the Lockian proviso to leave enough and as good of whatever is appropriated for others whose rights are equal to one's own. Since each must interpret these rules for himself, the idea of a natural agreement on property entitlements seems fanciful.

If natural property rules can't help in the resolution of conflicts of liberties, can we appeal to a natural hierarchy of the specific liberties? The difficulty here is that while some liberties are no doubt inherently more valuable than others, for instance the liberty of religious belief and practice compared with the liberty to drive on the left-hand side of the road, yet this natural order of values would not resolve conflicts of liberties at the same level, such as the conflict between one person's freedom of speech or movement and another's. There are no natural priority rules in such matters which could be successfully applied by individuals independently of a collectively agreed procedure. Furthermore, conflicts between one person's higher value liberty and another's lower value liberty cannot be resolved immediately in favour of the former, since from the point of view of the latter's life and interests the particular obstructed use of his lower level liberty may be of more importance to him than the value to the other of his higher level liberty. But in the state of nature we have only the impersonal hierarchy of values on the one hand together with a multiplicity of personal perspectives, each with its own legitimacy on the other. In such circumstances no one can be required to subordinate his personal perspective on the good to that of any other, since they have equal rights in the matter. The solution to the indeterminacy problem, then, involves the creation of a common perspective on the good which depends on the coming into existence of a collective life of a body of persons. This collective life consists in the members undertaking to pursue their natural interests together through determinate rules arrived at through a communal decision procedure. In other words, the indeterminacy argument as well as the assurance argument directs persons to associate with others in limited, and hence unavoidably territorial, formal complete associations.[9]

On the above arguments cosmopolitan ethical theory justifies from the reflective standpoint those very territorially bounded formal complete associations that human beings have always lived in and been formed by, only it requires the collective life of these associations to be reorganized, if necessary, on the basis of mutual respect for the equal value of their members. It is not unreasonable to assume that the so-called communitarian theorists' original community to which the social thesis applies is just such a political association, although for the most part the communitarians do not tell us specifically that this is so. At any rate it would be unreasonable for them to hold any other view, since the assurance and indeterminacy arguments can be used independently of cosmopolitan theory to show that all partial and informal associations need to be parts of a formal complete association; while history, of course, reveals a human world organized on that basis.[10]

We must now consider whether the assurance and indeterminacy arguments do not in a sense prove too much, by undermining the coherence of cosmopolitanism itself. The question is whether it continues to make any sense to attribute rights to persons universally and hence in a state of nature, if at the same time we also say that the conditions in a state of nature are such that no one can be reasonably required to respect the rights of others, and that in any case we cannot know what these rights are with sufficient determinacy. If persons cannot have duties to respect rights in a state of nature, how can we meaningfully attribute rights to them? For someone to have a right another must be under a duty in respect of it. Suppose we accept this conclusion and hold that rights can be possessed by persons only as members of a formal complete association. The difficulty then arises that we would lose the basis for claiming that formal complete associations should be internally organized so as to reflect the equal value of their members, since their equal value is an expression of their rights in universal society.

This conclusion is itself deeply unsatisfactory from an ethical point of view. For having arrived at it from the reflective standpoint, we cannot avoid the commitments involved in our move to that position. These consist in our self-understanding as human individuals with natural interests. From that perspective each knows himself and others as ends for themselves in that each has reason to organize his life from the point of view of his individual good. But we now recognize that we cannot translate that conception of our individuality directly into an ethical system according to which each individual is an end not for himself but for others also, because each is an end in himself. Yet the unavailability of the ethical point of view does not alter the necessity of elaborating the self-understanding we have affirmed from the reflective standpoint in terms of a universal state of nature. It only means that our conception of the state of nature must be one of a world without rights. This will be a 'Hobbesian' state of nature in which our natural liberty is, as Rousseau puts it, limited only by our power.[11] Natural right in this sense is not a right at all, but a universal liberty amounting to a total absence of obligation not to do whatever we can. Nevertheless, we can still construct an argument from the conditions of a 'Hobbesian' state of nature to the rationality for an individual, who is an end for himself, of pursuing his natural interests together with others as members of a formal complete association, provided that he can expect to be better off in terms of the satisfaction of his natural interests in such an association than he would be as an independent in a state of nature.

But now we can say nothing about the basis of association from an ethical point of view. All we can say is that whatever can be agreed by persons in their own interests according to their relative bargaining power will be rationally acceptable. This will mean that members of a particular community will be entitled to use whatever natural and social advantages they possess to maintain or shift the terms of cooperation in their favour *irrespective of the justice of such arrangements.* For the only alternative to that conclusion would be to declare that justice simply is whatever is in the interests of the stronger party, and we must surely accept that that is not a conception of justice at all. Our aim was to retreat to the reflective standpoint in order to obtain a better perspective on the actual moral beliefs and practices of our community. But the only result seems to be to deprive those beliefs and practices of all objective moral legitimacy.

A RAWLSIAN SOLUTION?

Is there a way out of these difficulties to be found in the resources of contemporary contractarian thinking of the Rawlsian type? Possibly. The idea of the reflective standpoint in this chapter is clearly modelled on the Rawlsian idea of the original position which persons, who are already engaged in some cooperative practice, adopt when they seek to reflect on the existing terms of their cooperation. It involves the formation of an abstract idea of persons as beings with the capacity to form and revise conceptions of the good, together with a notion of their general interests consisting in a set of primary goods that are valuable for each person whatever his particular ends turn out to be.[12] But this is merely going to reproduce the already discussed difficulties of ethical theorizing from the reflective standpoint, unless it is possible to generate the principles of just cooperation from the original position itself in a way which does not presuppose the existence of moral rights in some hypothetical universal society. If the terms of cooperation that are 'agreed' in the original position simply reflect principles of just interaction that are given independently of the contract, the idea of determining these principles through the procedure of an ideal agreement becomes pointless. We would have derived the principles in some other way, and would be committed to elaborating their implications immediately through the notion of a cosmopolitan society.

Contractarianism in its Rawlsian form does purport to derive the principles of justice from the notion of an agreement made under ideal conditions. It appears to be distinguished from the classic contract theory of the early moderns precisely by not presupposing a set of natural rights as the moral background to a contract that then becomes focused on the political conditions necessary for making those rights effective. The question is whether the ideal conditions, necessarily imposed on the contractual situation to ensure that it is not simply the idea of an agreement for mutual advantage which reflects the relative bargaining power of the contractors, do not reintroduce a belief in prior rights. These ideal conditions are the impartiality requirements for a valid agreement, which in their Rawlsian form involve a person choosing terms of cooperation from behind a veil of ignorance which detaches him from all knowledge of his *particular* characteristics and situation in the world, with the consequence that he has to think of himself and his interests from a purely general point of view, and hence reason about his good as though he were anyone. If objection is made to the particular formulation of the choice situation to be found in Rawls's *Theory of Justice* – that is to say the idea of a self-interested choice behind a veil of ignorance – exactly the same general feature, namely choice from the standpoint of anyone, is produced by the formula for an ideal agreement, that many believe to be superior, which is to be found in Scanlon's well-known article on contractualism.[13] What he emphasizes is not self-interested rationality plus a veil of ignorance, but a desire to cooperate on terms which no one can reasonably reject, where the idea of unreasonable rejection is defined as the exclusion of proposals on the grounds of their burdensomeness to oneself in particular. The unreasonable is therefore the partial, and reasonable proposals are ones which anyone could accept whatever his position in the world. But this requirement will yield agreement only if it means that persons must abstract from their particular interests and consider their good from a general point of view having regard to their general nature and interest as rational agents who desire to cooperate on terms which all such agents could acknowledge. In other words, they must choose as though they were anyone.

It is obvious that the central idea of the impartiality requirements – namely choice as though one were anyone – expresses a conception of persons as fundamentally of equal value and as having fundamentally equal rights from the point of view of their cooperation on terms which all can accept. Hence, if this equality of value and rights has to be understood as constraining the choice situation from the outside, then nothing is gained in presenting the argument for justice in a contractual form. The contract would be wholly redundant, and we would have to retrace the steps taken in the earlier section of this chapter in attempting to theorize a universal society based on natural rights. But does the notion of the equal value of the contractors and their equal rights have to be understood as external to the choice situation itself? The answer to this is no.

To understand this answer we must start again with persons who from the reflective standpoint know themselves as having already been formed as morally cooperative beings in accordance with some conception of valid cooperative norms. To have been formed as a morally cooperative being is to have learnt to pursue one's individual good together with others as a member of some community subject to the superior claims of the communal norms. Whatever the content of the norms, to have acquired a moral character is to possess a disposition in which the communal norms occupy a higher place in the hierarchy of reasons for action than those of one's separate individuality.

We are not to suppose that this general formula for the moral point of view is available to the cooperators prior to reflection. As unreflective, but morally socialized, beings they will have been taught only the hierarchical superiority of their community's particular moral commands. It is through the process of reflective distancing of themselves from their initial embeddedness in a particular morality that a more general perspective on their situation becomes possible. When they (or some number of them, or even a single individual among them) come to reflect on their existing norms, they will arrive in the manner described above at a conception of their general nature and interests as human beings independently of the formation of those interests in accordance with some particular morality. This abstraction from a *substantive* morality is a necessary implication of the process of distancing oneself from one's own substantive norms. All such norms are to be placed in brackets, because their adequacy is being called in question. But this is not to say that the moral point of view itself is also bracketed. The contractors know that they must cooperate on the basis of some norms which will have a higher place in the ranking of reasons for action than self-interest. They do not yet know what these norms are.

From the reflective standpoint persons know themselves, both as possessing separate individuality, and hence as having natural interests and being ends for themselves, and also as developing their capacity for self-conscious individuality only as members of some community which at the same time forms them for cooperation on the basis of moral norms. So they know themselves as having both an individual and a moral communal human nature, and further that these dimensions of their character are necessarily hierarchically ordered. Yet they do not know what principles such beings should cooperate on, and we are now to assume that if there are any principles whose validity can be established from the reflective standpoint, they must be derived in a way which is not independent of the contract itself. The contractors must acknowledge that they are bound to cooperate on terms which all can accept from the reflective standpoint, when there is no basis for what is acceptable other than the general knowledge they possess in that position of their general human nature and interests.

This nature comes in two parts: separate individuality and moral communality. If we take the first part only as the basis of cooperation, then we would have to endorse the notion of 'justice' as mutual advantage, which allows the terms to be determined by the relative bargaining power of the cooperators. But 'justice' as mutual advantage is incompatible with the other dimension of human nature which involves the hierarchical superiority of the moral norms. This is because 'justice' as mutual advantage must permit the norms of any collection of persons to change so as to reflect changes in their relative bargaining power. Hence any person or body of persons in the community will be entitled to seek to advance their interests in order to overturn the existing normative settlement and alter its provisions in their favour. No normative agreement could be stable under such conditions, for no one would accept the moral point of view from which the pursuit of self-interest is legitimate only within the constraints of the moral norms.

The contractors' commitment to the moral point of view as the necessarily higher element in their own nature reproduces the impartiality conditions of the Rawlsian contract which require persons to choose as though they were anyone. For the contractors' acceptance of the superiority of moral reasons over self-interested ones means that they form the idea of a normative agreement that will be binding on them whatever position they come to occupy in a society governed by such norms, and hence whatever their particular interests. They must think of the agreement as acceptable to them whoever they turn out to be. So the two bases of choice together – their individual and moral nature and interests – will yield the substantive moral conclusion, albeit of a high generality, that a morally legitimate community must be organized on the basis of the mutual respect of the members as equals and hence entitled to fundamentally equal rights. For as the moral principles must be acceptable to each person from the point of view of his being anyone, each must see himself as but one person among others having the same basic nature and value as them.

The difference between this form of contractarianism and the Rawls–Scanlon version is that the latter's impartiality conditions invite interpretation as an external constraint imposed on the contract, and hence as presupposing the principle of equal value instead of deriving it from the reflective standpoint itself. If the moral point of view in the above account were identical to the Rawls–Scanlon impartiality requirements, then, indeed it would also have to be understood as an external principle independently derived. But the moral point of view is just the idea that persons arrive at when they consider their nature from a general perspective as self-interested beings who pursue their good together with others under communally determined norms. When they move to the reflective standpoint and come to understand their general nature, they grasp also that the basis of any actual norms that they can endorse from that position cannot represent some external principle, but must be their own will to pursue, but now self-consciously, the cultivation of their nature as individual communal beings by cooperating on principles which all can accept from the general point of view they now occupy. The contractarian idea expresses this notion. It is the idea of the foundation of the moral community in the will of its members to pursue their good together as equals.

However, this account in no way excludes its being taken to apply directly to a universal society of all human beings in so far as such a society is understood as an informal moral community containing many partial associations within it through which its members could have their human nature developed by being socialized and moralized in accordance with reason-giving practices. What makes such an application of the idea unacceptable is the validity of the assurance and indeterminacy arguments, which require the contractors to recognize that they can fulfil their human natures only in communities which have the character of states. The validity of these arguments does not now call in question the principle of equal value itself, for that principle is not now to be understood as affirming the equal value of persons as ends in themselves, but only their equal value for each other as cooperators in some state. It is valid only as the general communal form through which they can self-consciously pursue the realization of their natures. Hence it is not tied immediately to the idea of a universal society of human beings, but is not incompatible with it, in so far as the idea of such a society can be derived through a further contractarian argument in which the contractors are immediately the separate states themselves and only indirectly their members.

STATES OR INDIVIDUALS

Here I return to what I said at the beginning of this chapter was its ultimate object – the possible choice between an individual – and a state-based conception of the international ethical order. The argument developed above seems to require that any such order should have as its primary elements states and not individuals, since the argument supports the general communitarian thesis that the ethical status of individuals is grounded in their membership of particular moral communities. Consequently ethical relations between individual members of different states cannot be immediate, for that would presuppose the existence of a world state, but must be mediated through the relations between their respective states.

However, a state-based contractarian view of an international ethical order must be distinguished from the traditional so-called society of states' theory of international relations.[14] On the latter view individuals have no rights; only states have rights. From the standpoint of the society of states the members of states have no independent ethical standing. It is only the state that has such standing and how it organizes itself internally is a matter for it to decide and of no concern to other states. Similarly, how a state, or its members, acts towards individual human beings, who are members of other states, is important ethically only in so far as it involves harm done to those states and not to the individuals.

This view cannot be considered acceptable even in respect of the present practice of our own existing international society. For our states have subscribed to international covenants and agreements which affirm the possession by individual human beings of human rights, and we engage in diplomatic activity in support of these commitments. We also acknowledge the existence, and engage in the prosecution, of a type of international crime called war crime. This is in part concerned with the treatment of prisoners of war, but involves also the distinction between combatants and non-combatants. For prisoners of war are effectively non-combatants. If the rules of international society make it a crime to kill non-combatants without good cause – in other words not as the unintended consequence of an assault on a lawful target – then this must be because non-combatants are the locus of ethical claims as individuals in their own right rather than as resources of the enemy state. For since a state is permitted by international law to wage war against other states in defence of its rights, and can do so only by destroying the resources of those states, it would not seem possible from the ethical standpoint of states' rights to make a distinction between lawful and unlawful military targets. All that could legitimately be demanded of belligerents would be the limitation of the damage they impose on each other to what was necessary for the conduct of the war.

If we are to accept the ethical validity of these elements in our present practice, we cannot nevertheless do so satisfactorily by simply adding on to the society of states' conception of international order the idea of a world society of which individual human beings are members and in which they have rights independently of their membership of states. For the argument of this chapter has been that a universal individual-based conception of ethical order is not a sustainable idea. In any case such a conception could not be coherently combined with the society of states' view, since the former affirms the independent rights of individuals which the latter denies.

If the idea of an unmediated world ethical society is to be rejected, and an international ethical order must be conceived as the cooperative practice of states, how is it possible to accommodate ethical standing for individuals within that conception? The answer to this is that a society of states, the members of which are from a domestic point of view ethical orders in their own right, will constitute a cooperative practice which will not consist solely in the common good of the states, but must comprehend in that idea the common good of the members of the several states. For the good of each state understood as an ethical order just is the common good of its members, with the consequence that in so far as this good is pursued cooperatively with other just states as the common good of the society of states, it will be translatable into the common good of all the individuals who make up the separate states. Thus, if we conceive a just domestic order to involve a system of equal rights and duties to be enjoyed by the individual members in their promotion of their natural interests, then the general society of these just states will be characterized by a recognition, through the mediation of its member states, of individual rights. These may be called human rights, since they are to be enjoyed by persons on the basis of their natural human interests and capacities. However, we must note that in terms of the argument of this chapter, persons are entitled to such rights, not in virtue of the inherent worth of their individual personality as ends in themselves, but through the way in which they are the necessary ground of particular ethical communities. Nevertheless, an international society, conceived in the above terms, would demand of its members that they acknowledge and respect the human rights of all persons, who through their membership of their states are members of the general society. A world society which recognizes the ethical status of individuals, and an international society in which no one participates except through membership of a state would be brought to a synthetic unity.

For this sketch of the idea of an international ethical order to be contractarian in nature along the lines developed in the substance of this chapter, it is necessary that there should be an international society already in place which did not arise through an actual contract, but on the contrary spontaneously or unselfconsciously, and that it should have a recognizably ethical form. In other words, there should be rules that are accepted as binding on the members, and hence as regulative of their pursuit of their self-interest. Thus when the members of this society come to reflect on the nature and basis of their cooperative practice they will arrive at the foundational principle of equality. Furthermore, to be consistent the members of each member state of international society must apply the same reflective procedure to their domestic constitution. From this we arrive at the conception of an international ethical order in which individual human beings are recognized to have rights, but only as these rights are mediated through their membership of states which are the primary rights-bearers of international society.

However, there would seem to be a crippling objection to this application of the contractarian idea, as it has been developed in an account of the ethical constitution of particular states, to an international society of states. The assurance and indeterminacy arguments, which support the claim that ethical life must take a coercive political form, would appear to establish that there could not be a world ethical order except in the shape of a world state. An international ethical society is by definition a multi-centred order. Thus if reasoning from the need for a cooperative determination and enforcement of the natural law is to conclude, as it does in its classical contractarian form, in an argument for the ethical necessity of the state, then there cannot be an international ethical order. To avoid this conclusion, we must be able to conceive of an ethical society which has a de-centralized form in which the execution of the law is to a considerable extent in the hands of the members themselves and not in those of a central organ of the whole society. Could there be such a society? Not only could there be such societies, but also they were at one time the universal form of human social life. I mean by this the stateless form of tribal society. There are no legislators, courts of law, or police forces in such societies. There exist only the customary practices of the tribe for the purpose of regulating the members' interactions in respect of their natural interests in life, liberty and resources. Each unit of the society is entitled to interpret and enforce its own claims. It is true that these units are not individual human beings so much as the families and clans to which they belong. But in this respect tribal society may be said to resemble international society with the families and clans forming the semi-independent segments.

A tribal society is a bounded coercive political association. Hence one cannot conclude immediately from the validity of the assurance and indeterminacy arguments that only a state satisfies their requirements. Perhaps the centralized state satisfies them better. But even if this were true, a centralized world state is not a serious possibility, and we should not think that, because we cannot have a world state, we cannot be members of a world-wide ethical order.

NOTES

1 A. Gewirth, *Human Rights*, Chicago, University of Chicago Press, 1982, ch. 1.
2 See in particular B. Williams, *Ethics and the Limits of Philosophy*, London, Fontana, 1985, ch. 4.
3 This objection is to be found in M. Sandel, *Liberalism and the Limits of Justice*, Cambridge, Cambridge University Press, 1982, pp. 122–32.
4 A particularly influential contemporary attack was in C. Taylor, 'Atomism', in *Philosophy and the Human Sciences*, vol. 2, Cambridge, Cambridge University Press, 1985.
5 R. Nozick, *Anarchy, State, and Utopia*, Oxford, Basil Blackwell, 1974, ch. 2.
6 D. Gauthier, *Morals by Agreement*, Oxford, Clarendon Press, 1986, ch. 7.
7 This is a term of art of my own construction. I distinguish four different types of communities: partial and complete, informal and formal. A partial community is one in which the good around which the community is formed is only a limited or particular human good, such as chess-playing. A complete community comprehends or aspires to comprehend in its collective life all the main human goods. An example of a complete community is a state. The distinction between formal and informal communities turns on the presence or absence of an institutional organization for the carrying on of the common life.
8 C. Brown, *International Relations Theory: New Normative Approaches*, London, Harvester Wheatsheaf, 1992, especially pp. 23–4.
9 Of course, in principle the assurance and indeterminacy arguments could be used to justify a world formal complete association. But in practice this is still not a serious suggestion.
10 This is not to say that there have not been throughout history, and above all now, flourishing transnational partial associations of all kinds. My claim would be that their flourishing depends on an order within and between states that is the product of state activity. Of course, order between states is often lacking also because of the activity of states, but it would be simple-minded to conclude that the transnational associations would be made better off by the abolition of states.
11 J.-J. Rousseau, *Du Contrat social*, *Oeuvres complètes de J.-J. Rousseau*, Paris, Bibliothèque de la Pléiade, 1959–64, vol. III, p. 365.
12 J. Rawls, *A Theory of Justice*, Cambridge, Mass., Harvard University Press, 1971, ch. 3.
13 T. Scanlon, 'Contractualism and Utilitarianism', in *Utilitarianism and Beyond*, A. Sen and B. Williams (eds), Cambridge, Cambridge University Press, 1982.
14 The Society of States' theory of international relations is the traditional political theory of those relations. Its most recent practitioners have been called the English School, which had as its most prominent members Martin Wight and Hedley Bull. See M. Wight, *Systems of States*, Leicester, Leicester University Press, 1977; H. Bull, *The Anarchical Society*, London, Macmillan, 1977.

11 Women, gender and contract

Feminist interpretations

Diana Coole

In this chapter my intention is to discuss the way feminist critiques of the social contract tradition are inflected through developments within feminist theory itself. Discussion of the tradition will thus serve as an illustration of theoretical developments within feminism as well as demonstrating the variety of approaches feminist scholars bring to bear in interpreting contractarianism.

Broadly, I see social contract theory, and feminist interest in it, as twofold. The first issue is one of citizenship: of who participates in the contract and of what terms it establishes for their social and political status. Corresponding with this is the careful textual analysis by feminists who have discerned within the canon an exclusion of women from civic life. Second, contract theory is about paradigmatic social relations within a liberal society. In its more recent versions these relate to morality more than political obligation, but they retain many of the same assumptions regarding the orientations and capacities of the individuals who participate. In this context, and in line with developments within feminist theory, there has been a shift from analysing the place of actual women within the contract to interpretations of contractarianism as a mode of discourse that privileges masculinity as a norm. I will consider both these dimensions in turn, before concluding with a brief discussion of feminists' pursuit of a more 'woman-friendly' alternative to contractual relations.

SOCIAL CONTRACT THEORY AS A DISCOURSE OF EXCLUSION

At first sight, social contract theory appeared to offer women a vehicle for sexual equality. Contrary to the natural, theological and ontological hierachies of pre-modern thought, now freedom, equality and rights for all individuals were the declared foundation on which relationships of authority were to be established via reasoned consent. If first-wave feminists were critical, it was only because the theory was applied inconsistently and thus failed to satisfy its own universalist premises.[1] It was not until a second wave of feminists began rereading the canonical works during the 1970s that a comprehensive feminist critique began to develop.[2]

This reading focused on certain slippages, contradictions and omissions noticeable within the classical texts, notably those of Hobbes and Locke, when they are read from the perspective of women. In Rousseau's work these would evolve into an explicit legitimation of women's exclusion from citizenship, but even among his predecessors it was possible to discern a quiet subversion of the radically egalitarian logic of contractarian argument. Although women's eventual enfranchisement would ostensibly overturn their exclusion, by allowing them to express the same hypothetical consent to the state as men during elections, the arguments and oppositions utilized by early liberal thinkers (in particular the public/private divide) continue both to exclude many women from active citizenship and discursively to construct them as bearers of feminine personalities and female bodies inimical to civic virtue.

The egalitarian premises of the early contract theories lie in their descriptions of the state of nature, a fiction introduced to refute the possibility of naturally stable or justifiable patterns of authority. Individuals, whether they be material bodies (Hobbes), moral works of God (Locke) or primordial savages (Rousseau), are sufficiently equal in status and ability both to mount credible challenges to any power and to aspire to power themselves. For although there are natural differences, these are neither great enough to ensure or legitimize lasting victory, nor distributed in any systematic way, such as along sex or gender lines. Yet in every case, women end up in patriarchal families and are more or less explicitly excluded from participation in the contract and full citizenship. The question is then how this transition occurs and whether it is intrinsic to the argument itself.

In Hobbes's state of nature women are equally as desirous, and as responsible for the war of all against all, as men. For 'there is not always that difference of strength, or prudence, between the man and woman, as that the right cannot be determined without war'.[3] The contract is then a device for institutionalizing peace, facilitated by our rational capacity to deduce the laws of nature and motivated by our fear of death and desire for commodious living. Apart from the sovereign to whom all rights are transferred, all individuals are now confirmed in their formal equality. If an absolute authority can protect us, it is rational to consent to its rule. Everyone can in principle make the calculation, register their consent and benefit from the law, since all can exercise the instrumental reason that prudence requires. The logic of the argument thus appears to support sexual equality.

However, although Hobbes's formal analysis refers to individuals populating the state of nature, he also describes it more historically as being composed of families. Like political associations, these are formally modelled on consensual, self-interested relations (despite the difficulties of children giving consent), but it is apparent not only that these operate patriarchally, but also that they can consistently do so only in so far as women have consented to such an arrangement, since they had begun in an initial state of equality. As in the state, so in the family, Hobbes insists that authority must be unified, but why should it be the woman who acquiesces? Hobbes does not tell us explicitly, but it is possible to offer a plausible reconstruction of his thinking by following through its logic in the light of certain comments he does make. Thus it is true that in the state of nature, men as a group are not strong enough to overpower women as a group, thereby precluding the stability of their rule without women's consent. However, most individual men can subdue most individual women – perhaps because, as Carole Pateman has suggested, the latter are defending their infants as well as themselves.[4] But Hobbes also contends that 'men are, naturally fitter than women, for actions of labour and danger'.[5] As in the historically more evident commonwealths by acquisition, it is then in the rational self-interest of the vanquished, in this case individual women, to submit and consent to being ruled in return for protection. Indeed this is also what weaker men do when they consent to their subordination as servants rather than slaves, and women's position seems hereafter to be most like that of conjugal servant. In civil society this male privilege becomes institutionalized in marriage laws, which must also apply to that minority of women who avoided the naturalistic imperative to submit.

Nevertheless, the structure of Hobbes's argument is distinct from the patriarchal ideology he was rejecting in so far as women's subordination is not based on a theory of natural servitude, but only on an inconsistent presupposition of natural inability that is smuggled in to explain why they will recognize the rationality of submitting to the stronger agent despite the fact that they might legitimately aspire to mount destabilizing assaults. Where they succeed, as with the Amazons, there is no reason in principle why authority patterns should not be different, at least in the state of nature. But as this sole example shows, Hobbes did not expect such exceptions to be common and nor would they endure within civil society.[6] The inferrence is then that women's subordination rests on rational consent, although it is no more voluntary than the submission of individuals to their conqueror. There is a hiatus within Hobbes's theory because the sexually egalitarian logic of his formal account is at odds with unexpurgated ideological and historical assumptions.

Although the structure of Locke's argument is similar to that of Hobbes, his state of nature is more benign and orderly due to the operations of natural law there. Unlike Hobbes, he also takes the crucial step of distinguishing between political association which is contractual and family relations that are natural; between public and private. However, women's location here is ambiguous because of a third set of relations, which are conjugal.[7] These are also contractual and voluntary and can indeed be terminated once their purpose has been accomplished, but that purpose is a natural one: the reproducing and rearing of children. The main concern of the marriage contract is nevertheless family property and here Locke follows Hobbes in insisting that there can be but one authority. Although everyone is endowed with natural rights in the state of nature, it is again primarily the women who submit here due, we can surmise, and once more following Hobbes, to recognition of their lesser capacity where men are 'abler and stronger'.[8] As in *Leviathan*, the argument remains implicit, but Locke seems to employ the same logic: that because of natural weaknesses, most women will find it rational to acknowledge their husband's authority and will place their property under it, although there may be exceptions where an individual woman is in a particularly strong position and things can in principle be otherwise. In Locke's case the example is not Amazons but queens.

Because women participate in both contractual relations through marriage, and natural relations through reproduction, they seem to occupy a boundary position which might have been resolved either way as far as their participation in the social contract is concerned. However, under the terms of the marriage contract, most consent to an inferior position within the family and although this need not necessarily restrict them to the private sphere, this seems most likely for a number of reasons.

First, their natural inability is now reinforced by economic dependence and legal subordination. Second, the primary function of the state is to preserve property, but the majority of women have handed over that responsibility to husbands. It will therefore be men who make the relevant decisions here, most notably those instituting a commonwealth to guarantee natural property rights. Even if we interpret property in its broader sense as encompassing natural rights to life and liberty as well as possessions, women do not seem to have much direct interest in the state's services. Much of their liberty, as well as their estate, has been transferred to the husband; they will benefit from the state's protection of their lives, but in practical terms their strong and able spouses would be of more immediate value. It would seem then to follow that women's interests are largely satisfied within the private sphere, where they have little direct concern with politics and where their husbands anyway take the important decisions, thereby mediating women's relationship with the state. If men's consent is shown to be voluntary because they can withdraw it by emigrating, women simply retreat into the private realm where the only consent they need give is to marriage.

Third, Locke, like Hobbes, realized that most political associations evolve historically rather than being instituted by contract, and here he suggests that it is 'obvious to conceive how easy it was. . . for the *Father of the Family* to become the Prince of it' and 'almost natural for Children by a tacit, and scarce avoidable consent to make way for the *Father's Authority and Government'*.[9] Private patriarchy is clearly assumed here and this would in most cases then slip imperceptibly into public patriarchy (using the latter term in its modern feminist sense of men's rule over women: in its seventeenth-century sense Locke could absolve himself of charges of patriarchalism by insisting that both women, and children on reaching adulthood, have consented to the father/husband's political authority, even if this is only 'tacit, and scarce avoidable'). Fourth, although Locke has not explicitly excluded women from the social contract, it seems unlikely that they would have had much opportunity to express consent. Following the initial agreement, when they would have had little motivation or authority to participate, few would inherit property and most would therefore be denied that most explicit opportunity for consenting. At best their acquiescence would remain tacit; they would not be full members of the political community but among the ranks of those who are obliged only to obey. Finally, although Locke begins with morally equal persons and holds an egalitarian psychology, each being born a blank slate on which experience writes, women probably fail to develop their rationality sufficiently to register consent. For despite each being born with the potential for reason, it requires development. A precondition and sign of this is autonomy, manifested as material independence and success. But marriage would seem to rob women of these credentials since domestic dependency deprives them of control over their working or its products, and thus of the symbols of autonomy, while their toils (both productive and domestic under conditions of early capitalism) would generally keep their reason immature due to lack of time for education and reflection. Although Locke nowhere says that women are naturally irrational, then, their natural infirmity will probably commit them to a situation where, having consented to marriage, they would be unable to sustain or develop the mature rationality needed for active expressions of citizenship.[10] Overall, then, women seem to be excluded from full citizenship, while their tacit consent to political association appears to be both inevitable and irrelevant due to their (subordinate) positioning in the private sphere.

Because Hobbes and Locke are not very clear about the status of women, who simply disappear from their arguments at crucial stages, feminist scholars have been obliged to reconstruct the missing steps according to asides or absences within their texts. Overall, as we have seen, a radically individualist logic is formally applied in presenting all persons as free to enter contracts, but because assumptions about women's natural incapacity slip in, their acts of self-interested and rational agency seem limited to marital, rather than social, contracts. Besides inconsistently importing naturalistic criteria of exclusion into modern theories whose foundations in principle precluded them, however, these allusions to natural infirmity mystified the historical and structural reasons why women were socially and economically disadvantaged and why many are indeed still obliged to accept patriarchal arrangements that negate more than a formal accession to citizenship.

In Rousseau's work, feminists have needed to look no further than *Emile* (chapter 5) to discover an explicit exclusion of women from participation in the social contract. Rather than allowing naturalist assumptions to slip in and subvert the egalitarian logic of his work, Rousseau is quite clear that there is a natural difference between men and women and that this manifests itself both in women's role and subservience within the family, and in the havoc they wreak should they gain a political voice. Nevertheless there is a crucial slippage in Rousseau's narrative of the natural state in his *Discourse on the Origin of Inequality*, where he moves from a state of nature originally populated by free and equal individuals, to a second stage of apparently natural patriarchal families. He bases his subsequent accounts of sex/gender relations on this latter golden age without explaining its origins, although they are clearly not contractual.

Although in The Social Contract Rousseau insists that the General Will must be an expression of the active and continuous consent of all citizens, lest it express mere particularity, it is evident from *Emile* that it does not include women although Rousseau nowhere acknowledges that a specifically masculine will must therefore result. Indeed he presents it as one of the characteristics of male citizens that they have the capacity for enlightened and autonomous judgments of a universal interest, whereas he describes women as lacking the ability to transcend their particular wills, which are (rightly) focused on the needs of their own families, and as therefore lacking in the autonomy, judgment and capacity for abstract reasoning that would qualify them to express consent. For not only does nature designate women's domestic role, where they service citizen-husbands and nurture citizen-sons, but it also endows them with the requisite gender characteristics. Femininity is described by Rousseau as a combination of modesty, chastity, docility, submissiveness, coquettishness, cunning, heteronomy and irrationality. It is to be reinforced nevertheless by an appropriate education and a firm male hand.

> A woman's education must therefore be planned in relation to man. To be pleasing in his sight, to win his respect and love, to train him in childhood, to tend him in manhood, to counsel and console, to make his life pleasant and happy, these are the duties of woman for all time, and this is what she should be taught while she is young.[11]

Because Rousseau's social contract entails active and ongoing participation, rather than being the one-off or tacit affair of Hobbes or Locke, women's exclusion has far more significant consequences for social arrangements generally. For Hobbes and Locke, few citizens would be politically active after the initial contract unless its terms were abrogated. But Rousseau's theory was presented as a call for popular (male) sovereignty and radical democracy. Because of this, and because Rousseau had constructed femininity as antithetical to citizenship, society had to be strictly regulated along gender lines. He operates with a set of clear oppositions here: masculine/feminine, public/private, culture/nature, universal/particular. The norms of feminine behaviour and the spaces appropriate to its expression are strictly delineated. Any transgression of their boundaries is profoundly subversive since effeminate men or virilized women would destroy the very foundations of the legitimate state.

If feminists have not had to look far for women's exclusion from public life in Rousseau, their task has been to insist that *The Social Contract* should be read in conjunction with *Emile*. The former alone gives the impression of being gender-neutral, yet it is clear from the latter that Rousseau's account of women there cannot be simply ignored as a piece of gratuitous misogyny, to leave *The Social Contract* unaffected. For although women do not participate in the social contract and General Will, they do have a vital, if indirect, contribution to make to the state, although they can make it only if their particular characteristics are safeguarded within the private sphere. Exercised in public, they would be both corrupted and an unruly, subversive force. But it is the love and compassion that women alone can inspire in their husbands and sons, which will be sublimated into the patriotism, fraternity and love of the law on which the republic depends. Indeed it is this very bonding, whose flourishing relies initially on the feminine virtues, that renders Rousseau's state a democratic community rather than the merely mechanistic aggregation that arises from the Hobbesian or Lockian contracts.[12] It is through marriage that men and women's complementary natures are brought together yet remain distinct, where women both engender the emotions that underpin citizenship, and protect the space where male citizens can harmlessly express and defuse them in their particularity before going on to give them more universalist expression in public.

Rousseau's emphasis on romantic love and the quality of matrimonial relations[13] is quite at odds with the contractual and self-interested relationship Hobbes and Locke described. For Rousseau, marriage can never be reduced to a contract between two only anatomically distinct persons who exchange goods and services out of self-interest. Complementarity and fidelity, rather than autonomy and rationality, are what distinguish private (natural and hierarchical) from public (free and equal) relations. Yet the latter must also draw on such qualities if they are to avoid the caprice and contingency of the liberal contractual state. In this Rousseau prefigures Hegel, who would also see the familial moment and its lessons of altruism and community as vital to the state, alongside the egoism contributed by (male) civil society. Although Hegel would be no more inclined than Rousseau to allow female citizenship, their acknowledgement that women's particular ethical modes do contribute to the ethos of a communitarian state beyond the alienation of bourgeois society, is missing from the harsher self-interested politics of Hobbes, Locke or liberal contractarianism generally.[14] In this they perhaps, ironically, anticipate recent feminist (and communitarian) suggestions that liberal political and ethical relations need restructuring to accommodate a different – more 'feminine' – voice, which would infuse an ethic of responsibility and care, a concern for concrete others, into the detached and impersonal individualism of the modern polity. Moreover Rousseau and Hegel also insist that human nature is not uniformly of the sort Hobbes and Locke had described, but is itself gendered and thus conducive to other than contractual, exchange relations. Although for them this excludes women from citizenship, the argument is amenable to reversal, whereby the paradigm of political relations might be remodelled by being regendered. I will return to this in my conclusion.

SOCIAL CONTRACT THEORY AS GENDERED DISCOURSE

So far I have focused on feminist interpretations of classic contract theorists to show how the tradition is implicated in excluding women from citizenship. However, the social contract also offers a paradigm for free and equal relationships within liberal states, thus raising broader questions about the style and ethics of association.[15] This shift in focus corresponds to a reorientation of feminist thinking which, having identified women's exclusion within existing theories and practices, now turns its attention to broader criticisms of those theories and practices themelves, perceiving them as fundamentally gender-biased in their presentation of a particular set of masculine norms as universal. Inclusion in this unreconstructed politics is then inadequate. This change of interpretative emphasis is associated with a broader movement within recent feminisms, from equality (between women and men) to difference (between feminine and masculine inscriptions).[16]

Declaring that a body of thinking is masculine, or privileges masculinity, has nevertheless to be carefully finessed, since otherwise feminists would only be conceding Rousseau's point about natural difference. While it is true that many are sympathetic to the idea of replacing so-called masculine political norms with a more 'feminine' version, they are reluctant to embrace any essentialist theory of sex/gender difference and a variety of strategies, of significance for how the contract tradition is read, are deployed to this end.

Most commonly, gender is presented as monotonously general (at least within the western liberal societies with which contract theory is concerned) yet contingent, by drawing on some theory of socialization. This explains how biological males come to acquire the specific personality traits, behavioural norms and values that are conventionally designated masculine. They are taught to, and internalized by, boys as the most appropriate orientation under conditions where it is men who act publicly and exercise power. However, feminists have developed more sophisticated versions of socialization theory by drawing on certain psychoanalytic and poststructuralist approaches. According to the former, gendered orientations are not simply imposed on already constituted subjects but are deeply stuctured within the personality from its inception. Unlike more orthodox Freudian accounts, object-relations theory has allowed this process to be understood as culturally modifiable because the gendered personalities it describes are the psychic effects of a particular sexual division of labour that yields mother-centred childrearing. Alternatively, a more Foucauldian approach would suggest that masculinity is demonstrated by men because they, as the gender which both inherits positions of power and constitutes the discourses that prescribe which norms are most valued, institute disciplines that construct themselves accordingly. Dichotomous sexual difference, as it is etched on to bodies as well as identities, is thus discursively produced within a context of power relations. In both cases, there is then a circularity whereby the sexual and discursive division of labour feeds on itself to reinforce an equation between sex and gender. However, the emphasis in the sort of postmodern accounts that thinkers such as Foucault have inspired is also on a disjunction between sex and gender, where socialization and identity fail or where the binary formula of sexual difference is transgressed. Here the focus moves on to the gendered nature of the representational system itself and its deconstruction. In this sense, social contract theory might be deploying certain gendered oppositions which continue to operate (and to suppress or marginalize, even while constructing, 'the feminine') even if women are included as equal citizens.

I will discuss these various approaches to the claim that social contract theory operates with masculinity as its norm, or code, in this section. In order to illustrate the contrast between them and the interpretations I discussed in the previous section, I will focus particularly on readings of Hobbes.

Since the early 1980s, a number of feminists have interpreted social contract theory, and *Leviathan* in particular, from a psychoanalytic perspective. This allows texts to be read on a deeper level, with overt exchanges between free and equal individuals being underlain by a subtext where unconscious motivations operate. Here, authors, actors and readers are all implicated in a complex drama of kinship relations – between mothers, fathers, siblings and infants – which allegedly explain or symbolize the (masculine) fears, anxieties and phantasies that underpin contractarian thinking. Because on this level actors are sexually differentiated and driven by irrational desire, this reading is both conducive to feminist interpretations and deeply subversive of the foundations of contract theory itself, which assume the presence of rational, conscious, calculating individuals who are transparent to themselves and capable of controlling their passions through reason. It is not then gratuitous that contract discourses are littered with familial terms and metaphors (patriarchy, fraternity, and so on), nor that they continue to strike so profound a resonance among their contemporary readers.

The first two discussions of Hobbes to be considered both draw on object-relations theory.[17] It will be useful briefly to summarize its relevant assertions at this point. Here the key to psychic development is a process of separating from the mother, in the course of which self- and gender-identity are established. As a consequence of the profound identification between the daughter and her same-sex mother, the girl remains longer in the primary relational mode, thereby establishing more fluid ego boundaries and a capacity to bond and empathize with others. Boys on the other hand separate sooner, evolving stronger and more rigid egos but more brittle and defensive gender-identities, since their masculinity is modelled on the absent father and establishes itself as being not-female, a rejection of the mother. Under these particular conditions of the asymmetrical family, boys thus typically evince the personalities and value systems that are conventionally called masculine. These are centred on autonomy, detachment, objectivity and a general hostility to others as a threat to one's ego boundaries, as opposed to the feminine characteristics of girls (compassion, cooperativeness, intimacy, relatedness, and so on) on whose negation masculinity is defined. Moreover, because of the infant's initial dependency on the mother, she is experienced as an omnipotent and capricious power. For the son in particular, women are associated with the fear and vulnerability she inspired and by the desire to control her.

In an article published in 1983, Christine Di Stefano used this approach to equate masculinity with 'a vigorous brand of dualistic thinking, a persistent and systematic amplification of the primal self-other oppositional dynamic', and patriarchy with 'men's attempts to overthrow female control over reproduction, while masculinity embodies a fundamental turn away from the mother'.[18] With this in mind, she then utilized what she describes as a method 'akin' to psychoanalytic explanation of symptoms, in order to reconstruct the hidden, masculinist levels of meaning operating beneath the surface of Hobbesian texts. The way Hobbes defines human nature and his account of its manifestations within the state of nature are especially relevant here:

> what we find in Hobbes's account of human nature and political order is a vital concern with the survival of a self conceived in masculine terms. The strict differentiation of self from others, identity conceived in exclusionary terms, and perceived threats to an ego thus conceived which will be minimally displaced and maximally dissolved by an invader, all recapitulate issues which are materially grounded in the experiential process of securing a masculine identity by means of struggle against a female maternal presence. The masculine dimension of Hobbes's atomistic egoism is powerfully underscored in his state of nature, which is effectively built on the foundation of denied maternity.[19]

On the one hand then, we find typically masculine egos operating in the state of nature, for whom 'relations' are based on combat or, subsequently, on limited and impersonal contractual exchanges. Since the founding contract does not change human nature or the ethos of interpersonal relations, it is these discrete egos which will also constitute civil society and its paradigms. Thus human nature and the socio-political relationships which are declared universal are in fact specifically masculine. On the other hand, sovereignty is defined, according to Di Stefano, in terms of a rejection of the intensely personal and complex bonds of maternal authority, favouring instead the impersonal and external reign of the father who is unconcerned with the particular identities of his subjects. The conception of authority itself is thus a gendered one that embodies male paranoia. Finally, great significance is placed on a passage in *De Cive* where Hobbes invites us to consider men as mushrooms, sprung from the earth into full maturity (i.e. not born of, or nurtured by, woman). This image is claimed to remain latent throughout *Leviathan*, thereby rendering men self-sufficient orphans and again denying the mother and a place for women or reproduction generally.

Aspects of this argument have recently been contested by Kathleen Jones,[20] although she relies on the same psychoanalytic approach and similarly concludes with assertions regarding the masculinity of Hobbes's basic concepts. Her main concern lies in his understanding of authority. Social contract theory, she argues, constructs authority as 'masculinized mastery', such that women would be misguided if they were merely to seek access to it, as opposed to developing a 'compassionate' alternative. Nevertheless, Jones takes issue with a simple conflation of Hobbesian individuals and masculinity, arguing instead that within the state of nature Hobbesian man 'seems remarkably infantile'.[21] Using a psychoanalytic 'misreading' to 'supplement' feminist equations, she finds in Hobbes an analogy between the state of nature and infancy, understood psychoanalytically as a stage of pre-Oedipal narcissism. While the type of authority that will prevail, and the type of personalities who are sufficiently autonomous to sanction it, are indeed conceptualized in masculine terms, then, natural men in their state of infancy must first mature. Initially they are overwhelmed by a sense of fragility and by their dependence on others for their survival, and as such they are in no position to authorize the sovereign.

Jones relies here on a correspondence between object-relations accounts of separation and Hobbesian ideas of individuation: only those who develop according to the masculine route of autonomous ego-identity will be sanctioned to enter the contract. Because this occurs over time, however, she must contest the significance that Di Stefano places on the mushroom metaphor and argue instead that Hobbesian individuals do in fact undergo a developmental process (which is gendered in the way described by object-relations theory) within the state of nature. Although they are educated for society here, they also acquire a legacy of haunting memories of dependence and vulnerability, especially *vis-à-vis* the mother and female body.

It matters significantly that the 'other' whom we have feared in our ontological and political infancy is a woman. It is separation from a woman, our distinguishing our bodies from hers, that triggers the process of individuation and codes the development of autonomy in masculine terms. We retreat to the stability of the order of father-Leviathans because it is a 'sanctuary from maternal authority'.[22]

If women were to institute a 'feminine' authority predicated on their capacity for relatedness, it would clearly take a different form. Even if we grant that in the state of nature masculine men are, to paraphrase Simone de Beauvoir, not born but made, however, this surely does not diminish the significance of their desire retrospectively to construct a myth of male autogenesis.

Jones makes further important, but more cultural, points regarding the gender of Hobbesian authority. On a symbolic level, she argues, 'the concept of sovereignty as unity negated the possibility of including divisible [i.e. reproductive, sometimes pregnant] bodies – women's bodies – in the scheme.'[23] Nor can this unity accommodate difference. The formal, unified and universal form authority takes in *Leviathan*, where it is authorized to speak for all, cannot accommodate the diversity and particularity of persons, such as their female embodiment or their gender. Nor can it acknowledge their connectedness, as well as separation, that is forged out of this specificity. (Seyla Benhabib similarly criticizes more contemporary contract theory in its Rawlsian form, where the veil of ignorance precisely requires that we ignore particularity. Under its conditions, 'the *other as different from the self* disappears.')[24] Ironically, what had seemed to be the radical aspect of Hobbes's theory, namely the ungendered nature of his individuals, is now seen as a further indication of its masculinism, where this is 'rooted in the universalizing form that authority as sovereignty took in his system, and not simply in the fact that women, as individuals, were not fully included as contract makers'.[25] While the *self-interested* nature of contractors is condemned by feminists as a particularly masculine mode, then, so is the commitment to *disinterested* rules of impartial justice.

A mix of psychoanalytic theory with a deconstructive approach to Hobbes's representational system is again exemplified in a brief reading by Benhabib. She describes the state of nature as a metaphor, or mirror, whereon bourgeois man projects his dreams and anxieties, but whose basic message is that in the beginning, man was alone. She, too, cites Hobbes's mushrooms here as denying the mother: 'The denial of being born of woman frees the male ego from the most natural and basic bond of dependence'.[26] However, despite this autonomy, Benhabib also describes Hobbesian individuals developmentally, perceiving them as narcissists who both exhibit unlimited desire and perceive others as threats. She then interprets their progress in Hegelian fashion: from narcissism, through self-loss in confrontation with the other (the 'sibling brothers') and a fight to the death, to the social contract where autonomy is recovered since all are bound by the law. The law establishes clear (ego and property) boundaries; it 'reduces insecurity, the fear of being engulfed by the other'. Although the law represents the (absent) father's authority, this is modelled on siblings' own masculine self-image, where according to this more Freudian interpretation, it is brothers rather than the mother who are the source of rivalry and otherness. The outcome according to Benhabib is then bourgeois rather than patriarchal, where it is fraternity that more appropriately signals the psycho-dynamics of authority relations but where there is always anxiety that the brothers will usurp power in a competitive situation that is only sublimated. As far as women are concerned, however, the 'point is that in this universe the experience of the early modern female has no place. Woman is simply what man is not; namely they are not autonomous, independent, but by the same token, nonaggressive but nurturant, not competitive but giving, not public, but private'.[27] It is not only that women are excluded from civic life then, but also that the discursive field constructs the female according to a series of oppositions which exclude her from history.

Feminists have been interested in this deconstructive approach because it discloses how masculinity operates as a powerful code for representational mastery, while the feminine is a metaphor for the disorderly and chaotic; for the differences that play within language to deny stable meaning. Kathleen Jones, for example, conveys the play of gendered oppositions at work within political thinking when she criticizes a Hobbesian understanding of authority:

> When political authority is defined as the rightful imposition of order on disorder, or the substitution of an artificial unity for a lived diversity in community, it excludes women and the symbolically female from its practice axiomatically. Women represent disorder.[28]

Although as far as I know no feminist has extensively deconstructed *Leviathan*, Michael Ryan did so from a Marxist perspective in order to show the equation between absolute meaning and absolute authority, and his conclusions are provocative in terms of the gendered codes mentioned above. According to Ryan,

> Hobbes demonstrates the relationship between the metaphysical concept of the logos as a point of absolute cognitive authority, from which laws issue in an unequivocal language that excludes all possibility of ambiguity or intention or interpretation, and the absolutist political concept of a sovereign who represents the whole state and who is the unique source of laws where authority is uncontestable. In Hobbes, metaphysical rationalism and political absolutism are mutually supporting, and this is made clear in the way an absolutist theory of meaning in language hinges with an authoritarian theory of law. The authority of the sovereign's law depends on the establishing of unambiguous proper meanings for words.[29]

Ambiguity and metaphor ('the unsanctioned transfer of meaning') are equated with sedition: they question unequivocal meaning and identity and thus the law and rationality. Yet if equivocation, fluidity and relationality are more fundamental – if all language is metaphorical and unstable because it is dependent, as post-Saussurean linguistics claims, on the play of differences – then so, too, given the language–politics equation, would sedition, popular sovereignty and civil disobedience be more fundamental than absolute rule. This reversal, Ryan argues, is inherent within the text, since *Leviathan* is itself a metaphor: Hobbes cannot avoid what he condemns, his own theory does not establish truth and clarity, but seditiously displaces other types of meaning and authority. Moreover without the absent sedition, there would be no requirement for sovereignty.

Although Ryan reaches a Marxist conclusion from this deconstruction, where permanent revolution is the equivalent of linguistic difference, gendered oppositions can clearly be discerned in this account, since it is the feminine within western discourses that is a metaphor for undecidability, disorder, multiplicity and sedition. Although on an explicit level both men and women are at war in the natural state, the gendered oppositions at work within the text tell a typically virile story, where men pass from nature to culture; from passion to reason; from chaos to order; from multiplicity to unity; from unstable patterns of power and passion to the civil law where meanings are stable and terminated in a final authority (a transcendental signifier). Thus in deconstructive terms, *Leviathan* is a narrative about the transition from a feminine to a masculine register, just as in psychoanalytic terminology it marks the shift from infantile maternal dependence to the autonomous masculinized ego; from polymorphous perversity and heterogeneity to the Law of the Father and homogeneity (where the Oedipus complex is equivalent to the social contract as a membrane or threshold between the two states. Although reversible, transgression of the contract heralds chaos, just as regression to the pre-Oedipal signals madness). If, for Ryan, Hobbes's thesis means displacing permanent revolution by absolute authority, for women it suggests a suppression of the difference and relatedness that might engender more 'feminine' authority patterns, under the monotonal speeches of the masculine, phallic one.[30] Yet it also gestures to the feminine as a permanent source of subversion.

Carole Pateman's use of psychoanalysis in *The Sexual Contract* (1988) is rather different from those described above, because she interprets Freud's story of the primal horde as a historical occurrence which she uses to reveal the sexual dimension of the social contract, rather than to explain its unconscious dynamic.[31] In fact her work combines aspects of both the approaches I mentioned in the introduction. Like Benhabib, Pateman interprets the tradition as displacing patriarchy in favour of fraternity (or more accurately: as displacing seventeenth-century patriarchy *qua* father-right, by modern forms of fraternal patriarchy *qua* male-right).

For Pateman, the social contract presupposes and sustains an integral sexual contract whereby the brothers acquire rights over women's bodies. 'Modern patriarchy is fraternal in form and the original contract is a fraternal pact'.[32] According to Freud, the brothers kill the father out of jealousy for his access to women which he denies them. He presents this as the origin of kinship relations: thenceforth each child relives the guilt of parricide through the Oedipus complex, whereby the boy renounces his mother and identifies with his father, thereby sustaining the incest taboo and acquiring a male identity. Pateman (problematically, in my opinion) conflates the original historical act with the social contract between brothers. According to her reconstruction, the primal patriarch must have possessed a woman to become a father in the first place and because of his unrestrained will, this must be interpreted as rape.[33] It is this sex-right that the brothers then inherit, sharing it through the non-incestuous kinship relations whereby women are exchanged, and constraining their rivalries through civil law, which now has a 'completely different basis' from the primal father's rule. This is the sexual contract, which in modern social contract theory is displaced on to the marriage contract, although this is not its sole manifestation. It is true then that patriarchy (*qua* father-right) is over-thrown, but what the brothers share is not a father but their sex-right over women.

Moreover, because women cannot therefore be the proprietors of their persons, since their bodies are at the disposal of men, they cannot exercise the possessive individualism which is the criterion of citizenship. Although women will gain access to the latter, Pateman argues that modern positions of subordination, such as that of the wife, are *created* through contract. Nor do women enter such contracts as abstractly equal individuals, but as embodied women whose bodies cannot be contracted out for use (such as sexual services or surrogate motherhood) while leaving the individual free, as contract theories and possessive individualism assume, both because their bodies are intrinsic to women's identity as women, and because they carry within them the subordination established by the sexual contract. 'In the victory of contract, the patriarchal construction of sexual difference as mastery and subjection remains intact and repressed'.[34] Pateman's conclusion is therefore both that modern patriarchy takes contractual (fraternal) form, and that contractual relations are inherently patriarchal (masculine), so that it would be disingenuous for feminists to adopt them as a model of free and equal gender relations.

In the course of her argument, Pateman criticizes Juliet Mitchell for arguing that the law of the father is established after the primal father's murder and continues within modern patriarchy. 'The social contract *replaces* the law of the father with impartial, public laws'.[35] However, Mitchell's claim is supported by Freud's own account in *Totem and Taboo*, in a *psychoanalytic*, rather than a *historical*, sense. It is the *symbolic* father and his law which is unconsciously reinstated in every child as it passes through its Oedipal phase to become a subject under the Law of the Father. Although civil relations may enter a new fraternal phase under modern conditions, as Benhabib and Pateman suggest, then, the unconscious law remains patriarchal. It is the law that breaks up the mother–child dyad and that imposes a symbolic order which is phallocentric.

It is the place of the father, not the actual father, that is... here
significant.... The little boy cannot *be* the father, but he can be
summoned for his future role in-the-name-of-the-father. The symbolic
father, for whose prehistoric death the boy pays the debt due, is the law
that institutes and constitutes human society, culture in the fullest sense
of the term, the law of order which is to be confounded with language
and which structures all human societies, which makes them, in fact,
human.[36]

The implication of this is that even if contractual relations include women,
the situation is bleaker than Pateman allows since it is not just historical
male sex-right, but the very foundations of civilization, of what it means to
be a subject, that construct her as an object of exchange and as a lack. 'This
is the story of the origins of patriarchy. It is against this symbolic mark of
the dead father that boys and girls find their cultural place within the instance
of the Oedipus complex'.[37] According to this 'socio-symbolic contract',[38] the
boy learns his place as heir to the father's law; only he will be allowed to
take the father's place, while girls are consigned to the family and to a
symbolic realm that has no name for them.

CONCLUSION: RENEGOTIATING THE CONTRACT

The responses of feminism to social contract theory have been, as this chapter
shows, primarily critical. The theory has been condemned for its exclusions
of women and deconstructed to reveal multiple levels of gendered thinking.
Both its individualism and its theory of justice have been identified with
specifically masculine norms. Nevertheless, feminists have been giving some
consideration to alternative modes and these might be described, following
object-relations theory and the ethical studies of Carol Gilligan, as expressing
a more feminine voice (although it should be noted that this is only typically
and contingently a woman's voice). In ethics, this is associated with an
orientation to care and responsibility for concrete others, yielding a massive
feminist literature debating how these traditionally private virtues might find
a place in the public realm.[39] In democratic theory generally, this is paralleled
by the question of how universality and difference are to be reconciled in a
postmodern, multicultural world.

Overall, contemporary democratic theorists, communitarians and feminists seem to be in broad agreement in challenging the liberal model of
contract, which institutes impersonal rules and authorities to which obedience is then due, on the one hand, and presents a model of self-interested
exchanges and rational choices as the paradigm for public relationships on
the other. In the democratic, discursive ethics which is their alternative,
conversation rather than contract (voices rather than choices) is the model,
intersubjectively enjoined by individuals or groups in their particularity.
Although consent remains essential, the goal is no longer consensus but

ongoing negotiation within a broadened public space; a dialogue among actual, encumbered, situated selves.[40] This may only mean empowering women's voices to participate, among others, in negotiating the form of public values and style of institutions; in enjoining an incessant debate concerning the very foundations of the social contract (regarding the processes of political association and the good life) and, more specifically, actually practising new ones. But many feminists also insist that these practices themselves entail an intrusion of 'feminine' (and mainly women's) orientations – towards relatedness; care for others in their otherness; reciprocal, collective life; compassionate judgement; openness to ambiguity – into the sterile politics of the 'neutral', impersonal, contractual, *masculine* state. From this perspective, questions concerning the social contract, and contractual relations more generally, cannot be separated from the social, psychological and discursive constructions of gender; as far as feminists are concerned, their purely formal analysis is only another example of a mystifying and masculine approach.

NOTES

1 This accusation was initially developed by Mary Wollstonecraft in her *Vindication of the Rights of Woman*, London, Everyman, 1929. Using Lockian arguments, she insisted that universal rights must include women; if their reason was deficient, this was due only to a mix of poor education, patriarchal culture and the mentally stultifying effects of domestic life. In this context she specifically challenges Rousseau's naturalism. However, Wollstonecraft's concern is with civil, more than political, rights, and she particularly draws attention to the discrepancy between attacks on aristocratic privilege in public, and support for the husband's authority in the home.

2 A pathbreaking article here was one published by T. Brennan and C. Pateman, '"Mere Auxiliaries to the Commonwealth": Women and the Origins of Liberalism', *Political Studies*, 1979, vol. XXVII. Detailed analyses of Hobbesian and Lockian texts include: M. Butler, 'Early Liberal Roots of Feminism: John Locke and the Attack on Patriarchy', *American Political Science Review*, 1978, vol. 72; L. Clark, 'Women and Locke: Who Owns the Apples in the Garden of Eden?', in *The Sexism of Social and Political Theory*, L. Clark and L. Lange (eds), Toronto, University of Toronto Press, 1979; M. L. Shanley, 'Marriage Contract and Social Contract in Seventeenth-Century English Political Thought', in *The Family in Political Thought*, J. Elshtain (ed.), Sussex, Harvester, 1982; D. Coole, 'Rereading Political Theory from a Woman's Perspective', *Political Studies*, 1986, vol. XXXIV; D. Coole, *Women In Political Theory: From Ancient Misogyny to Contemporary Feminism*, Sussex, Wheatsheaf, 1988, 2nd edn, 1993, ch. 4; C. Pateman, *The Disorder of Women*, Cambridge, Polity Press, 1989; C. Pateman, *The Sexual Contract"*, Cambridge, Polity Press, 1988; C. Pateman, ' "God Hath Ordained a Helper': Hobbes, Patriarchy and Conjugal Right', in *Feminist Interpretations and Political Theory*, M. Shanley and C. Pateman (eds), Cambridge, Polity Press, 1991.

3 T. Hobbes, *Leviathan*, J. Plamenatz (ed.), London, Fontana, 1962, ch. XX, p. 197.

4 C. Pateman, 'Hobbes', in *Feminist Interpretations*, Shanley and Pateman (eds), p. 65

5 Hobbes, *Leviathan*, ch. XIX, p. 195
6 Hobbes, *Leviathan*, ch. XX, pp. 197f.
7 J. Locke, *Two Treatises on Government*, P. Laslett (ed.), Cambridge, Cambridge University Press, 1960, II, 78
8 Locke, *Two Treatises*, II, 82
9 Locke, *Two Treatises*, II, 74, 75
10 This point Locke draws on C. B. Macpherson's deductions regarding lacunae among working-class men, who are also thereby excluded from full citizenship. See his *The Theory of Possessive Individualism*, Oxford, Oxford University Press, 1962.
11 J.-J. Rousseau, *Emile*, B. Foxley (trans.), London, Melbourne and Toronto, Everyman, 1911, p. 328.
12 The theme (minus the gender implications) is developed persuasively by L. Colletti in 'Rousseau as Critic of "Civil Society"', in his *From Rousseau to Lenin*, New York and London, Monthly Review Press, 1972.
13 S. M. Okin sums up this vision well, as 'the sentimental family'. See 'Women and the Making of the Sentimental Family', *Philosophy and Public Affairs*, 1982, vol. XI. For her fuller account of Rousseau's thinking on women, see S. M. Okin, *Women in Western Political Thought*, London, Virago, 1980.
14 Hegel discusses women and the family in both *The Phenomenology of Mind*, J. B. Baillie, (trans.) New York, Harper & Row, 1967, in the section on ethical life, and in *The Philosophy of Right*, T. M. Knox (trans.), Oxford, Oxford University Press, 1967, in the section on the family.
15 This is true both for classical contract theories and for more recent revivals of the tradition. J. Rawls's *A Theory of Justice*, Cambridge Mass., Harvard University Press, 1971, has attracted widespread feminist criticism in this context. See for example I. M. Young, *Justice and the Politics of Difference*, Princeton, NJ, Princeton University Press, 1990; S. Benhabib, *Situating the Self: Gender, Community and Postmodernism in Contemporary Ethics*, Cambridge, Polity Press, 1992.
16 Feminisms, plural, is a term now frequently used to denote the irreducible variety of forms that such thinking takes. Corresponding to it is an acknowledgement that despite greater emphasis on sexual difference, women are also highly diverse and perhaps sufficiently so that it is no longer legitimate to speak of them (us) as a whole. Pronouns become irresolvably problematic here and I have adopted a generalizing, third-person voice in this chapter while acknowledging its difficulties.
17 This Kleinian theory, with its emphasis on the pre-Oedipal mother–child relationship, has been enormously influential among feminists, especially as developed by N. Chodorow, *The Reproduction of Mothering*, Berkeley, Calif., University of California Press, 1978, and D. Dinnerstein, *The Mermaid and the Minotaur*, New York, Harper & Row, 1976. This is in spite of widespread criticism of the theory by feminists – for example, because it operates with a universal and binary account of gender that is insufficiently attuned to cultural and gender diversity.
18 Di Stefano, 'Masculinity as Ideology in Political Theory: Hobbesian Man Considered', *Women's Forum International Forum*, 1983, vol. 6, pp. 636, 635. I discussed this article at greater length in 'Rereading Political Theory', 1986, and it still seems to me that one of the outstanding questions posed by such an approach is why, given the generalized gender characteristics that are associated with modernity, these should be so well exemplified in contract theory yet so much less evident in for example dialectical theories, which would seem better to express a more feminine mode.
19 Stefano, 'Masculinity as Ideology', p. 637.

20 K. Jones, *Compassionate Authority: Democracy and the Representation of Women*, New York and London, Routledge, 1993, pp. 50–7.

21 Jones, *Compassionate Authority*, p. 47

22 Jones, *Compassionate Authority*, p. 51. The final phrase in quotation marks is from Dinnerstein. Jones's interpretation seems, however, to rely upon an elision of two rather different senses of dependency, since although the infant undoubtedly depends on its mother, natural man can be said to depend on others only to the extent that his survival may rely on their not exercising their natural rights against him, which seems a rather curious use of the term.

23 Jones, *Compassionate Authority*, p. 67.

24 Benhabib, *Situating the Self*, p. 161.

25 Jones, *Compassionate Authority*, p. 70.

26 Benhabib, *Situating the Self*, p. 156.

27 Benhabib, *Situating the Self*, p. 157.

28 Jones, *Compassionate Authority*, p. 21.

29 M. Ryan, *Marxism and Deconstruction*, Baltimore, Md, and London, Johns Hopkins University Press, 1982, p. 3.

30 Jones, *Compassionate Authority*, p. 70.

31 One of Lacan's criticisms of Freud is that he lapsed into real, rather than symbolic, time in mistakenly arguing for the existence of a historical parricide as the origin of the Oedipus complex in *Totem and Taboo*. See *Feminism and Psychoanalysis: A Critical Dictionary*, Elizabeth Wright (ed.), Oxford, Basil Blackwell, 1992, p. 294. This accounts for the disagreement between Pateman and the Lacanian Juliet Mitchell. Pateman also discusses Freud to classify him among those thinkers who legitimize women's exclusion from political power by invoking a natural sexual difference. As a result of the different routes that boys and girls take through the Oedipus complex, Freud concludes that girls have weaker superegos and thus a lesser sense of justice, rendering them a permanent threat to social order. See *The Sexual Contract*, p. 100, and '"The Disorder of Women"': Women, Love and the Sense of Justice', *Ethics* 1980, vol. 91.

32 Pateman, *The Sexual Contract*, p. 77.

33 Pateman, *The Sexual Contract*, p. 107. Two aspects of Freud's text do not fit with Pateman's account, however. First, Freud does not interpret parricide as the overthrow of the father's power as such: 'The dead father became stronger than the living one had been' under a psychological procedure of 'deferred obedience'. Second, Freud argues that the brothers guiltily renounced the fruits of their deed 'by resigning their claim to the women who had now been set free': Freud, *Totem and Taboo*, James Strachey (trans.), New York, W.W. Norton, 1950, p. 143.

34 Freud, *Totem and Taboo*, p. 187. This brief discussion of some of the key themes of Pateman's book cannot of course do justice to it. For a longer consideration and some of my hesitations about her account, together with Pateman's response, see D. Coole, 'Patriarchy and Contract: Reading Pateman', and Pateman, 'Contract and Ideology: A Reply to Coole', *Politics*, 1990, vol. 10.

35 Pateman, *Sexual Contract*, p. 104.

36 J. Mitchell, *Psychoanalysis and Feminism*, Harmondsworth, Penguin, 1974, p. 391

37 Mitchell, *Psychoanalysis and Feminism*, p. 403.

38 The term is Julia Kristeva's. See her 'Woman's Time', in *The Kristeva Reader*, T. Moi (ed.), Oxford, Basil Blackwell, 1986.

39 C. Gilligan, *In a Different Voice*, Cambridge Mass., and London, Harvard University Press, 1982. For bibliographical details of the huge literature which has followed on feminist ethics, see S. Krol and S. Sevenhuijsen (eds) *Ethics and Morality in Feminism. An Interdisciplinary Bibliography*, Utrecht, University of Utrecht, 1992.

40 Much of the influence here has been Habermasian, although feminists have
    generally contested his ideal of consensus and what they see as an overly
    rationalistic bias. See for example I. M. Young, *Justice*; S. Benhabib, *Situating
    the Self*; S. White, *Political Theory and Postmodernism*, Cambridge, Cambridge
    University Press, 1991; K. Jones, *Compassionate Authority*. Young inclines more
    to the idea of empowering women among other groups, but Benhabib, White
    and Young all suggest a link between communitarian politics and feminist ethics.

12 Gauthier's contractarian morality

Margaret Moore

The central aim of David Gauthier's *Morals by Agreement* is to derive principles of morality, or justice, from the starting-point of the agent as a rational, self-interested (non-tuist) utility-maximizer. 'Morality', Gauthier argues, '. . . can be generated as a rational constraint from the non-moral premises of rational choice'.[1] Self-interest, as Gauthier recognizes, is an unproblematic motive for human action. If Gauthier can demonstrate that the rules of morality further our interests, it is not difficult for him to explain the authority of morality, that is, why we would act in accordance with moral precepts.

Gauthier's argument takes the form of a hypothetical social contract. The liberal idea that legitimacy flows from agreement underlies contractarian arguments: the rules which constrain individuals' behaviour are legitimate only if they are consented to; and Gauthier can show that the moral rules generated by his argument would be consented to by rational agents because they are in each person's interests.

The contractarian project of demonstrating the legitimacy of principles or rules or institutions through agreement has received a great deal of attention recently.[2] There are many different arguments about what people find acceptable, and many different formulations of the contractarian project. Crucial to any contractarian argument is the underlying conception of the person and of practical reason. Obviously, different conceptions of what is essential to the person will yield different sets of principles or rules which would be acceptable to persons so described. It is also crucial that the parties to the contract are people with whom we can identify: if the argument is to have any relevance to us, in the real, empirical world, and legitimize rules or principles or institutions for us, the reasoning of the parties to the contract must be such that we can understand it and identify with it.

In his book *Theories of Justice*, Brian Barry argues that there are basically two types of theories of justice: justice as mutual advantage and justice as impartiality.[3] Both work from the intuitive idea of agreement or consent and thus both can be given a contractarian formulation.

The logic of mutual advantage theories is that everyone must gain from the agreement: the contract is acceptable, or agreed to, because advantageous to all the (self-interestedly rational) parties. But advantageous compared to what? In Hobbes's theory, the life of man in the state of nature is 'solitary, poore, nasty, brutish and short;'[4] and the agreement to set up rules to govern mutual cooperation and a coercive political authority to enforce those rules is advantageous relative to *that* state of nature.

Because, on Gauthier's theory, moral principles must be shown to be self-interestedly advantageous, it cannot generate duties to meet the needs of others or to rescue those in dire straits. Gauthier writes,

> the rich man may feast on caviar and champagne, while the poor woman starves at his gate. And she may not even take the crumbs from his table, if that would deprive him of his pleasure in feeding them to his birds.[5]

Although Gauthier does hope that people come to have some fellow feeling for each other, acts of charity or kindness cannot be demonstrated to be in the interests of each self-interested agent.

Nor is Gauthier's morals by agreement universal in its application. Because morality must be shown to be in everybody's interests, its rules come into play only when people engage in cooperative activity for mutual advantage. Gauthier's theory specifies the terms of that cooperation and what kinds of interactions are permissible or impermissible. But there is no *requirement* to interact with people, or animals, from which no benefit can be expected. This is explicit in Gauthier: 'Animals, the unborn, the congenitally handicapped and defective, fall beyond the pale of a morality tied to mutuality. The disposition to comply with moral constraints... may be rationally defended only within the scope of expected benefit'.[6]

Impartial theories of justice, by contrast, conceive of people, not as determinate individuals, with full knowledge of their talents and abilities and strengths, but as abstract persons, each one equal to the other, and the rules of justice as legitimate because impartial among the interests of persons, conceived in this abstract way. In Rawls's theory, for example, parties to the original position agree to the principles to govern the basic structure of society in ignorance of their natural endowment and position in society. Differences in natural endowment can be expected to affect differentially people's ability to secure goods for themselves, and so will affect the bargaining power of the parties to the agreement. For Rawls, these (natural endowments and bargaining power) are morally irrelevant: he seeks an agreement on the terms of the basic structure of society which is acceptable to all people viewed abstractly, as autonomous agents with a plan of life. Moral conceptions – conceptions of what is relevant and irrelevant to morality and morally valuable about the person – are thus incorporated into the theory, and structure the choice situation. As a result, the principles which Rawls arrives at, such as the requirement that the well-off be taxed in order to improve the lot of the worst-off in society, may seem closer to our intuitive conception of what morality involves. However, they would not be acceptable to Gauthier's rational non-tuists, nor to many concrete, determinate people in society (particularly those who are well-off), many of whom would not agree to taxes to improve the lot of the worst-off. Impartial theories may be more attractive conceptions of morality (universalist and inclusive), but, as Brian Barry points out, they do not show that morality is in our interests and so have difficulty explaining why people should act in accordance with morality.[7]

On Gauthier's conception of morals by agreement, the principles of justice or morality are principles of self-constraint which are instrumentally rational to the pursuit of self-interest, correctly understood. They are what rational agents would agree to as mutually beneficial to the pursuit of their individual self-interest. Specifically, Gauthier argues that rational agents would agree to cooperate with each other because this is mutually advantageous; that only bargains which proceed from a fair initial position and which divide the fruits of cooperation fairly (in accordance with his Principle of Minimax Relative Concession) would be agreed to by rational agents; and, furthermore, that rational agents would comply with the (fair) agreements that they make. At each stage of the argument, Gauthier is anxious to demonstrate not only the individual rationality of cooperation and compliance and the terms of cooperation, but also that the terms of cooperation can plausibly be described as moral principles.

Gauthier's quest to arrive at morals from the premises of self-interested reason is governed by his conception of morality. In Gauthier's view, a moral constraint has two features. First, it 'is internal, in operating through the will, or decision-making of the agent'.[8] If Gauthier can show that such a constraint is self-interestedly rational, he can link morality with the internal subjective motivational set of the agent. There is no difficulty in explaining why someone does something if we can show that it is in her interests. Second, Gauthier argues that the constraint must 'operate in a manner that satisfies some standard of impartiality among persons'.[9] At one level, any theory of mutual advantage is impartial in the sense that what is agreed to must be in the interests of each agent (otherwise they would not agree). They may agree for their own partial, self-interested reasons, but the terms eventually arrived at can be characterized as impartial in the sense that it advances everyone's interests and so is impartial between them. However, the two distinct components of Gauthier's conception of morality – rationality and impartiality – pull in different directions, and ultimately lead to two distinct conceptions or theories.

This chapter argues that Gauthier's quest to satisfy the impartiality requirement exerts pressure on his theory *away* from the premises of a pure mutual advantage conception and leads Gauthier to modify his argument in an impartialist direction. The integrity of Gauthier's derivation from the non-moral premises of self-interested reason is compromised at crucial points in his argument, namely, in his argument for keeping the agreements one makes, and bargaining from fair initial positions only. At crucial points in his argument, Gauthier departs from the assumptions of mutual advantage and attempts to derive principles which are impartially acceptable, and so could plausibly be described as *moral* principles. Moreover, in chapter VIII, 'The Archimedean Point', where Gauthier demonstrates the impartiality of his results, he suggests a more radical, more abstract (and more thoroughly impartial) justificatory conception than the one advanced hitherto. Ultimately, this chapter will argue, Gauthier is unable to reconcile the two elements of his moral theory: the rationality requirement (that it be acceptable to each individual self-interested agent); and the impartiality requirement of morality.

This chapter, then, questions the deduction of the principles of morality from the non-moral premises of rational choice: it questions whether the principles which Gauthier arrives at are the *rational* ones to adopt; and whether what rationally self-interested (non-moral) agents would agree to constitutes *morality*. It concludes by suggesting that the principles of morality cannot be demonstrated to be self-interestedly rational: there is an unavoidable gap between reason and morality, between what is acceptable from the standpoint of self-interested agents, who are not interested in the interests of others, and what is acceptable from the impartial standpoint.

IS IT RATIONAL?

Is it rational to keep one's agreements?

The structure of Gauthier's argument is similar to Hobbes's argument from mutual advantage in *Leviathan*. Hobbes argued that moral rules are instrumentally rational to the pursuit of each person's self-interest: they are, he wrote, 'theorems concerning what conduceth to the preservation and defence' of mankind.[10] Morality is presented in Hobbes as a system of mutually advantageous constraints on the pursuit of self-interest, and the sovereign or political authority is justified as a mechanism to ensure that individuals adhere to these constraints. In Hobbes's theory, political authority is an external coercive power to ensure that the parties to the initial contract comply with their agreement: coercion is necessary because, although cooperation is mutually advantageous, sometimes it is more rational (in self-interested terms) to agree to cooperate and defect when possible, than to keep one's agreements.

In contrast to Hobbes, Gauthier argues that the instrumental reasoning underlying the adoption of moral principles does not lead to problems of compliance: it doesn't justify cheating when this is instrumentally rational. He offers a non-political solution to the compliance problem: he argues that we must modify our view of what is rational in certain situations. In situations where cooperation is not involved, particular choices are rational if they maximize the agent's expected utility. But in situations where cooperation is involved, the standard conception of rationality as straight-forward utility-maximization should be modified. Gauthier points out that, in cooperative interaction, straightforward utility-maximization on the part of each agent will result in a sub-optimal outcome. The relevant question is not whether it is rational to comply or not to comply with a bargain in each particular case but whether it is rational to *dispose* oneself to comply with one's agreements. He argues that it *is* rational to adopt a disposition to choose cooperation over defection because the agent can expect actions based on this disposition to yield more utility than any other disposition or strategy.

Gauthier distinguishes between two types of dispositions. Constrained maximization is the disposition to uphold any agreements that one makes, while straightforward maximization is the disposition to straightforwardly maximize one's utility, and this involves defecting from the agreements one makes if that should prove to be more utility-maximizing. Gauthier's argument for the rationality of constrained maximization is this: if a constrained maximizer (CM) believes that the other party will cooperate, then the CM will too; but if the CM believes that the potential partner to a contract is a straightforward maximizer (SM), she will not cooperate. Therefore, when CMs meet, and recognize each other to be CMs, they will cooperate. In this way, Gauthier argues, CMs will have more opportunities for beneficial cooperative activity than SMs.

Gauthier's argument for constrained maximization raises many questions, not the least of which is its relevance for people in the real, empirical world. One line of criticism focuses on the psychological plausibility of Gauthier's agents.[11] Specifically, is it possible to *choose* dispositions? Is it possible to induce in oneself a disposition not merely to cooperate when one thinks one's partner will do so as well, but a disposition so strong that one will not defect even when there is no chance that defection will be penalized? Suppose, for example, that the sum of money from defection is so large that one will be immune from the consequences of defections – exclusion from further beneficial joint ventures is not much of a deterrent when one has the opportunity to leave the country or live very well on the proceeds of defection. This point is especially pertinent given that, on Gauthier's conception, the adoption of the disposition is justified in utility-maximizing terms, as a meta-strategy which is rational in certain situations. Why should we confine our attention to only two possible situations and two possible meta-strategies? There are other situations (e.g. large pay-offs) in which other strategies or dispositions might be effective in utility-maximizing terms.

The relevance of Gauthier's argument is jeopardized also by his assump-tion that CMs and SMs can recognize each other a fairly high percentage of the time. Gauthier writes: 'Suppose a population evenly divided between constrained and straightforward maximizers. If the constrained maximizers are able to co-operate successfully in two-thirds of their encounters, and to avoid being exploited by straight-forward maximizers in four-fifths of their encounters, then constrained maximizers may expect to do better than their fellows'.[12] In this crucial passage, Gauthier assumes, without argument, that people can detect the dispositions of others with a very high degree of accuracy. The assumption is unrealistic, especially when we recall that the only difference between a CM and a SM is the disposition they have induced in themselves regarding what it is self-interestedly rational to do. The motives of both are the same (self-interest). They diverge merely in having different conceptions of what it is rational to do in certain situations. How can people so accurately detect which people have adopted which rational meta-strategy – especially when, presumably, SMs seek to disguise their dispositions when interacting with CMs?

Moreover, the argument assumes that there is a fairly large number of CMs in the population in the first place. It is rational to become a CM only if there are enough other people in the population who are also CMs, for only in that situation will one benefit from one's disposition to keep the agreements one makes. If there are no other CMs, or very few, the CM agent will realize no benefit from her disposition, and, in fact may find herself the victim of defection and exploitation when she mistakenly interacts with SMs.

Both the threshold assumption and the assumption that agents can recognize the dispositions of others a high percentage of the time rely on Gauthier's idealized conception of *equally rational* agents. Being equally rational – with no psychological strengths and weaknesses[13] – they are all able to detect dispositions with roughly the same degree of accuracy. And, being equally rational, agents will presumably reason identically – they will all recognize the advantage of constrained maximization in overcoming prisoner's dilemma-structured situations – and so the emergence of the threshold number of CMs, indeed a population of CMs, can be explained.

But this serves only to reveal how strong, and implausible, the equal rationality assumption is. The assumption that people are rational or equally rational is used in game theory, in economics and in rational choice theory to mean only that agents are motivated to maximize their utility: it does not indicate that people have identical strengths and weaknesses, or identical powers of deception and insight. However, Gauthier is using the assumption to mask important differences between people, differences in their talents and abilities and preferences, those things on which rational agents usually *base* their decision about what it is rational for them to do, what will maximize their utility. In Gauthier's world, it seems, there are no good poker players; there are no people who find it rational to cultivate their considerable powers of deception rather than simply accept Gauthier's argument that the threat of being recognized will result in fewer opportunities for beneficial cooperation.

The abstraction involved in Gauthier's equal rationality assumption is extremely problematic for a mutual advantage theory, which claims to demonstrate the rationality of certain principles or actions or dispositions for each person, as she is, given her determinate abilities and beliefs and utility function. Indeed, Gauthier criticizes Rawls's impartialist conception on the grounds that it arrives at the impartial, moral standpoint only by abstracting from people's differences, people's natural endowments. This is problematic, according to Gauthier, because people's abilities and talents are part of who they are, part of their identity and must be incorporated in any theory of justice.

> In supposing that the just distribution of benefits and costs in social interaction is not to be related to the characteristics of the particular individuals who make up society, Rawls violates the integrity of human beings as they are and as they conceive themselves. . . . In his argument morality is divorced from the standpoint of the individual actor.[14]

And yet, it is essential to the success of Gauthier's argument for constrained maximization that the equal rationality assumption is interpreted in this strong and implausible way. If we allow that people are differentially talented (at deception, say, or the ability to detect deception), then it may well be rational for some individuals to defect from their agreements. And if there is enough uncertainty about dispositions, because there are some people who are good at hiding their dispositions, or others who have poor insights into the dispositions of others, then it will not be rational to adopt a constrained maximization disposition. And, if that is the case, then it is unclear how the threshold number of constrained maximizers required by Gauthier's argument could arise in the first place.

Is there a rational principle of distribution?

In his argument for a rational principle to divide the fruits of cooperation, Gauthier advances his Principle of Minimax Relative Concession (MRC principle), which he claims accurately reflects the process of bargaining. According to this principle, rational contractors would distribute the cooperative surplus on terms which required all participants to make equal concessions from their maximal claims.

Gauthier's central argument for both the rationality and fairness of the MRC principle is that it mirrors real bargaining processes where rational people seeks to minimize the concessions that they have to make in order to reach agreement. In Gauthier's view, an equal concession is rational assuming that both parties are equally rational. By this he means not only that his contractors are under no illusions about how to maximize their utility, and will do whatever is most advantageous for them, but also that they have 'no psychological strengths to exploit, or psychological weaknesses to be exploited'.[15] Since both parties to the contract are equally rational, what is rational for one will be rational for the other. Gauthier points out that both participants are utility-maximizers and would of course like to concede as little as possible in order to reach an agreement, but it would violate the assumption of equal rationality if one were to accept an agreement which required her to concede more than she had to, more than the other party to the agreement. It follows from this that neither will do so. Being equally rational, both recognize the futility of holding out for more, and so will settle on terms which minimize the concessions that each has to make. This is rational, because both parties to the agreement benefit from it (or else they wouldn't agree) and moreover they benefit to the maximum, because the terms of cooperation are such that neither could extract a greater concession from her partner. And the (equal) concession that each has to make to accommodate the interests of the other is fair in so far as the participation of both is necessary to producing the cooperative surplus.

Commentators on Gauthier's argument have pointed out that, while he does need a rational method to divide the fruits of cooperation, it is not crucial that the MRC principle is that principle. Some critics of Gauthier's work have argued that we do not have sufficient knowledge of bargaining processes to know whether or not focusing on concessions from maximum claims does mirror actual bargaining, as Gauthier claims;[16] while others have claimed that some people would benefit more from other principles of dividing the surplus and that utility-maximizers would argue for those principles which promised to divide up the cooperative surplus to her advantage.[17] These criticisms question whether there is a single rational solution to all bargaining problems, as Gauthier's argument requires, suggesting instead that the terms of cooperation are essentially contested.

What is noteworthy here is that Gauthier's argument for a rationally defensible and fair principle to dictate the terms of cooperation crucially depends on an equal rationality assumption. It is because he situates his agents equally with respect to their rationality – with respect to their reasoning powers, their psychological weaknesses and strengths and their motives – that he can arrive at an intuitively fair solution such as equal concession from the maximum claims. But, even if we allow that assumption, we must note that equal rationality does not imply equal bargaining power. Sometimes, bargainers are situated unequally with respect to their need to cooperate with each other. While Gauthier's argument might work in abstraction from considerations of context, such as how much one needs to make the bargain or what one's opportunity costs are relative to not bargaining with that person, it is quite clear that when such things are factored in, the results of actual bargaining can be highly unequal and intuitively unfair. The success of Gauthier's quest to derive moral principles from the premises of rational choice seems, then, to depend on his argument concerning the initial position or baseline from which bargaining can proceed. This is crucial to demonstrating whether what is rationally agreed to is also moral, or whether it merely reflects the threats and inequalities pervasive in relations between people.

Is it rational to bargain from a fair initial position only?

Gauthier's principle for the just distribution of gains from cooperation, the MRC principle, presupposes a baseline or determinate initial position to define the cooperative surplus. Gauthier argues that rational agents would assess the advantages or disadvantages of a bargain relative to what things would be like if that prospective bargainer was not around at all. This baseline is defined by Gauthier's 'Lockian Proviso', which 'prohibits bettering one's situation through interaction that worsens the situation of another'.[18]

By making non-interaction the baseline, Gauthier in effect 'purifies' the starting-point of the effects of past force or fraud. This is consistent with an important moral intuition – that agreements based on threats or coercion lack justificatory force. It represents an intuitively fair starting-point for bargaining because it embodies the (moral) idea of 'not taking advantage' of others.[19]

Why does Gauthier think that his rational contractors would agree to non-interaction, rather than, say, noncooperation, as the baseline? Gauthier begins his discussion through a parable of a slave-owning society, in which the Masters engage in coercion to force the Slaves to serve them. Gauthier points out that this society is sub-optimal: the Masters have to bear the costs involved in maintaining the coercive apparatus; the Slaves have to bear the even more unpleasant costs of being coerced. Gauthier then asks whether it would be rational for the Masters and the Slaves to agree to a bargain in which the Slaves continue to serve, but *voluntarily*. This is beneficial for the Slaves, for they are spared beatings; and beneficial for the Masters, who will continue to be served but without the costs of coercing the Slaves.

Gauthier argues that this bargain from an unfair initial position (one which does not satisfy the Lockian Proviso) is unstable: the slaves would soon fail to comply with the terms of their agreement. Gauthier imagines that one of the representatives of the ex-slaves would argue:

> It was only because of the power they held over us that it seemed a rational deal. Once that power was taken away, it became obvious that the fruits of co-operation weren't being divided up in accordance with that fancy principle of minimax relative concession. And so there wasn't any reason to expect voluntary compliance.[20]

The problem with this example is that Gauthier does not factor in the relative power of the Masters and the Slaves in considering whether the agreement is rational. If the former Masters do not dismantle their coercive apparatus, then it may well be rational for the Slaves to serve the Masters because this is better than being subjected to their coercion. The implicit threat is the return to the state prior to the agreement – not the state prior to *all* interaction. Indeed, this seems a natural starting-point from which to measure whether the bargain is rational or not.

In Gauthier's example, this scenario is not considered, because we are led to believe that the Masters have destroyed the instruments of coercion. But why would rationally self-interested, utility-maximizing Masters do this? For, if they are rational, as Gauthier supposes, they will be able to reproduce the reasoning of the Slaves and recognize what the Slaves would do once they are in a position of equality. The Masters would recognize that they should not make the agreement unless they are in a position to *ensure* compliance with the agreement, and one way to ensure compliance is to be prepared to reinstate the *status quo ante*. This suggests that it may well be rational to make an unfair agreement: it is certainly rational for the Masters, for the privileged position that they enjoy in the sub-optimal slave-owning society is better than equality with the ex-Slaves; and it may be rational for the slaves to agree to the Masters' admittedly unfair bargain because it is better than their present situation.

Gauthier's parable of the Masters and the Slaves is intended to demonstrate that unfair bargains are unstable, because it is not rational to comply with them. This conclusion is also reached through an analysis of strategic rationality which parallels his earlier analysis of constrained maximization.

Here Gauthier suggests that we can distinguish between two types of constrained maximizers: first, broad compliers, who will make and comply with any utility-maximizing agreements that they make; and second, narrow compliers, who will make and comply with fair agreements only ('fair' being defined in terms of the MRC principle and the Lockian Proviso).

Gauthier's argument for the rationality of narrow compliance is crucial to his demonstration that what rational self-interested agents would agree to is also moral or fair. He argues that it is rational to discourage sub-optimal predatory behaviour in the state of nature; hence, rational agents would exclude former predators from beneficial cooperation. This would have the effect of making the costs of predation (exclusion from beneficial cooperation) greater than its benefits, and thus would make prebargain predation irrational. Because predators know that they will be excluded from beneficial cooperation, they will have no incentive to engage in predatory activity; hence, they will adopt non-interaction as a baseline, and the fruits of force and fraud will not be factored into Gauthier's agreement.

But this argument is subject to the same difficulties as the parable of the Masters and the Slaves. Just as, in that story, Gauthier attempted to situate the Masters and the Slaves equally – by assuming that the Masters will dismantle their coercive weaponry, and, presumably, all knowledge of the *technology* of predation, – so, here, Gauthier attempts to situate the individuals equally by assuming that equally rational individuals will comply under the same conditions. He assumes that it is a violation of equal rationality if some individuals make unfair but mutually beneficial agreements.

The problem with this is that it abstracts completely from considerations of differential power and abilities, just as the Master/Slave parable does. Differential powers, in practice, in real-life bargains, translate into different points at which agreements – and compliance with agreements – become rational. Opportunity costs are a measure of this differential power. If X is sick or weak or old and has few opportunities for beneficial interaction, she might have to settle for an agreement which offers less than fair shares because no other opportunities present themselves. It might be rational for her to agree to an unfair, but still beneficial, bargain, because that is the best she can hope for in the circumstances.

Gauthier recognizes the importance of differential abilities on bargaining in his discussion of the scope of his principle. There he admits that his theory of justice as mutual advantage applies only when people enter into cooperative interaction with each other: if interaction with X doesn't promise to be mutually beneficial, then rational agents won't bargain with X; and she is outside the scope of morals by agreement. Similar considerations also apply *in* cooperative ventures: if someone has something which is valued by others, then she will have more options in bargaining, and this will affect whether she can afford to hold out for fair shares. Thus, it seems that whether the disposition to narrow compliance is rational or not depends on whether the person can afford to hold out for fairer terms, and that will be a function of the other opportunities available to her, which, in turn, will depend, at least in part, on whether she has things (talents, abilities, goods) which are in demand by others.

This point applies not only to productive powers but also to what is gained in predation: if I have control over the only fresh water well for miles around, then I may be precisely the person that you *need* to bargain with. You need access to what I control; you cannot afford to exclude me from future bargains – even though I may have acquired that control through superior force or fraud. This analysis suggests that a bargain would be preceded by a sub-optimal state of predation and defence against predation in an attempt to bring as many goods and powers to the bargaining table as possible.

The assumption of equal rationality does not imply equal productive or equal predatory powers; and because the parties to the bargain are not situated equally, it would seem that some may be rational to accept less than fair shares. Given differential opportunity costs implicit in differential powers, different people will find it rational to settle for different kinds of agreements, and some of these may incorporate the results of force and fraud. In his argument for the Lockian proviso and the rationality of narrow compliance, Gauthier employs the equal rationality assumption to argue that it would be rational for people to adopt a disposition to agree to and comply with fair agreements only. This is important to his project, because Gauthier seeks to arrive at principles which bear some resemblance to our intuitive sense of justice. But if the argument presented here is correct, then Gauthier's noncooperative baseline has to be seen as arising from a strategic struggle for relative advantage, and the resulting principles of distribution would reflect the threat advantage of successful predators.[21] This result threatens to jeopardize Gauthier's project of deducing *moral* principles from the starting-point of self-interested reason. Not only does it run counter to our most important intuitions about what is fair and just, but also it is difficult to see why the exercise of predatory powers (force and fraud) should constitute a morally relevant basis for distribution. Indeed, the justificatory force of Gauthier's morals by agreement depends on the notion of agreement or consent, but this is brought into question if the agreement itself is coercively structured by incorporating the results of force and fraud.

ARE GAUTHIER'S PRINCIPLES MORAL?

Because Gauthier's derivation of morals from self-interested reason employs no moral constraints or assumptions, he must demonstrate that what is agreed to by rationally self-interested contractors are *moral* principles. Therefore, Gauthier 'tests' the principles which are the outcome of his argument from an impartial moral standpoint which he calls the Archimedean point. In this chapter, Gauthier seeks to justify the deliberation process of the rational contractors on the grounds that it is *impartial*, and so claim that the principles which are the outcome of this procedure are moral.

Impartiality is embodied in Gauthier's Archimedean chooser who is not herself rationally self-interested – indeed, she has no particular identity, no particular talents or preferences or utility function of her own – but is motivated only to choose principles which impartially benefit all parties to a hypothetical agreement. The Archimedean chooser identifies with the interests of each party to the bargain, with full knowledge of the abilities, talents and preferences of each person, and attempts to maximize the utilities of each person. Gauthier argues that this will result in a point of convergence at which no one's utilities can be maximized further without making someone else worse off. This parallels Gauthier's description of bargaining in chapters IV to VII in which each agent is assumed to be utility-maximizing, and no rational agent would concede more than she has to. Not surprisingly, Gauthier argues that the Archimedean chooser would select the very same principles that his rationally self-interested maximizers would choose (constrained maximization, the Lockian proviso, Minimax Relative Concession).

However, in this chapter, as in the earlier argument, the problem of unequal power relations raises its head. Unequal power relations in society can affect the very abilities and talents that Gauthier's theory is sensitive to, and this threatens to vitiate the impartiality of his derivation. Imagine a severely class-divided society in which members of the lowest class are kept uneducated and ignorant, their talents undeveloped, so that they have very little to bargain with, and can perform only the most menial and degrading tasks. Would this be fair? Would the bargains entered into in this context be impartial and free, if the social structure itself is biased and individuals born into the lowest class have no other opportunities, no other options? Gauthier attempts to control for such coercively structured bargaining situations by modifying his conception of the Archimedean point:

> The principles chosen from the Archimedean point must. . . provide that each person's expected share of the fruits of social interaction be related, not to what he actually contributes, since his actual contribution may reflect the contingent permissions and prohibitions found in any social structure, but to the contribution he would make in that social structure most favourable to the actualization of his capacities and character traits.[22]

Not only must Gauthier's modified Archimedean chooser identify with each person concerned to maximize her utility, given her determinate abilities and talents, but also each person must be concerned with how the capacities and talents that she has will develop. She must consider this, Gauthier argues, because it is on the basis of the exercise of these talents that goods are distributed.

This modification seems justified from the standpoint of ensuring that his theory is truly impartial. It would seem unfair to tie the distribution of goods to talents, if there is no guarantee that these talents will develop under fair or impartial conditions. However, as Jean Hampton has argued in her important article,[23] it is not at all clear that proto-people, concerned with the development of their talents, would agree to the same rules or the same principles as determinate individuals, fully socialized, with developed factor endowments. If the social structure has favoured me, and I now possess rare and therefore lucrative abilities, why would I, a self-interested utility-maximizer, seek to change the social structure?

This is a question which Gauthier does not answer – indeed, he does not even seem to recognize the tension between these two aspects of his theory – and it probably cannot be answered within the context of his theory. The question raises the limitations of a theory of self-interested reason. What makes that conception so powerful, so promising, is that it claims to demonstrate why we, as we are, should act in accordance with morality; but, in considering the requirements of impartiality, we are led to consider who we are, and whether the conditions that have shaped us are truly impartial. And here the marriage of morality and self-interested reason begins to unravel, as the impartiality requirement questions who the self-interested 'self' is, and the determinate 'self' of self-interested conceptions would not agree to an impartial social structure.

CONCLUSION

It is crucial to Gauthier's conception of morality as part of rational choice theory that the principles he arrives at are both self-interestedly rational and acceptable from an impartial moral standpoint. To achieve this reconciliation of morals and reason, Gauthier attempts to purge his principles of the effects of unequal power relations in society. Specifically, Gauthier imports a very strong and implausible equal rationality assumption into his argument for constrained maximization and for the Lockian Proviso, which enables him to arrive at principles which seem fair and impartial. The equal rationality assumption functions to sanitize the bargain of all sense of context, and particularly contexts of unequal power. This is unfortunate because it is precisely the promise of sensitivity to context, and appeal to the powerful motive of self-interest which always operates within contexts, that makes Gauthier's project so compelling in the first place. Thus, the equal rationality assumption robs the theory of its relevance and its mutual advantage character: it seems plausible that real self-interested agents, who have unequal power and talents, would in fact arrive at principles which reflect their ability to threaten weaker parties to the contract.

Ultimately, the need to arrive at impartially acceptable principles leads Gauthier to modify his theory in an impartialist direction. In the chapter on the Archimedean point, Gauthier considers the effects of unequal power relations on the talents and abilities which his theory is sensitive to. As a result, the contract he describes is not one which rationally self-interested agents, with full knowledge of their abilities and preferences, would agree to, but a contract to determine what social structure would be impartially acceptable to abstract proto-people. This gap between the requirements of impartiality and the dictates of self-interest suggests, not surprisingly, that what is moral cannot be derived from self-interested reason; and that what is self-interestedly rational may not bear any resemblance to what is acceptable from an impartial moral standpoint.

NOTES

1 David Gauthier, *Morals by Agreement*, Oxford, Clarendon Press, 1986, p. 4.
2 B. Barry, *Theories of Justice*, Berkeley, Calif., University of California Press, 1989, pp. 3–9.
3 See, for example, Samuel Freeman, 'Reason and Agreement in Social Contract Views', *Philosophy and Public Affairs*, 1990, vol. 19, pp. 122–157; Thomas Scanlon, 'Contractualism and Utilitarianism', in *Utilitarianism and Beyond*, Amartya Sen and Bernard Williams (eds), Cambridge, Cambridge University Press, 1982, pp. 103–28; David Gauthier, 'The Social Contract as Ideology', *Philosophy and Public Affairs*, vol. 6, no. 2, pp. 130–64; Brian Barry, *Theories of Justice*.
4 Thomas Hobbes, *Leviathan*, C. B. Macpherson (ed.), Harmondsworth, Penguin, 1968, ch. 13, p. 186.
5 Gauthier, *Morals by Agreement*, p. 218.
6 Gauthier, *Morals by Agreement*, p. 268.

7 Barry, *Theories of Justice*, p. 7. However, Barry argues that impartialist theories *can* provide a motive for behaving justly. This is the 'desire to act in accordance with principles that could not reasonably be rejected' (p. 8).

8 David Gauthier, 'Morality, Rational Choice, and Semantic Representation', in *The New Social Contract: Essays on Gauthier*, Ellen Frankel Paul, Fred D. Miller Jr, Jeffrey Paul and John Ahrens (eds), Oxford, Basil Blackwell, 1988, p. 177.

9 Gauthier, 'Morality, Rational Choice, and Semantic Representation', p. 177.

10 Hobbes, *Leviathan*, ch. 15, p. 217.

11 Alan Nelson, 'Economic Rationality and Morality', *Philosophy and Public Affairs*, 1988, vol. 17, p. 158.

12 Gauthier, *Morals by Agreement*, p. 177.

13 Gauthier, *Morals by Agreement*, p. 156.

14 Gauthier, *Morals by Agreement*, p. 254.

15 Gauthier, *Morals by Agreement*, p. 156.

16 Gilbert Harman, 'Rationality in Agreement: A Commentary on Gauthier's Morals by Agreement', in *The New Social Contract*, Paul, Miller, Paul and Ahrens (eds), pp. 7–8; Nelson, 'Economic Rationality and Morality', p. 153.

17 Hampton, 'Can We Agree on Morals?' *Canadian Journal of Philosophy*, 1988, vol. 18, p. 341.

18 Gauthier, *Morals by Agreement*, p. 205.

19 Gauthier, *Morals by Agreement*, p. 205.

20 Gauthier, *Morals by Agreement*, p. 191.

21 Jan Narveson accepts that Gauthier's argument for non-interaction as the baseline is flawed, and that the rational baseline should incorporate predatory gains. However, Narveson is not troubled by this, because, he writes, exercising predatory power in the state of nature 'was not wrong, because nothing was wrong'. Jan Narveson, 'Gauthier on Distributive Justice and the Natural Baseline', in *Contractarianism and Rational Choice*, Peter Vallentyne (ed.), Cambridge, Cambridge University Press, 1991, p. 144. However, Narveson's sympathetic interpretation ignores the fact that Gauthier's project is a justificatory one, and it is difficult to see how the exercise of predatory powers (force and fraud) constitutes a morally relevant basis for distribution.

22 Gauthier, *Morals by Agreement*, p. 264.

23 Hampton, 'Can We Agree on Morals?', pp. 344–52.

13 Justifying 'justice'

Contractarianism, communitarianism and the foundations of contemporary liberalism

Paul Kelly

Such has been the influence of Rawls's *A Theory of Justice*,[1] that any discussion of contemporary liberalism must start with his contractarianism and its communitarian critiques.[2] In this chapter I want to trace the impact of the communitarian critique on liberal political theory after Rawls's *A Theory of Justice*. The chapter will begin by rehearsing the standard communitarian objection to liberalism. But in the second section I will also be focusing on Ronald Dworkin's liberal critique of Rawls's strategy in *A Theory of Justice* and *Political Liberalism*,[3] which claims that the continued adherence to the social contract renders Rawls's theory incapable of grounding liberal political principles. I will be concentrating on the recent work of two key liberal thinkers, John Rawls[4] and Ronald Dworkin,[5] because they represent the main strands of response to communitarianism within contemporary liberal theory.[6] Rawls attempts to accommodate the communitarians' rejection of the atomistic individual while maintaining a contractarian theory, whereas Dworkin argues that the moral schizophrenia implicit in Rawls's revised contractarianism undermines the possibility of justifying a genuinely liberal political theory. These attempts to accommodate what is of value in the communitarian critique have given rise to a distinction between *political* and *philosophical* or *ethical* versions of liberalism. Therefore, I will be arguing that whilst the communitarian critique has not provided much by way of a positive agenda for normative political theory it has changed the terms of debate within contemporary liberalism. In conclusion I will provide an assessment of this debate and argue that any adequate liberal theory must abandon contractarianism.[7]

A THEORY OF JUSTICE AND THE COMMUNITARIAN CRITIQUE OF CONTRACTARIANISM

The subject of Rawls's *A Theory of Justice* is nothing less then the principled justification of a liberal polity. He presents this liberal project in terms of a theory of distributive justice applicable to those institutions which comprise the 'basic structure of society'. The 'basic structure' of society covers all the major institutions of the political constitution as well as social and economic institutions, such as the monogamous family and competitive markets.[8] All of these institutions together define individuals' rights, duties, prospects and opportunities. The subject matter of the theory is the 'basic structure' of society, the point of the theory is to provide a set of principles which regulate the 'basic structure' such that the terms of association within a society are fair and consequently the society is well-ordered. Rawls defends two principles of justice to regulate the 'basic structure' of a well-ordered society, these are the equal liberty principle and his conception of democratic equality which comprises both fair equality of opportunity and the difference principle.

However, what is distinctive about Rawls's enterprise is the way in which he attempts to defend his conception of 'justice as fairness' by recourse to the social contract tradition. He writes:

> My aim is to present a conception of justice which generalizes and carries to a higher level of abstraction the familiar theory of the social contract as found in Locke, Rousseau, and Kant. In order to do this we are not to think of the original contract as one to enter a particular society or to set up a particular form of government. Rather, the guiding idea is that the principles of justice for the basic structure of society are the object of the original agreement. They are the principles that free and rational persons concerned to further their own interests would accept in an initial position of equality as defining the fundamental terms of their association. These principles are to regulate all further agreements; they specify the kinds of social cooperation that can be entered into and the forms of government that can be established.[9]

Rawls's theory is contractarian in the sense that the terms of association in a just or liberal polity are those that individuals would agree to as fair, because they are principles that would have been chosen in a hypothetical fair original agreement. His assumption is that political and social arrangements can be legitimized only if society is conceived of as a voluntary scheme of fair social cooperation in which individuals are regarded as free and equal. The social contract method is crucial for Rawls because it provides a justification which accommodates this conception of individuals as free and equal. Such a conception when fully worked out is, he argues, more likely to be consistent with our fundamental intuitions about the priority of the person, and it was precisely its inability to make sense of these intuitions which lead Rawls to reject utilitarianism.

A liberal polity structured in accordance with Rawls's two principles of justice is justifiable not because it maximizes welfare, but because it would be chosen in a hypothetical initial contract. Even though the contract situation can only be hypothetical, the contractarian method serves two purposes; first, it provides a mechanism for choosing the two principles of justice; and second, it aims to show us why we ought to accept the terms of association specified by the two principles. It achieves this second task by showing that the principles do not disadvantage us in order to advantage someone else, as utilitarian principles might, and because they recognize our status as equals.

While the contractarian method imbues the whole of Rawls's conception of 'justice as fairness', the main focus of discussion and criticism has been his account of the hypothetical contract and in particular the 'original position' and the 'veil of ignorance'. The 'original position' is the hypothetical situation of choice under which individuals choose among the rival candidate principles of justice, those principles which ought to apply to the 'basic structure' of society. As these principles apply not only to the distribution of political benefits but also the distribution of the benefits of 'social cooperation',[10] certain constraints have to be imposed on the situation of choice if it is to be a fair choice and not advantage any particular party. The 'veil of ignorance' is designed to bridge the gap between an individual's self-interested motivation and the requirements of impartiality which are built into the principles of justice. If individuals were left simply to maximize their mutual advantage there would be no reason for them to adopt the perspective of impartiality which underlies Rawls's liberalism. Thus, in order to make the 'original position' a fair situation of choice, Rawls introduces the idea of a 'veil of ignorance'. This blocks out all those aspects of a person's knowledge of themselves and society which would lead them to attach an undue weight to their own position. The 'original position' has to be recognized as a fair procedure if the principles chosen within it are to be accepted as just. The device of the 'veil of ignorance' provides for this by excluding from the choosers knowledge of their class or social position, their fortune, assets, talents or abilities, their conception of the good or their life plan, or specific features of their psychology. Furthermore, the choosers behind the 'veil or ignorance' do not know the circumstances of their own society, its political or economic situation or level of culture and civilization. Finally, they do not know to which generation they belong. In this way Rawls argues: 'no one is in a position to tailor principles to his advantage'.[11] Given these particular constraints on choice Rawls believes that the parties in the 'original position' would choose his two principles. And in so far as we can adopt the stance of the 'original position' as a thought experiment we can see why we should accept Rawls's two principles of justice as an account of fair terms of social cooperation. The crucial question raised by communitarians such as Sandel is whether we can adopt the stance of the original position?[12]

Michael Sandel argues that we cannot adopt the stance of the 'original position' and therefore we have no grounds for accepting Rawls's two principles or any other liberal principles chosen in such a hypothetical contract. His argument is addressed to both the contractarian method and the conception of liberalism it is supposed to justify, but I shall focus primarily on the critique of contractarianism. The first part of the argument against Rawlsian contractarianism is that it presupposes an implausible conception of the moral subject, the second part of the argument extends this critique of 'justice as impartiality'[13] into a 'motivation' problem.

The communitarian argument is that 'justice as impartiality' can have the priority it does only if individual subjects are conceptualized in a particular Kantian way, that is, as a subject distinct from its constitutive attachments. Sandel's claim is that Rawls's choosing subjects behind the 'veil of ignorance' are similarly detached or 'unencumbered selves'. They are deprived of knowledge of the particularities of their identity and that of their community, and of any conception of the good by the device of the 'veil of ignorance'. These 'unencumbered selves' stand in a proprietorial relation to their particular attributes. Thus one's projects, beliefs, moral values and rational life plans are things that a subject can stand in the same sort of relation to as they can to some external attribute such as an article of property. This conception of the moral subject as separate from his contingent attachments and the consequent conception of morality as a standpoint divorced from and impartial between rival conceptions of the good or well-being creates a number of serious problems for Rawls's contractarian method.

Most obviously, Rawls uses this conception of the person to ground principles of justice which are impartial between individuals' beliefs and conceptions of the good so that the resultant liberal polity will be neutral in its dealings with such individuals. It is only by adopting such an abstract conception of the moral subject that Rawls can provide an Archimedean point within the 'original position' from which genuinely impartial and universal principles must be chosen. But in appealing to this Kantian conception of the moral subject, Rawls is himself adopting a particular and by no means uncontestable conception of the subject. Against this Kantian view of the subject as pre-socially individuated – one whose identity is prior to his desires, beliefs and constitutive commitments – Sandel contrasts a conception of the self as situated in particular social relationships and practices so that the possibility of practical reason is itself only conceivable in the context of such communal practices or shared conceptions of the good.[14] Communitarian arguments typically refer to both Aristotle and Hegel as sources of the view that identities are embedded in, or the product of, communal attachments. The point here is that Rawls's conception of the subject is just as much a consequence of a particular philosophical anthropology as that of Aristotle, Hegel or contemporary communitarians, and that it violates the neutrality of his starting-point, namely that the *right* is prior to, and therefore neutral between, conceptions of the *good*.

However, the communitarians are not simply offering alternative conceptions of personal identity in order to show that we have a choice between Rawls's 'unencumbered selves' and Aristotelian accounts of the person. Rather the point is to show that Rawls's adoption of a radically individualistic contractarian methodology undercuts the possibility of grounding his conception of justice as 'impartiality' or 'fairness'. The social contract is used to show the practical necessity of the impartial perspective. This requires a conception of the subject as a pure chooser shorn of all contingent or empirical components of his identity. Such a person, it is argued, could not but choose the impartial perspective of justice as fairness.

Yet it is precisely at this point that the contractarian device fails. For if the subjects in the original position are denied all the forms of self-knowledge precluded by the 'veil of ignorance' then they cannot be said to engage in a rational discussion or bargain about how to proceed, therefore, how can we be said to choose the principles behind the 'veil of ignorance'? The contract is not interactive in the way in which one ordinarily understands contracts in law for example.[15] Thus the subjects behind the veil of ignorance do not so much decide in a voluntaristic sense on which principles are to be chosen, instead they decide on them in a cognitive sense, in the same way in which one might come to *decide* the validity of an argument. Instead of the terminology of choice and will, a more appropriate terminology for what goes on behind the 'veil of ignorance' is discovery, coming to awareness, or gaining recognition. This might not in itself seem a devastating criticism of Rawls's enterprise, but it does seriously undermine his recourse to a contractarian justification. For if we have no grounds for bargaining behind the 'veil of ignorance' because we have no grounds for individuating perspectives, then equally we have no clear grounds for maintaining the idea of the separateness of persons. Each individual behind the 'veil of ignorance' becomes identical with every other,[16] and where there is no difference we can assume an identity. The significance of this is not simply that it seems to embody precisely the defects that Rawls attributes to the idea of the 'impartial spectator' in utilitarian theory, but also that in so far as any representative individual can cognitively recognize the force of the two principles, then the whole idea of the contract becomes redundant. This is because for Rawls's method to provide us with reasons it would have to show that we already accept a constitutive conception of the community when we think about justice otherwise we would have no grounds for accepting the constraints of the original position. Sandel concludes his argument thus:

> what begins as an ethic of choice and consent ends, however unwittingly, as an ethic of insight and self-understanding. . . . The secret to the original position – and the key to its justificatory force – lies not in what they *do* there but rather in what they *apprehend* there. What matters is not what they choose but what they see, not what they decide but what they discover. What goes on in the original position is not a contract after all, but the coming to self-awareness of an intersubjective being.[17]

The point of Sandel's critique is to show that Rawls's social contract theory and the conception of the person upon which it is premised is incoherent and cannot justify his liberal theory of justice as impartiality. Consequently we can abandon not only his method but also his substantive theory. This seems an over hasty conclusion and one that many liberals have been unprepared to accept. Why not, as Brian Barry and T. M. Scanlon suggest, simply abandon Rawls's 'original position' contractarian device whilst retaining his commitment to one version of 'justice as impartiality'? Rawls just makes life difficult for himself by adopting such an abstract and philosophically implausible account of the person in order to ground an impartial perspective. If we abandon this device, so the argument goes, we can just sidestep Sandel's critique. This is obviously an attractive solution but is it sufficient to avoid the communitarian critique? If we concentrate narrowly on the 'original position' then it would appear that by abandoning that device we can still provide an alternative 'contractualist' justification for 'justice as impartiality'.[18] But this would be to misunderstand the full import of the communitarian critique.

The critique of the Rawlsian subject is intended to show not only that there is some incoherence in the idea of such a radically abstract chooser, but also that there is an unbridgeable gap between the moral perspective of impartiality in the 'original position' and the person outside the 'original position' who is in full knowledge of his beliefs, values and interests. This creates a problem of 'motivation': why should real people in full knowledge of their identities acknowledge the purchase of such a radically abstract moral identity and therefore acknowledge whatever principles are chosen behind the 'veil of ignorance'? What is more, this motivation problem remains even if we abandon the 'original position' altogether, for we will still be faced with the requirement to show why we should adopt the impartial perspective and accord it priority over the personal perspective?[19] To justify any conception of 'justice as impartiality' we need to show not only a connection bridging the gap between these two perspectives, the personal and the impartial, but also a connection which prioritizes the impartial. It is this problem which is at the core of the communitarian critique, and it is with this problem that contemporary liberal theory has had to wrestle. The next section will show how this problem has been central to the subsequent development of liberalism and how it has given rise to a bifurcation between *political* and *ethical* liberalism in the recent work of Rawls and Dworkin. This section will also assess the role of contractarian foundationalism in response to the communitarian critique.

POLITICAL *VERSUS* ETHICAL LIBERALISM

The communitarian critique of the social contract device leaves liberalism with a 'motivation' problem: how to connect the personal perspective with the impersonal perspective of the public realm. Communitarians such as Sandel have assumed that not only is the contractarian method undermined but also the whole liberal enterprise of drawing jurisdictional boundaries between private and public life. The claim is that resolving this 'motivation' problem is not possible with the conceptual resources of liberal political theory, instead the problem has to be overcome by combining the personal and impersonal perspectives within a shared conception of the common good. These shared conceptions of the common good provide the resources from which identities are formed, therefore the person is seen as a social creation and not independent of such constitutive communities. Given this fact communitarians argue that moral and political theory does not take the form of showing how the two distinct realms of the personal and the political can be reconciled, rather it proceeds by articulating the shared resources of a community or tradition. The ideas of will and contract play no useful part in this enterprise.

Whilst the communitarian critique of social contract theory has some merit, the positive agenda of communitarianism is deeply problematic. Not only is the project of grounding a shared common good no more easy than attempting to reconcile the claims of the personal and impartial realms, but the aspiration of returning to such a shared common life runs up against two problems. First, most societies that might serve as potential constitutive communities look pretty unpleasant; second, there is the problem of the fact of pluralism in most modern western societies. Pluralism challenges not only the possibility of gaining consensus on a conception of the good but also the possibility of reconciling constitutive communities with the political structures of modern nation-states.

It is precisely this problem of pluralism which undercuts the force of the communitarian critique and provides the original motivation for contractarian theories such as Rawls's. The very attraction of the contractarian device was that it appeared to provide a ground for liberal political principles in circumstances where there is no consensus on a shared common good. Whereas utilitarian, perfectionist and communitarian theories define or identify the good and then try to deduce the political implications of institutionalizing that 'good', the contractarian method enabled liberal theory to determine a procedure from which rules of association could be derived which provide each individual with a reason for acknowledging the normative priority of those rules, but without expecting any convergence among individuals on such a common good. This procedural version of liberalism is obviously attractive as a means of realizing a liberal polity in a society characterized by pluralism.

Rawls claims in his new book *Political Liberalism* that it was his failure to take seriously enough in *A Theory of Justice* the problem of pluralism – precisely that which had originally motivated his theory – that prompted him to reconsider the foundations of his argument.[20] However, while Rawls does not respond directly to the communitarian challenge, his reinterpretation of his theory accommodates many of the substantive communitarian charges. What will be clear in the subsequent account of Rawls's conception of his theory as *political* rather than *metaphysical* is that while making concessions to the communitarians, the recognition of the fact of reasonable pluralism causes him to retain a substantively contractarian argument. The remainder of this section will examine, in the light of Ronald Dworkin's arguments, whether Rawls's *political* conception of 'justice as fairness' provides a sufficiently secure basis for a liberal theory of justice.

The main problem with *A Theory of Justice* that *Political Liberalism* is supposed to address arises from his conception of a well-ordered society in the former book. Rawls had assumed there that since the two principles of justice comprising 'justice as fairness' were chosen in the 'original position' they would become part of the comprehensive morality of a society for that reason. However, this runs up against the problem of reasonable pluralism among comprehensive doctrines in modern societies. This reasonable pluralism is according to Rawls 'the normal result of the exercise of human reason within the framework of the free institutions of a constitutional democratic regime'.[21] Reasonable pluralism precludes the possibility of a public morality for the foreseeable future and perhaps even as a goal, but leaves the problem of what terms of association can be justified given this fact. Rawls maintains that his theory of 'justice as fairness' still provides the only justifiable terms of association given this fact, but only when it is recognized as a *political* rather than a full or comprehensive moral doctrine.

While the goal of Rawls's 'new' theory is to accommodate reasonable pluralism, in recasting his theory as a *political* as opposed to a *metaphysical* theory he is also making a significant concession to the communitarians. As a *political* theory the task is no longer that of showing how the 'original position' can connect the personal and the impartial perspectives. Instead Rawls argues quite explicitly that the formal contractarianism of the 'original position' and 'veil of ignorance' serve only as devices of representation.[22] He acknowledges that individuals have conceptions of the 'good', and that some of these will be reasonable, and it is ultimately out of these reasonable comprehensive doctrines that the resources to justify liberal principles will be found. By using the 'original position' as a device of representation and disclaiming any *metaphysical* conception of the person he avoids having to define the moral perspective in Kantian terms as impartiality. Instead the impartial perspective is adopted only for specific political purposes, and the justification for adopting it is found in the variety of reasonable comprehensive moral doctrines, many of which would not identify the moral realm with the perspective of impartiality. Therefore, as Sandel originally claimed, Rawls is acknowledging that the priority of 'justice as fairness' is recognized from within the perspective of some reasonable comprehensive doctrine and is not a matter of will or pure choice behind a 'veil of ignorance'. Rawls writes:

> All those who affirm the political conception start from within their own comprehensive view and draw on the religious, philosophical, and moral grounds it provides. The fact that people affirm the same political conception on those grounds does not make their affirming it any less religious, philosophical, or moral, as the case may be, since the grounds sincerely held determine the nature of the affirmation.[23]

The difference between Rawls and communitarians is that Rawls recognizes a plurality of such reasonable comprehensive doctrines in modern pluralistic societies.

It is precisely because of this fact of pluralism that 'justice as fairness' has to be developed as a free-standing view, or one that does not presuppose any particular moral, psychological or epistemological doctrines, and around which an 'overlapping consensus' of reasonable comprehensive doctrines can form. Consequently, Rawls claims that his theory is intended as a *political* theory only, one that is addressed to a particular set of political problems – fair terms of association in circumstances of reasonable pluralism, in order to secure stability across generations – and consequently one that has to be presented as neutral between the moral claims of these reasonable comprehensive doctrines. This explains why the theory is presented in such an abstract fashion and with so many philosophical disclaimers. Rawls's notion of the theory as free-standing means that neutrality is built-into his very conception of a *political* theory: it has to be distinguished from the comprehensive doctrines that exist in a society if it is to ground an 'overlapping consensus'.

This free-standing conception of justice is possible because it is derived from the 'shared fund of implicitly recognized basic ideas and principles'[24] which underlie the public culture of modern liberal democracies. Rawls trades on the idea that a democratic culture is composed of concepts and principles which can be articulated in a variety of ways and which are no longer seen as being closely tied to any one comprehensive moral view. Any *political* theory has to draw on the resources of this shared public culture as its ultimate starting-point. Once again Rawls's argument can be seen as a response to the communitarian charge that the abstraction of his argument led him to present both states and individuals as if they sprang fully formed on to the world stage, and that his principles of justice applied *sub specie aeternitatis*.

The concept of an 'overlapping consensus' is crucial to Rawls's *political* conception of 'justice as fairness'. Rawls intends that his theory still has a moral justification, so he distinguishes between a *modus vivendi* and an 'overlapping consensus'. The first is merely a compromise based on a fortuitous balance of forces within a society. No single party has the strength to impose its moral views coercively so all the rival perspectives agree to differ and tolerate one another. However, should circumstances change a *modus vivendi* would soon collapse as the principle of toleration is merely prudential. Rawls's idea of an 'overlapping consensus' is intended to establish a consensus on a principle of toleration, by trying to show how the core values underlying 'justice as fairness' are implicit in reasonable comprehensive doctrines, and that they have the priority they do because of the circumstances of reasonable pluralism in which final consensus on one particular comprehensive morality is unlikely and perhaps even impossible. It is this connection with the core values of reasonable comprehensive doctrines which provides the moral justification not the social contract device, and it is this moral justification which over time is designed to secure stability.

As long as citizens recognize reasonable pluralism as a fact of political life, and the need still to establish fair terms of cooperation to avoid continual recourse to force and coercion, they will have, according to Rawls, good reason for adopting a contractarian method for publicly justifying their terms of association. So Rawls's theory despite its concessions to communitarianism is still substantively contractarian. However, whereas his original theory used the contractarian devices of the 'original position' and 'veil of ignorance' to bridge the personal perspective and the moral perspective of impartiality for each individual, the contractors in his new theory are the reasonable comprehensive doctrines and the contractual agreement is not designed to bridge the gap between the personal and the moral perspective but rather to separate the full moral perspective from the *political* perspective. In this way Rawls's argument becomes more like the traditional idea of the social contract as analogous to a commercial contract, in which the parties put to one side the possibility of realizing all their preferences and adopt an artificial perspective that does not represent the full substantive view of either partner, but does provide a perspective from which to judge the terms of their relations, whether these be commercial or political. The point here is that by presenting his theory as a free-standing *political* theory, Rawls's claims that 'justice as fairness' does not have to be shown to follow directly from the full moral perspective of citizens, instead it is an artificial perspective they adopt for *political* purposes. It is for this reason that Rawls builds neutrality into his conception of 'justice as fairness' from the very beginning. By designing the theory as free-standing or neutral it avoids as far as possible drawing directly on any citizen's full moral perspective. Each citizen has a reason provided by her, or his full moral perspectives for adopting the *political* perspective, that is the desire to live together peaceably on fair terms of association, but by avoiding showing that the *political* perspective follows from the full moral perspective of a citizen Rawls thinks he can accommodate a plurality of such reasonable comprehensive doctrines. To use Dworkin's terminology, 'The political perspective, on this view, is discontinuous in substance but not in motivation'.[25] The genius of Rawls's theory is that he does not merely rely on self-interest as the motivation in the *political* realm. Thus if successful his theory will be more attractive to those who balk at the extreme parsimony of economistic or rational-choice conceptions of the social contract.

Dworkin contrasts what he calls Rawls's *discontinuity* strategy with an alternative *continuity* strategy which rejects the social contract device and any attempt to build neutrality into a liberal theory from the very beginning. The aim of this *continuity* strategy of justifying liberal principles is the converse of Rawls's *political* theory. Instead of distinguishing the realm of the *political* from full personal moral perspective, Dworkin claims that attempts at a full justification of liberal principles such as 'justice as fairness' have sought to show a connection between liberal egalitarianism and the full moral perspective – hence continuity. Dworkin's point is that an adequate defence of liberalism must abandon the contractarianism implicit in Rawls's *political* theory and in alternative contractualist defences of liberalism.

This contrast between *continuity* and *discontinuity* or non-contractarian and contractarian justifications of liberalism is not simply based on the desire of some liberal philosophers for a 'more integrated moral experience'.[26] Rather it is derived from a deep-seated philosophical critique of both Rawls's *political* theory and contractarian or contractualist devices more generally, as possible foundations for a liberal political theory.

Dworkin's critique of the *discontinuity* strategy is in three parts. First, he argues that contractarian arguments sacrifice what he calls *categorical force* to *consensual promise*, this is particularly true of Rawls's *political* conception of 'justice as fairness' which explicitly makes an 'overlapping consensus' of reasonable comprehensive doctrines the standard of justification. Second, the conception of public reasonableness, which is central to the gounding of a free-standing or neutral *political* theory, is used by contractualists as if it were less problematic than the idea of a public morality. Third, Dworkin rejects the idea that appealing to principles and ideals latent in our public culture is any use in justifying liberal egalitarianism or 'justice as fairness'.

By claiming that *discontinuity* theories sacrifice *categorical force* to *consensual promise*, Dworkin claims that social contract theories look in the wrong place for a justification of liberal principles. *Political Liberalism* is presented as a theory around which an 'overlapping consensus' can be formed. The task of political theory for Rawls, and according to Dworkin for the whole social contract tradition, is to provide some grounds on which people of profoundly differing views can come to some consensus on how to live together. This is certainly an urgent and weighty consideration for any realistic theory to accommodate, but should it be the primary concern? Dworkin suggests not. There are two reasons why we should balk at *consensual promise* being the goal of a theory. First, the terms of the consensus might simply reflect the existing distribution of power in society so that the consensus is no more than a *modus vivendi* brought about by no group being strong enough to impose its will on all others. Such an arrangement, as Rawls points out, is inherently unstable over time and has no moral status whatsoever. Social contract theories that fail to incorporate some principle of equality into their initial choice situation can achieve no more status than that of a *modus vivendi* and consequently cannot provide a compelling moral justification for those who want to challenge existing inequalities. The point about liberal theories of justice is that they are traditionally advanced as both critiques of existing inequalities and criteria for political reform, consequently such theories claim a validity that is independent of the values currently held within a society.[27] If liberalism abandons this claim then it loses all force in the face of theories that assert contrary values and principles. This leads on to the second reason why we should not be satisfied with *consensual promise*. Dworkin writes: 'Liberals insist that political decisions be made on liberal principles now, even before liberal principles come to be embraced by everyone, if they ever will be'.[28] Rawls's strategy of presenting a theory which it is hoped will become the focus of an 'overlapping consensus' puts off the goal of achieving liberal objectives until such a time, if ever, when an 'overlapping consensus' among reasonable comprehensive doctrines emerges. We have no guarantee that this process will be any easier or quicker than providing an alternative constructivist defence of a liberal morality. So it appears we have to postpone talk of the obligatoriness of liberal principles until they can become the focus of consensual agreement. This is surely not what Rawls intends: that we can have no reason for recognizing the priority of liberal principles until they become the object of an 'overlapping consensus'. Yet by focusing justification on consensual agreement social contract theory does at least traditionally claim that obligation is based on the contract. Crude contractarianism which tries to build agreement on self-interest certainly assumes that obligations are not prior to the contract. Indeed such theories are premised on the view that if one could gain all one wanted without cooperating with others there would be no reason to assume any obligations at all. Few contemporary theorists take seriously this crude version of contractarianism because it begs too many questions. However, even hypothetical contract theories such as Rawls's still have a similar problem justifying obligations because they still take the form of a collective agreement, apart from the obvious difficulty of a counterfactual agreement, creating a real obligation. Even if such a collective agreement is likely to be forthcoming, given certain constraints of the sort built into a hypothetical contract arguments, that does not necessarily entail that an individual has a reason to act as if the agreement has already been achieved. And given the problem of pluralism such agreement is much less likely than in the abstract world of hypothetical contracts.

Consensual promise is no doubt important in maintaining a stable political regime over time, but surely only if that order has some other claim to legitimacy. Liberalism is not simply concerned with maintaining stability in any political order: stability is only one among a number of core liberal values. Similarly, the point of a philosophical justification of liberalism is to provide individuals with a reason to respect or institutionalize core liberal values in circumstances where they are insufficiently recognized. The point that Dworkin is making is similar to the 'motivation' problem that is developed in the communitarian critique of Rawls's earlier contractarianism in *A Theory of Justice*. Sandel, for example, claims that Rawlsian individuals need a reason to enter into the 'original position' and accept the moral constraints of the 'veil of ignorance', such a reason cannot be provided if individuals are purely self-interested. Indeed it cannot be provided unless they already accept the moral obligations that the contract is supposed to justify. This is saying no more than that even if a consensus could be established behind the 'veil of ignorance' (which Sandel doubts for other reasons) we still need a reason to go behind the 'veil of ignorance' and that reason cannot simply be the promise of a consensus on principles of justice. We need another kind of reason than *consensual promise*, and this reason is what Dworkin is referring to when he claims that an adequate moral foundation for liberalism requires a *categorical force*, that is, a moral reason which will motivate individuals here and now to act on principles in the absence of an 'overlapping consensus'. Thus an adequate foundation of liberalism will have to focus on a different set of reasons, those which are prior to contractarian reasons, because they are the reasons one needs in order to accept the reasons provided by the contractarian strategy. Rational choice contractarianism of the sort advanced by David Gauthier[29] is therefore not in a position to provide an adequate justification for liberal principles unless it begs all of the complex questions about moral motivation which are raised by the communitarians and with which modern liberal theories have been wrestling.

Rawls, in his most recent work, thinks he has overcome the 'motivation' problem by locating the moral reason for accepting the contractarian or *discontinuity* strategy of *political liberalism*, within the reasonable comprehensive doctrines of citizens in modern liberal democratic societies. The *categorical force* of *political liberalism* is to be found in these reasonable comprehensive moral doctrines which provide the reason for accepting the neutral contractarian method. In effect Rawls is using communitarian reasons for accepting contractarian reasoning!

However, in order for Rawls to have overcome the 'motivation' problem identified by the communitarians he has to be able to show that individuals not only have a reason for accepting 'justice as fairness' but also have reasons for giving those *political* reasons a moral priority. This is a much more difficult task than merely pointing out how diverse comprehensive moral viewpoints can accommodate the claims of Rawls's *political* liberalism. Contemporary political problems posed by abortion, blasphemy, incitement and pornography merely highlight the extent to which groups within democratic communities challenge the priority of a liberal constitutional settlement to such questions, without wholly rejecting other aspects of a liberal constitutional regime. Catholics opposed to abortion or Muslims incensed by blasphemy are expected to compartmentalize the political implications of their morality in order to accept the liberal distinction between the *political* realm and purely private matters. The point is not that people with such beliefs and commitments will *not* be able to accept Rawls's *political liberalism*, but that they will not necessarily have a reason for granting such liberal principles priority in such difficult cases.[30] Consequently, appeals to comprehensive moral perspectives will not overcome the motivation problem unless those perspectives will grant the required priority to liberal principles. Again we are back with the communitarian criticism of his original contractarianism in *A Theory of Justice*.

One might wish to defend Rawls here by noting that he specifically refers to 'reasonable' comprehensive doctrines. Obviously, the plurality of opinions and beliefs that are held in any modern society will include those that are stupid, wicked and groundless, and no political morality has to take them too seriously. But the crucial point is that even excluding such views there is still considerable diversity and how, given that, can we distinguish those that are reasonable and those that are unreasonable? Rawls's whole enterprise of identifying the *political* realm as a realm of public reasonableness depends on his being able to provide a neutral conception of 'reasonableness'. Rawls's problem is similar to that of other 'contractualists' such as Scanlon and Barry who appeal to a public conception of 'reasonableness' as the grounds for justifying some conception of 'justice as impartiality'. The point made by these 'contractualist' theorists is that given what Rawls calls the 'burdens of judgement',[31] namely the view 'that many of our most important judgements are made under conditions where it is not to be expected that conscientious persons with full powers of reason, even after free discussion, will all arrive at the same conclusion',[32] we have a reason for compartmentalizing our full comprehensive moral viewpoints and instead adopting a narrower conception of 'public reasonableness' where we act on principles that others who similarly suspend their full moral judgements could not reasonably reject. Consequently, a reasonable comprehensive doctrine is going to be one that accepts the 'burdens of judgement' and adopts Rawls's *political* perspective. But this merely reinforces the communitarian's point that liberals can overcome the 'motivation' problem only by presupposing a liberal conception of the good which then makes the social contract redundant. Here the conception of the good is the idea of 'public reasonableness', and individuals will have a reason for accepting the perspective of 'public reasonableness' only if their personal perspective already contains the same perspective. Given that Rawls confines his discussion to reasonable comprehensive doctrines it should be no surprise that the 'reasonable' individual's full moral perspective provides reasons for accepting the constraints of the *political* realm. Thus, far from accommodating the pluralism of modern democratic societies as he suggests in *Political Liberalism*, the pluralism Rawls is really addressing is much narrower, namely the pluralism of comprehensive liberalisms – Kant's, J. S. Mill's, and so on.

As Dworkin and others[33] have pointed out, it is not possible to identify a conception of 'reasonableness' which does not itself draw on substantive ethical beliefs and values. I will for example be able to recognize the 'reasonableness' of the *political* perspective only if I have a moral reason for adopting that neutral perspective when addressing moral matters. If for example I judge abortion wicked, then I will ordinarily think it unreasonable for others to reject my views. What I need if I am to be persuaded to adopt the *political* perspective is a reason which connects my personal moral perspective with the *political* perspective. Once again we are back with the communitarians' 'motivation' problem: individuals need a reason to adopt the neutral political perspective of 'public reasonableness' that cannot be provided from the same neutral perspective. The conception of 'public reasonableness' needs a moral content if it is going to override such substantive moral beliefs and obligations; it needs to be shown to be a direct implication of the moral point of view. This *discontinuity* strategy of social contract arguments cannot provide, for it cannot provide us with a reason for adopting the contractarian perspective without appealing to some prior moral motivation which makes the contractarian device redundant. Again Dworkin's point is similar to that made by the communitarians: we need to show how the political principles of liberalism connect with our moral views such that they have priority over other moral commitments. Consequently, we cannot avoid an ethical defence of liberalism if we are going to provide any defence at all for liberal principles. The *discontinuity* strategy employed by contract theories cannot provide the *categorical* force needed to justify the priority of liberal principles when they clash with other aspects of the moral perspective.

So the *discontinuity* strategy of social contract arguments fails on two counts; first, it cannot provide an individual with a reason to adopt the contractarian perspective in the first instance, therefore it cannot provide an individual with a reason for acting on liberal principles unless those principles have already become an object of consensus; second, it cannot provide individuals with reasons for adopting the neutral perspective of 'public reasonableness' because it makes neutrality a premise of any justification of liberal principles, rather than a conclusion, so that unless one has already adopted the perpsective of neutrality for other reasons the *discontinuity* strategy will not overcome the 'motivation' problem.

Although Rawls's argument is ultimately susceptible to the same critique as contractualists such as Barry and Scanlon, it differs in a significant fashion. The 'contractualists' put faith in the possibility of constructing a neutral conception of 'public reasonableness' which has some kind of unspecified universal validity. Rawls on the other hand bases his conception of 'public reasonableness' on the resources latent in the shared public culture of democratic societies. This has, according to many critiques, given his overall argument a much more limited appeal. However, far from helping Rawls avoid the need for a full ethical justification of liberalism, according to Dworkin it merely highlights more starkly why 'egalitarian liberalism' cannot avoid recourse to ethical justification.

Dworkin's argument is quite simple: in circumstances of pluralism where the need to justify liberalism arises, there will be conflicting accounts of the principles *latent* in a community's traditions and history. If one single interpretation were available that encompassed all aspects of a community's history and traditions completely we would not need the kind of theory Rawls and other liberals offer. Given that there are conflicting accounts of the principles and values *latent* in a community's public culture we need some way of arbitrating between those accounts, particularly when there are important conflicts of principle. There are two alternative ways of settling such conflicts; we can choose the interpretation with the biggest following, but in the absence of a just constitutional framework for democratic decisions we have no reason to prefer majoritarianism; or else we can appeal to some criteria on which an interpretation of our public culture as embodying 'public reasonableness' is shown to be better. But showing one interpretation to be better than another requires us to specify in what ways it is better. This obviously cannot then depend merely on a further appeal to values latent in our 'public culture'. If we want, as Rawls does, to show that one account of justice – 'justice as fairness' – is a better interpretation of the values latent in our 'public culture' than alternatives such as utilitarianism or libertarianism, then we must ultimately appeal beyond the resources of that 'public culture' to show why one interpretation is better (because more just) than the other. Consequently, when discussing questions of political morality we cannot avoid appeal to criteria of truth and validity which are not merely part of a community's traditions. That is not necessarily to appeal to an abstract external criterion of truth or justice, but it is to look elsewhere than mere 'congruence with a community's traditions'[34] for our account of such values. In other words there is no escaping the need for substantive ethical argument if one is to provide a justification of liberal principles. The same argument applies equally well to simple communitarian views which assert that moral and political theory is merely the articulation of the shared resources of a community, as if this can be done without recourse to precisely the sort of abstract political theorizing they so much dispise.

CONCLUSION: *POST*-CONTRACTARIAN LIBERALISM

The argument so far has shown that an adequate defence of liberalism cannot be provided by contractarian arguments even in a revised form. We have also seen that the current debate between *political* and 'contractualist', and *ethical* versions of liberalism draws on the main philosophical point of the communitarian's critique of social contract theory. However, the character of the argument so far has been negative. It has not shown that a non-contractarian defence of liberalism can be provided. Communitarians have argued that undermining the contractarian method of liberalism undermines the possibility of defending liberal principles; this view is obviously rejected by non-contractarian liberals such as Dworkin. Whilst there is not the space to consider how Dworkin or anyone else can provide such a *post*-contractarian justification of liberal equality,[35] I can briefly indicate the form such an argument will take and show that liberalism can accommodate the communitarians' one substantive point without having to swallow all of the implications that they usually draw.

First, an adequate defence of liberalism must adopt a *continuity* strategy that connects liberal political principles with other aspects of ethical motivations broadly conceived, that is not only with personal welfare but also with morality. Liberal principles need to be shown to form an essential component of a good life. This sort of language is certainly reminiscent of communitarianism, but it departs from communitarianism in the sense that the good life that liberals are concerned with is one that can be justified as better than others and not simply a received inheritance of a shared culture. Again, identifying the good requires substantive moral argument: it is not merely received, even if that argument begins from the resources of a shared cultural heritage. What the communitarians claim is that we cannot engage in constructive moral argument about our shared moral inheritance, we simply appeal to it as a source which enables us to bridge the 'motivation' problem. But as Dworkin points out, even starting from a shared inheritance still leaves the need for constructive moral argument about the way that inheritance should be interpreted. This is where moral and political theory come in; they are not merely there to uncover our common inheritance, but instead are there to construct the best account of that inheritance and in this the arguments must appeal to criteria of validity which are themselves the outcome of substantive philosophical argument. What is wrong with communitarianism is that either the argument stops with an appeal to community, as in the case of Sandel, as if this concept did not need explanation and justification, or else appeal is made to a conception of community as a moral source significantly different from the liberal conception of community which is difficult to sustain in the modern world, as in the case of MacIntyre. In either case we cannot avoid ethical argument about the nature of community as a moral source nor constructive argument about the nature of the good life.[36] Consequently, an adequate argument for liberal principles or even a communitarian conclusion will have the abstract philosophical character that so many communitarians wish to reject.

The second point that can be made about *post*-contractarian foundationalist liberalism concerns its constructivist character. Here the *post*-contractarian argument becomes closer to Rawls's original idea of reflective equilibrium.[37] Given that the justification of liberal principles and their connection with the best account of a good life is a matter of theory construction and the criticism of alternative theories, the emphasis of the argument moves from its foundations to its structure and implications. Whereas much of the discussion of *A Theory of Justice* initially centred on the conception of the person and the social contract device, the real value of the theory from the *post*-contractarian perspective is to be found in the fully worked out account of 'justice as fairness'. *Post*-contractarian liberalism will therefore proceed primarily by developing a complete theory of justice and its connection with other components of ethics and contrasting these with alternative theories.

These general comments about the possibility and future character of liberal political theory must necessarily remain vague and tentative. That said, it is possible to conclude with some confidence that contrary to the premature triumphalism of communitarians, substantive liberal political theory will not disappear with the decline of social contract theory. Communitarian theories have yet to provide more than a critique of contractarianism, as such they neither make much contribution to normative political theory, nor pose much of an obstacle to it.

NOTES

1 J. Rawls, *A Theory of Justice*, Oxford, Oxford University Press, 1971.
2 M. Sandel, *Liberalism and the Limits of Justice*, Cambridge, Cambridge University Press, 1982. See also A. MacIntyre, *After Virtue*, London, Duckworth, 1981; M. Walzer, *Spheres of Justice*, Oxford, Basil Blackwell, 1983; C. Taylor, 'Atomism', in *Philosophy and the Human Sciences: Philosophical Papers*, vol. II, Cambridge, Cambridge University Press, 1985, pp. 187–210, and *Sources of the Self*, Cambridge, Cambridge University Press, 1989. My chapter focuses on the communitarians' philosophical critique of liberalism; for an insightful though polemical critique of the rejection of liberal values see S. Holmes, *The Anatomy of AntiLiberalism*, Cambridge, Mass., Harvard University Press, 1993.
3 J. Rawls, *Political Liberalism*, New York, Columbia University Press, 1993.
4 See especially *Political Liberalism*.
5 R. Dworkin, 'Foundations of Liberal Equality', in *The Tanner Lectures on Human Values*, vol. XI, Grethe B. Peterson (ed.), Salt Lake City, University of Utah Press, 1990, pp. 3–119.
6 Also see B. Barry, *Theories of Justice*, Berkeley, Calif., University of California Press, 1989; T. M. Scanlon, 'Contractualism and Utilitarianism', in *Utilitarianism and Beyond*, A. Sen and B. Williams (eds), Cambridge, Cambridge University Press, 1982; T. Nagel, *Equality and Partiality*, New York, Oxford University Press, 1991.
7 By implication this argument will also apply to the contractarianism of D. Gauthier in *Morals by Agreement*, Oxford, Clarendon Press, 1986, although I will not develop this line of argument.
8 Rawls, *A Theory of Justice*, p. 7.
9 Rawls, *A Theory of Justice*, p. 11.
10 Rawls, *A Theory of Justice*, p. 7.
11 Rawls, *A Theory of Justice*, p. 139.
12 Sandel, *Liberalism and the Limits of Justice*.
13 The contrast between theories of justice as 'mutual advantage' and as 'impartiality' is derived from Barry, *Theories of Justice*, pp. 3–9. Rawls describes his own theory as 'justice as fairness' but it fits into Barry's characterization of the 'justice as impartiality', and as it is being used here as a paradigm for other similar liberal arguments I will describe it as a theory of 'justice as impartiality'.
14 This argument is most clearly made in MacIntyre, *After Virtue*, chaps. 14–16.
15 See R. Dworkin, *Taking Rights Seriously*, London, 1977, pp. 150–84.
16 Sandel, *Liberalism*, p. 131.
17 Sandel, *Liberalism*, p. 132.
18 See Scanlon, 'Contractualism and Utilitarianism', p. 127.
19 See Gauthier, *Morals by Agreement*. For an excellent critique of Gauthier's full-knowledge contract see M. Moore, *Foundations of Liberalism*, Oxford, Clarendon Press, 1993, pp. 79–111.
20 Rawls, *Political Liberalism*, p. xvi.
21 Rawls, *Political Liberalism*, p. xvi.
22 Rawls, *Political Liberalism*, pp. 22–8.
23 Rawls, *Political Liberalism*, pp. 147–8

24 Rawls, *Political Liberalism*, p. 8.
25 Dworkin, 'Foundations of Liberal Equality', p. 17.
26 Dworkin, 'Foundations of Liberal Equality', p. 20.
27 A similar point is made by Jospeh Raz in 'Facing Diversity: The Case of Epistemic Abstinence', *Philosophy and Public Affairs*, 1990, vol. 19, pp. 3–46, when he argues that we cannot avoid recourse to concepts like truth and validity without leaving the commitment to the priority of liberal values groundless in the face of challenge.
28 Dworkin, 'Foundations of Liberal Equality', p. 25.
29 Gauthier, *Morals by Agreement*. See also M. Moore's Chapter 12 in this volume.
30 As Dworkin points out with admirable force and clarity in his book *Life's Dominion: An Argument about Abortion and Euthanasia*, London, Harper Collins, 1993, liberals have no alternative but to engage directly with the moral claims of those who would deny the propriety of a liberal settlement of such complex and often tragic issues.
31 Rawls, *Political Liberalism*, pp. 54–8.
32 Rawls, *Political Liberalism*, p. 58.
33 Similar criticisms are made by Jean Hampton in 'The Moral Commitments of Liberalism', in *The Idea of Democracy*, D. Copp, J. Hampton and J. Roemer (eds), Cambridge, Cambridge University Press, 1993, pp. 92–113.
34 Dworkin, 'Foundations of Liberal Equality', p. 34.
35 I will give this issue an extended treatment in my forthcoming book on Dworkin's legal and political theory.
36 Much of Dworkin's recent work has been devoted to explaining and defending his two models of a good life: the *challenge* and the *impact* models. This distinction features significantly, in the Tanner Lectures and *Life's Dominion*.
37 Rawls, *A Theory of Justice*, pp. 46–53.

14 Economic justice

Contractarianism and Rawls's difference principle

Rex Martin

In the first section of this chapter, I attempt very briefly to sketch an underlying or root idea of economic justice, the origins of which can be found in Locke. And I claim that this same idea can be found in both Adam Smith and Marx. The second section turns, then, to the accepted understanding of Rawls's second principle of justice, in particular, to that part called 'the difference principle' or sometimes the 'maximin' principle – that is, to the part which requires the maximal well-being of the worst-off group. In this section I attempt, first, to provide the main lines of Rawls's justificatory reasoning (on contractarian grounds) in favour of this principle and, second, to show that his principle, as seen in the light of this reasoning, incorporates the root idea developed in the first section.

The third section develops an alternative version of Rawls's difference (or maximin) principle. This alternative version, in sum, is designed to achieve pareto efficiency as constrained by egalitarianism. This version too can be seen to incorporate the root idea of economic justice. I will show in the third section that the alternative version can be supported by contractarian reasoning, of the sort Rawls used to support the difference principle. And I will argue the superiority of the alternative theory over Rawls's difference principle. Thus, the pareto efficiency-egalitarian principle emerges as the preferable account of economic justice when seen from the perspective of Rawlsian contract theory. The chapter concludes with a brief reflection on the general line of argument taken.

THE ROOT IDEA OF ECONOMIC JUSTICE AS FOUND INITIALLY IN LOCKE

Locke's overall account is embedded in an imagined state of nature – when, as he put it, 'all the World was *America*'.[1] Here things available for use by all but owned by no one in particular can be annexed to a given individual through labour, under the conditions Locke sets forth in chapter 5 of his *Second Treatise.*

In the course of developing his views on property in this particular chapter, Locke ultimately fixed upon a standard-of-living criterion that would require (for all persons, if natural justice is to be maintained) a standard of living that was higher, *or at least not worse*, than it would have been at the *relevant* level of ordinary comfort in the rude condition set by relatively unimproved nature (before money was introduced). This criterion (which Locke introduced newly minted in section 41 of his *Second Treatise*) is at two points a better one than the old 'enough, and as good' criterion with which he had begun.[2]

First, it allows us to take account of the difference money could make (that is, in a better standard of living) by not confining comparisons of distributive economic justice wholly to persons existing within the rudimentary conditions and under the standards of the primeval forest (persons existing, that is, exclusively in the initial state of nature, before money was introduced). The 'enough, and as good' criterion does not have this virtue: it operates only in very special circumstances – in a highly restricted environment, like the initial state of nature.

This leads directly to the second point. The revision introduced is in no way arbitrary. It is still faithful to Locke's initial remarks, for the original constraint of 'enough, and as good for others' can plausibly be regarded as but a *special case* of this new criterion. It is the case that would obtain in the rock-bottom conditions of the initial state of nature (before money). Here widespread acquisition and use (be it of acorns or of small landholdings) leaves newcomers to the scene no worse off than they would have been without such acquisition by others, for they have 'enough, and as good' remaining to them.

The notion of economic justice we have extracted from Locke's theory (the increasing-standard-of-living criterion, with the proviso added that none is to be made worse off) would command a surprisingly wide assent today. It is deeply rooted in existing theory; for there is in effect already something of a consensus about economic justice. We can point to a single, common, underlying idea of economic justice which can be found in Locke, in Adam Smith, and in Marx.

The root idea here, put very crudely now, is that the arrangement of economic institutions requires, if it is to be just, that all contributors benefit or, at least, that none is to be left worse off. Thus, the root idea requires that if some individuals (say, those in the top 20 per cent) improve their standard of living (measured in terms of real income and wealth), others should do so as well; no group, not even those least well-off, should be left behind. All should continually improve their lot in life together. None at least is to be left worse off.

Admittedly, Locke confined his benchmark for these comparisons to the levels of subsistence in a rudimentary state of nature (allowing for two main levels there: a lower level appropriate to a hunter/gatherer economy and a second, somewhat higher but still quite modest level appropriate to very small-scale private landowning). He did not shift the benchmark up, as I have just done, or at least suggested could be done, to levels of subsistence above those found in that rudimentary state. Nor did he allow, as I have just done, for constantly shifting such benchmarks up and then still further up as economic conditions improve. But I think the logic of his increasing-standard-of-living criterion would definitely allow for such moves.

The changes I have marked are, one could plausibly say, changes explicitly introduced by later theorists. They are changes introduced as western society moved from agriculture (which is where Locke found it) to commerce (as Smith famously envisioned it) to heavy industry (as Marx both criticized and commended it). They are changes introduced as these later theorists reflected on the sheer fact of increasing standards of living for all (or at least the possibility of such increase).

I will not, in this chapter, do more than merely assert that Smith and Marx (as well as Locke) do subscribe to this root idea. What does seem important at this stage is to say that the root idea plays an important role in the theory of each of the theorists named.

Of course, significant differences come in the way each thinker embeds this root idea in an overall theory. Locke puts it in a state of nature, and thus within the context of a theory of natural rights; Smith lodges it in an open and competitive market (in a 'natural system', as he called it) and then puts that ultimately within the confines of a rather utilitarian scheme of justification; and Marx embeds it in a system of proper socialist ownership of the means of production and that, in turn, is set within his theory of historical materialism.

RAWLS'S DIFFERENCE PRINCIPLE

We turn now to our own time, specifically to the theory of justice of John Rawls. In Rawls's view justice is, or should be, a virtue of society, specifically of its 'basic structure'. The problem for Rawls, then, is to choose a basic structure and not simply a favoured distribution to individuals on given occasions. Thus, he is looking for a feasible set of basic political and social and economic arrangements (which would include such things as the arrangements concerned with the ownership and management of the means of production) that could be shown to satisfy the demands of justice, as these are given in his theory.

What Rawls requires of these institutions is not only that they exhibit the principle of (i) equal basic liberties and (ii) fair equality of opportunity but also that (iii) they work together in such a way as (a) to encourage contributions that (b) increase the production of goods and services, which in turn are so distributed as to (c) improve continually the level of income and wealth of *all* the various income groups involved.

We might, following Rawls, describe (i) and (ii) as *prior* demands of justice and (iii) as a secondary demand, one that is to be fulfilled in the context of fulfilling these prior demands and without sacrifice by them. Rawls claims, then, that in a just or well-ordered society resultant inequalities in economic or social positions and in income and wealth can be allowed – indeed, should be allowed – subject to meeting these conditions. Since the principle in question justifies differences in income and wealth Rawls calls it the 'difference principle'.

A society that met this particular set of standards – from (i) to (iii) – would be 'thoroughly just', in Rawls's view. But to be 'perfectly just', it would also, at some point, have to *maximize* the level of income and wealth of the least well-off group in particular (say, the bottom one-fifth). This last point (the point about maximizing the minimum) is not intended to identify a benefit for everyone. Rather, the relevant effects here are the effects on a 'representative' person within that target group; they are effects on an ideal-type *average* individual in the bottom group.

It should be evident, then, that the root idea (as described at the end of the first section) is one we can plausibly ascribe to Rawls. For he seems committed to the principle that 'every income group is to benefit or, at least, none is allowed to become worse off'. Indeed, Rawls says this, quite explicitly, at a number of points.

Thus, Rawls's well-known idea that we should *maximize* the minimum level of economic well-being (which is how his difference principle is usually cited) does not give the whole story here but merely describes the optimum case, which ideally would be achieved in the long run. Here, after a series of reciprocal improvements, a point is reached where it is no longer possible to improve the lot of any one group (including the target group) without worsening the lot of at least one other group.[3] At this point the goal has been reached: the least well-off group has reached its maximum level of income and wealth.

One difficulty with the reading just given should be noted immediately. Rawls does not think that we must always be engaged in reciprocal improvements, up to the point of reaching the goal identified. For we may sometimes have to redistribute goods and services to take care of *injustice*. Here, in order to rectify a present injustice (or in order to compensate those disadvantaged *now* by past unjust arrangements), some resources may have to be shifted from the better-off (and to their overall detriment) into the hands of those less well-off. Since the better-off in such cases would end up, at least temporarily, with a reduction in their net benefit, we cannot realistically commit ourselves to improving literally *everyone's* well-being continually (nor be required to in Rawls's theory).

But does this account of rectifying injustice require a rejection of the reading I have been giving? I think not.

Perhaps the following observation may prove helpful in clarifying this particular point. Where Rawls is concerned principally to describe normal or standard patterns of just distribution (without regard to prior maldistributions), his theory incorporates the root idea which we earlier developed from the texts of Locke (and have attributed to Smith and Marx). Here, in other words, we are being asked to assume (in order to see what picture would result) that a society simply satisfied the difference principle and the other demands of justice. And here my reading holds good, with nothing further required to be said. But where it is assumed that past injustices have occurred and that rectification or redress of these defective patterns is thereby in order, Rawls seems willing to say that a pattern of reciprocal benefit is not required, until the maldistribution has been corrected. And here my reading holds good, *after* the correction has been made.

This said, any significant difference between Rawls and the other theorists named (for example, Locke) would again come mainly in the way that Rawls incorporates the root idea in his overall theory. At least in *Theory of Justice*, he does so by locating it within a 'well-ordered society' organized in accordance with certain recommended principles of justice that, in turn, are themselves justified by a social-contract type of reasoning. We turn to that line of reasoning now.

Rawls's contractarian method of justification is very complex. I will be able to mention only a few of its main features in what follows. One feature that is often emphasized – and that Rawls has continued to include even in his more recent writings – is that the 'parties' to the contract are placed (in what he calls the 'original position') behind a thick 'veil of ignorance'. Here they are instructed in subsequent reasoning to ignore their own *particular* traits (traits that distinguish them from all or most other people), to be unaware of (or, at least, to ignore) their actual place in society, and so on.

Thus, extreme uncertainty (as to outcomes for any given individual) would characterize the deliberations in the original position setting, in which individuals are called upon to construct and then choose the principles of justice that they would prefer to govern the society in which they are to spend their lives. Given this high degree of uncertainty, it might be sensible to reason about such principles in the following way: each individual thinks that, since he, or she, does not know how or where he, or she, might end up, it behoves them all to set things up so that the worst controllable outcome (for any one of them) is the best of a bad lot (the best, that is, of the set of worst outcomes). Everybody, then, starts from this particular vantage point, from the highest-level minimum; and those not worst off can go up from there.

This line of reasoning, which has its home in rational choice theory (and can be found in economics and in politics), is sometimes called *maximin* reasoning (that is, reasoning literally on the principle of maximizing the minimum). The standard line of interpreting Rawls's difference principle (at what I have called its goal or optimum outcome) has been that it was supported justificatorily and was rationalized by maximin reasoning. This maximin line of reasoning was attributed to Rawls by his initial expositors (and often, then, they severely criticized him for holding to it), and more recent critics have continued to view maximin as the standard pattern of justification intended by Rawls for the difference principle.[4] This line has, in the view of most, been encouraged by Rawls himself (and can be found, clearly enough, they think, in *Theory of Justice* and in later texts of his).

There are, as might be imagined, many plausible objections to maximin reasoning. Thus, critics have argued that maximin reasoning is inherently suspect, or that it might not be appropriate to use in the setting provided by Rawls's original position or, even if it was appropriate, that such reasoning may not support Rawls's difference principle, or support it uniquely among alternative principles (some of which may be utilitarian in ultimate provenance). Accordingly, doubts about maximin *reasoning* tended to translate into doubts about the maximin *criterion* itself; that is, into doubts about Rawls's favoured way of characterizing the difference principle.

But, contrary to what most of his interpreters and critics suppose, Rawls does *not* claim that his difference principle is itself supported *specifically* by maximin reasoning. At least, he makes no such claim in his published writings. Rather, maximin reasoning seems to have a secondary role in his account, as developed in *Theory of Justice* and thereafter. It is brought in only *after* his principles of justice have been established on *other* grounds; it is then employed by him to defend the *whole set* of these principles. Here the main use of the maximin argument is to rule out or to constrain utilitarian alternatives to Rawls's preferred principles of justice. For it is his view that utilitarians and others, especially in the setting afforded by the original position, would allow (though they should not, given maximin reasoning) the sacrifice or attenuation of some of the demands of justice, of the *prior* demands especially, or would do so for some people at least.

The question we must now face is this: precisely what is the *initial* line of justificatory reasoning that Rawls relies on in the case of the difference principle? Interestingly, he answers this question rather clearly. In Rawls's theory, the argument specifically and peculiarly designed for the purpose of supporting the difference principle *in particular* is the one based on the idea of collective asset; it is an argument for reciprocal benefit of the sort that would be developed in the original position.[5] It is this argument that he calls the 'compelling' one for the difference principle.[6]

Let me sketch the main lines of this particular argument. We could imagine the following characteristic line of reasoning occurring in the original position. All the parties to the deliberation about justice might agree that it was reasonable to attempt to achieve a higher index of wealth and income for *all* representative persons at the various income levels (higher, that is, than existed at some initial point). Each realizes that inequalities in position and attendant wealth may well be involved in such an achievement. But no one wishes to accept an inferior position for oneself, even though it might prove to be for the common good in a particular society. Each person sees, then, upon reflection, that it would be unreasonable for *anyone* to have to take or be forced to take an inferior position as their lot in life. So, granting that inequality in positions is both highly likely (perhaps inevitable) and very useful, each would want income- and wealth-generating positions to be open to all on some reasonable principle of equality of opportunity.

Now, Rawls believes that significant inequalities in outcome (inequalities sufficiently great to affect one's lot in life) stem in important ways from differences in people's natural endowments and in their initial social circumstances. Accordingly, to even begin to secure a reasonable measure of fair equality of opportunity, one must in a theory of justice somehow deal with these fundamental sources of inequality.

One plausible proposal here is to attempt to make for fair equality of opportunity by rearranging the social contingencies so as to mitigate the undue advantage or disadvantage that accrues to individuals from their initial social circumstances. But beyond this, the proposal takes a basically laissez-faire approach. The reasoning here is that once a fundamental rearrangement is achieved respecting the *social* contingencies that play on one's formative years and that can continue to give undue advantage even after that, then the resulting distribution of positions (and income and wealth) is the correct one – for every individual and for the society – and should not be disturbed.

It could reasonably be contended against this proposal, however, that the individual's natural endowment (with whatever stimulation or encouragement it gets from social circumstances) still has too much sway. Why is it fair, one asks, to factor out and then attempt to reduce the gap between people as regards their social circumstances (and the undue advantage/disadvantage this brings) but to ignore such a gap in the case of their *natural* endowments? For the two sets of factors – one's social circumstances and one's natural endowment – seem to be equally 'arbitrary from the moral point of view'. Nonetheless, such factors powerfully affect a person's life prospects, advantageously for some and disadvantageously for others.[7]

Accordingly, another interpretation of reasonable equality of opportunities is fashioned to meet this objection. It differs from the initial proposal in two important respects. First, it recognizes a broader set of limiting factors over which the issue of fair equality is to be canvassed by requiring consideration of important differences in natural endowments as well as in social starting-points. And second, it replaces an approach that lets the results lie, after a conscientious effort has been made to 'cut' the gap in initial advantage (attributable to *both* these considerations), with a non-laissez-faire approach that further sorts these results. Rawls calls this new approach the 'democratic interpretation' of the notion of equal opportunity. It is the approach he favours.[8]

The democratic interpretation arises out of reflection on the reasonableness of providing fair equality of opportunity. And the main argument for it begins, as we have seen, with the fact that people have different natural endowments and are born into and grow up in different social circumstances. No one can be said to be responsible for – hence, to deserve – these factors in their own case.[9]

The argument now continues: since these initial differences are both morally arbitrary and undeserved on the part of the individual involved, each person could agree that the initial social circumstances, and the natural endowment of each, can and should be developed to benefit everyone. This might not be a view that we could expect individuals to take in the everyday world, but it is a view that it would be reasonable to take in what Rawls calls the 'original position'. The point here is simply that, behind the 'veil of ignorance', no one would prefer *disadvantageous* deviations from equal (or from lesser and unequal) shares, were he, or she, on the losing end, and hence would veto such deviations. Thus, only deviations advantageous to all would survive the veto (that is, only such *advantageous* deviations could achieve the required unanimity).[10]

Society can be arranged (and should be, from the perspective of the original position) so that no representative individual is hurt and none unduly helped by that individual's own 'luck' in the natural 'lottery' (as measured by one's initial draw of natural endowment and social circumstances). Rather, all are to use their natural assets and to exploit their social circumstances not merely for their own advantage but also for the good of everyone.[11] Rawls's point, then, is that it is reasonable in the original position for persons to regard 'the distribution of natural abilities as a collective asset' and to constitute society accordingly, such that 'each person can participate in the total sum of the realized natural assets of the others'.[12]

The democratic interpretation combines fair equality of opportunity – conceived as the taking of remedial steps, conscientiously, to reduce the initial inequality in advantages accruing to individuals from two main sources – with the principle of everyone's benefit, which further reduces the resultant inequality between them. The object of this two-step procedure is to minimize the gap between persons by taking account of both starting-points and end results.

Society must be arranged so that everyone's circumstances are improved in the relevant way(s), and no one's life prospects are further worsened by the inequality in initial circumstances and the resultant inequality in positions. The gap in advantages remains, but everyone benefits from it, even the least-advantaged individuals. (Or to be precise, everyone is to benefit from the distribution of positions implicated in a particular scheme of differential advantage.)[13]

As some people improve their situations, others should continue to improve, to become better-off. No one should be hurt or left behind without recourse. Mutual or reciprocal improvement is a continual process. This is the understanding of the difference principle – the principle that concerns the distribution of resultant benefits – that we have reached so far by deploying the idea of collective asset as its justification and rationalization.

The idea of collective asset provides a rationale for the main features of Rawls's second principle of justice. It underwrites both fair equality of opportunity, in its 'democratic interpretation', and the principle of distributive economic justice – that is, the difference principle, in the rather simplified version that we have used in this section of the chapter. We can get to the usual specification of the difference principle by repeatedly deploying the simplified version (the principle of everyone's continual benefit) up to the optimum point, where the least well-off are as well off as they can be (without making any *other* group worse off).[14]

An aside: people do not first hit upon the idea of collective asset and then argue from there. Rather, they first fashion the requirement of a reasonable equality of opportunity, and then the collective asset idea arises from reflection on that. Ultimately, if one accepts the democratic interpretation of fair equality, one also accepts collective asset (as providing the best rationalization and justification of that interpretation, when seen from the original position or contractarian perspective). The idea of collective asset is the Rawlsian solution to the problem posed by differential starting-points and by the fact that these unmerited initial differences can never be reduced to allow for more than a passable measure of equality of opportunity.

There are, however, significant difficulties with the Rawlsian difference principle, as developed in this section. For there is no guarantee that following the principle of everyone's benefit, up to the point where no further improvement can be made in the average well-being of the target or bottom group (that is, without lowering the average well-being of some other group), will in fact achieve the *maximum* well-being of the target group, in the sense of 'maximum' that Rawls intended. This can be shown graphically. For example, consider Figure 1.

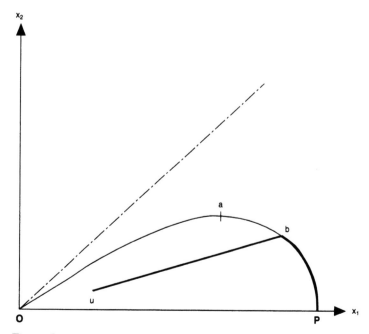

Figure 1

Here x_1 is the axis line that measures well-being for the better-off group and x_2 is the axis for the less well-off group. The dotted line (running at a 45 degree angle) is the equality line; it represents the points of absolute equality between the two groups. The space on and below the curve OP represents the available economic options in a particular society, given its resources, reasonable expectations of development, etc. (subject, of course, to the constraint of meeting the prior demands of justice). The darkened line on OP is the pareto-optimal 'zone'; in it no improvements for any group are possible without worsening the prospects of at least one other group. The point *a*, on the OP curve (and in the pareto-optimal zone), is the point of maximum well-being for x_2 within the available space.

Point *a* (in Figure 1) is Rawls's optimum or goal point. It maximizes the well-being of the target group. Now, select a point within the available space (but not *on* the OP curve or terribly close to it). It would be possible to select moves within the available space that made each group better off and to continue selecting such moves (up to the point that the pareto-optimal zone was reached) without necessarily intersecting the OP curve at point *a*. Or even coming tolerably close to it. Line *ub* is one example of such a possibility. Indeed, there are infinitely many such examples.

Another consideration is also telling here. Rawls's difference principle has two main elements, or two variant emphases that can be struck: one emphasizes maximizing the prospects for wealth and income of the least well-off group; the other emphasizes improving the situation, in those respects, of that group (and all other groups along with it).[15] The problem is that the maximin formulation (the usual way in which Rawls's difference principle is stated and understood) does not appear amenable to the latter emphasis. For, if what is required is the maximizing of the life situation (as measured in income and wealth) of the least well-off group, then any arrangement of income and wealth that fell short of that – even one in which their life situation was being continually improved – would be unacceptable by that criterion.

However desirable it might be to have it do so, it is not clear how the maximin criterion does or even could – simply on its own (which is how it is usually stated) – justify situations that are less than maximal. Or how the maximin criterion, as optimum point or goal, could be understood to govern policies in the sub-OP space.

Now, there does appear to be, in Rawls's account, a criterion governing policies in such situations – namely, that the prospects of the least well-off are being improved (under the everyone's benefit principle). But I have already indicated that following such policies will not guarantee that the optimum goal will be reached. Our problem has now come full cycle.

There is, in sum, a tension between Rawls's 'improving' criterion and the textually favoured maximin one. More important, it is not clear how they are to be brought together and given a unified treatment.

One could say here: well, then, when at some sub-optimal point let us simply choose those policies that aim at maximin and that have the most likelihood of achieving it. But how does one make this simple idea operational in Rawls's theory?

Rawls has not dealt with this particular problem in his *published* writings. There is, however, one attempt by him to do so in his *unpublished* work. In concluding this section, I'll turn to that attempt briefly.

Here Rawls envisions a situation very like that represented in Figure 1. He suggests that if the two groups were to move along the curve *Oa*, then they would satisfy the requirement of everyone's continual benefit, up to the point of encountering the pareto-optimal zone. And at that precise point, they would be at point *a*, the optimum or goal point = the maximin point.

What Rawls suggests is perfectly true. But it lacks generality. It fails to tell us how policies should be constructed in the vast remainder of the available space, the part that lies below the OP curve. It is also arbitrary, for he gives us no good reason why a society can be, or *should* be, expected to stay on the *Oa* curve exclusively.

After all, if a society were in effect to follow Rawls's principle of everyone's benefit and were to do so, for example, by moving along the line *ub* in Figure 1, that society would be 'thoroughly just' in so acting. There would be no injustice to rectify were this to happen. Now, suppose it actually had happened: a society finds itself, before it adopts a Rawlsian theory of justice, on the *ub* line (slightly to the northeast of *u*). What is it *now* to do in order to reach the Rawlsian optimum or goal point? Again, we reach a problem already encountered: the problem of making Rawls's theory fully operational in the vast remainder of the available space, the part that lies below the OP curve.

Let us note one further point. Rawls does emphasize, in his discussion here, that the point *a* (the maximin point on the entire OP curve) is the stopping point for those moving along the *Oa* curve. Point *a* is also, interestingly, the point closest to the equality line that one could get to upon reaching the pareto-optimal zone, the zone of *all* stopping points for those following the principle of everyone's continual benefit. Rawls does not state the point about equality in precisely the way I just have, but my statement of it adequately captures the gist of his observation for present purposes.[16]

Interestingly, in his published writings after *Theory of Justice* Rawls makes a somewhat similar claim about point *a* and the equality line. Here he notes that, where there are only two relevant classes, the difference principle (or 'maximin,' as he calls it there) 'selects the (Pareto) efficient point closest to equality'. He continues, 'Thus, in this instance at least, [the difference principle] has another interpretation'; but he adds, 'I do not know, however, whether the focal point can be defined sufficiently clearly to sustain the second interpretation. . . when there are three or more relevant classes.'[17]

There is, thus, a failure of generality here too, for the observation Rawls makes (about nearness to the equality line) explicitly holds *only* for a two-income-class situation. Thus, his own theory (as formulated in *Theory of Justice* and thereafter) would not cover the situation we have been envisioning throughout, where there are, say, *five* such equal-sized groups. And this very same failure of generality probably holds for Rawls's discussion (in his unpublished treatise) of improving moves along the *Oa* line, as summarized above.

Nonetheless, there may be some virtue in following Rawls's lead by using some sort of equality metric (as yet unspecified) as a constraint on policies designed to follow the principle of everyone's continual benefit. It is to this particular problem that we turn in the next section.

AN ALTERNATIVE VERSION OF THE DIFFERENCE PRINCIPLE

In this section I will offer a sketch of an alternative version of the difference principle, a version that can meet the problem identified. Then I will turn to the issue of how the difference principle, in this version, can be justified.

The ground we will traverse in the paragraph that follows is already familiar, so we can proceed quickly there. But we will need, after that, to slow our pace somewhat.

Again we are concerned with the distribution of income, wealth, and social/economic position that representative persons from different classes (x_1, x_2, etc.) could reasonably expect to receive over a normal life under some particular attainable or feasible basic structure arrangement. And, again, we assume that any basic structure selected will feature an arrangement of main political and social and economic institutions that will, as a set, satisfy the prior demands of justice, as given by the principles of (i) equal basic liberties and (ii) fair equality of opportunity, understood here as the taking of remedial steps, conscientiously, to reduce the initial inequality in advantages accruing to individuals from two main sources (social circumstances and natural endowment). And in considering policies for suitable distributions here we, of course, confine ourselves to those that are consistent with meeting the prior demands of justice.

These policies should be designed to give results that exhibit, or can reasonably be expected to exhibit, 'chain connection'. And, in such cases, we further stay within the 'zone' where *all* the income classes (x_1, x_2, etc.) can actually benefit. Figure 2 illustrates these two notions (chain connection and the zone of reciprocal improvement) and shows how they can be distinguished.

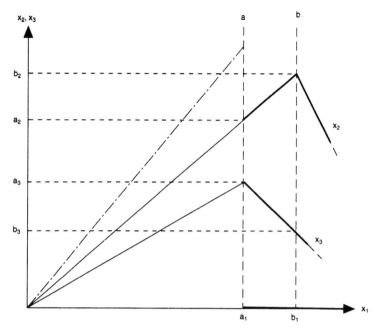

Figure 2

In Figure 2 the respective profiles (in terms of income, wealth, and social/economic position) are given in a society with three income classes. For example, at *a* each class has a particular income level, which can be coordinated, roughly, with the wealth and position of its members. Here the 'curve' of the best-off class is, for simplicity of treatment, taken to be identical with the horizontal axis. Chain connection means that so long as the 'curve' of the least well-off class (here x_3's) shows improvement, all the other classes do so as well. In this figure, then, chain connection holds.

Between *a* and *b*, you'll note, we don't have reciprocal improvement (for x_3's curve is dropping); beyond *b* both x_2's and x_3's curves are dropping. But everything to the left of *a* exhibits such improvement for all the classes. This is the zone of 'positive contributions'. Thus, we stay throughout to the left of *a*.

In a situation where there are two or more beneficial options for change, we should choose that one which is 'efficient' (that is, which is *most* beneficial). The 'argument' for this claim is given simply by an idea we are already familiar with, by the notion of everyone's continual benefit, understood in such a way as to be compatible with what is called pareto efficiency (as in Figure 3).

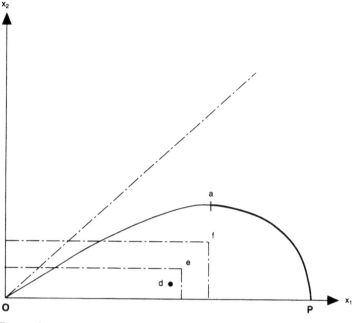

Figure 3

In Figure 3 imagine a point *within* the box defined by point *e*. In relation to that point (which we can arbitrarily call *d*) both points *e* and *f* mark solutions that are reciprocally improving (for the classes involved), but only *f* is 'efficient'.

That is, within the box defined by *f*, there is only one point which is the *most* beneficial solution for *all* the classes there. That point is *f*. So, clearly, if one box is wholly within another, then at least one point in the exterior box has to be more beneficial than any point in the interior box and, since *f* is the most beneficial point in the exterior box it is the 'efficient' point within that whole domain. So we select *f*.

If more than two classes were involved, we would have to represent their situation in a more complex way (as in Figure 2, for example). I presume, though, that no significant difficulty is posed on this particular score for my account of Figure 3.

Next, we come to a more problematic (and realistic) situation. Where there are two or more options for improvement, each one of which is 'efficient' relative to the other, we should choose that option which *minimizes* the difference (in income level, etc.) between that of the best-off income class (x_1) and that of the worst-off income class (x_n).

An aside: in a grouping of, say, two income classes, the worse-off half would be designated x_2; in a grouping of three such classes, the worst-off class would be designated x_3, etc. In every case, though, the size of various

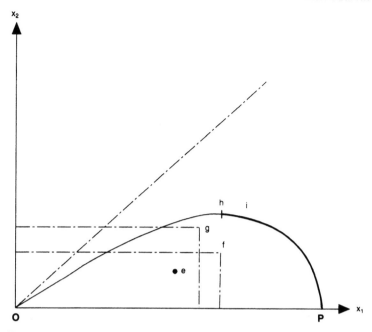

Figure 4

classes in a given grouping would be identical; thus in a grouping of four such classes, each class would be the same size (25 per cent of the whole).

Now, we go to Figure 4 (above) to illustrate the selection pattern I have described for this more complex (and realistic) situation.

Suppose that in Figure 3 we had moved only from *d* to *e*. So, now we are at *e*. Relative to point *e*, both solutions, *f* and *g*, mark improvement and each, relative to the other, is 'efficient'. For, note, neither box is wholly contained in the other, though *e* is in both.

The one that minimizes inequality (that is, is nearer the 45 degree 'equality' line) is to be selected here; that point is *g*. If more than two classes were involved, we would have to represent their situation in a more complex way (as in Figure 2, for example). I presume, again, that no significant difficulty is posed on this head for my account of Figure 4.

One final step. Imagine we were at *g* (in Figure 4) and two further options presented themselves (*h*, *i*), each on the darkened line. Again we'd move to that one which is nearer the equality line (*h*, say, the point at the far left end of that line). This choice favours that 'efficient' solution which *minimizes* the inequality (in income, etc.) between the best-off and the worst-off classes.

Now, let me put this final step in somewhat different words. At some stage, we could conceive options which, if any one were taken, we would be at a point (on a 'curve', so to speak, or in a region) where no further reciprocally improving changes were possible. Here the only way members of any one class could be better off (say, the members of x_2) would be for those in another class (say, x_1) to be worse off. When this point, this 'curve' or frontier, has been reached, we have reached the 'pareto-optimal' zone. Obviously, options to *move* to such a frontier can be taken, but no further moves within it are thereafter allowed (for none could be reciprocally improving). In all four of my figures, that zone is marked by the darkened lines.

In moving to that zone, the same rule holds as was followed in the discussion of the problematic (but realistic) choice situation in Figure 4. Under the conditions spelled out at the very beginning of this section, a pareto-optimal 'solution' that conformed to the rule for changes in Figure 4 would be *identical* to a Rawlsian Difference Principle solution, at its optimum or maximin point.[18]

Thus, we have a likely alternative version to Rawls's second principle of justice. That alternative can now be summarized and stated more fully: social and economic institutions in the basic structure are to be arranged so that (a) the offices and positions are open to all under conditions of fair equality of opportunity, (b) the resulting distribution of economic goods is efficient (or, ideally, is pareto optimal), subject to the constraint that (c) the inequality between the best-off income class and the least well-off one is minimized. Regarding priorities, (a) is 'lexically' prior to (b) and it, in turn, is 'lexically' prior to (c).[19]

The version I have just described is, of course, one I am recommending. A person could quite plausibly regard this version as simply another *characterization* of Rawls's difference principle. Rawls has not, so far as I know, regarded it this way himself. Accordingly, it is probably better at this point to consider it as an alternative, perhaps a competing, version of economic justice, one which could nonetheless be developed in a Rawlsian contractarian frame. In concluding this section of the chapter, I want to provide a brief assessment of Rawls's theory of economic justice (and of the alternative version I have been advocating).

Let me begin by noting that the alternative version has several virtues. Not only does it incorporate the root idea of economic justice, thereby retaining one of the strong features of Rawls's own account, but also it solves the problem encountered at the end of the second section. The alternative version leaves no gap, either conceptually or in language, between the two emphases – the maximizing one and the 'improving' one – that Rawls characteristically builds into one or another of his various formulations of the difference principle. The alternative analysis draws at every point on a single unifying intuition: everyone's continual benefit – an idea rationalized and justificatorily supported by the notion of collective asset – constrained, of course, by a definite egalitarian metric.

Moreover, the alternative version specifies a general case, where more than two income groups can be considered and where the whole range of available sub-optimal situations can be considered (and not merely those on the so-called OP curve in Figure 1). Unlike Rawls's difference principle (in its maximin version, as usually stated) the alternative version can justify mere continual improvement. And it gives, within the entire sub-optimal area (in particular, in the space *below* the OP curve in that figure), a clear directive for policy choices such that we could expect their long-term drift to be in the direction of intersecting that curve at the maximin point (*a*), or at least coming tolerably close to it.

And none of the key assumptions of the alternative version is contrary to Rawlsian contractarian ones. Thus, it assumes (when describing the standard operation of the difference principle) that chain connection is satisfied, that there are two or more index groups (x_1, x_2, etc.) of equal size, and that we stay within the zone of 'positive contributions'.

In short, my argument has shown a clear superiority for the alternative theory over Rawls's own version of the difference principle, on two main grounds. First, it affords *greater generality* in that *n* income groups, and not merely two, can be considered throughout the *entire* range of available sub-optimal situations (as well as at the maximin point, *a*). Rawls's theory, as he has developed it so far, fails to achieve generality at precisely these points (as I argued at the end of the second section). Second, the alternative theory has *better justificatory support* from within Rawls's own contractarian theory in drawing not only on the *same* contractarian justificatory pattern as the Rawlsian difference principle itself (in particular, the idea of collective asset)[20] but also on the strong egalitarian resources that exist within the Rawlsian theory of justice.

This last point, which largely distinguishes Rawls's own difference principle from the alternative version, is important. For the egalitarian metric is crucial to the success of the latter version. Without it, the 'virtues' identified a few paragraphs back could not be obtained (and the problems identified at the end of the second section would be left unsolved). And with it, we can demonstrate that, at an efficiency frontier (at the point of achieving pareto *optimality*), the alternative version is mathematically equivalent to Rawls's own difference principle (in its maximin emphasis).

The equality metric is itself a plausible one, with respect to egalitarian concerns. Moreover, it has features that would commend it to Rawls himself, given some of his remarks about relating the maximin point to an equality line and given that the minimizing of inequality between groups would survive the veto power of the equal 'parties' who represent different but equal-sized groups in the original position. Or, to put this same point differently, the parties there have an equal status and they would not create or perpetuate inequality unnecessarily; thus, they would not opt for principles allowing a *surplus* of inequality, that is, an inequality greater than is required to achieve compensating reciprocal benefit among feasible efficient schemes. It seems, then, that no further defence of this metric, or of its egalitarian plausibility, is required – at least for Rawlsians.

Let me mention one final virtue of the alternative theory. It provides a plausible interpretation and understanding of Rawls's idea of reciprocity.

For Rawls, the identification of a situation as one of reciprocal benefit required satisfaction of the benchmark idea, the idea that, in a given social world, mutual continual benefit has occurred 'with respect to an appropriate benchmark of equality defined with respect to that world'.

For, if we assume in our basic structure (in our social world) the satisfaction both of the prior demands of justice and of the effective operation of the pareto efficiency-egalitarian principle, and this has been so from one generation to the next, then we have as the backdrop or starting-point – the foundation – of our *present* choices a set of economic and other arrangements that expresses an appropriate equality 'with respect to that world'. And when we now act to change the set of existing institutions or to make long-term policies, then (in so far as these changes affect income and wealth) we will in time get results that represent mutual continual benefit, as measured against that benchmark.

These results reflect the effective operation of the pareto efficiency-egalitarian principle, and they in turn become part of the 'appropriate benchmark of equality' for the *future* operation of the selfsame principle in that particular social world. In sum, Rawls's notion of reciprocity is suitably captured, in my judgment, in the idea that a society's economic arrangements, in both their present foundation and future result, continue to reflect the effective operation of the pareto efficiency-egalitarian principle.

If this is so, if Rawlsian reciprocity is satisfied, there is reason to believe that those less well-off in such arrangements will not suffer from socially destructive envy or alienation. And those better-off (presumably including those who have exhibited and used traits of intelligence, energy, and so on in an economically productive way) will not be jealous of their talents or feel ill-used by others. For the top 20 per cent, say, are in fact better off than others in such arrangements and can reasonably look forward to even further improvements in their material well-being (and to *continuing* to be better off than others). There is no guarantee here, of course. Some may fall from the top group and others may move into it, over time; but what I've said is true for most (or at least a great many) of those in that group.

A BRIEF REFLECTION OVERALL

Let me turn now, in concluding, to a somewhat larger picture. I've made a quick but I hope plausible case, largely on inductive grounds, for saying that there is a root idea of distributive economic justice. This root idea can be stated, in simplest terms, as 'every income group benefits or, at least, none is to become worse off'. When carefully stated, this idea becomes the principle of pareto efficiency, as developed in Figure 3. And I've suggested that this root idea is not in any way idiosyncratic; for it has, historically, been supported on natural rights, utilitarian, Marxist and contractarian grounds.

For Locke the root idea of pareto efficiency is, I would suggest, something like a criterion for distributive economic justice in the rather limited sense that his increasing-standard-of-living account was intended to be fully suitable for ruling out claims of injustice. But for Smith and Marx – and here I merely assert the point – it is more like a crucial bit of evidence for, a necessary evidential accompaniment of, the claim that a particular set of economic arrangements is just (or at least more nearly just than another). For Rawls the root idea quite simply identifies a course of action that is itself paradigmatically reasonable.[21] And, in my alternative account, that idea when constrained by egalitarianism, and with an appropriate background, becomes a sufficient condition for distributive economic justice.

What seems clear in all this is that the root idea is important and very central. Arguably, then, any theory of distributive economic justice will need to accommodate it in significant ways. What is not clear, however, is which *theory* of economic justice one is to go with and which view of the root idea one is ultimately to hold. Indeed, it is very hard to know what perspective to take in trying to answer such questions.

Rawls's theory (or the alternative version) seems to have great appeal to Europeans and Americans today. If this is true, and I suspect it is, there are many features of our history and institutional arrangements and intellectual traditions that would make it so. These things function, then, as part of the real underpinning of the theory in either its Rawlsian or its alternative version.

In the end, the contractarian mode of justification (supposing that it is in fact logically efficacious) may have its appeal on these very same, or on roughly similar, grounds. For what will count in favour of that mode is how well and how convincingly it can marshal the underpinning elements so as to reach a perspicuous conclusion about what, upon reflection, justice demands *for us*.

I'm inclined to think, though, that other justifying narratives are likely to prove better at this than contractarianism has (a conclusion Rawls himself appears drawn to in his book, *Political Liberalism*, 1993). In my view a narrative that is more wholeheartedly and robustly grounded in our complex *democratic* political tradition will be among the main contenders. It may well offer one of the best, if not the best, available justification – a justification that would be convincing to us, upon reflection, and one that would seem reasonable (perhaps even eminently plausible) to persons in other cultures or in other times.

I cannot say. For following out this particular lead would take us into yet another story, better told on another day.[22]

A POSTSCRIPT ON SOURCES AND ACKNOWLEDGEMENTS

The discussion in the second and third sections is developed at much greater length in my book *Rawls and Rights*, Lawrence, University Press of Kansas, 1985 (hereafter *R&R*), in chapters 4 and 5 especially and also 8. The discussion in these sections sometimes draws verbatim on *R&R* (and the four figures used in this chapter are adaptations of figures in that book). Chapter 5 of *R&R* is, in turn, a longer version of certain sections of the paper 'Two Interpretations of the Difference Principle in Rawls's Theory of Justice', which Prakash Shenoy and I published in *Theoria*, 1983, vol. 49, pp. 113–41. I owe to Shenoy both the idea for the alternative version (in the third section of this chapter) and much of the formalism developed for it there and in *R&R*.

Let me mention also two recent, important studies (and defences) of Rawls's theory of distributive economic justice. They are: Edward F. McClennen, 'Justice and the Problem of Stability', *Philosophy and Public Affairs*, 1989, vol. 18, pp. 3–30; Joshua Cohen, 'Democratic Equality', *Ethics*, 1989, vol. 99, pp. 727–51.

Finally, I want to thank not only Prakash Shenoy but also Ann Cudd, Howard Kahane, Donna Martin and David Reidy for their help on the present chapter (or on earlier versions of it). I have benefited as well from the discussion and criticism (of my argument in *R&R*) to be found in two unpublished papers: 'Pareto Efficiency, Egalitarianism, and Difference Principles' (by Julian Lamont, University of Wollongong, Australia) and 'The Revisionist Difference Principle' (which I read, on a blind-review basis, for the *Canadian Journal of Philosophy*).

NOTES

1 John Locke, *Second Treatise* (1690), §49.
2 Locke, *Second Treatise*, §27.
3 In his book *Political Liberalism*, New York, Columbia University Press, 1993 (hereafter *PL*), pp. 16–8 (see esp. n. 18), Rawls distinguishes between 'mutual advantage' and 'reciprocity'. The former takes as its benchmark 'each person's present or expected future situation as things are [now]' (*PL*, p. 17); the latter (which Rawls prefers) takes as its fundamental point of comparison that 'everyone benefits judged with respect to an appropriate benchmark of equality defined with respect to that world' (*PL*, p. 17). Unfortunately, Rawls leaves very vague exactly what this particular idea of equality amounts to. I think my exposition in this chapter of his theory of distributive economic justice is compatible with the benchmark he had in view, vague as it is. And, to mark this compatibility, I have typically referred to 'reciprocal' (rather than to 'mutual') benefits.
4 For Will Kymlicka, see his book *Contemporary Political Philosophy: An Introduction*, Oxford, Clarendon Press, 1990, ch. 3, pp. 61–6. For D. D. Raphael, see his book *Problems of Political Philosophy*, 2nd edn, London, Macmillan, 1990, pp. 147–8.
5 See John Rawls, 'Reply to Alexander and Musgrave', *Quarterly Journal of Economics*, 1974, vol. 88, pp. 633–55, at pp. 647–8; see also his 'Distributive Justice: Some Addenda', *Natural Law Forum*, 1968, vol. 13, pp. 51–71, at pp. 59, 69, 71.
6 See John Rawls, 'Some Reasons for the Maximin Criterion', *American Economic Review*, 1974, vol. 64, pp. 141–6, at pp. 144–5. Rawls goes so far as even to *reject* the maximin argumentation for the difference principle as representing a philosophical 'misunderstanding'. See his paper 'Social Unity and Primary

Goods', in *Utilitarianism and Beyond*, A. Sen and B. Williams (eds), Cambridge, Cambridge University Press, 1982, pp. 159–85, at p. 175 n. 15.

7 See John Rawls, *A Theory of Justice*, Cambridge, Mass., Harvard University Press, 1971 (hereafter *TJ*), pp. 72 (for the passage quoted), 74, 75.

8 For the phrase 'democratic interpretation' see *TJ*, p. 75. Technically, it is an interpretation of the *entire* second principle of justice (the principle that combines fair equality of opportunity with a standard for distributive economic justice), as I shall make clear shortly.

9 'It is one of the fixed points of our moral judgments that no one deserves his place in the distribution of natural assets any more than he deserves his initial starting place in society' (*TJ*, p. 311). See also Rawls, 'Distributive Justice: Some Addenda', p. 67.

10 See *TJ*, pp. 102 and 137. See also Rawls, 'Kantian Constructivism in Moral Theory', *Journal of Philosophy*, 1980, vol. 77, pp. 515–72, at p. 551.

11 The quoted terms are drawn from Rawls; see *TJ*, pp. 74, 75, 104 and his paper 'Distributive Justice', in *Philosophy, Politics and Society*, P. Laslett and W. G. Runciman (eds), 3rd series, Oxford, Basil Blackwell, 1967, pp. 58–82, at p. 68.

12 For the first passage quoted see *TJ*, p. 179, also p. 101; for the second see p. 523. At this latter point in his book Rawls is discussing what he calls 'social union' (see *TJ*, sect. 79, esp. p. 529 and n. 4 on pp. 523–5). 'Social union' is a broader term than 'collective asset', and it is the term he normally employs in his later writings.

13 See *TJ*, pp. 302–3. On the important point about not sacrificing anyone's life prospects see also pp. 178, 180, 183.

14 The development of and main argumentation for the collective asset idea is found in Rawls, *TJ*, pp. 72–5, 101–4 (see also n. 12 above). To this main argumentation should be added his paper 'The Basic Structure as Subject', in *Values and Morals*, A. Goldman and J. Kim (eds), Dordrecht, Reidel, 1978, pp. 47–71, at sects 5, 7 and 8. (This paper is reprinted, as Lecture VII, in John Rawls, *Political Liberalism*, New York, Columbia University Press, 1993.) In 'Basic Structure' Rawls attempts to address issues respecting natural endowment that are raised by David Gauthier; see also Rawls, 'Reply to Alexander and Musgrave', pp. 647–8. For further discussion of the relationship of the collective asset idea to individual desert see the second section of ch. 8 of R. Martin, *Rawls and Rights*, Lawrence, University Press of Kansas, 1985 (*R&R*).

15 The 'final statement' of the difference principle speaks of 'the greatest benefit of the least advantaged' (*TJ*, p. 302). At other points, Rawls speaks quite comfortably and naturally in the 'improving' idiom (e.g. in *TJ*, pp. 75, 103; in 'Basic Structure', pp. 64–5; in 'Social Unity and Primary Goods', pp. 171–2; these examples could be multiplied). It is important to note also that Rawls's justification of inequality (in income, wealth, social position) presupposes that representative members of the least well-off group are better off (or at least no worse off) under either emphasis, the maximizing one or the improving one, than they would be under 'a hypothetical initial arrangement in which all the social primary goods are equally distributed [which would include that] income and wealth are evenly shared' (*TJ*, p. 62). This standard is met by all points in the so-called available space in Figure 1.

16 See Rawls's unpublished treatise, 'Justice as Fairness: A Briefer Restatement', Cambridge, Mass., Harvard University [Department of Philosophy], 1989, sect. 18. Rawls's graphic representation (adapted as Figure 1) is found on p. 46A.

17 Rawls, 'Reply to Alexander and Musgrave', p. 648 (including n. 7); see also 'Social Unity and Primary Goods', p. 173 n.12. For additional discussion of the two class situation see Rainer Stuhlmann-Laeisz, 'Gerechtigkeit und Effizienz: Eine Untersuchung zum Verhältnis des Unterschiedsprinzips zu dem der Pareto

Optimalität in Rawls' Theorie der Gerechtigkeit', *Allgemein Zeitschrift für Philosophie*, 1981, vol. 6, no. 1, pp. 17–30.

18 For a proof of this contention, see the Appendix in *R&R*, pp. 197–201. (I should add that this Appendix is entirely the work of Prakash Shenoy.)

19 By 'lexical', I mean what Rawls meant. 'This is an order [correctly called 'lexicographical'] which requires us to satisfy the first principle in the ordering before we can move on to the second, the second before we consider the third, and so on' (*TJ*, pp. 42–3). It is the order we follow when we look up words in a dictionary. Say, we wanted to find 'word' there; we'd first go to 'w', then to 'wo', and so on, until we had the word we wanted.

20 See *R&R*, ch. 5, sect. 3, pp. 97–101, for the main argument here; see also pp. 76–81, 164–6, 169, 177–80.

21 For discussion of this claim, see *R&R*, ch. 4, sect. 1, pp. 63–7.

22 I have tried to elaborate the contemporary notion of democracy and its institutions, in the context of what I call a democratic system of rights, in my book *A System of Rights*, Oxford, Clarendon Press, 1993; see esp. chs 5–7, 12, and the Appendix. The main ideas here are conveniently summarized in my paper 'Basic Rights', *Rechtstheorie*, 1993, Beiheft vol. 15, pp. 191–201.

Index